SECOND EDITION

CONSUMER
Behaviour

South African Psychology and Marketing Applications

T0338238

SECOND EDITION

CONSUMER
Behaviour

South African Psychology and Marketing Applications

Content editors
Alet Erasmus   Mercy Mpinganjira

Authors
Elrie Botha   Gift Donga   Danie du Toit   Lene Ehlers
Bertha Jacobs   Tania Maree   Virimai Mugobo   Richard Shambare

OXFORD
UNIVERSITY PRESS
SOUTH AFRICA

OXFORD
UNIVERSITY PRESS

Oxford University Press is a department of the University of Oxford.
It furthers the University's objective of excellence in research, scholarship,
and education by publishing worldwide. Oxford is a registered trade mark of
Oxford University Press in the UK and in certain other countries.

Published in South Africa by
Oxford University Press Southern Africa (Pty) Limited

Vasco Boulevard, Goodwood, N1 City, Cape Town, South Africa, 7460
P O Box 12119, N1 City, Cape Town, South Africa, 7463

Consumer Behaviour 2nd edition

First published 2013
Second edition published 2019

ISBN 978 0 19 041242 5

Epub ISBN 978 0 19 041169 5

Second impression 2019
Typeset in ITC Century 10pt on 12pt
Printed on 70gsm Woodfree paper

Acknowledgements
Publisher: Janine Loedolff
Editor: Lee-Ann Ashcroft

Manuscript development: Liezl Roux
Designer: Natalie McCulloch

Cover design: Judith Cross

Permission researcher: Janaee Barkhuizen

Project manager: Nicola van Rhyn
Typesetter: Thomson Digital
Printed and bound by: CG Direct (Pty) Ltd.

The authors and publisher gratefully acknowledge permission to reproduce copyright material
in this book. Every effort has been made to trace copyright holders, but if any copyright infringements
have been made, the publisher would be grateful for information that would enable
any omissions or errors to be corrected in subsequent impressions.

TABLE OF CONTENTS

CONTENTS

PREFACE

In the highly competitive, global market place in which we find ourselves, the intricate interaction between the consumer and business, is undeniable. While consumers are spoilt for choice, they have also become more discerning, pursuing multiple platforms and channels to satisfy their product needs. Businesses and brands can therefore only thrive if consumers continue to perceive their offerings as appealing, reliable, and good value for the money in terms of the time and effort spent, compared to alternatives in a particular context.

This book presents the theory related to consumer behaviour, acknowledging the psychological processes of consumer decision-making and marketing applications. The four sections in the book aim to contextualise the content within a South African perspective. The first section introduces consumer behaviour as a discipline. It and explains how the consumer decision-making process cannot be isolated from marketing processes, -practices or the retail environment. The tempo at which text books are revised nowadays is testimony of the how fast these related disciplines are evolving.

The second part attends to the internal influences on consumers' decisions, as a result of motivations that are highly personal and deeply rooted in the consumer's psyche, and are difficult to change. Theoretical support is given for: the relevance of consumers' underlying motives when acting in the market place; storage and retrieval of information in memory; influence of consumers' perceptions (whether realistic or not) regarding their behaviour; fundamental characteristics and theoretical viewpoints on the relevance of personality in consumers' behaviour; and the undeniable implications of attitude during consumers' evaluation of products and services as well as post purchase evaluation.

The third section attends to external factors that influence consumers' decisions and behaviour in the market place. Inevitably, the marketing related effects that influence consumers' behaviour are dealt with. Social and cultural factors, including family and household influences are explained to demonstrate how consumer behaviour and attitudes are shaped. Situational influences that may be very supporting but overwhelming for consumers to deal with are also covered.

The fourth section deals with the complexities of the consumer decision-making process, and deals with topics such as market segmentation, communicating with consumers, the evolution and use of consumer decision-models as well as consumerism. A unique addition to the new edition is the chapter on changes in retailing that explain how the act of purchasing has transcended to new levels with exciting options that now drive retailers to continue to surprise, excite and amaze consumers in order to keep them satisfied.

Every chapter concludes with an end of chapter summary as well as self-assessment questions, case studies, and suggestions for additional learning. Teaching instructors using this book, have access to ancillary material that can be found on the companion site, Learning Zone (learningzone.oxford.co.za).

Enjoy the book!

Alet Erasmus and Mercy Mpinganjira

PART ONE
INTRODUCTION

Chapter 1   Introduction to consumer behaviour

CHAPTER 1

INTRODUCTION TO CONSUMER BEHAVIOUR

Alet Erasmus

LEARNING OBJECTIVES

After reading this chapter, you should be able to:

- explain what consumer behaviour entails
- distinguish between the various levels of complexity of consumer decisions
- identify and discuss the different stages of an extensive consumer decision-making process
- explain how the various stages of the consumer decision-making process differ for consumer decisions in terms of complexity
- interpret and apply consumer-related concepts correctly in any discussion of consumer behaviour
- discuss the evolution of the marketing concept over time.

Key terms

cognitive dissonance	etic perspective	product orientation
compensatory strategy	evoked set of products	psychological perspective
complex purchase decision	external influences	relationship orientation
consumer	general dealer	retailer
consumption	habitual decision	retro marketing
controllable market forces	impulsive purchase decision	sales orientation
cultural perspective	individual influences	simple purchase decision
customer	manufacturer	societal marketing concept
customer or consumer	non-compensatory strategy	socio-cultural factors
orientation	non-personal information sources	sociological perspective
decision-maker	personal information sources	uncontrollable market
decision rules	personal or social marketing	forces
department store	orientation	
economic perspective	production orientation	
emic perspective		

John and Andrew have just completed their studies and are both eager to start their careers. Both have grown up in the city and attended the same college, completing the same degrees. John has joined a company where he will be interacting with important business clients on a daily basis and has to make a good impression. His visual appearance therefore has to be quite formal although he is not given a clothing allowance to afford the new clothes. To date, his clothing style has been informal as part of the student environment. Andrew is joining another company where employees have to abide to specific specifications in terms of the style and colour of their workwear. He also has to pay for his work clothes himself, despite the dress code. Although the two gentlemen agreed on the budget that they could devote to their new wardrobes, and even though they visited the same store to do their shopping, it took John much longer to complete the task of choosing suitable clothing items. Why is this so?

1.1 INTRODUCTION

In this chapter, we define and discuss **consumer** behaviour to shed more light on this dynamic field of study, which draws from multiple disciplines. Literature on the topic of consumer behaviour aims at explaining consumers' choice of products and services and buying behaviour in the marketplace. The abundance of research published in various scholarly journals over the years demonstrates researchers' interest in this dynamic field. Topics of investigation range from context-specific research (for example, an investigation of the internet adoption of consumers in developing countries) to global investigations that involve varying populations and samples (for example, a study of the consideration given by households to environmental issues in their day-to-day **consumption** decisions). Research findings are continually used to explain the latest trends in the market and how they affect consumer behaviour. This explains why textbooks about consumer behaviour are revised regularly.

For some time now, scholars have encouraged a discussion of consumers' behaviour within their environments, because existing theories and models mostly originated in first-world economies such as the US and the UK. These theories and models do not always apply in developing contexts (for example, South Africa and other African countries) that are less affluent, unless certain amendments are made to them. Literature used in tertiary institutions should therefore acknowledge and incorporate the characteristics of consumers in the context where the academic offering is made, for example reflecting on consumption practices in African countries if the institution is based in South Africa. One cannot assume that findings obtained in more developed countries are generalisable and relevant to other contexts. This textbook aims to address this shortcoming in South Africa.

1.1.1 Consumer behaviour defined

Consumer behaviour is a simple term that describes a multitude of mental and physical processes associated with consumer decision making. It entails the way in which consumers deal with purchase decisions in different contexts with the aim of satisfying their product needs and requirements. Consumer behaviour includes all the related activities of consumers and buyers of products from the pre-purchase phase, when they begin thinking about purchasing a product or consuming a service, through the actual purchase phase, to post-purchase evaluation.[1]

In the example discussed in the opening case study of this chapter, John and Andrew are consumers with the same purchase objective, although their levels of experience are not the same owing to the difference in their backgrounds. Their needs subsequently differ in terms of the type and amount of information required to make an informed, responsible purchase decision. Their eventual behaviour in the marketplace can be explained from different perspectives (for example, economic, social and/or psychological) that would shed light on different aspects of the decision process.

1.1.2   The contribution of multiple disciplines to the field

The first major textbook on consumer behaviour, by Howard and Sheth,[2] was published in 1968 during a period of increased awareness of consumers' needs in the marketplace. One of the challenges that consumer behaviour as a field of study has had to acknowledge over time is its intricate involvement with other disciplines[3] that are all strongly associated with pertinent theoretical perspectives and relevant theories. The advantage of this interaction, however, is that it provides an opportunity to incorporate different viewpoints in our understanding of consumer behaviour. The section that follows explains some of the different theoretical perspectives.

Studying consumer behaviour from an **economic perspective**[4] allows for an investigation of consumers' behaviour from a rational viewpoint. This viewpoint assumes that consumers formulate needs and wants in terms of concrete and rational criteria. A limiting assumption of the economic perspective is that consumers in a specific market are considered to be homogeneous, and essentially alike in nature. If this were true, it would be possible to anticipate the buying decisions of South African consumers in a specific product category. For instance, from an economic rational perspective, a person applying for a loan would also consider interest costs and loan duration, which are concrete and rational facts about credit, before concluding a credit transaction. However, evidence in the marketplace indicates the contrary. As an example: a consumer might consider it extremely important to have a new dress for a special occasion and hence not worry about the interest added to the purchase price if the dress is purchased on credit. In terms of real-life circumstances, buying decisions are influenced by multiple factors, which makes it difficult to anticipate consumers' buying decisions than it would be if we could simply rely on economic principles.

Individual differences in consumers' behaviour are accounted for through the incorporation of **psychological perspectives**, which acknowledge individual consumer traits (or distinguishing characteristics) that will be discussed in following chapters, for example, motivation, personality, attitude and

Figure 1.1 A consumer may purchase a new dress for a special occasion on credit

perception, in terms of addressing consumers' product preferences and consumer behaviour at a personal level. In marketing, the character of a brand[9]
is often intentionally shaped in accordance with specific personality traits to
attract specific market segments, assuming that consumers would be lured by
products or brands that might support or enhance their personalities. Familiar,
prominent people such as sportsmen with specific, appropriate characteristics
are often approached by brand managers to introduce and promote certain
products (for example, Wayde van Niekerk endorsing luxury watches to signify his attention to time). Consumers are also inclined to frequent stores that
support their self-image and to avoid stores that are not aligned with their
self-image. In one study,[6] participants were shown examples of product displays exhibiting the same brands of towels in different interior stores, ranging
from sophisticated specialised stores to cheaper **department stores**. Upper-
income participants in the study unequivocally indicated that they would
rather pay more for the same product in a sophisticated retail outlet than pay
less for it in a department store. One person indicated that she would rather
'drop dead' than be seen in the cheaper department store because the image of
the store was inferior according to her standards. Similarly, other consumers
might be hesitant to enter upmarket stores for fear of feeling uncomfortable
when entering the store.

The use of psychological perspectives in consumer behaviour research has
considerable potential to explain the influence of consumers' emotions on their
behaviour in the marketplace. It can, for example, be applied in research in an
investigation and interpretation of consumers' continued use of credit to the
point of incurring excessive debt, in spite of urgent warnings in the media about
the dangers of doing so. The psychological theory of 'temporal choices',[7] for
instance, explains this phenomenon by proposing that the temptation of immediate ownership of a product (such as a new desktop computer or iPod) can
exceed a consumer's concerns about the obligation of having to pay multiple

instalments with interest in the future. In the same way, several other theories and approaches can be used to explain consumers' behaviour, making consumer research extremely interesting.

Sociology and social psychology provide theoretical frameworks that enable an understanding of consumer socialisation as well as consumers' behaviour based on their affiliation and association within groups. For example, it considers the influence of consumers' families, cultural affiliation, peer groups (for instance, their fellow students), age groups, professional societies and lifestyle segments on their behaviour.

A consumer does not operate in isolation, which explains the relevance of sociological interpretations of issues such as consumers' socio-economic status, lifestyle and socio-psychological aspects of consumption,[8] which are explained in this textbook. Consumers' judgements of products based on the shared meaning that they attach to certain images, brands or products (for example, our perception of luxury brands such as BMW and Ferrari, or our perceptions of the healthiness of fast-food) fit well within socio-psychological frameworks such as symbolic interactionism[9]. Consumer-related studies could therefore use **sociological perspectives** and **socio-psychological perspectives** during the design of the measuring instruments including the most suitable scales for questionnaires and the interpretation of the findings, for example when investigating teenagers' preferences for certain clothing brands or households' eating habits.

Cultural anthropology[10] provides avenues with which to understand the consumption behaviour and product needs of specific cultures and sub-cultures, for example nationalities, ethnic groups and religious groups. It also provides theoretical frameworks within which to analyse and interpret cross-cultural influences in societies, something which has become increasingly relevant in modern day global societies. Although globalisation has, to a large extent, blurred boundaries, consumers across the world are not homogeneous and probably never will be. Consumer behaviour theories may be universal in nature to explain consumers' adoption of the behaviour of other cultures. An approach that considers the viewpoints of other cultures is known as an **etic perspective**[11] (for example, when the eating habits of other cultures are investigated or incorporated in meal planning). However, when a discussion is specific to one culture, such as South African cuisine, it adopts an **emic perspective**.[12] Explaining how norms and values are maintained within a specific cultural group such as the Xhosas is an example of an emic approach.[13] In an interesting study by Parker and Keim,[14] an emic perspective was used to investigate differences in perspectives about overweight and obesity among women, while other researchers[15] were interested in the unique African female body shape for the sake of the correct body dimensions for the South African fashion industry.

Over time, scholars have begun to distinguish between the needs and behaviour of consumers in developing countries and those in developed countries,[16] and to refrain from assuming that the models and perspectives that have been applied in more affluent countries necessarily apply to all societies. A **cultural perspective** acknowledges long-term influences on consumers' consumption practices (for example, the influence of the cultural group to which a consumer belongs)

Figure 1.2 Pretzels originated in southern France where monks (610 AD) baked thin strips of dough and shaped them to look like a child's arms folded in prayer. These baked goods are also associated with Lent.[21]

and accentuates a deeper understanding of the meaning of products, brands and symbols in a cultural context.[17] In a plural society (that is, a society that consists of several cultural groups, such as major urban areas in South Africa), consumers construct new identities because they adopt new roles that they are exposed to over time, thereby creating alternative identities within brand cultures.[18] The so-called Black Diamonds in South Africa[19] are an example of how affluent black consumers have created a unique sub-culture with pertinent characteristics as a result of their exposure to and adoption of a Western lifestyle.

A sensitive understanding of cultural values and taboos may help prevent disastrous blunders in marketing, such as using a brand name that is offensive to a part of the community or using colours that have contradictory meanings to different cultural groups. South Africa is a multi-cultural society, which means that manufacturers and **retailers** must be particularly sensitive towards different market segments such as ethnic or religious groups.[20]

APPLICATION

Retailers have to consider the grouping, presentation and advertisement of foods that are meant for certain specific market segments, such as kosher products for Jewish consumers and halaal foods for Islamic ones. It would, for example, be insensitive to display pork products such as bacon and ham next to kosher foods on a shelf in a store. The time of presentation is as important: turkey and gammon are typically eaten for Christmas, while hot cross buns are popular among Christians for Easter, and will not attract much attention when offered during the rest of the year.

1.2 A CRITICAL LOOK AT CONSUMER DECISION MAKING

Consumer decision making is an integral part of consumer behaviour and is of particular interest to marketers, who wish to influence consumer decisions, while retail and industry have a vested interest in consumers' needs and requirements. Consumer facilitators, on the other hand, aim to guide consumers towards making informed and responsible purchase decisions in a marketplace that can be overwhelming at the best of times. It is difficult to predict consumers' decisions because they differ in terms of how and why they are made, the type of decision, who the **decision-makers** are and where consumers are located.

1.2.1   Simple versus complex decision making

A consumer decision is mostly a process rather than a single action. Literature indicates that consumer decisions could be:[22]

* fairly swift (for example, an **impulsive purchase decision** that a person makes at the point of purchase without any prior consideration such as buying a chocolate when paying for groceries at the checkout point)
* a routine or **habitual decision** that is based on multiple and/or similar decisions made in the past (for example, buying your favourite brand of tea every month)
* a more complex and lengthy process that involves considerable deliberation over time (for example, buying a car or an outfit for a special occasion).

A consumer decision is generally described in terms of its complexity and the subsequent involvement of the consumer during the decision-making process. Although literature generally provides examples of so-called **simple purchase decisions** and **complex purchase decisions**, the complexity of the buying decision eventually depends on more than merely the product type.[23] An interplay of factors may influence it, including:

* a consumer's skills and ability to handle the buying decision (for example, an art student who has to purchase a new computer without any prior experience or knowledge of computers would find the buying decision far more complex than an information technology (IT) student)
* a consumer's involvement during the decision process owing to a particular interest in the process or a lack thereof (for example, a motor car mechanic is knowledgeable about car repairs and would be quite demanding when his own car needed to be serviced or repaired at a dealer)
* the variety of products that are available to choose from (for example, the art student may be overwhelmed by the array of computers available to choose from in the store)
* the context in which the decision is made (for example, a person from a rural area who enters a hypermarket in a large city will find grocery shopping more complex than a city dweller who is familiar with large department stores).

Considering the potential influence of consumer characteristics, product type and the context in which a consumer decision is made, it makes more sense to describe consumer decisions in terms of a continuum of complexity that ranges from simple to complex buying decisions (see Figure 1.3).

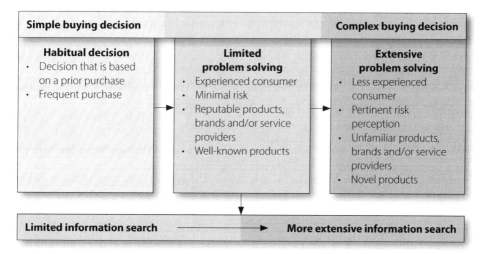

Figure 1.3 Simple versus complex buying decisions

A consumer decision may be simple if:[24]
* the consumer has a reasonable degree of experience and skill with which to perform the task
* the product holds minimal risk (for example, a pair of socks that is of little importance and will probably not evoke much criticism if it fails expectations)
* the product is easy to replace (for example, a tube of toothpaste)
* the product is not visually conspicuous (for example, a toothbrush)
* the consumer chooses a reputable brand and does not have exceptional expectations, knowing that it will not cause problems and will evoke little critique, if any, from others).

A consumer decision becomes more complex when:
* the individual has limited or no experience in handling such a decision
* the decision encompasses some form of risk, such as uncertainty about whether the product will perform as expected, concern that it might cause physical harm (for example, a gas heater), the likelihood that it might not be easy to use and concern that others might criticise the product
* the product is novel (for example, a new cellphone with unfamiliar technology, brand or service provider)
* many product alternatives exist that are highly similar, which confuses the evaluation process.

Habitual routine decisions are those that are repeated frequently, almost without the consideration of alternatives.[25] These decisions may be simple, for example purchasing fuel for a car. They may, however, also be more complex decisions that are made regularly, which means that the consumer has become an expert over time and thus possesses the skills to deal with similar tasks, for example when a professional tennis player replaces his tennis racquet. They may also represent the type of decisions where certain products, brands or service providers are trusted to such an extent that only a few or no alternatives are considered. An example would be choosing a veterinarian to take care of a sick pet or relying on a reputable computer brand.

1.2.2 Handling consumer decisions

Simple consumer decisions[26] are generally handled without seeking much additional information from external sources. These decisions are mostly framed in accordance with previous experiences, that is, within existing knowledge frameworks. However, when confronted with more complex consumer decisions, progressively more information is required from external sources to expand existing knowledge in a consumer's memory during the evaluation process. **Personal information sources** like friends and family or salespeople may be sufficient to support or influence a buying decision and are particularly valuable because they are generally trusted. An additional advantage is that a consumer can discuss specific issues and individual problems with people who probably know and understand the situation. Family members may even act as gatekeepers who control the purchases of other, less experienced members of the family. Unfortunately, the advice of salespeople is not always trusted because **customers** are inclined to believe that they are primarily concerned about increasing their number of sales and thus their commission.[27]

Non-personal information sources[28] such as technical reports, advertisements or electronic media are particularly useful when dealing with complex factual information such as product specifications because the information can be read over and over again. Mostly, it takes time and effort to access the relevant information sources. Written information can be detailed and even difficult to comprehend, especially concerning technical specifications and user instructions, which explains why consumers often simply do not read the documents properly.

1.3 THE CONSUMER DECISION-MAKING PROCESS

A consumer decision-making process is typically distinguished in terms of various stages, namely inputs (influencing factors that would determine the process of decision making), the transformation or processing stage, and outputs (the post-purchase evaluation that would result in consumer satisfaction or dissatisfaction).[29]

1.3.1 Inputs

Consumer decisions are not made in isolation and are ultimately influenced on two levels:

- On a personal or internal level,[30] a consumer's existing knowledge, which is based on a combination of someone's learning and prior experiences as well as personal characteristics such as motives (Chapter 2), intellectual capacity (Chapter 3), perception (Chapter 4), personality (Chapter 5), and attitude (Chapter 6), determines the way in which consumer decisions are handled.

- On an external level,[31] a consumer is influenced by marketing-related and socio-cultural factors:
  - **Controllable marketing forces**[32] are the marketing-related factors that can be manipulated by an organisation, for example the elements of a company or a store's marketing mix such as product characteristics, price, promotion and distribution channels.
  - **Uncontrollable marketing forces** refer to factors that are difficult to predict in terms of relevance and magnitude, such as economic conditions at a given point in time (the economic slump around 2000 had devastating consequences on economies world-wide), public policy, forces of nature, competition in the marketplace (imported goods have increased in availability in South Africa in recent years, making it difficult for local producers to survive) and the availability of national resources (South Africa's water and energy supplies are ongoing concerns).
  - **Socio-cultural factors**[33] include lifestyle and cultural context-related factors such as social status (Chapter 7), cultural and sub-cultural impacts (Chapter 8) and family influences (Chapter 9). These influences are not equally important to every consumer, or in every purchase situation. As a result, consumers attend to the first step in the decision-making process in different ways.

The consumer decision-making process can be described in terms of specific stages, as portrayed in Figure 1.4.

1.3.2 Transformation or processing

The process stage of consumer decision making involves three distinct phases:[34]

- *Need recognition:* This simply refers to a consumer realising a need, for example a cool drink to quench thirst, a new pair of tennis shoes or an electrician to fix lightning damage. A consumer's perception of how complex, urgent or risky the problem is differs from one context to the next.[35] For example, a person might not be able to afford the expense at the point when the need arises. It also differs from one consumer to another for various reasons. Some needs may be more serious or urgent, such as attending to damage caused to a home's electricity supply by lightning. Other needs are less serious, not necessarily requiring immediate attention, such as replacing a dead tree in the garden.
- *Information search:* The extent of the pre-purchase information search will depend on the urgency or seriousness of the product need.[36] While a limited information search might be required for some products, the pre-purchase information search during a complex buying decision might call for an extensive information search that involves different sources and visiting various stores for guidance. This process might be frustrating if a consumer struggles to get relevant information or finds it difficult to interpret the information that is needed to conclude a satisfying, informed purchase decision. An abundance of product information and many alternatives is not necessarily an advantage and may complicate the process. A consumer never considers all the product alternatives in the marketplace simply because it is

not possible or practical to do so. An overload of product choices is mostly overwhelming and confusing (see Figure 1.4).

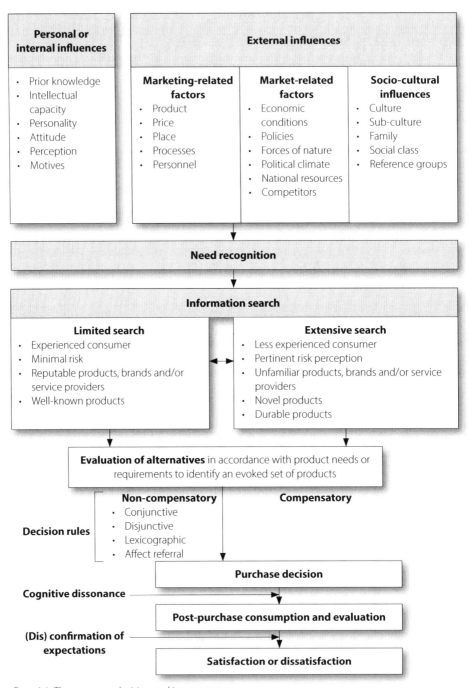

Figure 1.4 The consumer decision-making process

- *Evaluation of alternatives:* Different routes may be taken to evaluate alternative options during decision making. Typically, a consumer identifies a number of possibilities, the so-called **evoked set of products**[37] or services which is a short list of three to seven possible product choices. This enables a less intimidating and confusing evaluation process. This evoked set usually includes products or brands that a consumer likes and is more familiar with (for example, limiting the selection to plain, informal, long-sleeved, button-up shirts, between R300 and R500 each, of specific brand names). The consumer then identifies more acceptable alternatives (for example, the preferred colours and more desirable brand names, within the price range) and rejects products that are less acceptable (for example, striped fabric, too expensive, less popular brand name) or not exciting enough (for example, white shirts). The evoked set of products eventually consists of products that are all potentially acceptable. Some of these may be chosen based on previous positive experiences (for example, a black shirt), while the rest might represent new possibilities.

A consumer applies one or more **decision rules** or decision strategies[38] to identify the most suitable alternative from the evoked set of products:

- When using a **compensatory strategy** to identify the chosen product, a consumer assigns a score to each relevant product attribute to identify the product with the highest weighted score. This means that the chosen product may have certain less desirable features because certain initial negative judgements (scores) were offset by others that were very favourable, such as an excellent price and a popular brand name.
- **Non-compensatory strategies** do not allow one positive attribute to compensate for one or more negative features of a product or service. Four options exist when using this strategy:
  - When applying the conjunctive rule, the consumer assigns certain minimum acceptable levels (cut-off points) for each product feature that is considered. If a product has any feature that does not meet the minimum requirements, it will be disqualified (for example, a product that is too expensive). The conjunctive rule is useful to reduce the number of alternatives when many options exist. An additional decision rule is subsequently used to identify the final choice.
  - The disjunctive rule is similar to the conjunctive rule. In this case, products that meet or exceed the minimum cut-off point that was set for every product feature are retained (for example, retaining all products that are cheaper than expected). Thereafter an additional decision rule is used to select the final product.
  - The lexicographic rule often follows the decision rules that were discussed above, in order to identify the final product choice (for example, to identify the most suitable product after application of the conjunctive rule). A consumer evaluates all potentially suitable products individually by considering product features in order of importance, for example starting with maximum price affordable. Having eliminated all of the products that

are too expensive, the consumer then compares the remaining options in terms of the second-most important feature, for example colour.
— The so-called affect referral rule is applied when a consumer considers an entire product based on overall perceptions gained from experience or prior exposure to similar products (for example, receiving compliments when wearing a specific colour, or winning others' admiration when wearing a specific brand).

1.3.3   Outputs

The actual consumer decision eventually represents the product or service that a consumer chooses as the most suitable in a specific context[39] (context being what the consumer considers to be the most important criterion for the purchase). When buying a new high-definition plasma television, for example, one consumer might go for the cheapest television, another might choose a specific brand based on prior experience, another might purchase the most energy efficient appliance, while the next consumer might focus on the most desirable technological features or the size. These consumers have different expectations and might all experience uncertainty about whether they made the right choice.[40] For example, consumers might ask themselves the following questions:

* Will this relatively cheap television set function properly and will it have a reasonable service life?
* Will this brand really live up to its reputation in terms of functional performance and service life expectancy?
* Will the energy saving promoted by this television brand be significant in terms of our households' energy consumption?
* Was it worth paying more for an appliance with so many additional technological features?

This is known as **cognitive dissonance**.[41] It is a feeling of discomfort or uncertainty that a consumer experiences immediately after a purchase has been concluded.[42] It is more likely to occur after purchasing a relatively expensive product (such as a cell phone or a computer) or a visually significant product (such as an evening dress for a special occasion or a car). The major cause of this discomfort is attributed to a consumer's awareness of all the positive attributes of the products that have not been selected and the realisation that this decision cannot be reversed easily. The final choice is generally made from an evoked set of products that do not necessarily differ significantly. The final product mostly represents some compromise, as consumer decisions are not necessarily rational. The decision rule that was applied to reach the final decision may therefore also contribute to this feeling of discomfort.

Several strategies can be applied to reduce cognitive dissonance. Here are some examples:

* Seeking information that supports the purchase decision, for example sales figures that indicate that Brand X is the most popular in the country
* Gaining confirmation from friends who have had positive experiences with a similar product

- Applying a defence technique to justify the purchase, for example reasoning that a cheaper product will perform the same basic functions as more expensive models

The level of cognitive dissonance that is experienced may also differ from one consumer to the next. High-dissonance consumers are perhaps more uncertain about their choices and are subsequently more anxious. Low-dissonance consumers may be more certain about their choices or less involved and therefore less anxious. Dissonance experienced by a consumer who is uncertain about whether the purchase is really necessary or the right choice, may be based on feelings of guilt, for example concern about excessive spending.

Whatever the cause of the dissonance, positive feedback of some sort is needed to relieve it. This may occur:

- once the consumer starts using the product and concludes that it performs according to expectations
- when someone else admires the product or sanctions the product choice, indicating that it was a wise decision
- when concrete evidence that supports the product choice is produced.

Cognitive dissonance[43] is generally relieved shortly after a purchase. During post-purchase consumption of the products, consumers get the opportunity to compare their actual experience with the purchased products with their initial product expectations. This post-purchase evaluation process[44] may continue for some time. For example, if Jane's newly purchased computer is supposed to give excellent service for five years, she will continue to evaluate the performance of her computer during this period. If the computer performs as expected, her pre-purchase expectations are confirmed. If, for some reason, the computer does not meet her expectations, it implies disconfirmation of her expectations.[45] If the computer performs better than expected, positive disconfirmation occurs (which reflects a cognitive discrepancy, as the product did more than merely performing as expected, it exceeded expectations), which typically culminates as consumer satisfaction (an emotion that will highly likely influence future decisions). On the contrary, a product that fails consumers' expectations causes negative disconfirmation of expectations (the cognitive discrepancy is negative in this instance) that may cause consumer dissatisfaction (an emotion) unless the consumer finds a good reason to explain the negative disconfirmation, such as a service provider who fitted the wrong parts or lightning damage that caused a series of problems with a particular household appliance.

Consumer satisfaction therefore reaches a maximum level after the purchase and while the product is used. In some cases, a consumer may only experience consumer satisfaction after a considerable amount of time has passed since the purchase, for example when the computer that was expected to last five years, breaks down after three years. Consumer (dis)satisfaction is an emotion that influences a consumer's attitude and will inevitably influence future purchases. A satisfied consumer is more likely to return to the store that has provided excellent service in the first place. Similarly, a satisfied consumer will purchase the same brand of product in the future, thus becoming a brand-loyal customer.

This explains why some consumers become brand loyal and eventually own several products that carry the same brand name. Loyal customers eventually use the brand name or the name of the store as an heuristic, i.e. an indicator of quality or good service, to reduce uncertainty as well as cognitive dissonance.[46]

1.4 MARKETING AND RETAILING APPLICATIONS

The excerpt that follows, which describes the findings of a research project,[47] demonstrates the application of decision rules during consumers' evaluation of products in a complex product category and provides a demonstration of its consequences for the outcome of the purchase decision.

DISCUSSION

Juggling product attributes during consumer decision making

A survey among millennial consumers (thus consumers born after 1980) that focused on environmental concerns, specifically consumers' inclination towards voluntary simplistic behavioural practices,[48] revealed that this age group regarded material simplicity as very important. Therefore, the initial answer was that they would try to prevent wasteful consumption when purchasing clothing, generally trying not to purchase clothes unnecessarily. Further investigation in the same study, however, indicated that these millennials' ecological awareness was weak. Therefore, their decision to prevent waste was not necessarily related to concern about the environment, but could have been due to financial restrictions. Although the initial indication was that they were sensitive about environmental issues because they wished to reduce waste, one could not assume that the predominant reason was to conserve the environment. Consumers are, in fact, constantly juggling product attributes and an investigation of one attribute may provide an incomplete or even incorrect answer.

Discussion questions

1. The findings of the study indicated that consumers' eventual purchase decisions were based on a prioritisation of product characteristics. Explain the relevant decision rule that would have resulted in elevating the importance of cost and reducing the importance of ecological concern during product evaluation.
2. Explain how application of the affect referral rule may have led to a product choice that prioritised the consideration of environmental issues.
3. How could consumers reduce cognitive dissonance that developed following their rejection of local brands that were clearly more environmentally friendly?
4. Explain why a consumer might be satisfied with a purchase (for example, a pair of shoes), although the product itself might not necessarily be the best compared with other options in the same store within the same price range.

1.5 THE EVOLUTION OF THE MARKETING CONCEPT

The section that follows explains how the marketing concept, which is very important in terms of how businesses distinguish themselves from others in the market place and attempt to address their target markets' needs, has changed over time. The marketing concept commenced as an economically driven, rational, perhaps even manipulative approach by retailers and marketers with a primary focus on increased sales and profit margins, but evolved to become a more informative and supportive approach that acknowledges consumers' needs and requirements. It will become clear that much has been done over the years by social consumer organisations and through legislation by governments to acknowledge consumers' needs, to support and protect vulnerable consumers, and to prevent exploitation of consumers.

1.5.1   An historical overview

The marketing of goods and services has changed considerably over the years, with increasing emphasis being placed on consumers' needs and requirements. During World War II, many factories closed down, and the production of goods and services literally came to a halt, which resulted in a shortage of consumer goods. When conditions improved during the second half of the 1940s, a **production orientation**[49] followed to ensure increased production of goods to overcome the shortage of products at the time. The philosophy during the production era was to manufacture and sell whatever products the market demanded. Production was unfortunately not well planned in terms of consumers' product-specific needs and quality requirements. Subsequently the market became over-stocked with low quality products and products that consumers showed no interest in.

During the **product orientation** era that followed in the 1950s, particular attention was devoted to the quality of products.[50] Unfortunately, many of the products that came on the market were not designed with consumers' needs in mind. Although many of these products initially served as a major source of excitement, for example sewing machines with more than 200 decorative stitches, owners soon realised that they had paid for technology that they were barely using.

During the 1960s, a **sales orientation**[51] demonstrated manufacturers' revised effort to sell the abundance of goods on the market. Their over-emphasis on sales is referred to as transaction-oriented efforts. This approach involved aggressive, persuasive sales techniques that were used to take products literally to consumers' doorsteps and to boost sales, for example through door-to-door selling. A sales orientation is typical when product supply exceeds consumers' needs or during trying economic times, when the buying capacity of consumers slows down. Special offers, 'no deposit' transactions and incentives such as free holidays are often used to enhance sales during such an approach. Chapter 14 deals with ways in which consumers in South Africa are protected from exploitation, misinformation and abuse by over-enthusiastic marketers and how they are assisted today. Through the promulgation of the National Credit Act and the Consumer Protection Act as well as various consumer organisations that are operating across the country, vulnerable consumers are protected against abuse and fraudulent practices. At the same time, the pressure that could be exerted by retail, industry and marketing to boost sales is restricted.

For those interested in consumer behaviour, the 1960s will probably be remembered best for the birth of the **customer** or **consumer orientation**.[52] This era followed the initiatives of John F. Kennedy, a presidential candidate of the US who propagated a Consumer Bill of Rights as a fundamental part of his presidential campaign. When elected, his emphasis of consumers' rights in the marketplace mobilised a social consumer movement and the so-called **societal marketing concept**[53] in the US. To this day, the aim of the consumer movement is to address consumers' needs and to promote the well-being of society. At its core, the societal marketing concept aims to protect consumers and to prevent exploitation of vulnerable consumers by over-enthusiastic marketers or confusing and intimidating sales campaigns. The consumer orientation forms part of the market orientation of the 1970s, which acknowledged the duality of all market transactions. This duality implied an awareness that marketing strategies are essential for an organisation to survive competitive rivalry and to achieve long-term success in a highly competitive marketplace, but that it is equally important to maintain good relationships with complex consumer markets by providing satisfying service offerings.[54]

Within a marketing orientation, the efforts of companies would be dominated by a customer orientation, which elevates customers' needs and aims to retain customers without pressurising them. This ideology actually restricts innovative marketing practices since it is argued that consumers' behaviour and responses should not be pre-empted because that would stimulate consumer needs and desires. 'Real world' consumers, however, do not necessarily know what they want. It is therefore difficult to delay marketing activities until favourable consumer responses are achieved. In **retro marketing**,[55] consumers are cleverly 'tricked' into becoming interested in new product developments through ingenious marketing techniques that are not necessarily manipulative. Generally, old brands are revived in this way by relying on nostalgia to gain consumers' interest. For example, a novel product is introduced and is then marketed as an exclusive idea in a non-threatening, entertaining manner to attract the attention of potential customers.[56]

The **relationship orientation** has been evident since the 1990s.[57] It focuses on the responsibility of retailers to secure long-term, profitable relationships with customers and other stakeholders, trying to satisfy the needs of all. The main focus of this orientation is on customer care. Relationship marketing is crucial because it costs about five times more to attract a new customer than to retain an existing one.

At present, a **personal** or **social marketing orientation** is gaining momentum as a result of technology such as the internet and cell phone connectivity. Time saving and access to a global network of brands, products and services can probably explain consumers' use of online shopping. Notwithstanding, online shopping is not equally established in all countries across the world such as in African countries yet, due to problems with infrastructure, access to appropriate technology, lack of consumer competence and perceived value of personal interaction in retail stores.[58]

RESEARCH BOX 1.1

The involvement of various disciplines such as economics, psychology, cultural anthropology and sociology in scholars' understanding of consumer behaviour explains the abundance of research in this field as well as the diversity of research projects. Researchers adopt a specific theoretical approach within their field of interest. For example, they may choose to explain consumers' decision making from a cultural perspective or use theories of psychology to investigate consumers' attitudes towards environmental issues when choosing food products.

In addition, consumer behaviour research could be quantitative in kind, which means that findings are expressed in numbers, for example percentages, and statistical procedures are used to analyse the findings more extensively, for example to detect significant differences in the purchasing behaviour of different consumer groups such as men and women. A survey may be done to gather suitable information from a selected population. This may involve the completion of questionnaires, containing various questions and scales, by a carefully selected sample of consumers. Findings will then produce figures that could indicate what percentage of consumers in a particular geographic area are in favour of campaigns that are used to promote environmental awareness amongst shoppers and whether there is a significant difference in the awareness of consumers who differ in terms of their level of education. Over the years, various scales have been developed and tested to investigate specific phenomena (such as attitudes and perceptions). These scales can be used by other researchers to investigate the same phenomena in a different context. In other words, the voluntary simplicity scale that was developed in the US can be used and verified in a South African context.

Quantitative research therefore provides empirical evidence of consumers' behaviour, which is valuable for the manufacturing industry, retailers and marketers, who need to know that the money they are investing in a new product is worthwhile. However, quantitative research usually does not explain adequately why consumers behave in a certain manner. Qualitative research, in which consumers are asked open-ended questions by means of interviews, focus group discussions or written narratives, may help to expose the underlying reasons for consumers' behaviour. Consumers may, for example, be asked to tell a story or to draw pictures that are analysed and interpreted by researchers through an identification of concepts and themes. This fairly intricate type of research process involves smaller numbers of consumers in a research project, but provides a valuable understanding of consumers' behaviour.

SUMMARY

Consumer behaviour as a field of study comprises much more than consumer decision making, and refers to the behaviour of individuals and groups before, during and after their choice of products or services. The field of study is complicated by the fact that evidence about consumer behaviour cannot be generalised across all contexts and that all consumers do not behave in the same way. This explains why textbooks and publications that originated in relatively affluent parts of the world do not necessarily reflect the behaviour of consumers elsewhere in the world. Similarly, personal differences, for example in age, level of education, experience or attitude, cause pertinent behavioural variances among individual consumers, even members of the same family.

This chapter explained the basic concepts related to consumer behaviour and discussed consumer decision making as a process involving inputs, which materialise in terms of outputs that, in turn, may realise as consumer satisfaction (or the contrary). The chapter further aimed to explain the contribution of different disciplines to this field of study as well as theoretical viewpoints on consumer decision making. Subsequent chapters elaborate on specific aspects of consumer behaviour.

ADDITIONAL RESOURCES

Self-assessment questions

1. How would a consumer go about making a rational purchasing decision? Refer to case study of John and Andrew at the beginning of the chapter. How might they go about making rational purchasing decisions with regards to the clothing they need to purchase for work?
2. How would an emotional purchase decision differ from a rational decision?
3. Do you think that rational decisions always completely exclude emotional influences? Explain.
4. Why are various disciplines such as psychology and sociology relevant to a discussion of the behaviour of consumers?
5. Why is a purchase of a specific product, such as the purchase of a computer, not necessarily regarded as a complex purchase decision for every consumer?
6. Discuss a complex buying decision that involves an evoked set of three possible alternatives in terms of the application of a compensatory rule.
7. Does confirmation of a customer's expectations of a guest house's service necessarily imply that the service is good?
8. Explain the cognitive dissonance experienced when purchasing a wedding gift for special friends.
9. Explain how changes in the marketing concept have been to the benefit of consumers.

EXPERIENTIAL EXERCISE

You have recently purchased a new computer. Because you were on a tight budget, you had to shop around to get the best possible deal and eventually ended up at a small retailer where the salesperson was very friendly and helpful. After a week, unexpected problems with the computer occurred. Upon your return to the retailer, you found that it had closed down.

1. Explain how you would go about finding a service provider that could help you with your problem.
2. Explain which information would be required for a service provider to assist you.
3. Reflect on the emotions that you would have experienced during the incident, for example the anger at the upset caused after your initial excitement about your new possession.

CASE STUDY 1

Multi-tasking in a complex market place

Lynn and Mary are two newly enrolled first-year students who have just moved into a self-service commune near the university that they will be attending. Lynn comes from a small town and has always done all her shopping at the local **general dealer** in her home town. Mary, her new friend, has lived in Johannesburg all her life. She owns her own car and is familiar with the area where the commune is situated, the different shops and city life in general.

Mary asks Lynn to join her on a shopping trip to the nearby mall because she needs to buy a comfortable pair of shoes. She asks Lynn if she would mind going to the supermarket on the lower level while she goes to the shoe store on the upper level. She thinks that it will save time if Lynn does the grocery shopping for the commune while she looks at shoes. Mary provides Lynn with a shopping list that has been drawn up by the students as well as the money that they have all contributed. Before they part, Mary remembers that they also need a toaster for the commune, so she hands Lynn extra money to purchase 'the best four-slice toaster she can find within their budget' and says to meet her in the coffee shop near the entrance to the mall in half an hour.

Discussion questions

1. Discuss the complexity of the errands that Lynn has to deal with.
2. Explain why the complexity of these errands would have differed for Mary.
3. What product characteristics would you expect in the evoked set of products that Lynn might identify when evaluating the toasters in the store?
4. Explain Lynn's evaluation of the toasters in the store when applying the compensatory rule and using the criteria that you identified in your answer to question 3.
5. Explain Lynn's evaluation of the toasters in the store while applying the lexicographic non-compensatory rule and using the same criteria.
6. Explain how Mary would have evaluated the toasters on the shelf using the affect referral rule.
7. When they meet up for coffee, both Lynn and Mary are concerned about their purchases. Explain the cognitive dissonance experienced by Mary versus the cognitive dissonance experienced by Lynn.
8. Why might the supermarket experience have been quite stressful for Lynn?

REFERENCES

1   Donoghue, S., Strydom, N., Andrews, L., Pentecost, R. & De Klerk, H.M. 2016. Differences between black and white South Africans in product failure attributions, anger and complaint behaviour. *International Journal of Consumer Studies*, 40: 257; Schiffman, L.G. & Wisenblit, J.L. 2015. *Consumer behaviour*, 11th ed. New Jersey: Prentice Hall.
2   Howard, J. & Sheth, J.N. 1968. *Theory of buyer behaviour*. New York: J. Wiley & Sons.
3   Solomon, M.R. 2018. *Consumer behaviour: Buying, having, being*, 12th ed. New York: Pearson, 25; De Mooij, M. & Hofstede, G. 2011. Cross-cultural consumer behavior: A review of research findings. *Journal of International Consumer Marketing*, 23: 181–192.
4   Lamb, C, Hair, J, McDaniel, C, Boshoff, C, Terblanche, N, Elliott, R & Klopper, H. 2015. Marketing, 5th ed. Cape Town: Oxford University Press, 76, 61–63; Dobson, J. 2003. Method to their madness: Dispelling the myth of economic rationality as a behavioral ideal. *Research in International Business*, 17(1): 181.
5   iSpot.tv. n.d. Panetene TV commercials. Available at: https://www.ispot.tv/brands/dWp/pantene (accessed on 31 July 2018).
6   Sonnenberg, N.C. & Erasmus, A.C. 2008. Exploring the role of retailer image and store brands as extrinsic cues in young urban consumers' choice of interior textile products. *Advances in Consumer Research* (Latin American ed.), 2: 71–76.
7   Ranyard, R., Hinkley, L. Williamson, J. & McHugh, S. 2006. The role of mental accounting in consumer credit decision processes. *Journal of Economic Psychology*, 27: 571–588.
8   Lamb et al., op. cit., 49–54, 207; Fischer, R. 2006. Congruence and functions of personal and cultural values: Do my values reflect my culture's issues? *Personality and Social Psychology Bulletin*, 32: 1 419–1 431.
9   https://www.google.co.za/search?q=Daniel+Craig+Land+Rover+advertisement&tbm=isch&source=iu&ictx=1&fir=OI92OjNgBkt6nM%253A%252CZfAC5sFfH1K4GM%252C_&usg=__1dadq_vQtI0xpyuuKaQAyHj9p1Q%3D&sa=X&ved=2ahUKEwj25Nnfw8bcAhWHCMAKHX9xCIYQ9QEwAHoECAUQBA#imgrc=OI92OjNgBkt6nM:
10 Lamb et al., ibid., 107; Nilsson, D. 2007. A cross-cultural comparison of self-service technology use. *European Journal of Marketing*, 3/4(41): 367.
11 Solomon, M.R. 2010. *Consumer behavior: Buying, having, being*, 8th ed. New Jersey: Prentice Hall, 549.
12 Schiffman & Wisenblit, op. cit., 98, 106.
13 Lamb et al., op. cit., 108.

14 Parker, S. & Keim, K.S. 2004. Emic perspectives of body weight in overweight and obese white women with limited income. *Journal of Nutrition Education and Behavior*, 36(6): 282.

15 Mastamet-Mason, A., De Klerk, H.M. & Ashdown, SP. 2012. Identification of a unique African female body shape. *International Journal for Clothing Science and Technology*, 5(2):105.

16 Yakup, D., Mucahit, C. & Reyhan, O. 2011. The impact of cultural factors on the consumer buying behavior examined through an empirical study. *International Journal of Business and Social Science*, 2(5): 109–114.

17 Sonnenberg & Erasmus, op. cit., 71; Schroeder, J.E. 2009. The cultural codes of branding. *Marketing Theory*, 9(1): 123; Nilsson, op. cit., 367.

18 Schroeder, J.E. & Salzer-Morling, M. 2006. *Brand culture*. New York: Routledge, 54.

19 Truffert, A. 2015. South Africa: The rise of the 'Black Diamonds'. Available at: http://www.butterflylondon.com/south-africa-the-rise-of-the-black-diamonds/ (accessed on 14 June 2018); Nieftagodien, S. & Van der Berg, S. 2007. Consumption patterns and the black middle class: The role of assets. Stellenbosch Economic Working Papers: 02/07 Department of Economics and the Bureau for Economic Research. University of Stellenbosch. Available at: http://www.ekon.sun.ac.za/wpapers/2007/wp022007/wp-02-2007.pdf (accessed on 14 June 2018); Bevan-Dye, A.L., Garnett, A. & De Klerk, N. 2012. Materialism, status consumption and consumer ethnocentrism amongst black generation Y students in South Africa. *African Journal of Business Management*, 6(16): 5579.

20 Lamb et al., op. cit., 109, 110.

21 Wikipedia. n.d. Pretzel. Available at: https://en.wikipedia.org/wiki/Pretzel#/media/File:Fastenbrezel.JPG (accessed on 31 July 2018).

22 Erasmus, A.C., Donoghue, S. & Dobbelstein, T. 2014. Consumers' perception of the complexity of selected household purchase decisions. Available at: https://repository.up.ac.za/handle/2263/42268?show=full (accessed on 21 June 2018); Schiffman & Wisenblit, op. cit., 47, 48; Lamb, C.W., Hair, J.F., McdanieL, C., Boshoff, C., Terblanche, N., Elliot, R., & Klopper, H.B. 2010. *Marketing*, 4th ed. Cape Town: Oxford University Press, 525.

23 Erasmus et al., ibid., 302; Kardes, F.R., Cline, T.W. & Cronley, M.L. 2011. *Consumer behavior Science and practice*, international ed. Australia: South-Western Cengage Learning, 64; Solomon, 2010, op. cit., 307; Schiffman & Wisenblit, op. cit., 47, 48.

24 Erasmus et al., op. cit., 302; Solomon, ibid.

25 Schiffman & Wisenblit, op. cit., 366; Koch, J., Einsend, M. & Petermann, A. 2008. How complexity impacts path dependent decision making: The mediating role of heuristics. Available at: http://www.acrwebsite.org/search/view-conference-proceedings.aspx?Id=14117 (accessed on 14 June 2018).

26 Lamb et al., op. cit., 86–89.

27 Solomon, 2018, op. cit., 427–429; Erasmus, A.C. & Gothan, A.J. 2004. The complex role of a salesperson in an appliance sales context. *Journal for Family Ecology and Consumer Sciences*, 32: 94–104.

28 Lamb et al., op. cit., 86–89; Schiffman & Wisenblit, op. cit., 161–163.

29 Lamb et al., ibid., 5–9, 25–26; Babin, B. & Harris, E.G. 2013. *Consumer behaviour*, student ed. Mason, OH: South-Western Cengage Learning, 288.

30 Lamb et al., ibid., 95, 102, 184; Du Plessis, P.J., Rousseau, G.G., Boshoff, C., Ehlers, L., Engelbrecht, M., Joubert., R. & Sanders, S. 2007. *Buyer behaviour: Understanding consumer psychology and marketing*, 4th ed. Southern Africa: Oxford University Press, 9.

31 Jobber, D. 2010. *Principles and practice of marketing*, 6th ed. London: McGraw-Hill, 111; Parumasur, S. B. & Roberts-Lombard, M. 2012. *Consumer behaviour*, 2nd ed. Cape Town: Juta, 327.

32 Lamb et al., op. cit., 39, 564; Parumasur & Roberts-Lombard, ibid., 327.

33 Lamb et al., ibid., 106; Schiffman & Wisenblit, op. cit., 63; Terblanche, N.S. & Boshoff, C. 2003. The controllable elements of the total retail experience: A study of clothing shoppers. *International Journal of Economic and Management Science*, 6(1): 143–157.

34 Lamb et al., ibid., 84–92; Schiffman & Wisenblit, ibid., 47, 48; Solomon, 2010, op. cit., 7.

35 Lamb et al., ibid., 95–99, 106.

36 Ibid., 86–89.

37 Jobber, op. cit., 137; Schiffman & Wisenblit, op. cit., 370; Koch et al., op. cit.
38 Lamb et al., op. cit., 89–90; Kardes et al., op. cit., 63, 64; Hawkins, D.I. & Mothersbaugh, D.L. 2010. *Consumer behavior: Building marketing strategy.* New York: Mc Graw Hill, 564; Schiffman & Wisenblit, op. cit., 372, 373.
39 Lamb et al., ibid., 106; Schiffman & Wisenblit, ibid., 374; Sonnenberg, N.C., Erasmus, A.C. & Donoghue, S. 2011. Significance of environmental sustainability issues in consumers' choice of major household appliances in South Africa. *International Journal of Consumer Studies,* 35(2): 72, 74.
40 Lamb et al., ibid., 240.
41 Lamb et al., ibid., 91; Schiffman & Wisenblit, ibid., 189, 374; Lindquist, J.D. & Sirgy, M.J. 2006. *Shopper, buyer, and consumer behavior: Theory, marketing applications, and public policy implications,* 3rd ed. Ohio: Thomson, 107.
42 Ibid., 91, 92.
43 Schiffman & Wisenblit, op. cit., 189, 374; Hawkins & Mothersbaugh, op. cit., 363.
44 Schiffman & Wisenblit, ibid., 374.
45 Ibid., 123.
46 Lamb et al., op. cit., 384.
47 Sonnenberg et al., op. cit., 71–76.
48 Naidoo, P. 2018. South African millennials' propensity to adopt voluntary simplistic clothing purchasing and consumption choices. Master's dissertation. University of Pretoria.
49 Lamb et al., op. cit., 11; Jobber, op. cit., 37; Kirca, A., Jayachandran, S. & Bearden, W. 2005. Market orientation: A meta analytic review and assessment of its antecedents and impact on performance. *Journal of Marketing,* 69(2): 24–41.
50 Lamb et al., ibid., 12.
51 Ibid.
52 Ibid., 13.
53 Lamb et al., ibid., 14; Sheth, J.N., Sisodia, R.S. & Sharma, A. 2000. The antecedents and consequences of customer centric marketing. *Journal of the Academy of Marketing Science,* winter, 28: 55–66.
54 Lamb et al., ibid., 13, 154; Jobber, op. cit., 108, 259.
55 Jobber, ibid., 194.
56 Dobson, J. 2003. Method to their madness: Dispelling the myth of economic rationality as a behavioral ideal. *Research in International Business,* 17(1): 198.
57 Lamb et al., op. cit., 15.
58 Lamb et al., ibid., 64–65, 118; Chong, A.Y. 2013. Mobile commerce usage activities: The roles of demographic and motivation variable. *Technological Forecasting and Social Change,* 80: 1354.

PART TWO
INTERNAL FACTORS

CHAPTER 2

CONSUMER MOTIVATION

Elrie Botha

LEARNING OBJECTIVES

After reading this chapter, you should be able to:

- define motivation
- explain the different theories of motivation
- name the factors influencing consumer motivation
- describe each of the factors influencing consumer motivation
- demonstrate how the motivational conflicts are applicable to consumer behaviour.

Key terms		
achievement	extrinsic motivation	power person
aesthetic person	goal setting	rational
affiliation	growth	relatedness
conscious	hierarchy	religious person
economic person	instrumentality	social person
emotional	intrinsic motivation	theoretical person
equity	motivation	unconscious
existence	power	valence
expectancy		

OPENING CASE STUDY

The Mokoena family decided four years ago to upgrade to DSTV premium. At that stage their daughter had just started high school and their son had just turned five years old. They were not going out much and therefore reasoned that spending a bit more on in-house entertainment was okay. Mr Mokoena enjoys the variety of channels and Mrs Mokoena loves her soapies, which she can watch on catch-up whenever she has time.

One day, Ghuguletu, their teenage daughter, asks if they can rather switch to Netflix as all her friends are watching it and they talk about it all the time, which makes her feel left out. She also finds the advertisements from Netflix on social media, Youtube and television fun and interesting. However, the rest of the family is reluctant at the time because they enjoy DSTV as they know it. Mr Mokoene does not know much about Netflix and his daughter can only tell him that it has a lot more options in terms of movies and shows. She is, however, uncertain about the costs involved and how much data it would use to download or stream shows.

A few weeks later, with the economy being negative and everyone having to cut back on their spending, the Mokoena family start considering cancelling their DSTV subscription to save money. Ghughuletu immediately reminds them about the Netflix option, which might be cheaper. Mr Mokoena, however, points out that the data necessary to make the downloads might be expensive and Mrs Mokoena does not want to sacrifice her soapies.

After a couple of months, Mr Mokoena upgrades to unlimited data because he needs to be available online 24 hours a day for his job and he has also noticed that there are some affordable options. Mrs Mokoena also hears from some friends about some interesting soapies that they are watching on Netflix, which will also interest her. Bonganie, the little brother, does not understand the problem because all his friends have Netflix and according to him, it is logical to switch. After much deliberation, Mr Mokoena finally decides to cancel the DSTV subscription and get Netflix instead.

2.1 INTRODUCTION

For centuries, philosophers have been intrigued with why people do what they do and what motivates them to behave in a certain manner. The Greek philosopher Aristotle (384–322 BC) suggested that motivation is a movement that originates from envisioning the real or apparent good. This envisioning or imagining of the consequence can inspire people to move towards the positive or avoid the negative.[2] According to Sigmund Freud (1856–1939), the founding father of psychoanalysis, people are driven (or motivated) to experience pleasurable effects and to avoid pain. Over time, different views and opinions about motivation have emerged. The role of an industrial psychologist or behavioural scientist is to understand the motivation of the consumer and how to influence this behaviour.

Figure 2.1 Aristotle[1]

In this chapter, we focus on defining motivation. We look at theories of motivation that are relevant to the consumer environment. We also examine factors that influence consumer motivation and explore a view on motivational conflict.

Figure 2.2 Sigmund Freud[3]

2.1.1   Defining motivation

Motivation can be defined as the factors that influence the behaviour of humans. Motivation either pushes a person towards certain behaviour or pulls that person away from other behaviour. Emotion plays an important role in motivation as it determines its strength or intensity. Consider the example of Mildred, a single woman in her late 50s. Her only daughter has moved from Cape Town to Johannesburg with her husband and one-year-old baby boy. She misses them so much that she decides she is going to look for a job in Gauteng and leave everything behind in Cape Town to move closer to the people that are important to her. Her emotion towards her family strengthens her decision. Her motivation to relocate is a result of the pushing factor of being close to her family rather than pulling away from something that she does not like in her current job. Factors such as personality and attitude also have an impact on motivation. These factors will be investigated in Chapter 5 and Chapter 6.

The term 'motivation' comes from the Latin word *movere*, which means 'to move'. Looking at what moves or motivates consumers is important when it comes to influencing their buying behaviour. Lifestyles have become increasingly busy and people need to make decisions based on the information available to them. Making choices has become more and more complex, with broader product ranges, more competitors and wider ranges from which to purchase. Complicating matters even further is the fact that the internet closes the distance between the consumer and the product. As a result, suppliers' need to influence the motivation of consumers is greater than ever before. As we saw with the Mokoena family's choice of entertainment, consumers are challenged with goals, situations, values and numerous other things regarding the choices they can make. We will discuss some of the factors that have an impact on consumers' behaviour in section 2.3. We will also explore the various theories of motivation in order to build a foundation for understanding the motivation of consumers and the factors that have an impact on it.

2.2 THEORIES OF MOTIVATION

Many of the different theories of motivation that exist have a direct link with consumer behaviour. Some of the theories that are considered important in the science of consumer behaviour are discussed below.

2.2.1   Maslow's hierarchy of needs

In 1943, psychologist Abraham Maslow (1908–1970) published his need hierarchy theory of motivation, which he based on his experiences working with patients during the Great Depression of the 1930s. According to him, human motivation is based on five basic needs. People have the same needs as animals on three levels, which are categorised as lower-order needs. However, there are two levels (levels four and five) which refer to higher-order needs that distinguish humans from other species. The different levels of needs, categorised according to Maslow's **hierarchy**, are shown in Figure 2.3.

As seen in Figure 2.3, the lower-order needs consist of the following:

- *Physiological needs:* These include the need for water, food, sex and sleep. These needs relate to the biological functioning of the body.
- *Safety needs:* These are the needs for safety and security, both physically and psychologically. They include a safe place to stay, job security, and freedom from physical and emotional abuse. Once the physiological needs have been satisfied, it is important for the individual concerned to know that there is a good chance that these needs will always be satisfied, which is why financial security is also important.
- *Social needs:* These include the need to belong and to be accepted by others. People search for companionship in various ways, including forming

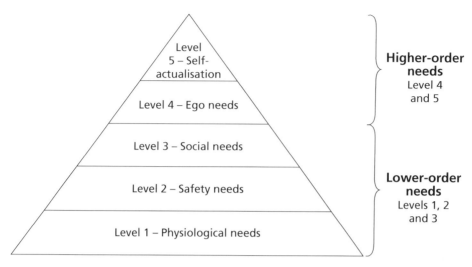

Figure 2.3 Maslow's hierarchy of needs[4]

romantic relationships, making friends, belonging to a church or social groups and being part of a team at work.

The higher-order needs consist of the following:

- *Ego:* This is the need to acquire self-esteem and to be ambitious. In order to be recognised by others, a person must achieve and be successful. This recognition leads to self-respect and confidence. This can be achieved by successfully completing a course or a degree or something similar.
- *Self-actualisation:* This refers to the need to be able to give back to society what was learnt and experienced during a person's lifetime, while being creative and spontaneous. When people speak of self-actualisation, they mean fulfilling their full potential.

Maslow maintained that the lower-order needs must be fulfilled before people are able to consider satisfying their higher-order needs. However, critical analysis of this reasoning reveals that it is not necessarily always true in reality. Extreme circumstances such as war may affect the relative importance of the various needs. For example, some of the people who were forced to live in concentration camps during World

Figure 2.4 Social needs are important and therefore people search for companionship. Making new friends is one of the tactics to fulfil this need.

War II found that satisfying their needs for the companionship of family and friends (that is, their social needs) was more important to them than fighting for food (that is, satisfying their physiological needs). Victor Frankl (1905–1997), an Austrian neurologist and psychiatrist who was also a Holocaust survivor, is an example of a person who endured incarceration in a concentration camp where he did not have access to the things required to satisfy his basic lower-order needs (physiological and safety needs), but was able to satisfy his higher-order needs by finding meaning even in the most difficult circumstances.

Maslow understood the hierarchy as steps following one after the other in a particular order. He believed that the first need level should be satisfied before the next one would act as a motivator. His hierarchy suggests that you should not, for example, try to sell an expensive house, which represents a safety need, to a starving family before the physiological needs of that family have been addressed. Making available bursaries for academic courses that pay for tuition fees (in other words, satisfying an ego need) is not a viable solution if the student does not have money with which to buy food (in other words, to satisfy his or her physiological needs) during the period of study. A gallery selling attractive art, which appeals to people's need for self-actualisation, is more likely to be successful in a neighbourhood or community where the people have satisfied their lower-order needs, such as enough food and safe housing, than in a community where these needs have not been met.

DISCUSSION

The Gauteng-based radio station 947 uses a phrase: 'If you love Jo'burg, 947 loves you'.

1. On which level of Maslow's hierarchy of needs do they focus?
2. Why do you think this is an important need to focus on, especially in today's world where technology replaces activities where people previously needed to get together?

2.2.2 McClelland's need theory

American psychological theorist David McClelland (1917–1998) stated that motivational needs are learnt throughout a person's life and that different individuals rate different needs as more important than other needs. For one person, the need for **power** may be more important than the need for **achievement**, while another person may rank his or her need for achievement as more important than the need for **affiliation**. He focused on three internal needs (see Figure 2.5):

* The need for power
* The need for affiliation
* The need for achievement

Figure 2.5 presents McClelland's need theory schematically. One need does not follow another need in a set order, as is the case in Maslow's hierarchy of needs. For each person, one of these three needs is dominant and may be followed by any other need. For example, the need for power and achievement may be evident in a successful businessman, while a salesman may have a strong need for affiliation and achievement. The three needs can be understood as follows:[5]

- *Need for affiliation (nAff):* This is the need to spend time with others and to be part of a group, and the desire to be accepted by others. A person with a strong nAff might be satisfied in a client service or interaction position.

- *Need for achievement (nAch):* This is the desire to overcome obstacles and accomplish goals. A person with a high nAch need should try to avoid high-risk as well as low-risk situations as it is important to ensure that he or she experiences success.

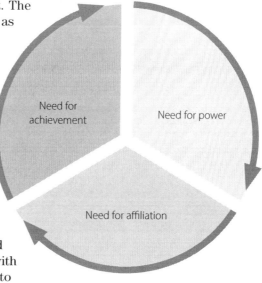

Figure 2.5 McClelland's need theory[6]

- *Need for power (nPow):* This is the need to influence or control others, or to coach and encourage others. It can be divided into two categories:
  1. The individual need for power, which is often selfish and is perceived as being undesirable
  2. Institutional power or social power, which strives to further the goals of the group.

It is important to remember that there is no particular order of importance for the three needs discussed under McClelland's theory. Each consumer has a different need as dominant factor. Good advertisements focus on all three needs. For example, an energy drink might be presented as giving the person who consumes it the energy required to lead the conversation at an important business meeting (in other words, it is portrayed as enabling that person to satisfy his or her need for power). This person may then be shown driving away in an expensive car (satisfying the need for achievement), and then partying with friends that evening (meeting the need for affiliation) without getting tired. Thus, the advertisement uses images of all three needs being satisfied in order to reach as many consumers as possible. This is easier to accomplish in a television advertisement as the scenes can follow on each other and therefore display the different motivations.

DISCUSSION

Take a few magazines and page through the advertisements.
1. Determine which refer to the different needs of McClelland.
2. Do most refer to one, two or all three needs?

2.2.3 The ERG theory of Alderfer

Clayton Alderfer (1940–2015), an American psychologist, further developed Maslow's hierarchy of needs by categorising the lower-order and higher-order needs into his existence, relatedness and growth (ERG) theory in the late 1960s. Alderfer proposed that more than one need can be satisfied at the same time. There is also no hierarchy indicating the importance of the various needs, suggesting that all needs are equal. The three sets of needs are illustrated in Figure 2.6.

As seen in Figure 2.6, Alderfer's theory consists of three concepts:[8]

* **Existence** (E): This refers to a person's physiological and materialistic well-being.
* **Relatedness** (R): This refers to a person's need for good relationships with others.
* **Growth** (G): This refers to a person's need to grow and use his or her abilities to increase his or her competence.

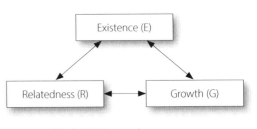

Figure 2.6 Alderfer's ERG theory[7]

As Alderfer argued, more than one need can be satisfied at the same time. For example, an advertisement for a new easy-to-cook chicken-in-sauce portrays the satisfaction of all three needs by using the image of an inviting and friendly family (R) looking neat and well-dressed (E), with the mother presenting the cooked chicken to her family, while boasting about the cooking skills she used (G) in providing them with this nutritious meal (E).

Kim and Drumwright[9] refer to social network platforms which enhance the social relatedness aspect of consumer motivation. People like and share products that friends upload and this create a feeling of relatedness. For example, when Lillian uploads a photo to Instagram of her family enjoying the hot chocolate that she has just prepared for them, using a specific new brand of hot chocolate, her friends might be influenced to try the new product. Alternatively, attention on social media can have negative results for companies or brands. For example, if Zindile received terrible customer service when she returned a faulty garment to a specific store, she may decide to post a message about the specific garment as well as the store on her Facebook profile. Many of Zindile's friends might now think twice before purchasing this specific brand's clothing or visiting this specific store again.

In Figure 2.7, an example of ERG is demonstrated.

2.2.4 Adams's equity theory

In 1963, John Stacey Adams, a workplace and behavioural psychologist, developed his equity theory, which is based on the belief that it is important to strive

Figure 2.7 Using an image like this in an advert demonstrates ERG in a

for fairness and justice. **Equity** occurs when a person perceives him- or herself as being treated equally or fairly when compared to another person in a similar position. A person's motivation is driven by a sense of inequality in an effort to find equality and fairness[10]. For example, a new staff member joins a company, and is offered a slightly higher salary than the current staff on the same level, in order to attract the new staff member. The existing staff members were comfortable with their salaries until they realised that the new staff member is earning more than them even though they are on the same level as this new employee. The existing staff now feel that they are not being treated equally, which creates a feeling of unfairness. This might motivate them to talk to their managers about the situation or even consider looking for another job.

The input should be a fair trade in terms of what is received. In other words, it should be characterised by an even exchange. For example, when a couple decides to save for their child's education, they would expect the fair trade to be that enough money will be available to them on the day when they need to withdraw it to pay for the child's studies. Consider the retail industry: imagine you saved to buy an expensive leather jacket before the winter starts, only to find it on a 50% sale two weeks later. Although you were prepared to pay the full price and feel happy with your purchase, when you realise that it was possible to pay half of the price, you feel less happy.

The equity theory can be applied to the seller–buyer relationship.[11] It refers to the perception that what we believe is equal to 'relevant others'. Since each consumer expects to be treated fairly and equally, in the same way as other consumers who are similar to him or her, two views are important and should be considered:
- *Fair trade:* Whatever is put in should ensure a specific output.
- *Equality in terms of others:* A person should be treated the same as other people who are similar to him or her.

For example, when consumers take their motor vehicles for a maintenance service, they believe that they will receive good-quality service as they schedule the visit based on the correct kilometre reading (that is, fair trade), and that they will pay the same that every other consumer with a similar service request pays (that is, equality in terms of others). Should the consumer not receive equitable treatment, he or she will be motivated to make use of a different service provider.

Certain bank clients with strong financial portfolios could potentially receive preferential treatment. Clients with less strong portfolios might also want to be treated in this preferential manner. This could encourage them to open additional investment accounts or to purchase other products.

2.2.5   Vroom's expectancy theory

Victor Vroom (1932–), a professor at the Yale School of Management, introduced his expectancy theory in 1964. The theory proposes that people are motivated by the results they expect from an action. This theory differs from need theories as it claims that motivation is based on the outcome of how much a person wants a reward. It is rather the person's input that will lead to achieving the outcome than pursuing a need.[12] It implies that people tend to analyse the costs and benefits of possible behavioural actions. If the value of any of these elements (valence, instrumentality and expectancy) is zero, the equation's sum is zero. The three elements that influence the motivational process are presented in Figure 2.8.

Figure 2.8 The three elements on which Vroom's expectancy theory is based

As seen in Figure 2.8, the three elements or perceptions are as follows:
* *Valence:* This refers to the value or the degree of satisfaction an individual expects to receive from an outcome.
* *Instrumentality:* This is a person's belief that his or her action or input will lead to a specific outcome.
* *Expectancy:* This refers to the probability that the outcome will be achieved. This probability is based on past experiences, self-confidence and the perceived difficulty of achieving the outcome.

For example, the Black Friday sale is an important item on the retail calendar. Consumers are motivated to endure the long queues because they expect to be satisfied with the savings (that is, valence) they will be making. They know which shop offers the best savings on the products they prefer (that is, instrumentality) and that they should start early when the shops open to beat the mad rush in order to get the best items (that is, expectancy).

2.2.6   Goal-setting theory

For the purpose of this discussion, we will focus on the model that Dr Edwin Locke, the pioneer of goal-setting theory, developed in the 1960s. In 1968, Locke wrote an article entitled 'Toward a theory of task motivation and incentives',[13] in which he explains that people are motivated by clear goals and appropriate feedback. According to Locke, the following reasons make **goal setting** important:

- Goals direct attention towards the need that is set as a goal.
- Goals regulate effort because they motivate the person to act.
- Goals increase persistence because the person has a clear picture of the end result in his or her mind.
- Goals help create plans and actions to achieve the end result.

There are five key principles of goal setting specified by Locke:
1. *Clarity:* A goal should be clear and specific.
2. *Challenge:* People are motivated by the reward of achievement.
3. *Commitment:* The goal should be understood and bought into.
4. *Feedback:* Feedback helps the person in question to clarify his or her expectations, adjust the level of goal difficulty and receive recognition.
5. *Task complexity:* A goal should not be too easy or there might be no challenge involved. However, when a goal is too difficult, the person might give up before he or she has even started.

Consumers set various goals, for example saving money, losing weight and starting a new hobby. If a consumer, for example, decided to set a goal to save money for retirement, that person would start focusing his or her attention on this particular goal. The person would make some effort to obtain information, perhaps by searching for it on the internet or by talking to others who may be able to help. Even if he or she does not find the right solution immediately, the person will persist in working towards his or her goal. That person will put plans of action in place in terms of how to start saving and which would be the best way to go about this process.

Figure 2.9 Vroom's theory indicates that motivation is about the expected outcome.

By implementing the key principles, a consumer can strengthen his or her resolve to achieve a goal. For a consumer to save as much money as possible, there should be clarity on how much money that person would like to save for his or her retirement as well as how much time is available because without this, the person will never know how much money is enough for retirement. The person's understanding of this goal will ensure that he or she does not deviate from the action plan and is committed to saving the planned amount every month. The person will receive feedback in the form of bank statements indicating the growth of his or her savings within a particular time frame. If the person aims too low in terms of the amount he or she wants to save, the person might give up because he or she will realise that this amount will not be enough for his or her retirement. If the person aims too high, the target might be too difficult to reach and he or she will also give up.

APPLICATION

'Walk for your health' competition

An industrial psychologist who is tasked with the wellness aspect of the company's employees, decides to introduce a 'Walk for your health' competition at the company. The different departments of the company will compete with one another to see who can log the most steps in 30 days. Those staff members who are interested in this competition will receive a pedometer which they will wear to track the number of steps they take each day. Departments will be encouraged to come up with creative ways of increasing their totals through, for example, taking walks during lunch, going for group runs after work and on weekends, choosing the printer and bathroom which are furthest away from where they are seated etc. There will be weekly check-ins from a fitness consultant who will keep track of and reveal the progress of the different teams as well as provide training tips. The department who logs the most steps during the 30 days will win a day cruise on a yacht as well as vouchers to spend at their favourite fitness store to continue their fitness journey.

2.2.7   Overview of motivation theories

Table 2.1 gives an overview of the theories that have been explained.

Table 2.1 Theories of motivation

	Maslow's hierarchy of needs	McClelland's need theory	Alderfer's ERG theory	Adam's equity theory	Vroom's expectancy theory	Goal-setting theory
Definition	Motivation is based on a hierarchy of five needs.	Motivation is based on three needs. The order of importance of these needs is different for each person.	Motivation is based on three needs, of which more than one can be satisfied at a time.	Motivation is driven by a sense of inequality in an effort to find equality and fairness.	Motivation is based on the results a person expects from an action.	Motivation occurs by clear goals and appropriate feedback.
Pioneer's details	Psychologist: Abraham Maslow	American psychological theorist: David McClelland	Psychologist: Clayton Alderfer	Workplace and behavioural psychologist: John Stacey Adams	Business school lecturer at Yale School of Management: Victor H. Vroom	Psychologist: Edwin Locke
Brief explanation	Before a person can satisfy a higher-order need such as painting a picture, he or she must be satisfied relatively permanently in terms of the lower-level needs, such as living in a safe environment and having enough food to eat.	A person has a need for affiliation, achievement or power. One of these needs is always stronger than the others. The dominant need is different for each individual.	People have the need to exist, grow and relate to each other. All needs are equal and a person can satisfy more than one need at a time.	Equity occurs when a person perceives that he or she is being treated equally or fairly when compared with a person similar to him or her. The input should be a fair trade in terms of what is received. In other words, it should be an even exchange.	The theory is based on the outcome of how much a person wants a reward and beliefs that his or her input will lead to achieving the outcome rather than pursuing a need. As such, it implies that people tend to analyse the costs and benefits of possible behavioural actions.	The five key principles of the theory include clarity, challenge, commitment, feedback and task complexity.

2.3 CONSUMER MOTIVATION

In this section, we will examine some of the factors that play a role in the motivation of the consumer.

2.3.1 Individual differences

Consumers are diverse in personality, values and demographics. Personality will be discussed in Chapter 5 and demographics are considered under market segmentation (Chapter 11). One of the individual differences that influences consumer behaviour and is values. A value is a principle or belief that is ingrained in the individual's being. According to Eduard Spranger, a German philosopher and psychologist, there are six value orientations:[14]

- The **theoretical person**: This person values knowledge and the deeper meaning of things. As a consumer, he or she would like to know more about issues such as how the product works, where the raw material comes from or what the impact on the environment would be. There was no real evidence in the opening case study to suggest that anyone in the Mokoena family was a theoretical person, for example Mr. Mokoena was not really aware of the finer details of how Netflix works and his daughter was not readily able to provide more information either – Mr and Mrs Mokoena simply knew that they liked their DSTV package. If anyone had been interested in information on how it works, what options are available, how much it would cost, how much data it would use etc., then that person might have been considered to be a theoretical person.
- The **economic person**: This person is driven by the utility motive that something should be useful or practical, and as a consumer wants to see evidence of value for money. He or she will not buy something that he or she does not need or that is unnecessarily expensive. Mr Mokoena had some of the characteristics of an economic person as he wanted value for money when switching to Netflix and he wanted to make sure that it would not cost too much in terms of data usage.
- The **social person**: This person experiences meaning in relationships with others. To motivate this consumer, personal interest will have to be established and a relationship will have to be built to add value. He or she can also be convinced to buy a product by showing the benefits of this product for society or the family. Mrs Mokoena was convinced to switch when she realised her friends were watching series on Netflix that she would also enjoy and would then be able to discuss with them. This could indicate that she also has some of the characteristics of a social person.
- The **power person**: This person needs to be in a position of power. Focusing on the importance of the consumer and giving him or her superior choices will impress the consumer who is driven by power. If Mr Mokoene had been a power person he would have been impressed by a sales consultant or representative of Netflix who contacted him to discuss the service, costs, data usage and other information regarding the service with him.
- The **religious person**: This person's behaviour has a spiritual foundation. These individuals believe that things happen for a reason. Such a consumer will be less influenced by facts and encouragement from marketers.

- The **aesthetic person**: This person values beauty or the experience of beautiful things. As a consumer, this person is influenced by tasteful displays and creative selling skills. The manner in which Netflix advertises their product was attractive to Ghuguletu. We could consider that she has an aesthetic value orientation.

People may have more than one value orientation. Some value orientations may be stronger or more significant than others to different consumers. In the case of the Mokoena family, the social value seems strongest, with the mother and children interacting with their friends about the content they watch. Ghuguletu also displays some aesthetic values and Mr Mokoena relates to the economic person.

2.3.2 Rational and emotional motives

Most consumers are influenced by both rational and emotional motives, but one is usually more dominant for an individual. In Chapter 3, you will learn about the left (rational) and the right (emotional or creative) brain hemispheres. The **rational** motivational approach focuses on facts, logic, durability and quality. **Emotional** motivation focuses on subjective criteria such as fun, pleasure and beauty. The most effective advertisements use a mixture of rational and emotional motivations. For example, a consumer who wants to install a new blind in his or her house will consider how good it looks (emotional motivation) as well as the quality (rational motivation) of the available products[15].

2.3.3 Intrinsic and extrinsic motives

Intrinsic motivation refers to the pleasure a person gets from an activity. It is a motivation from within and not influenced by any external rewards, for example entertainment. **Extrinsic motivation** is a means to an end and is motivated from an external reward. A focus on intrinsic motivation usually lasts longer than a focus on extrinsic motivation, as it is a motivation from within not influenced by external forces. For example, buying a fast car for the thrill of its

Figure 2.10 An example of intrinsic motivation

speed is intrinsic motivation. If you buy the fast car because it can get you from point A to point B quickly, then the motivation is extrinsic.

2.3.4   Conscious and unconscious motives

Consumers are aware of certain needs, but are completely unaware of others. For example, a student who has to buy a textbook for a particular module will go to a bookshop and buy it on the spot as he or she has a **conscious** knowledge of the fact that he or she wants to buy the book. The student likes to be organised and present his or her work neatly, but might not think of this need when buying his or her study material (stationary). However, if the student sees a display of assignment covers, coloured pens and paper while browsing through the bookshop, this might trigger the **unconscious** need to organise his or her study material and the student might be prompted to buy these items.

2.3.5   Situational impact on motives

The situation or occasion for which the consumer is shopping can have an impact on the motivation of the person. If a consumer is buying a gift for his or her daughter, it will be a different experience from buying a gift for his or her boss or co-worker, and different factors will influence the consumer. Shopping for new clothes is normally pleasurable, but if you are shopping for a new outfit for a funeral, it might affect the way you approach the shopping experience.

Figure 2.11 The situation or occasion for which a consumer is shopping can have an impact on the motivation of the person.

2.3.6   Urgency motives

The urgency of the need influences a consumer's behaviour. If you know you need new shoes for the winter when it is still a few months away, you can take your time and look for the best offer until you find the pair of shoes that suits your particular needs. If, however, you were shopping for a pair of shoes to wear to a function the following day, your behaviour would probably be slightly different. You would go directly to the shop you know is most likely to have the right shoes even though it is more expensive, when you would normally have shopped around for a better deal.

2.3.7   Polarity influence on motives

Positive influences push consumers towards certain behaviours, for example going for a flu shot before the winter starts and drinking extra supplements to enhance your immune system. On the other hand, negative influences motivate the consumer to avoid negative consequences, for example buying a deodorant to prevent body odour. Marketers usually emphasise the positive aspect or influence of a product rather than the negative aspect. As a result, advertisements for deodorants usually focus on the positive aspects (such as enhancing the confidence of a person which could lead to attracting other people) rather than the negative aspects (such as the occurrence of body odour if a deodorant is not used).

As discussed, different factors have an influence on the motivation of consumers. These factors do not operate in isolation, but can be combined. Some factors have a stronger influence than others at a specific point in time, while another factor might be stronger on another occasion. It sometimes also happens that these motivations are in conflict with each other. In the next section, we will take a closer look at conflicting motivations.

APPLICATION

Student housing

At the entrance of the university's administrative building, a poster advertising private housing for students is posted. It is five one-bedroom flats with covered parking in a secure complex. The wifi is included and there are barbeque facilities that the tenants can use. Some of the comments from parents and students are listed below. See if you agree with the value orientations that might influence the consumer:

Person	Consumers' comments	Possible motivational factors
Student 1	I love the building, it is modern and beautiful.	Emotional
Student 2	This is much closer to the university than where I am currently staying. I will save on petrol and the renewal of my lease is due this month. Instead of renewing I can take up this offer.	Economic person Situational
Parent 1	I was looking for private, affordable accommodation for my child. This seems fair and wifi is included, which can cost a lot.	Economic person Rational
Student 3	The barbeque area is a real added benefit; I can just imagine all my friends getting together. Everyone will love visiting me.	Social person
Parent 2	Oh wonderful! I was so worried that we would not be able to find accommodation close to the university. This seems to be the perfect place, just when we needed it.	Urgency

2.4 MOTIVATIONAL CONFLICT

Decisions are not always easy to make. Most of the time, decisions depend on multiple factors that all have a direct impact on the decision-making process. Sometimes motivational influences complement and strengthen each other, but it may also happen that motivational factors are in conflict with each other and therefore complicate the decision-making process. Three scenarios can play out, as outlined in Figure 2.12:

- *Attraction–attraction:* The consumer has a desire or a need for something and finds this item on a sale. The item is easy to buy and therefore fulfils the consumer's desire or need. For example, towards the end of winter, summer clothing for the new season is already starting to come into the shops. It is still really cold and Mary loves the leather jacket (that is, attraction) for sale at the department store. The store needs to make space for the summer clothes, so there is a winter sale and the jacket is marked down. Mary can now afford to buy the jacket (that is, attraction).

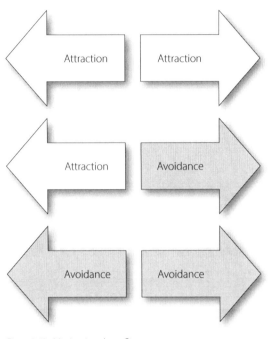

Figure 2.12 Motivational conflict

- *Attraction–avoidance:* The consumer really wants a particularly pricey item, but does not want to spend too much money on it. For example, Samuel wants new soccer togs because he was chosen for the first team (that is, attraction). However, he has to buy the new togs with his pocket money. He would rather save the money so that he can spend it on his summer holiday (that is, avoidance).
- *Avoidance–avoidance:* The consumer does not want a particular product or service and is also not happy to pay the cost of this item. For example, Mark is standing in the queue at the pharmacy. He has to buy flu medicine. He is feeling awful and not in the mood to pay for expensive medicine that does not taste great and will probably not make him feel better immediately.

2.4.1   How retailers make use of conflict situations
Retailers could make use of conflict situations as follows:
- *Attraction–attraction:* Retailers could advertise sale items with clearly marked signs to increase interest. Interesting displays can be used to match items, adding to the consumer's attraction towards the products, for example a denim on discount with matching boots, which have also been marked down. The customer was looking for a new denim and pair of boots for a specific occasion and now both are on discount.
- *Attraction–avoidance:* Consumers might be faced with the motivation to buy a product, but do not have enough money to do so immediately. The retailer could use methods such as 'buy now, pay later' to increase the likelihood of deciding to buy the product.

RESEARCH

With reference to Adam's equity theory, a study done by Gershoff, Kivetz and Keinan[16] investigated the perception of fairness when the production process was altered to exclude or degrade certain features. This process, called versioning, is often done to increase the welfare of the organisation and the consumer. Six studies indicated that consumers perceive the process of versioning as unfair and unethical, and believed that it resulted in an inferior version of the original product. Their views were so strong that they even lead to a decrease in the intention of consumers to buy the brand again.

One of the factors influencing consumer motivation is the emotional state of a person. Di Muro and Murray[17] report on three consequential choice studies that used scent and music to influence the mood of consumers. They found that consumers in a positive mood tend to choose products congruent with their level of arousal as well as the valence of their current affective state. For example, people who are in a relaxed mood (pleasant, low-arousal mood), prefer relaxing products. People who are feeling excited (pleasant, high-arousal mood) prefer exciting products. However, consumers who are experiencing negative moods prefer products that are incongruent with their affective state. For example, people in an unpleasant, low-arousal mood prefer pleasant, high-arousal products, while people who are in an unpleasant, high-arousal mood prefer pleasant, low-arousal products.

- *Avoidance–avoidance:* Spending money on insurance is not necessarily a pleasant action, but when the marketer uses figures of theft and losses balanced against a small amount to be paid to know your assets are insured, the consumer might be more willing to buy the product.

SUMMARY

Consumers are faced with numerous decisions each day and their motivation plays a role in which choices are finally made. In some cases, the motivation is to avoid an action, while in other cases, it is to react. Various factors have an influence on the motivation of consumers. Factors such as individual differences, emotions, intrinsic or extrinsic motives, conscious or unconscious motives, the situation, urgency, and positive or negative polarity have to be considered. These factors are all based on theories about motivation.

Sometimes the consumer experiences motivational conflict. The product or service is attractive to him or her, but it could be that the cost is too high. It could also be that it is an attractive offer in terms of the product or service as well as the price. In some cases, the product or service is not attractive and the consumer also does not want to pay for it, but is obliged to do so. It is important to have an understanding of the factors that motivate consumers since this information influences the way in which products and services are marketed.

SELF-ASSESSMENT QUESTIONS

1. Explain the similarities between Maslow's hierarchy of needs and McClelland's need theory.
2. Which theory indicates that making plans can help a person to achieve a goal?
3. Linda decides to join the gym because there is a special after the December holidays and she loves the new modern lay out. Which consumer motivation factors are relevant in her decision making?
4. Which factor has an impact on motivation if a consumer decides to buy a new suitcase at an airport because his or her suitcase's handle has just broken?
5. What sort of motivational conflict occurs if a consumer has to buy life insurance?

EXPERIENTIAL EXERCISE

You are the human resource manager of a retail company. You have been tasked with encouraging the sales managers to determine the goals of their teams and to motivate them to achieve it.
1. Explain how you would do this.
2. Which motivational theories would yield the best results?

CASE STUDY 1

Volunteers at a pet rescue centre

Three friends volunteer at a pet rescue centre on weekends. Although the plan was not to get involved and adopt any of the pets, they are having the following conversation:

Mary: The Labrador is so lovable, I hear they are real family dogs and good with children. My kids will enjoy having one.

Thabo: Yes, I also heard that, but I wish I could adopt that beautiful boer bull, he will win all the prices at the dog show. I would be such a proud owner.

Lindsey: I hope the two of you can take care of these dogs. At least I have a huge garden with lots of space for dogs to play. I will also be able to buy them the best food and toys.

Discussion questions

1. According to McClleland, which need is the strongest?
2. Based on the discussion between the friends, who has the strongest power need?
3. Based on the discussion between the friends, who has the strongest affiliation need?
4. Based on the discussion between the friends, who has the strongest achievement need?

CASE STUDY 2 (ADVANCED)

Marketing legal tobacco in the southern hemisphere

You are a marketing adviser and one of your important clients is the third-largest tobacco distributor in the southern hemisphere. Illegal trading of cigarettes is one of the largest threats that this company experiences. Many of the company's consumers are people from the lower-income group, and with legislation and taxes increasing the cost of cigarettes and other tobacco products, the company does not know how to motivate consumers to buy its legal yet more expensive products instead of illegal tobacco products. By going back to motivational theories, help them to find an effective solution.

Discussion questions
1. Which motivational theories could have an impact on this scenario?
2. What motivational factors could be considered?
3. Do you foresee any motivational conflict? If so, what?

ADDITIONAL RESOURCES

Visit the following websites:
- http://www.businessballs.com/maslow.htm
- http://www.mindtools.com/pages/article/human-motivation-theory.htm
- http://www.yourcoach.be/en/employee-motivation-theories/erg-motivation-theory-alderfer.php
- http://www.buzzle.com/articles/equity-theory-of-motivation.html
- http://www.mindtools.com/pages/article/newHTE_87.htm

REFERENCES

1 https://en.wikipedia.org/wiki/Aristotle#/media/File:Aristotle_Altemps_Inv8575.jpg (accessed 20 November 2018).
2 Bernacer, J. & Murillo, J.I. 2014. The Aristotelian conception of habit and its contributionto human neuroscience. *Frontiers in Human Neuroscience*, 8: 883.
3 https://en.wikipedia.org/wiki/Sigmund_Freud#/media/File:Sigmund_Freud,_by_Max_Halberstadt_(cropped).jpg (accessed 20 November 2018).
4 Maslow, A.H., Frager, R.D. & Fadiman, J. 1987. *Motivation and personality*, 3rd ed. Upper Saddle River, NJ: Pearson.
5 De Mooij, M. 2011. *Consumer behavior and culture: Consequences for global marketing and advertising*. London: SAGE, 160.
6 McClelland, D. C. 1985. Human motivation. Glenview, IL: Scott, Foresman.
7 Alderfer, Clayton P. (1969). "An empirical test of a new theory of human needs". Organizational Behavior and Human Performance. 4(2): 142–75.
8 Yang, C., Hwang, M. & Chen, Y. 2011. An empirical study of the existence, relatedness, and growth (ERG) theory in consumer's selection of mobile value-added services. Available at: https://www.researchgate.net/publication/266035490_An_empirical_study_of_the_existence_relatedness_and_growth_ERG_theory_in_consumer%27s_selection_of_mobile_value-added_services (accessed on 5 July 2018).
9 Kim, E. & Drumwright, M. 2016. Engaging consumers and building relationships in social media: How social relatedness influences intrinsic vs extrinsic consumer motivation. *Computers in Human behavior*, 63: 970–979. Available at: http://dx.doi.org/10.1016/j.chb.2016.06.025 (accessed on 5 July 2018).
10 From 'Pulse'. *Essentials* magazine of June 2018.
11 Osmonbekov, T. 2015. The impact of inequity, relationship-technology fit, and trust in conflict. Working paper series 15-01. Northern Arizona University, the W.A. Franke College of Business.
12 Lunenberg, F.C. 2011. Expectancy theory of motivation: Motivating by altering expectations. *International Journal of Management, Business and Administration*, 5(1): 1.
13 Jain, S. 2009. Self-control and optimal goals: A theoretical analysis. *Marketing Science*, 28(6): 1 027–1 045. Available at: http://www.wiwi.uni-bonn.de/kraehmer/Lehre/Beh_IO/Jain-SelfControlOptimalGoals.pdf (accessed on 5 July 2018).

14 Werner, A. 2018. Work-related attitudes and values. In Bergh, Z., *Introduction to work psychology*. Cape Town: Oxford University Press, 334.

15 From 'Sheet street'. Page 30 of *Essentials* magazine of June 2018.

16 Gershof, A.D., Kivets, R. & Keinan, A. 2012. Consumer response to versioning: How brands' production methods affect perceptions of unfairness. *Journal of Consumer Research*, 39(2): 382–398. Available at: http://www.jstor.org/discover/10.1086/663777?uid=2&uid=4&sid=21102051840077 (accessed on 5 July 2018).

17 Di Muro, F. & Murray, K.B. 2012. An arousal regulation explanation of mood effects on consumer choice. Available at: http://papers.ssrn.com/sol3/papers.cfm?abstract_id=2144802 (accessed on 5 July 2018).

CHAPTER 3

LEARNING AND INFORMATION PROCESSING

Elrie Botha

LEARNING OBJECTIVES

After reading this chapter, you should be able to:

- define learning
- explain the different theories of learning
- evaluate the how the theories of learning explain consumer behaviour
- discuss the influence of the brain on learning
- describe memory and consumer behaviour
- demonstrate how different methods of learning and memory can be enhanced.

Key terms

classical conditioning	operant conditioning
cognitive learning	positive reinforcement
negative reinforcement	social learning
neuron	

OPENING CASE STUDY

Jo-Ann was always curious about online shopping, but was too scared that something would go wrong to try it. One day after walking through the entire mall without finding the shoes she was looking for, her friend Lebo told her that it was not difficult to shop online and that she would show her how. After carefully looking at the steps Lebo took, Jo-Ann decided to try it. She found the perfect pair of shoes on a well-known web site and made the purchase. Three days later, her shoes arrived as promised. Jo-Ann was really happy and tried another purchase for a dress. This time, it arrived on time, however the dress did not fit well and she had to return it. It took more than a month to get the refund. She tried one more time, ordering a handbag at a special price from a web site that came up in her Facebook feed. After a week, she enquired about the status of her purchase. She was told it was still en route and given no indication of when to expect the delivery. After a month of waiting, she tried to cancel the order and get a refund. However, the shipping company told her that according to their records, her handbag had been delivered. So she lost her money. As a result of this, when her brother, Peter, suggested that they buy a gift for their mother for her birthday online, Jo-Ann was reluctant and shared her experiences with him. She had learnt to be careful when making purchases online.

3.1 INTRODUCTION

Every day, consumers are faced with a huge amount of information from advertisers and marketers who want to influence their decision-making process. Consumers are constantly observing, processing and storing information in their memories ab out the experiences they have. This information is available for them to retrieve at a later stage. For example, in the opening case study, Jo-Ann learnt that online shopping is not always successful and that one has to look carefully at delivery specifications and refunds. She stored this information in her memory and was able to advise her brother on the pitfalls.

Consumers are constantly involved in a process of learning and memorising information. It is important to understand this process as consumers can store positive as well as negative experiences.

3.1.1   Defining learning

Learning is a change in behaviour and knowledge as a result of an experience. A consumer can practise learning as an adaptive or problem-solving activity. In other words, learning results in a change of behaviour when an individual adapts to what was learnt or solves a problem based on previous experience. Learning is not always immediately evident, but occurs as a result of an individual's long-term memory. As you saw in the opening case study, Jo-Ann learnt through experience that online shopping can be effective, but that you need to make sure that it is a reputable company from which you order.

3.2 LEARNING THEORIES

Different learning theories can be used to explain how consumers learn. The most important theories are discussed below.

3.2.1   Classical conditioning

Physiologist Ivan Pavlov (1849–1936), who won the Nobel Prize in 1904 for his work on digestion, came across an interesting phenomenon during his experiments with dogs and their digestive systems. He realised that as soon as dogs saw someone coming in with food, they started to salivate. It was a natural occurrence for dogs to salivate when they smelt food. Presenting dogs with food was an unconditioned stimulus (US) and the dogs' salivation was an unconditioned response (UR). Being a scientist and curious to investigate this phenomenon, Pavlov experimented by using different stimuli such as bells, whistles and lights. For example, he started ringing a bell just before the dogs received their food. As a result, the dogs began to associate the ringing of the bell with being given food. Once this association had been formed, Pavlov tried ringing the bell without presenting the dogs with food. He found that the dogs started to salivate anyway, just from the stimulus of hearing the bell. Even after a few occurrences when the bell was rung without food being presented, the dogs still salivated upon hearing the bell. The ringing of the bell was therefore a conditioned stimulus (CS), which triggered a conditioned

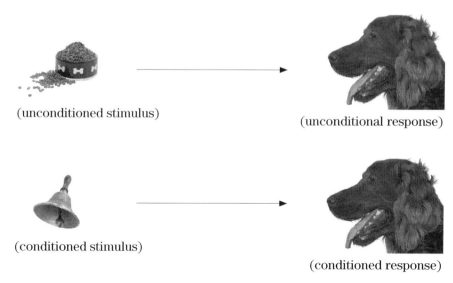

Figure 3.1 Pavlov's dogs are an example of classical conditioning.

response (CR) of salivating. This learning process is known as **classical conditioning**.

In the same way as Pavlov's dogs learnt to react to the stimulus of a bell, humans react to stimuli such as sound and visual cues when making a decision as a consumer. For example, consider the 'going green' advertising and marketing campaigns that have been urging consumers to purchase environmentally friendly products. Solar heating, energy-saving lightbulbs, recycled packaging and organically produced food are only a few examples. Opting to buy environmentally friendly products is not always cheaper at the till, but it holds the promise of saving money as well as our planet in the long run. When consumers are faced with a decision to buy a heater and the choice includes one that has a 'green' sticker claiming that the heater uses relatively little energy, does not emit any greenhouse gases and is safe for children and pets, this sticker will act as the conditioned stimulus leading to the conditioned reaction of buying the item in question. Gift bags or notebooks made from recycled paper is another example – people might rather buy these items as they are conditioned to help save the planet.

Figure 3.2 Eco friendly symbol[1]

3.2.2 Operant conditioning

American psychologist, behaviourist, author, inventor and social philosopher B.F. Skinner (1904–1990)[2] elaborated on the work of Pavlov. He became famous for the theory of operant conditioning. He investigated the outcome of the possibility that an animal involved in a particular study does not only react to external stimuli, but can also 'operate' or function by exploring its surroundings. This is called operant conditioning. **Operant conditioning**, also referred to as instrumental conditioning, is driven by the consequences of behaviour rather than by external stimuli. Skinner designed an experiment to evaluate the behaviour of rats by using different conditioning methods.

He built a cage, now known as the Skinner box (see Figure 3.3), in which he could control the levels of light, heat and sound to which a laboratory-bred rat was exposed (pigeons were also used in some experiments). A feature of the Skinner box is a lever set low on one of the walls. When this lever is pressed, a food pellet is released into the tray just below the lever.[3]

During Skinner's experiments, a rat was placed in the box. After a while, the rat started to explore its surroundings. When the rat accidentally pressed the lever, a food pellet would appear, which it would then eat. The rat did not make an immediate connection between the lever and the food, but after another accidental press which caused food to appear, it continued pressing the lever to obtain more food. The rat's operant behaviour was thus reinforced by the positive result of receiving food. **Positive reinforcement** encourages behaviour by giving pleasant rewards (for example, a food pellet) in exchange for a certain

Figure 3.3 The Skinner box[4]

behaviour (pressing a lever). When Skinner stopped releasing food when the rat pressed the lever, the rat stopped pressing the lever as it was no longer rewarded for its operant behaviour.

Skinner then investigated the power of **negative reinforcement** to change behaviour. He did this by sending a mild electric current through the floor of the box. This current could be turned off by pressing the lever. Once again, the rat learnt this by accidentally pressing the lever which then turned off the electric current. After a short while, the rat learnt to press the lever as soon as it felt the electric current again. Negative reinforcement encourages behaviour by avoiding unpleasant consequences.

Operant or instrumental conditioning, which is based on positive and negative reinforcement to encourage behaviour, is often used to influence consumer decision making. For example, when a consumer needs to buy a regular household item such as laundry detergent, offering a free sample of a new product in the range could encourage consumers to try it and buy it in future. As a further example, if a woman bought foundation and received a free sample of face powder, after using the free sample and liking the product, she might be eager to purchase it. Because she liked the product, she was positively reinforced and was therefore encouraged to buy it. Cash-back offers also provide positive reinforcement. For example, a car manufacturer may offer consumers who buy a certain car in a particular month, a cash-back payment of R30 000; another example is the various reward systems that are presented at retail stores, such as loyalty points offered on purchases for which the client can then claim discounts on subsequent purchases or receive a percentage of the cost of the purchase to spend on future purchases. Clicks is an example of a retailer that has a reward system. Consumers who are ClubCard members earn points on all of their purchases. In some instances, bonus points are also offered. These points can be redeemed for discounts on future purchases. In conjunction with this reward system, ClubCard members are also eligible for specials.[5] Figure 3.4 is an example of positive reinforcement.

Negative reinforcement is used to encourage consumers to make a decision to avoid an unpleasant outcome. This can often be seen in advertisements used to encourage brand loyalty, where the warning is that should consumers stray from the known brand, the danger exists that they will be unhappy with their purchases or service from the unknown brand. If the consumer upgrades to a different brand of cell phone, for example, and does not like the picture clarity of that phone or its features, he or she is negatively reinforced and will probably go back to the known brand upon their next upgrade.

Figure 3.4 Positive reinforcement

APPLICATION

Reward systems

A good example of a reward system is Discovery Health's Vitality. Search for the benefits online and identify the positive and negative reinforcements: https://www.discovery.co.za/vitality/how-vitality-works.

3.2.3 Cognitive learning

Learning results from acquired knowledge and not only from reactions to different stimuli. It involves the ability to reason and to reach a conclusion. People use active mental processes to think and to gain insight into a situation, and then make decisions based on this process. Behaviour is not only a response to stimuli, but a response that can lead to a goal. In the opening case study, Jo-Ann firstly responded to the stimulus that she could not find suitable shoes in the shops in the mall and therefore tried online shopping. This led her to achieve her goal of having the perfect pair of shoes. This form of learning is called **cognitive learning**. It is based on the learning model of American psychologist E.C. Tolman (1886–1959), which states that a desired goal can be reached through objects in the environment. Through his research, Tolman demonstrated that behaviour is based on learnt facts and not merely on reactions to stimuli.[6] For example, if you have learnt that sales on clothing for the season take place more or less in the middle of the season, you might wait to buy new clothes and take advantage of the opportunity to buy what you need at a reduced price.

Figure 3.5   There are many factors to consider when purchasing a house.

Table 3.1 Factors to consider when choosing between option A and option B

Price of house	R1 200 000	R1 600 000
Features	Three bedrooms, two bathrooms, living area, kitchen, study, two garages	Three bedrooms, two bathrooms, one guest toilet, living area, dining room, kitchen, study, two garages, lapa and swimming pool
Location	Less safe neighbourhood; close to schools and shopping area	Good neighbourhood; quite far from schools and shops
Other factors	Close to parents' houses; needs a bit of paint and work done to the bathroom ceiling	Swimming pool is not enclosed with a fence or fitted with a net

Cognitive learning within the consumer is usually evident in more complex decision-making processes as opposed to impulsive or quick decisions. For example, consider a couple who wants to buy a house. Factors such as price range, size and location all play a part in their final decision. Information about the two options (A and B) that the couple must choose between is given in Table 3.1. Option B is more expensive than option A, but it also offers more in terms of size. Both houses are in a good neighbourhood, while option A is closer to schools and a shopping centre. Previously they have learnt that being close to schools is an advantage, but they also know that they want to stay in a safe neighbourhood. They have also learnt that being close to their parents helps when they need support with babysitting.

The couple's goal is to buy an affordable house where they can be happy and safe. Considering all of the factors available in Table 3.1, they need to use what they have learnt before in order to make an informed decision. They know that living close to schools and their parents is a benefit. They know that a good neighbourhood is safer and the price needs to be considered, as it will influence their repayment each month. This is a rather complex decision and all available information needs to be taken into account.

Another example is a young man who wants to buy his first car. He might receive advice from his parents and he is likely to ask the salesperson specific questions in order to get enough information to make an informed decision. Cognitive learning takes place when he asks about the fuel consumption, service plan, the cost of replacing tyres, the engine capacity, what options there are in terms of colour choice and many other factors that could influence his final decision.

3.2.4 Learning in a social context

Canadian psychologist Albert Bandura (1925–) introduced the social learning theory. He was elected president of the American Psychology Association (APA) in 1973. According to Bandura, people learn by observing other people (think of children imitating older siblings or grown-ups). Bandura's theory is also referred to as observational learning because people learn through observing others. Social learning is achieved through observation; visual or verbal cues are stored and used later in applicable situations. There are four steps in the process of **social learning**:

- *Attentional processing:* This refers to the amount of attention that is given to the person or action, by the person observing the situation.
- *Retentional processing:* The information is processed and retained as a visual image or code that can be recalled when necessary. A person can practise the behaviour in his or her mind. This process is known as symbolic rehearsal.
- *Reproduction processing:* The person can now reproduce or display the symbolic rehearsal if the environment requires it.
- *Motivational processing:* Feedback from the environment will motivate the process. If the behaviour is rewarded, it will be reinforced; if not, it might not be used again.

For example, a girl watches her mother applying her make-up, paying particular attention to the process. She stores the mental image. In her mind, she rehearses the process. Over the weekend, she decides to reproduce this image before she goes out with friends. If the feedback from her friends is positive and they think she looks pretty, she will try it again, but if they laugh at her because her make-up is not applied skilfully, she might not try it again soon.

As an example, consider the four steps in the process of social learning illustrated in the opening case study concerning Jo-Ann, her friend Lebo and her brother.

- *Step 1: Attentional processing.* Jo-Ann observed her friend Lebo while she was linking onto the online shopping portal.
- *Step 2: Retentional processing.* Jo-Ann was able to recall the steps to shop online.
- *Step 3: Reproduction processing.* Jo-Ann was able to repeat the action of online shopping with different products and web sites.
- *Step 4: Motivational processing.* The first time, Jo-Ann's behaviour was rewarded with a successful purchase. The second and third time, however, were negative experiences and caused her to distrust online shopping.

Consider the taxi industry of South Africa. The consumer who uses taxis as transport needs to learn how to use the hand signals indicating where he or she wants to go. If he or she observes fellow passengers and pays attention to which signal means what, the visual image is retained and reproduced when necessary. If the outcome is positive and the hand signal was used correctly, it will be used again.

Another form of social learning is to observe the behaviour of a role model or someone who inspires people. Advertisers often use the image of an influential person, such as a sports idol, a movie star or a politician, to give a testimonial on how effective a particular product is. Consumers want to have the same result as these successful people, and therefore observe and re-enact the behaviour by buying and using the product.

Figure 3.6 Environmental learning motivated by a parent

From the various theories of learning considered above, it is evident that consumers learn in different ways and that these theories are all applicable in different contexts. Some theories are based on consumers who use direct cognitive application, while others are related to a consumer's observation or reactions to stimuli. However, the brain plays a major role in all of these processes. In the section that follows, we will explore the influence of the brain in more detail.

3.3 THE INFLUENCE OF THE BRAIN

Learning is a cognitive process; even if behaviour is activated through stimuli in the environment, the brain has to process the information and the memory has to store it. The age-old nature versus nurture debate (whether what we do is the result of hereditary factors or is learnt) remains relevant in the study of consumer behaviour.

Human behaviour is influenced by both genetic and environmental learning. Evidence of environmental learning can be seen by considering the behaviour of people who are motivated by famous people or children looking up to their parents or other role models. The influence of genes can be observed through physical attributes such as eye colour and height as well as personality factors. When planning advertising campaigns, the impact of both of these on the behaviour of consumers must be considered. The brain determines the learning process relevant to consumer behaviour, therefore a basic understanding of how neurons communicate will allow marketers to begin to make use of neuroscience and neuromarketing to sell their products and services.

3.3.1 Neuroscience

The brain plays a vital role in the learning process of the consumer. Once information has been processed, it needs to be stored. This is where memory plays a fundamental role.

In terms of consumer behaviour, neuroscience studies the brain's response to advertising stimuli to understand the decisions consumers make as well as to establish which part of the brain is active during that decision-making process.[7] Research on neuroscience and marketing has been published mostly in neuroscience journals, therefore this valuable contribution to the field of consumer behaviour has often been overlooked.

Neuromarketing studies the subconscious decisions consumers make in order to improve the effectiveness of marketing. Technologies such as magnetic resonance imaging (MRI), electroencephalogram (EEG) and neuroimaging are used to measure changes in brain activity and to identify the parts of the brain that are activated when the consumer is observing products or making decisions. Neuromarketing can be applied in research, product design and packaging, pricing, in-store design and advertising.

According to Professor Judy Illes, Director of the National Core of Neuroethics at the University of Columbia, the field of neuroscience is evolving at an unprecedented rate.[8] Her concern is that vulnerable consumers may be exploited if neuromarketing does not adopt a code of ethics to safeguard both consumers and the science of neuromarketing itself.

APPLICATION

The use of babies in adverts

Consumer psychologists have established that advertisements that have people in them attract more interest. This is even more so when there is a picture of a baby. Through eye tracking, they have discovered that when the baby faces front, people focus more on the cute child than on the product. However, when the baby faces in the direction of the product, people tend also to look at the product. Find examples at https://imotions.com/blog/neuromarketing-examples/

3.3.2 The communication process

Communication in the body takes place through the interaction of **neurons**. Figure 3.7 is an annotated diagram of a neuron. Each human is born with more than one hundred billion neurons, which are specialised in shape and size according to the kind of information that they transmit. Neurons can be divided into three types:[9]

- *Sensory neurons:* Sensory neurons involve the senses – hearing, smell, touch, sight and taste. These neurons collect information from the outside environment and send it to the brain.
- *Motor neurons:* These nerve cells form part of a pathway along which impulses pass from the brain or spinal cord to a muscle or gland. The brain communicates the information to the muscles and organs so that they know how to react.

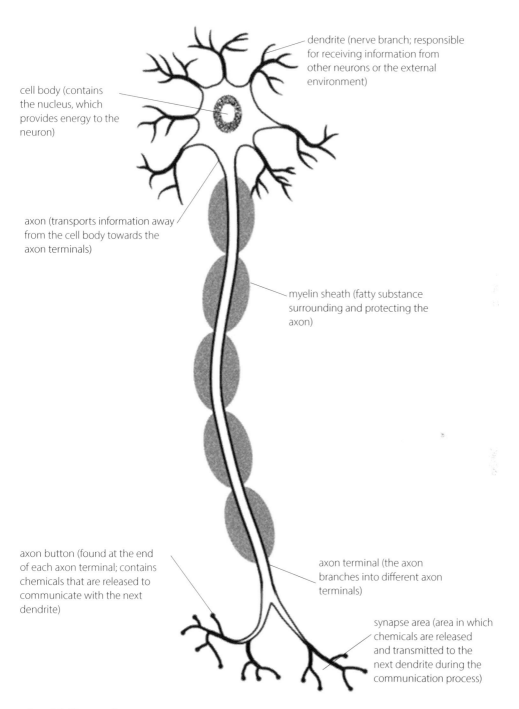

dendrite (nerve branch; responsible for receiving information from other neurons or the external environment)

cell body (contains the nucleus, which provides energy to the neuron)

axon (transports information away from the cell body towards the axon terminals)

myelin sheath (fatty substance surrounding and protecting the axon)

axon button (found at the end of each axon terminal; contains chemicals that are released to communicate with the next dendrite)

axon terminal (the axon branches into different axon terminals)

synapse area (area in which chemicals are released and transmitted to the next dendrite during the communication process)

Figure 3.7 Diagram of a neuron

* *Association neurons:* These neurons have the function of linking information. They assist in remembering, perceiving and thinking.

It is almost impossible to comprehend the speed and accuracy of the communication process. For example, if you put your hand on a hot stove, the sensory neurons receive the information from your skin, relay it to your brain, and your brain sends a rapid message back via the motor neurons to the hand muscles to snatch your hand away before it gets burnt. This happens so fast, you are not consciously aware of it. The association neurons take all of this information and store it so that you will remember not to repeat the mistake.

About 80% of complex thoughts are processed in the cerebral cortex. The cerebral cortex is the outer part of the brain and is often referred to as the grey matter. A strong nerve fibre, the corpus callosum, divides the cerebral cortex into a left and a right hemisphere. Each hemisphere is unique in its function, but needs to communicate with the other hemisphere in order to fulfil its tasks. The left hemisphere controls the right side of the body and the right hemisphere controls the left side of the body. The left side of the brain focuses on analytical thinking and logical processing as well as the learning of new habits and the expression of language through verbal communication. The right hemisphere is capable of processing multiple stimuli entering the brain. It can interpret complex visual images and focuses on graphic displays. The right side of the brain is considered to be the more creative side.

Marketers must consider the messages entering both hemispheres of a consumer's brain when advertising a product or setting up a marketing display. This will ensure that the maximum effect is reached. A good example is a typical television commercial for a car, which shows the beautiful places you can go, with strong visual images to influence the right side of the brain, but also focuses on the safety, fuel efficiency and ample space offered by the vehicle in order to impress the analytical, factual side of the brain.

3.4 MEMORY

Memory is the storing of information received from experiences, stimuli and learning. The inability to retrieve the information that was stored results in the phenomenon called forgetting. When Jo-Ann's brother suggested online shopping for their mother's birthday gift in the opening case study, she recalled the experiences she had had with previous online shopping. She was able to retrieve the information from her memory to give advice to her brother.

Memory has three stages or types:
* Sensory memory
* Short-term memory
* Long-term memory

Figure 3.8 illustrates the different stages or types of memory. These will be discussed in more detail in the section that follows.

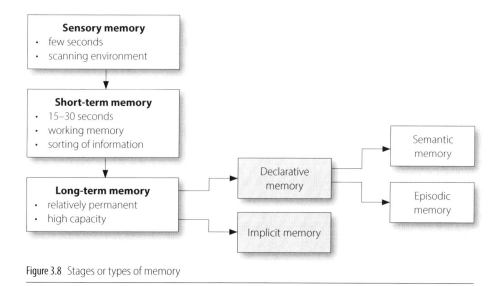

Figure 3.8 Stages or types of memory

3.4.1   Sensory memory

Information enters the memory from all five senses at once. This information is processed in just a few seconds. It is either retained to continue to the next stage of memory or it is disregarded as unimportant and is released. Imagine walking into a bustling shopping mall on a Saturday morning. Your eyes observe people moving around and the displays in the shop windows; your ears hear the background music being played, people talking and laughing, a baby crying and trolleys moving; your nose smells fresh coffee from a nearby coffee shop, perfume from the lady passing you and cigarette smoke on the clothes of another person; you taste the peppermint you just started chewing and you feel the coldness of the trolley handle on the skin of your hands. All of this enters your sensory memory. Each impression lasts for only a second or two. Back at home, you might not remember anything more than the smell of the coffee and the music that was being played because you had an interest in those stimuli and they were routed to the next stage: the short-term memory.

3.4.2   Short-term memory

The short-term memory holds information for only 15–30 seconds, but it needs to comprehend and decide where best this information can be stored while simultaneously receiving new information from the sensory memory on a constant basis. For example, the information received from the nose signalling that fresh coffee is being brewed nearby might lead an individual to go looking for the coffee shop. The information received from the ears in the form of music might only be retained as a thought such as, 'This mall plays enjoyable music' without any detail about the specific melody. This depends on the process called encoding, which moves information to the long-term memory. Encoding refers to the way information is held, for example the visual impression of a salesperson's friendly face or the confident sound of his voice.

3.4.3 Long-term memory

The long-term memory is relatively permanent and has a high capacity to store information. The way in which the information is encoded or stored determines the way the information needs to be retrieved in order to be remembered. Long-term memory can be either declarative or implicit. Declarative memory refers to conscious memories of events or facts, for example a personal experience at a specific time or place. Declarative memory can be divided into:

- episodic, and
- semantic memory.

Episodic memory would be, for example, when a consumer can remember the different buying options explained by a financial person when he applied for finance to buy his first car. Semantic memory refers to the conscious recollection of factual information and general knowledge about the world we live in. For example, the fact that Nelson Mandela was president of South Africa after the apartheid era is something most people know. However, if you ask them how they know this, they cannot tell you.

Implicit memory refers to past experiences that influence behaviour, although it is not possible to recollect the specific experience. For example, you always buy freshly baked bread from the bakery on Sundays, but you cannot necessarily remember how this ritual started.

DISCUSSION

Based on the recency effect, people tend to remember the first or the last words of an advert the best. Advertisers will therefore place the most important information at the beginning or at the end of an advertisement.

Discussion question

Watch a few TV commercials and make a note of the information shared right at the beginning and at the end of the commercial. Based on your observation, do you agree or disagree with the above statement about the use of memory in advertising?

3.5 METHODS USED TO ENHANCE LEARNING AND MEMORY

In the battle to grab the attention of consumers, to retain this attention and finally to ensure that consumers remember the product when making the buying decision, it is valuable to understand the methods that can be used to enhance the learning process and to improve consumers' memory function. Some of these methods are discussed below.

3.5.1 Repetition

Repetition of information that is important for the consumer to remember, such as a telephone number or the name of a specific model, increases the chances that the information will be processed and transmitted from the short-term memory through to the long-term memory. However, this method is more successful when the consumer is in need of such a product or service at that time.

The advertisement in Figure 3.9 illustrates the repetition[10] of the product name.

Figure 3.9 The use of repetition in a print advertisement

3.5.2 Visuals

One of the ways in which information is encoded in memory is via visuals. Showing visual images of how a product can be used assists the consumer in recalling the information if faced with a similar situation. This technique also contributes to brand awareness by linking a visual effect to all products under a specific brand.

The advertisement in Figure 3.10 uses visual examples to suggest to consumers how the product can be used.

Figure 3.10 Insurance road-side assist: the use of visuals in a print advertisement[11]

3.5.3   Self-referencing

Relating information to a person's own situation helps to improve the storage of information in the long-term memory. For example, when selling medical insurance to a young couple with a two-year old baby, it would be advantageous to refer to benefits that could assist their family, such as having a medical doctor on standby at night in case the child falls ill, or having access to an emergency number that could be used if they required roadside assistance. When the couple needs to recall various medical insurance options, this particular one should pop up in their memories as it would appeal to their particular situation.

Discovery Health is a company that offers medical aid cover in South Africa. Over time, the company diversified by introducing products such as Discovery Life, Discovery Insure and Discovery Invest[12]. People can relate to the company's well-known name in health care, and therefore store this information in their memories to use when they need to make a purchase decision related to the new products.

3.5.4   Elaborative rehearsal

This method links new information to something the consumer already knows and is familiar with. For example, consumers are aware that eating fruit and vegetables on a regular basis increases their intake of vitamins, minerals and antioxidants. If this existing knowledge is linked to a new frozen fruit product found in supermarkets, consumers are more likely to take note of the new offering. The frozen fruit offers an easy and convenient way to prepare fruit smoothies and healthy desserts, while retaining the nutritional value and health benefits of fresh fruit.

The print advertisement in Figure 3.11 promotes a skin-care range based on Rooibos extracts. People are more likely to buy this product if they know that Rooibos is a natural, healthy ingredient.

Figure 3.11 The use of elaborative rehearsal in a print advertisement

3.5.5 Chunking

When items are organised together, it becomes easier to remember them. One example of this is when a telephone number is repeated in numbers and in words, such as '082-PRE-SALE'. The telephone number in the advertisement in Figure 3.12 is given as 0800 CURVES. This is a form of chunking, which helps consumers to remember information.

3.5.6 Humour and exaggeration

Consumers remember advertisements more effectively if humour has been used. In addition, when a particular aspect of an advertisement is amplified or exaggerated, it stands out in consumers' memories. An example of television advertisements that do this are the Volkswagen advertisements that show how many items can be packed inside, even the huge teddy bear[13].

Figure 3.12 The use of chunking in a print advertisement

RESEARCH BOX 3.1

Once consumers have learnt that they can trust a brand, it is not easy to change their intent to purchase that brand, as was demonstrated in two experiments by Herbst, Finkel, Allen and Fitzsimons.[14] The intention to purchase is affected via heuristics rather than elaborative processes, as seen in the two experiments: fast (versus normal pace) end-of-advertisement disclaimers negatively influence consumers' intent to purchase from trust-unknown and not-trusted brands. The speed of the disclaimer had no effect on intent to purchase from trusted brands.

Finkelstein and Fishbach[15] saw a shift in feedback response towards consumers. They found that as consumers gained expertise, they responded better to constructive negative feedback. The commitment of novice, inexperienced consumers increased with positive feedback.

SUMMARY

In this chapter, we examined the learning process of consumers. We considered different learning theories, including classical conditioning, operant conditioning, cognitive learning and social learning. Examples of how these theories are applicable in consumer behaviour were provided. Neuroscience was touched on and the importance of upholding ethical standards in the fast-growing field of neuromarketing was briefly discussed. The influence of the brain was emphasised by looking at how communication occurs through the neurons as well as the left and right hemispheres of the brain. The three stages or types of memory (sensory memory, short-term memory and long-term memory) were examined. Ways of enhancing the learning process and memory function were discussed to indicate how these developments can influence consumer decision making. Looking back at the story of Jo-Ann, her friend Lebo, her brother and her experience of online shopping, it is evident that consumers remember situations and learn how to react the next time they are faced with a similar occurrence.

SELF-ASSESSMENT QUESTIONS

1. A consumer is offered a free sample-size hand lotion with the purchase of a magazine. The consumer likes the hand lotion and decides to buy the full size. To which learning theory does this situation relate and why?
2. Discuss the function of each of the three types of neurons.
3. Why would you not achieve the full potential impact on consumers if you only used visual graphics to advertise your product on a flyer?
4. What methods of enhancing learning memory can be used in advertising?
5. Use an example to explain the difference between semantic memory and episodic memory.

EXPERIENTIAL EXERCISE

1. You have traditionally used the same brand of coffee for more than three years. Describe the processes that could persuade you to try another brand.
2. Would you be less inclined to try the new brand if you were going through an extremely busy period at home and at work? Explain why and how your hectic schedule would lead to your deferring the decision to try the new coffee.

CASE STUDY 1

Choosing the right primary school

Mr and Mrs Harvey's son is going to primary school next year. They need to make a decision as to which school to enrol him in. All the schools are scouting for young learners and, as a result, try to influence prospective parents. The Harveys consider the choice made by some of their friends with older children who enrolled their children in more expensive schools, as the assumption is that this guarantees a high-quality education. Mrs Harvey agrees that this is a good way to make the decision. On the other hand, Mr Harvey is not convinced as he remembers that although his parents made the decision to enrol him in an exclusive primary school, he was extremely unhappy there. In an attempt to make the best decision, the Harveys make a list of all the facts linked to each available option.

Discussion questions

1. Reflect on the above scenario and provide an example of social learning (learning that is based on the example of others).
2. Give an example of operant conditioning (positive and negative reinforcement) in this scenario and explain why it is an example of this.
3. Give an example of cognitive learning (using facts to make a decision) in this scenario.

CASE STUDY 2 (ADVANCED)

Project team: A new app for buying second-hand books

You are part of a project team that has to market a new app for buying second-hand books. You have a market for academic text books for tertiary students and a market for general fiction and non-fiction for the broader public.

Discussion questions

1. Choose any two methods that would enhance the learning process and memory function of the consumer.
2. Explain to the rest of the team why you chose these methods and how you would apply them in your marketing campaign.

ADDITIONAL RESOURCES

Visit the following web sites for more information on the concepts discussed in this chapter:

- http://www.consumerpsychologist.com/cb_Learning_and_Memory.html
- http://www.ehow.com/info_12030739_operant-conditioning-vs-classical-conditioning-advertising.html
- http://www.consumerpsychologist.com/intro_Consumer_Behavior.html
- http://www.wisegeek.com/what-is-consumer-behavior.htm
- http://managementinnovations.wordpress.com/2008/11/25/consumer-learning/
- http://mpra.ub.uni-muenchen.de/24064/
- http://www.psych.upenn.edu/kable_lab/Joes_Homepage/Publications_files/Yoon%20et%20al%202012.pdf
- http://nmasa.co.za/
- https://www.neuralsense.com/

REFERENCES

1 https://www.google.co.za/search?q=advertisements+of+environment+friendly+products&tbm=isch&tbo=u&source=univ&sa=X&ved=2ahUKEwiKo_bUhsLcAhWJJ8AKHSQ1Cq8QsAR6BAgFEAE&biw=1023&bih=599#imgrc=TCmWBxYXEHrdQM:
2 Cherry, K. 2018. BF Skinner biography: One leader of behaviourism. Available at: https://www.verywellmind.com/b-f-skinner-biography-1904-1990-2795543 (accessed on 4 September 2018).
3 Ibid.
4 https://www.google.co.za/search?q=Skinner+box&source=lnms&tbm=isch&sa=X&ved=0ahUKEwiG9MbfopfdAhVEJcAKHSkPBEEQ_AUICigB&biw=2560&bih=1313#imgrc=ODQimeDoaKyT6M:&spf=1535717887510
5 https://www.google.co.za/url?sa=i&rct=j&q=&esrc=s&source=images&cd=&cad=rja&uact=8&ved=0ahUKEwitzNfag4DYAhXJCsAKHTb4DpwQjRwIBw&url=http%3A%2F%2Fall catalogues.co.za%2Fmtubatuba%2Fclicks&psig=AOvVaw0n2mzjwytrPvFQLGzON9IZ&ust=1513015364406114
6 New World Encyclopedia. 2016. Edward C. Tolman. Available at: http://www.newworldencyclopedia.org/p/index.php?title=Edward_C._Tolman (accessed on 2 August 2018).
7 Camerer, C. & Yoon, C. 2015. Introduction to the *Journal of Marketing Research* special issue on neuroscience and marketing. *Journal of Marketing Research*, LII: 423–426.
8 Loiacono, C. 2009. Can brain science manipulate consumers? Available at: http://www.publicaffairs.ubc.ca/ubcreports/2009/09apr02/manipulate.html (accessed on 2 August 2018).
9 Botha, E. 2018. Biology in work behaviour. In Bergh, Z, *Introduction to work psychology*. Cape Town: Oxford University Press, 96.
10 https://www.shutterstock.com/image-vector/oatmeal-ad-milk-splashing-mixed-berries-642327187
11 By minagephotography.shutterstock.com.

12 https://www.google.co.za/url?sa=i&rct=j&q=&esrc=s&source=images&cd=&cad=rja&uact=
8&ved=0ahUKEwjz4PWthIDYAhWpJsAKHWOeDdcQjRwIBw&url=https%3A%2F%2Fsky
insurance.co.za%2F&psig=AOvVaw0VsfCTQdpTkm3qy7ojl_07&ust=1513015562280412

13 https://www.google.co.za/url?sa=i&rct=j&q=&esrc=s&source=images&cd=&cad=rja&uact=8
&ved=0ahUKEwitj–ehYDYAhXGB8AKHW4sDm0QjRwIBw&url=https%3A%2F%2Fwww.
pinterest.com%2Fpin%2F246290673344101714%2F&psig=AOvVaw1QsKMGKhJivi_Ja3TKr
Vfd&ust=1513015789975175

14 Herbst, K.C., Finkel, E.J., Allen, D. & Fitzsimons, G.M. 2012. On the dangers of pulling a
fast one: Advertisement disclaimer speed, brand trust and purchase intent. Available at:
http://faculty.wcas.northwestern.edu/eli-finkel/documents/InPress_HerbstFinkel
AllanFitzsimons_JCR.pdf (accessed on 2 August 2018).

15 Finkelstein, S.R. & Fishbach, A. 2012. Tell me what i did wrong: Experts seek and respond to
negative feedback. Available at: http://blogs.cuit.columbia.edu/sf2559/files/2011/08/
FF_JCR_Feedback.pdf (accessed on 2 August 2018).

CHAPTER 4

CONSUMER PERCEPTIONS

Danie du Toit

LEARNING OBJECTIVES

After reading this chapter, you should be able to:
- define perceptions
- explain the perception process
- describe the functions of perceptions
- describe consumer perceptions
- understand how to get the attention of consumers
- understand the strategic implications of consumer perceptions for marketing.

Key terms		
absolute threshold	differential threshold	perceptions
attention	expectations	reaction
attitudes	gestalt psychology	sensation
beliefs	interpretation	sensory receptors
brand	memory	social media
depth psychology	neuropsychology	stimulus

OPENING CASE STUDY

Consumers are constantly exposed to consumer brands. Every day of their lives, consumers are bombarded with information. They surround themselves with brand names and are exposed to even more brand names by advertisers trying to make them aware of their products. Just think of the amount of information the average consumer has been exposed to by the time he or she leaves home every morning. Many people wake up to the sound of their **smartphone** alarms; when they open their eyes, the first things they see are the screens of their smartphones. They then drink a cup of Jacob's coffee with Huletts sugar and Parmalat milk. For breakfast, they might have Kellogg's corn-flakes with milk warmed in an LG microwave oven. They brush their teeth with Colgate toothpaste. They then put on their Adidas shirts, Levi jeans and Converse shoes, glancing at their Jeep watches to see if they are still on schedule. If they happened to switch on their Samsung flat screen televisions, even more brand names would try to get their attention.

4.1 INTRODUCTION

Consumer **perceptions** have to do with the way in which consumers view and react to the products that are available to them. As illustrated in the opening vignette, consumers are constantly exposed to marketers promoting their **brands**.

Usually, consumers are not even aware of all of these brand names or even of regular advertisements. The information that people are exposed to is called a **stimulus**. At a physiological level, a person perceives these stimuli through his or her senses: sight, sound, smell, taste or texture. When a consumer not only becomes aware of a stimulus, but also has a **reaction** to the stimulus, it is called perception.

In this chapter, we define consumer perceptions and discuss the process of perception as well as the functions of perceptions. We also consider marketing communication and consumer perceptions, focusing on how marketers get their message across to consumers and their efforts to ensure that the perceptions of consumers lead to positive reactions. We conclude by summarising the strategic marketing implications of this information.

4.1.1 Defining perceptions

Initially, perceptions were defined mainly as physiological phenomena. The emphasis was thus on the biological aspects; what happens in a person's brain when his senses pick up a stimulus. After some time, more complete definitions were constructed. Perception can be defined as the process by which stimuli activate sensory receptors (eyes, ears, taste buds, skin and nose).[1] A stimulus is any physical object or event to which a person is exposed. Perception can further be described as the process by which stimuli are selected, organised and interpreted, or the process of assigning meaning to what is sensed.[2] Perception has a subjective nature, which means that every person reacts to stimuli on his or her own terms. Recent definitions have explained perception as the act of absorbing by means of the senses and/or the mind.[3] Perception hence not only relates to basic senses, such as the visual, flavour and taste attributes of stimuli, but also includes formal learning and experiences. What a consumer has learnt and experienced in the past about a product will influence his or her perception of the product or service. Perceptions can therefore be defined as a person's awareness of, reaction to and **interpretation** of stimuli. The study of perception thus includes complex aspects of consumer behaviour, such as learning and motivation. Perceptions are important because consumers' purchasing decisions are, at least to some degree, based on their perceptions.

4.2 THE PROCESS OF PERCEPTION

The perception process starts with the way in which a person senses the stimuli to which he or she is exposed, and then makes meaning of those stimuli. The stimuli are then processed. The processed stimuli might then impact on the person's decision making.

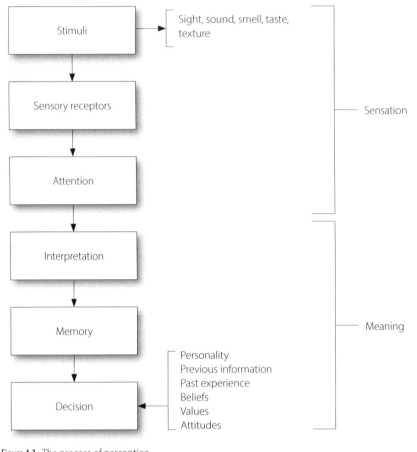

Figure 4.1 The process of perception

Figure 4.1 is a schematic illustration of the perception process.

4.2.1 Stimuli

The perception process starts with a person being exposed to stimuli. The person's sensory receptors pick up the stimuli through his or her senses (sight, sound, smell, taste and touch).

Visual stimulus – sight

A visual stimulus reaches a person through his or her eyesight. Colour is extremely important in visual stimuli. Not only does colour determine whether a person becomes aware of stimuli or not, but colour also affects his or her emotional response to the stimuli. In any form of marketing, the consumer's emotional response has a major impact on the purchasing decision.

The three main colour qualities of importance in a visual stimulus are as follows:[4]

- *Hue:* which refers to the pigment contained in colour (for instance, red, orange and yellow are seen as 'warm' colours, whilst green, blue and violet are seen as 'cool' colours)
- *Saturation:* which refers to the chroma or richness of a colour (a pale pink, for example, is very different from a deep, rich pink)
- *Lightness:* which refers to the depth of tone; it refers to whether the colour is light or dark (for example, light blue and dark blue).

When marketers decide which colours to use in marketing communications, they must consider whether the intention is to get the consumer interested or to encourage the consumer to take his or her time when making a decision. Socio-economic status has also been found to have an impact on the colour preferences of different consumers. People in the high-income bracket tend to prefer deep, rich colours. Thus, colours used for products and in advertising need to be carefully selected depending on the desired reaction and the market segment at which the product or advertisement is aimed.

Form is equally important. Research has shown that people generally prefer objects with curved shapes to angular objects.[5] Participants in a study were shown photographs of cars from the 1950s to 2009.[6] Generally, the cars of the 1950s had very curved forms, whereas the cars of the 1970s and 1980s were more angular. Thereafter, cars became more curved again.

Participants in this study showed a definite preference for the cars of the 1950s and cars made after 1980. The implication is that consumers have a more positive reaction towards round shapes in advertisements as well as in products. This preference can be explained by evolutionary psychology. It is believed that sharp transitions in contour are often indications of danger. Examples cited are the pointy shapes of the teeth and fins of a shark, cliffs and the thorn of a rose. All of these angular forms are associated with danger. In another study, it was found that objects with sharp design properties are likely to induce fear.[7] Should one then conclude that curved shapes make more marketing sense than angular shapes? The answer is probably simply that marketers should be more aware of the effect of shape on consumers. It has been theorised that angular shapes might increase arousal, which might trigger appreciation and an eagerness to explore innovative and challenging properties.[8] Some designs, for example A4 paper and doors, need to be angular for practical reasons. Research suggests that a design principle should not be changed too abruptly. Advanced shapes, which might be perceived favourably as novel and innovative, must still be familiar enough to be manageable.[9]

Auditory stimulus – sound

An auditory stimulus is one that reaches a person as sounds through his or her ears. A sound must be loud enough to be perceived. It must also be clearly distinguishable from background sounds if it is to be noted. Sound in the form of music is important to marketers, as it impacts on mood and behaviour. The consumer is usually unaware of the effect of music. Slow music, for instance, can increase sales in stores because it encourages leisurely shopping, whilst fast music tends to energise people and make them shop more quickly. Songs that consumers like and are familiar with can bring about a positive mood. Music that they do not like can have the opposite effect.

The type of music played in a store influences the type of products bought. For example, classical music tends to encourage the purchase of more expensive wines.

Scent stimuli – smell

Some basic emotions are linked to smell. The fragrance of freshly baked cookies might, for instance, bring back childhood memories.

Taste stimuli

Taste stimuli are of particular interest to the food and beverages industries. The growing health consciousness amongst consumers poses a particular challenge to producers to create healthier products that still taste good. People from different cultural groups differ vastly regarding taste. For marketing purposes, it is important to understand when a consumer is likely to accept or reject a stimulus. A recent study found that consumers accept or reject food based on the relationship between the intensity of perceptible attributes and the degree of acceptance.[10] Perceptible attributes refer to the sensory evaluation of the food: its taste, smell and presentation. The degree of acceptance refers to how acceptable consumers find the food in terms of taste, smell and presentation. Perceived health issues and cultural acceptability also play an important role.

Sushi is a good example. Until a few years ago, many South Africans may have viewed the idea of eating raw fish as disgusting, whilst many now perceive sushi as delicious and a healthy meal choice.

Touch stimulus – texture

A touch stimulus refers to the feeling or texture of a product. Less is known about the impact of touch on marketing than the impact of the other senses. Differences between cultures with regard to touch are also important. Marketers often provide samples in advertisements in an effort to include these other senses, which are not engaged by a visual advertisement, as well as to differentiate their product.

In using the sample, the consumer's senses of smell, sight and texture are engaged.

A sample can succeed in ensuring that the stimulus is noticed. However, it can also have negative effects if, for instance, the consumer finds the smell of the product distasteful.

4.2.2   Sensory receptors

The **sensory receptors** of the consumer receive the stimulus. The consumer sees, hears, smells, tastes or feels the stimulus. As described in the introduction to this chapter, consumers are exposed to many stimuli at any given point in time. Jia, Shiv and Rao[12] refer to research indicating that the human brain processes 11 million bits of information per second. A stimulus must thus be sufficiently intense in order for the consumer to become aware of it. It was found that there is an **absolute threshold** for stimuli to enter into a person's awareness.[13]

The absolute threshold refers to the minimum intensity needed for a person to become aware of the stimulus. If sounds are too faint, or images or words are too small, the person will not realise that they exist. The **differential threshold** refers to the intensity difference between two (or more) stimuli needed for a person to realise that the two stimuli are different. If the difference is too small, the person will perceive the two different stimuli as the same stimulus. This is particularly important when producers deliberately change the taste of a product. If the change is too small, consumers will perceive the new product as the same as the previous product.

Much has been written about subliminal perception. It has been described as presenting a stimulus that is below the threshold level of a person's awareness.[14] A stimulus that is below this level is so faint that the person who is exposed to it is not consciously aware of it. A message could, for example, be shown on the screen in a cinema or on television for a fraction of a second. The message will not be registered consciously by the consumer, but it will make an unconscious impression. Figure 4.2 illustrates the concepts of the conscious and the unconscious minds with regard to the threshold of perception.

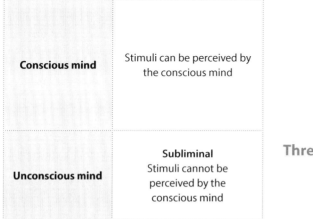

Figure 4.2   An illustration of threshold of perception

Research indicates that consumers can form preferences for particular products or services simply by repeated exposure to an associated stimulus that is accessible by the individual's sensory receptors. There seems to be no need to engage with the stimulus or even to create a conscious awareness of it. Preference is based on affection or what a person is attracted to.

It has been shown that if the affect is subliminal, it has an even greater impact on preference. A person might, for example, drive past billboards advertising a product and without deliberately reading the billboards or even noticing the advertisement consciously, the person might be influenced by it.

Affective (feeling) and cognitive (thinking) processes have been shown to be independent of each other, thus preference need not necessarily make logical sense.[15] A person might, for instance, have a fondness for a particular type of car. He might read reviews reporting many problems with this model, thus receive negative cognitive information about it, yet still allow his feelings to determine his preference. Deliberately using subliminal advertising to alter consumers' preferences towards products unconsciously (in an attempt to influence behaviour) may be questionable in terms of ethical practice as it could be seen as a manipulative practice Furthermore Elgendi, Kumar, Barbic, Howard, Abbott and Cichocki[16] reported contrasting results in the support of the effectiveness of subliminal messages on consumer behaviour. This indicates that we might not understand this phenomenon well enough to use it responsibly.

4.2.3   Attention

The consumer's attention to a stimulus is necessary for the stimulus to have any impact on the purchasing decision. Apart from the fact that people are exposed to more stimuli than they can possibly respond to, people's attention span is also becoming shorter and shorter. Consumers quickly lose interest, even if the marketer manages to get their attention in the first place. In addition, consumers are well informed and are becoming more sophisticated. Marketers are thus faced with the challenge of attracting and keeping the attention of consumers.

A strong brand is obviously a good starting point to do this. A brand is more than just the image of the product or service. It encapsulates the value proposition, in other words, the unique offering to the consumer that differentiates the product. Its history, previous experiences, **expectations** and quality all come into play.

APPLICATION

A car is a car, right?

On the surface, similar models of Toyotas and Hondas look alike and offer similar features. They are, however, branded completely differently. What comes to mind when you think of Toyota? For most people, the answer is reliability. In the eyes of the consumer, Toyota's value proposition is to offer a reliable car. Many consumers are aware of the attention the company gives to the quality of the cars they produce as well as how involved they are in the quality standards of their suppliers. Thus, the consumer who considers purchasing the Toyota is likely to be impressed by its reliability.

Honda, on the other hand, does not build unreliable cars, but it is not reliability that gives the company an edge. When most consumers think of Honda, engine technology comes to mind. Honda has a history of building engines, whilst, compared to Toyota, the company is relatively new in the car market. It is possible to find Honda engines in boats, motorcycles and other machines. However, it is unlikely that one would find a Toyota engine in a boat or motorcycle. Two very similar cars, two very different brands.

Brand alone is not enough to attract and keep the attention of consumers. Research has found that product design is equally important; consumers pay attention to attractive designs.[17] However, an attractive design is more persuasive when coupled with a strong brand. In January 2009, as part of a brand overhaul, PepsiCo in the US introduced a redesigned Tropicana orange juice carton in an attempt to modernise the package. The image of an orange, which formed part of the original package design, was removed and replaced with a glass of orange juice. The rationale related to showing the inside of the orange (i.e. the juice) and not the outside of the orange (i.e. the peel) as the juice was likely to be perceived as more appetising. By the end of February 2009, the new design was abandoned and replaced with the original one, as brand identification was impacted so strongly by this simple change in the design that consumers could not find the orange juice in grocery stores. This resulted in a 20% decrease in orange juice sales with an estimated cost of $27 million. This is regarded as one of the most significant events in the beverage industry.[18]

Humour is almost always a successful way of attracting the attention of consumers. The campaigns of Nando's and Kulula are good examples of South African advertisements that are funny and cheeky. These advertisements were successful and contributed towards differentiating the brand names of the companies.

Up to this point in the process, perception has been purely sensory: we have only considered the impact of **sensation**. The next steps in the perception process concern how a person makes meaning from what was picked up through his or her senses.

4.2.4 Interpretation

Interpretation is the first phase in forming meaning from what a person has become aware of through his or her senses. Interpretation is about creating meaning from the stimuli; the person tries to grasp the message or consequences of information. It has been found that consumers are more individualistic than in the past; they are less influenced by the views of others in forming their own perceptions.[19]

Part of interpreting a stimulus is placing it in a category or schema. The human brain can be compared to a filing system: it 'files' and retrieves related stimuli together, as illustrated in Figure 4.3.

Thus, if a consumer sees a certain brand name, the qualities and emotions associated with that brand name are all retrieved from the 'file'. Many sought-after brands place their names on totally unrelated products, hoping that the positive view that consumers have of the original product will carry over to the new product. Land Rover and Jeep, for example, both have clothing ranges. Clothes are totally unrelated to any qualities that the motor vehicles may be perceived to have, yet consumers seem to want the association with the brand name. Many consumers who are unlikely to ever ride in,

Figure 4.3 This image depicts how the brain works to retrieve information from 'files'[20]

let alone own, a Ferrari, may own an expensive Ferrari cap. Motorbike manufacturer Harley Davidson has even placed its name on an aftershave.

New developments in medical science have allowed marketers to understand consumer attention better. It was found, for example, that exposure to adverse stimuli activated specific parts of the brain, causing the person to feel emotions such as fear, anxiety or disgust. Through subliminal processing, masked stimuli (stimuli that are hidden and thus difficult to discern) can elicit automatic responses. From these medical studies of the parts of the brain that govern perception, it was learnt that some information can influence reactions without the person being consciously aware of it. Usually, people become aware of a stimulus, process the stimulus and then react to the stimulus. This is called the cortical process. However, it has been found that it is also possible to bypass cortical processing.[21] That means that a stimulus can affect a person's reactions and behaviour without the person realising it.

The consumer interprets the stimulus in order to make meaning of it. Marketers try to ensure that consumers interpret a stimulus in a favourable way. For example, it was recently found that if consumers knew that luxury cars that originated in a developed country were actually manufactured in a developing country, they perceived those cars as not adhering to the same quality standards as the identical models that were manufactured in a developed country.[22] This interpretation of information could damage the brand name.

Another example comes from the health market. Research has found that novel ingredients in new products are not perceived to be as attractive as known ingredients. For example, Omega-3[23] has been on the market for a while as an ingredient of fish oil, and its history and benefits are well known. If producers add Omega-3 to new products, such as bread and margarine, consumers are likely to interpret it in a positive light.

4.2.5 Memory

Memory refers to a consumer not only thinking about a message and its meaning, but also remembering it. If it is stored in memory, the consumer can retrieve and utilise the message when making a purchasing decision. Marketers have to ensure that a stimulus is strong enough and differentiated enough to make a big enough impression to be stored in memory. If the message is not stored in memory, the consumer cannot recall it and thus cannot utilise it during decision making.

4.2.6 Decision

The purchasing decision is the final step in the perception process. After becoming aware of a stimulus, paying attention to it, storing it and retrieving previously stored information, the decision to purchase an item is based not only on what was received during the sensory process but also on the consumer's personality, previous information received about the product, past experiences with the product or similar products as well as the consumer's beliefs, values and attitudes.

APPLICATION

Tumi chooses a jersey

Tumi is standing undecided in a clothes store. She came to buy a jersey and is finding it difficult to choose between two she really likes. If she looks at the decision on a purely practical level, the black jersey is the best choice because it is cheaper and will go with most of her clothes. She thinks that black is an elegant colour and implies status. This makes the black jersey more attractive. She also remembers that her grandmother, of whom she was very fond, often wore a black jersey. The black jersey thus brings back some pleasant memories. However, her past experience with a black jersey was that it gathered particles quickly and looked worn after a short period of time. This is causing her to have doubts about buying the black jersey. The blue jersey, on the other hand, is more expensive and would not match many of her outfits. The blue jersey, however, has a popular brand name. She knows that her friends would notice the brand name and would be impressed and slightly jealous. Wearing the brand name would also imply status. She decides to take the blue jersey.

4.3 FUNCTIONS OF PERCEPTIONS

Primitive man's perception of a situation often determined his survival. If he was hungry and went 'shopping' (in other words, went looking for food), he could be faced with a decision such as whether to eat a mushroom, which might be poisonous, or whether to attack a buffalo with primitive weapons. Taking or not taking either action might have fatal: die or be killed, or starve to death. The decision was ultimately based on the person's perception of the situation, the risks involved and the odds of the outcome being successful.

Clever marketers have known for some time how to utilise this primitive function of perception. Images of food stimulate hunger and a desire to eat. Early findings of research on transparent packaging indicate that seeing actual food (through, for example, a transparent window incorporated in the packaging design) is more effective in obtaining consumers' attention and creating positive expectations compared to only seeing images of food.[24] Further research has highlighted that transparent packaging increases consumers' expectations with regard to freshness, quality, taste and innovation as well as their willingness to purchase the product.[25]

People have come a long way since primitive times. However, consumers still rely on their perceptions to guide them and to stop them from taking actions that might harm them. The consciousness amongst many consumers about healthy food is an example of how consumer perceptions still protect their health and quality of life. Not that long ago, researchers stated that health is the most significant trend in the global food and drinks market.[26] While consumers want to eat more healthy food, it was also found that they are not willing to compromise on taste: they want healthy food that tastes good.[27]

Consumer perceptions also protect mankind from harmful decisions through their awareness of producers who are perceived to be socially responsible. Such producers are seen as taking care of the environment, and focusing on aspects such as animal rights and social issues (for example, transformation in South Africa).

During the so-called mass market era, the emphasis was on producing large volumes of what people needed as cheaply as possible. Developed countries are, however, now in the post-mass market era. Consumers today mainly buy to a greater extent what they want, not what they need. They also want to differentiate themselves by what they buy and the services they use. The authentic consumer has been described as a person who is no longer trying to keep up with other people, but is expressing him- or herself through his or her possessions.[28] His or her belongings and what he or she consumes play a role in determining his or her identity. 'We are, to some extent, what we possess'.[29] Some possessions are not only manifestations of a person's self-concept, but an integral part of his or her self-identity. Consumers' quest for authenticity leads them to discover themselves, not only who they are but, more importantly, who they aspire to be and feel that it is within their power to become. They perceive consumption as a growth function; through their acquisition of possessions that they value, they express themselves more comprehensively and their possessions thus become an indication of their own growth. They take note of products or services that enhance their individualism and differentiate them or make them feel part of a small elite.

Whereas consumers in the mass-market era suffered from a scarcity of cash, little choice and the limited availability of products, the new consumer suffers from scarcity of time, attention and trust. Marketers thus need a different approach. They need to ensure that consumers understand the marketing message quickly. According to research, today's consumers can be described as individualistic, involved, independent and well informed. Consumers' perception of product quality affects how much they are willing to pay for the product. Marketers thus often try to position a product as high quality. Consumers do not pay attention to the quality they expect, but to quality that fascinates.[30] Consumers will thus hold the perception of a product being of superior quality only if it far exceeds what they expected.

In addition to expectations regarding quality, consideration needs to be given to consumers from Generation Z (popular term used to refer to young adults born from 1995 onwards) who have different expectations than those from previous generations and behave differently as consumers. They are more focused on innovation and expect smart technology to influence their experiences. Widely available electronic processes that offer greater autonomy and faster transactions as well as technology that enables informed shopping decision making are some of the expectations of consumers from this generation.[31]

Things are still very different in developing countries. Although consumers in these countries are also aware of the social responsibility of producers as well as the importance of healthy food, environmentally friendly producers and quality products, affordability often overrides these considerations. Many consumers in developing countries can hardly afford the staples required to survive. Developing countries have specific challenges and issues. For example, many consumers in these countries only buy products to satisfy their basic needs. Although consumers in developing countries are less conscious of issues such as social responsibility, they still prefer to buy from producers with a good reputation for it.[32] They are, however, less inclined to compromise on product price and quality. They will support the socially responsible producer if the product and quality are the same as those of similar producers. Although there are cultural differences between countries concerning perceptions of social responsibility, most people are positive about companies that are perceived to make it a priority.

Consumers' perceptions concerning counterfeit products are currently a major issue. The ethical and economic impacts of counterfeit products are well known. The perception of consumers concerning these products plays an

Figure 4.4 Without taking a closer look, consumers could be misled into thinking they are buying the fragrance Lady Million by Paco Rabanne.[33]

important part in sustaining these practices. Figure 4.4 shows a product that is made to look like a fragrance from a well-known designer label.

Some counterfeit products look, on the surface at least, very similar to the original product. A common but misleading practice of marketers of unknown brands is to try to make their products look similar to those of the market leader in the hope of fooling consumers into thinking they are buying the more popular brand. Marketers who do this can be, and often are, prosecuted for trademark or copyright infringement.

In summary, the function of perceptions is to guide the consumer's decisions to adapt to the environment in the best possible way. This means that the context in which consumers make purchasing decisions must be considered. The product perceptions of people living in developing countries vary greatly from those in developed countries, as their contexts are so different. Apart from context, personal factors (in other words, the preferences, values and needs of consumers) are also important in understanding perceptions and their function.

4.4 THEORIES THAT ARE RELEVANT TO PERCEPTIONS

Various theories of psychology may be helpful in understanding the application of consumer perceptions in marketing and in consumer behaviour. The theories most often cited in consumer behaviour literature are from gestalt psychology.

Gestalt psychology asserts that a person usually tries to organise stimuli in order to make them meaningful. A single stimulus is usually not seen in isolation, but is organised and integrated into the context of the things around it. The process is called perceptual organisation. In order to organise stimuli into something meaningful, consumers would not perceive a stimulus in isolation, but differentiate between a figure and its background. This is called figure and ground.[34] The person interprets stimuli in the context of the background. The figure is intended to be the focal point of attention and perception, and the background becomes hazy and undefined. The background should not distract from the figure. If, for instance, a marketer wants to show a person enjoying a chocolate, the person eating the chocolate is the figure. If the person is in a place where many activities are taking place, viewers might focus on the background instead.

Another principle borrowed from gestalt psychology is that of closure. Individuals have a need to organise perceptions so that they form a meaningful whole. Even if a stimulus is incomplete, the person's need for closure will lead him or her to see it as complete. This principle is often used in advertisements to get the attention of consumers: if a letter of a word or an obvious part of a picture is left out, the person's need for closure will urge him or her to complete the word or picture and thus give attention to the advertisement.

The visual gap is being filled by our perception. People's need to organise the information into a meaningful whole urges them to pay attention to the images.

Neuropsychology has only recently been applied to assist with the understanding of perception in marketing. Brain functions are monitored to understand how marketing messages trigger neurological reactions, in other words, to help researchers understand what happens in the brain when a person is exposed to stimuli. As will be discussed further in section 4.5, researchers have found that messages that are processed in the instinctual, primitive part of the brain, which deals with survival, are often the most compelling. If any of the survival instincts, such as fight (the urge to react with aggression), flight (the urge to get away from the situation), hunger or the need to protect its offspring are triggered, the perception process is set into motion.

Neurolinguistic learning programming (NLP) is a field built on the notion that what people perceive through their senses is filtered by their unique expectations and preferences. NLP has shown that people differ in their sensory preferences. Some people are more visually orientated, whilst others rely more heavily on some of their other senses. The sense preferences of consumers impact on their perceptions of a stimulus as well as on the effectiveness of a marketing effort in terms of the senses that the marketer targets.

Depth psychology, which deals with the understanding of the unconscious mind, has the potential to be utilised much more in understanding consumer behaviour. As is now widely known, consumption has, to a large degree, to do with an unconscious need for fulfilment. For example, if a person unconsciously identifies with the hero in an advertisement or becomes angry with the villain, his or her unconscious anger is projected onto the villain and he or she is more likely to pay attention to the advertisement.

RESEARCH BOX 4.1

Ongoing research is essential to build theory and to ensure a scientific approach to consumer behaviour. There are many ways to do research about consumer perceptions. Both qualitative and quantitative research methods are utilised regularly.

Quantitative research usually consists of questionnaires asking consumers about their perceptions of specific products or services. The answers are then analysed to help marketers understand trends in consumer perceptions. For instance, older men might have a negative perception of a certain shoe brand, whilst younger men might have a positive perception of it. This type of information assists marketers in targeting their advertising campaigns at the correct segment of the market.

Qualitative research is used to get an in-depth understanding of certain aspects of consumer perception. Bearing in mind that the perception process is largely unconscious, consumers might unwittingly give wrong information in questionnaires. In-depth interviews and focus groups are often utilised for qualitative research on consumer perceptions. In-depth interviews consist of trained interviewers interviewing one consumer at a time to get a clear understanding of the consumer's perceptions. Focus groups consist of small groups of consumers who are asked to discuss their perceptions of a certain product.

4.5 MARKETING COMMUNICATION AND CONSUMER PERCEPTION: GETTING THE ATTENTION OF CONSUMERS

Marketers strive to influence the perceptions of consumers. Their aim is to create positive perceptions of their products.

Marketers are concerned with the following questions:

* How is it possible to get the attention of consumers?
* How is it possible to encourage consumers to develop a positive perception of a specific product or service?
* How is it possible to convince consumers to purchase a specific product?

4.5.1 The changing nature of consumer perception

Consumer expectations are changing. For many decades, consumers wanted low-priced, mass-produced products. In the current post-mass market era, consumers are much more discerning. For many years, the philosophy of marketing was to bombard the consumer, hoping that the message would eventually get through. Ultimately, the general belief amongst marketers was that what was known would be loved (even if the consumer was irritated to wit's end in the process). A consequence was a seemingly endless repetition of the same television advertisements. With the disintegration of the mass market, this philosophy has changed dramatically in the last few years. It is now known that perception is much more than sensory exposure. Marketers have realised that some consumers find meaning in consumption and that consumers are becoming increasingly sophisticated. This has resulted in the need for a totally new approach to marketing, since bombarding consumers with the same message repeatedly is clearly not going to work as well as it did in the past.

For some consumers, the marketplace is their soul.[36] Consumption has even replaced religion as their main source of solace and comfort. The main purchasing decisions of such consumers are dictated by a need to satisfy an inner hunger rather than an external appetite. They want to express their individuality through the products and services they use, which means that the marketing message directed at them must be noticeably different from the message communicated to consumers whose main purchasing drive is to buy products in order to survive.

4.5.2 Communicating with the new consumer

The way to reach consumers in a post-mass market era is through new messages in new media. Electronic media have not simply replaced printed media with the principles remaining the same. E-shopping and **social media** marketing are more than just new marketing media. How people buy, what they buy and why they buy have all changed. The principles of marketing have shifted. Electronic media are immediate and at everyone's disposal. Consumers are now connected to each other and able to tell literally the whole world about their experiences, good and bad, as they happen. In this way, consumers shape each other's perceptions. If, for instance, a person has problems with her new television set and she tags her friends in a Facebook post about how disappointed she is, her friends' friends will also read about her bad experience. They will form a perception of the product and the after-sales service of the company based on her comments. Every consumer thus has the power to shape perceptions, which impacts on consumer behaviour.

Research has shown how wine brands have created authenticity to form unique brand identities.[37] In order to create authenticity, marketers have to manage the paradox of remaining relevant while also remaining true to the original concept of the product. For example, clothes that were fashionable in a certain era may become fashionable again, but in a modernised way. The problem arises that authenticity is often more contrived than real. Producers sometimes use myths to create it. For example, the producers of Dom Pérignon champagne tell the story of the monk, Dom Pérignon, who produced champagne by accident. They emphasise the time-honoured ways that are still used to produce the champagne as well as its natural ingredients. These claims may be based on real events, but they are also stylised attributes used to create an aura around the brand that differentiates it from others.[38]

Myths and stories are also used to promote mass market products. They create the appearance that a brand actually exists above commercial considerations and that there is a real commitment to quality.

APPLICATION

Thandi's holiday

Thandi is 16 years old. She has just returned from a holiday with her parents to Victoria Falls in Zambia. She had a wonderful time. She sent all of her friends and e-friends photos and descriptions of everything she was experiencing. She told them about the early morning elephant ride in the African bush, she sent photos and a movie clip of the exhilarating experience of doing one of the highest bungee jumps in the world, and she told them about watching the sunset over the Zambezi River from the deck of the Royal Livingstone Hotel. She did all this while these events were actually taking place. Her friends probably passed this information on to their friends and followers, and might also have told their parents about Thandi's holiday. Thandi's experience touched many people. She, and ordinary people like her, probably unwittingly did more marketing for Sun International than any clever and expensive advertising campaign.

Thandi also immediately told all of her friends about her frustration with Vodacom because her international roaming function did not work, despite the company's promise that it would. In addition, she complained to them about her dad's Standard Bank cash card, which did not work in Zambia, even though her father had arranged it with the bank in advance, and that their return flight on South African Airways was delayed for five hours for no apparent reason. Her comments probably did more damage to these companies' reputations and sales than they will ever know. She shaped perceptions. The damage that this caused cannot be fixed by a clever advertisement or special deal.

The scenario described above illustrates the new social reality that shapes and forms perceptions. Companies are by and large not ready to deal with social media marketing. It is a form of marketing that they participate in, whether they want to or not. Most companies have not woken up to this new power of the consumer and they are not used to the immediacy of actions required. Most companies also do not utilise the marketing opportunities it brings properly.

In utilising social media marketing to get consumers to decide to purchase a specific product or service, it is becoming more and more important to get consumers to talk about the product or service and to share their excitement about it with others. Although social media marketing is important, it is only significant in some markets and not in others.

Research suggests that marketers should create 'buzz', not 'hype'.[39] In other words, marketers should rather get consumers excited about a product ('buzz') than attempt to persuade consumers to purchase the product by trying to convince them of its good qualities ('hype'). Hard selling or trying to push consumers into purchasing something is becoming less and less successful.[40]

Mike Pike, well-known South African social media marketing expert, says that social media marketing is relationship based. He likens social media marketing to a car salesman visiting a particular bar for the first time. It would be inappropriate for him to get onto a chair and shout out to everyone there that he is a car salesman and that anyone interested in buying a car should contact him. He would typically start talking to people, introduce himself and build relationships. When he goes to the bar for the fifth time and sees some people with whom he has built a relationship, he might mention casually that he is a car salesman and they might ask for his business card. Many companies in the mass market frame of mind approach social media marketing totally inappropriately. They do not understand the dynamics of the process yet and are still applying the principles that worked in the mass marketing era.[41]

An interesting study reported that men and women pay attention to different aspects of a stimulus.[42] It was found, fairly consistently across cultures, that men are attracted to visual and physical attractiveness, whilst women are attracted to wealth and status. Although the definitions of physical attractiveness, wealth and status differ from culture to culture and depend on environmental factors, this finding was consistent. Even women who themselves possessed high wealth and status still preferred men who had it. This shows that it is a deep-seated evolved adaptation. Marketers should take note of this difference in preference between the genders when compiling advertisements and in particular, when choosing models and settings for advertisements. This finding not only has implications for advertisements, but also for the types of products to which men and women tend to pay attention. It was found that men were, in general, more interested than women in possessions that gave an indication of their status, such as luxurious cars, but they also found some exceptions.[43]

The image in Figure 4.5 is probably aimed at male consumers, utilising a woman's physical attractiveness to draw attention to a marble kitchen top.

Figure 4.5   An example of an image aimed at attracting the attention of male consumers[44]

4.6 STRATEGIC MARKETING APPLICATIONS

When compiling a marketing strategy, marketers need to consider the impact of the perceptions of consumers on their marketing efforts. Perceptions are therefore important to marketers for several strategic reasons, including the following:

- *The consumer's perception is his or her reality:* Consumers behave according to their perceptions. These perceptions guide their purchasing decisions.
- *Social media marketing is here to stay:* Most companies do not really understand the speed with which news and experiences spread. Marketers must be able to utilise electronic media to their advantage. Marketing strategies need to be revised to enable marketers to react quicker and to be part of this development. They need to take cognisance of the power and influence of the consumer, and adopt a different approach from the one used in the mass market era. Many companies do this by participating in social media discussions as a way of dealing with both positive and negative consumer perceptions.
- *Social responsibility and environment:* These issues are important. Consumers want to know that companies are socially responsible and environmentally friendly. In South Africa, transformation is currently an important aspect of social responsibility. Companies who do not show sufficient employment equity are excluded from some deals. Many consumers in developing countries can barely afford the basic necessities and they are therefore more price sensitive than consumers in developed countries. They are nevertheless also concerned about social responsibility. Some consumer segments in developing countries, mainly higher-income groups, are as focused on social responsibility and environmental issues as those in developed countries.
- *Health is big business:* Consumers want food that is perceived to be healthy, but at the same time, they do not want to sacrifice taste. Marketers need to be aware of this trend and capitalise on it. They should highlight the health aspects of their products.
- *Brand perception:* Marketers need to protect their brand and ensure that consumers are aware of their value proposition. Marketers must ensure that what gives them an edge is clear in consumers' minds so that it guides their purchasing decisions.
- *Success of marketing:* By measuring changes in perceptions, marketers can determine the success of their marketing campaigns.

SUMMARY

Perceptions can be defined as a person's awareness of, reaction to and interpretation of stimuli. It is more than the physiological reaction and also includes complex aspects of consumer behaviour, such as learning and motivation. Perceptions are important because consumers' purchasing decisions are, at least to some degree, based on their perceptions.

The perception process starts with a consumer being exposed to a stimulus, which is detected by the consumer's sensory receptors. The stimulus can be visual, auditory, smell, taste or touch. The stimulus must have sufficient intensity to be noticed and for the consumer to pay attention to it. The consumer then interprets the stimulus to make sense of it. The stimulus is fitted into the consumer's schema of knowledge and is stored in memory to be retrieved when needed to assist with purchasing decisions. Consumers might also be influenced by subliminal stimuli, in other words, stimuli of which they are not consciously aware.

Perceptions have the function of guiding decisions. Thus, consumer perceptions of a brand are of utmost importance to marketers. In the post-mass market era, consumers are more likely to buy what they want rather than to have their purchasing decisions guided by what they need. Social responsibility and environmental issues are becoming increasingly important. However, in developing countries, widespread poverty means that price is still the major driver of purchasing decisions. Health is also of growing importance to consumers. Products or even ingredients of products that are perceived to have health benefits have an advantage in the market. Marketers need to understand how to market health benefits effectively.

Today's consumers are informed and involved, and they want to have a say. Companies miss important marketing opportunities if they are not attuned to social media marketing.

SELF-ASSESSMENT QUESTIONS

1. Define consumer perceptions.
2. Reread the application box on page 87. Explain how Tumi went through the perception process to arrive at the purchasing decision. Indicate clearly how she went through each phase.
3. Describe the colour dimensions that marketers should be aware of when considering visual stimuli.
4. Explain the concept of threshold in sensory perception.
5. Explain how social media has changed marketing. Why is it not enough to give a dissatisfied customer a gift or a special deal?
6. Explain how marketers can utilise consumers' survival instincts to influence their perceptions.

EXPERIENTIAL EXERCISE

Your task is to interview three consumers to determine their perceptions of a consumer product. You may choose persons you know for the interviews. The purpose of the exercise is to gain insight into the perceptions of consumers, how these perceptions are formed, what influence these perceptions and how likely these perceptions are to change.

A suggested format for the interview:

1. Explain the purpose of the interview.
2. Get agreement from the person to partake in the interview.
3. Select a consumer item the person recently bought (it could be a toiletry item, such as shampoo, or food, such as sugar, maize meal or sardines, or a luxury item, such as imported chocolates).
4. Ask them how often, for how long and why they buy that specific item.
5. Explore why they prefer the product above competing brands and how these perceptions were formed (why they believe what they believe about the product).
6. Explore the reasons which influence their preference for the product: quality, price, packaging (label colour or design, ease of use, environmental friendliness), image of the manufacturer (in terms of issues such as environmental friendliness, social responsibility or ethical standards); in case of food items: health, taste or feeling associated with the product, status which use of product implies or expression of individuality.
7. Explore the likelihood of their buying another, similar product. If loyal to the brand, how their perceptions could be changed to buy another product.

This exercise could potentially be done during class with students interviewing each other and reporting back on their findings.

CASE STUDY 1

Introducing a Kenyan coffee into the South African market

Lion Coffee is a Kenya-based coffee-producing company. The company exports coffee to several African countries and now wants to enter the South African market. Lion Coffee manufactures various types of filter coffee. Their market research has indicated that Lion coffee has a stronger smell than the filter coffee currently on the market. Initial trials showed that a sample of South African coffee drinkers prefers the taste of Lion coffee to other brands. Lion coffee would be slightly more expensive what is currently available in South Africa.

Discussion questions

1. How would you advise Lion Coffee to penetrate the South African market? Who would be their likely clients? How would they distribute their products?
2. Develop a comprehensive marketing plan to support the sales and distribution plan.
3. Part of the marketing plan is an advertising plan, including media to be used. Decide which consumer perceptions need to be influenced, for example regarding instant coffee vs filter coffee, or filter coffee vs tea and other drinks. Decide which senses would be employed. Develop a slogan for the product to increase consumer awareness.

CASE STUDY 2

I want a cool drink and I want it now

It is a hot summer day. John is thirsty. He knows exactly what he wants. He walks into the supermarket and goes past the shelves with sweets and food, hardly noticing any of them. He heads straight for the fridge and sees the red cooldrink can through the glass door. He takes the can and walks back past the shelves with sweets and food towards the till without really noticing anything. While standing in the queue, he notices chocolates on the shelf next to the till. Apparently without thinking twice, he grabs one and pays for the chocolate and the cooldrink.

Discussion questions

1. Does John want or need a particular brand of cooldrink? Why?
2. What factors could be involved in John's choice of a cooldrink instead of another brand, water or any other drink? Could the cooldrink company's marketing campaign possibly have had any impact?
3. Did the perception process have any relevance to the seemingly impulsive choice to buy a chocolate?
4. Did any marketing efforts possibly play a role in the purchase of the chocolate or was it purely incidental?

ADDITIONAL RESOURCES

- Consumer perception is active: http://www.youtube.com/watch?v=PnGaKYUAtQw
- Gestalt in sensation and perception: http://www.youtube.com/watch?v=nxpat5aalSw
- Various tips, models and theories on marketing, consumer behaviour and perceptions: http://www. businessballs.com
- Research on impact of consumer perceptions on performance of a business: http://www.iresearch-services.com/influence-of-consumer-perception-on-the-performance-of-a-business/
- Consumer behaviour and perceptions: https://smallbusiness.chron.com/role-perception-consumer-behavior-67136.html
- Consumer perceptions of packaging: https://www.emeraldinsight.com/doi/full/10.1108/07363760610655032
- Consumer perceptions of web advertisements: https://www.sciencedirect.com/science/article/pii/S0747563210000725

REFERENCES

1   Hoyer, W.D. & MacInnis, D.J. 2012. *Consumer behaviour*, 6th ed. Stamford, CT: South-Western Cengage Learning, 80.

2   Solomon, M.R. 2011. *Consumer behaviour*, 9th ed. Upper Saddle River, NJ: Pearson, 83.

3   Troy, D.J. & Kerry, J.P. 2010. Consumer perception and the role of science in the meat industry. *Meat Science*, 86(1): 214–226.

4   Hoyer & MacInnis, op. cit., 81.

5   Westerman, S.J., Gardner, P.H., Sutherland, E.J., White, T., Jordan, K., Watts, D. & Wells, S. 2012. Product design: Preference for rounded versus angular design elements. *Psychology and Marketing*, 29(8): 603. DOI: 10.1002/mar.20546.

6   Carbon, C.C. 2010. The cycle of preference: Long-term dynamics of aesthetic appreciation. *Acta Psychologica*, 134(2): 240.

7   Bar, M. & Neta, M. 2007. Visual elements of subjective preference modulate amygdala activation. *Neuropsychologia*, 45(10): 2 191–2 200.

8   Carbon, op. cit., 234.

9   Ibid, 233–244.

10 Costell, E., Tárrega, A., & Bayarri, S. 2010. Food acceptance: The role of consumer perception and attitudes. *Chemosensory Perception*, 3(1): 42–50.

11 https://www.inc.com/guides/201105/how-to-use-samples-to-promote-your-product.html.

12 Jia, J.S., Shiv, B. & Rao, S. 2014. The product-agnosia effect: How more visual impressions affect product distinctiveness in comparative choice. *Journal of Consumer Research*, 41, August: 342. DOI:10.1086/676600.

13 Solomon, op. cit., 9.

14 Hoyer & MacInnis, op. cit., 86.

15 Zajonc, R.B. 2001. Mere exposure: A gateway to the subliminal. *Current Directions in Psychological Science*, 10(6): 224–228.

16 Elgendi, M., Kumar, P., Barbic, S., Howard, N., Abbott, D. & Cichocki, A. 2018. Subliminal priming: State of the art and future perspectives. *Behavioural Sciences*, 8 (54): 13–14. doi:10.3390/ bs8060054.

17 Landwehr, J.R., Wentzel, D. & Herrmann, A. 2012. The tipping point of design: How product design and brands interact to affect consumers' preferences. *Psychology and Marketing*, 29(6): 422–433.

18 Lee, J., Gao, Z. & Brown, M.G. 2010. A study of the impact of package changes on orange juice demand. *Journal of Retailing and Consumer Services*, 17: 487–488. doi: 10.1016/j.jretconser.2010.08.003.

19 Lewis, D. & Bridger, D. 2000. *The soul of the new consumer: Authenticity – what we buy and why in the new economy*. London: Nicholas Brealey, 15.

20 https://www.dreamstime.com/brain-files-archiving-data-encephalon-office-vintage-colors-image104516237

21 Bar, M. & Neta, M. 2006. Humans prefer curved visual objects. *Psychological Science*, 17(8): 645–648.

22 Fetscherin, M. & Toncar, M. 2010. The effects of the country of brand and the country of manufacturing of automobiles: An experimental study of consumers' brand personality perceptions. *International Marketing Review*, 27(2): 164–178.

23 Lähteenmäki, L., Lampila, P., Grunert, K., Boztug, Y., Ueland, Ø., Åström, A. & Martinsdóttir, E. 2010. Impact of health-related claims on the perception of other product attributes. *Food Policy*, 35(3): 237.

24 Simmonds, G. & Spence, C. 2016. Thinking inside the box: How seeing products on, or through, the packaging influences consumer perceptions and purchase behaviour. *Food Quality and Preference*, 62: 340–341. doi: 10.1016/j.foodqual.2016.11.010.

25 Simmonds, G., Woods, A.T. & Spence, C. 2017. 'Show me the goods': Assessing the effectiveness of transparent packaging vs. product imagery on product evaluation. *Food Quality and Preference*, 63: 18. doi: 10.1016/j.foodqual.2017.07.015.

26 Lähteenmäki et al., op. cit., 230.

27 Verbeke, W. 2005. Consumer acceptance of functional foods: Socio-demographic, cognitive and attitudinal determinants. *Food Quality and Preference*, 16(1): 45–57.

28 Lewis & Bridger, op. cit., 79.

29 Hawkins, D.I., Best, R.J. & Coney, K.A. 2006. *Study guide for consumer behavior: Building marketing strategy*, 9th ed. Ventura, CA: Academic Internet Publisher, 432.

30 Lewis & Bridgeop. cit., 11.

31 Priporas, C., Stylos, N. & Fotiadis, A.K. 2017. Generation Z consumers' expectations of interactions in smart retailing: A future agenda. *Computers in Human Behavior*, 77: 374. doi: 10.1016/j.chb.2017.01.058.

32 Arli, D.I. & Lasmono, H.K. 2010. Consumers' perception of corporate social responsibility in a developing country. *International Journal of Consumer Studies*, 34(1): 46–51.

33 https://www.mindshareworld.com/ireland/news/are-instagram%E2%80%99s-fake-ads-symptom-bigger-problem; https://www.iol.co.za/business-report/economy/counterfeit-goods-threaten-sa-economy-16720574https://www.mindshareworld.com/ireland/news/are-instagram%E2%80%; 99s-fake-ads-symptom-bigger-problem

34 Hoyer & MacInnis, op. cit., 99.

35 https://www.google.co.za/search?hl=en&biw=1366&bih=603&tbm=isch&sa=1&ei=9hGNW9HQ GYv5gQbehaJw&q=coca+cola+bottle+with+knife+and+fork&oq=coca+cola+bottle+with+knife +and+fork&gs_l=img.3...9021.15068.0.15372.31.19.1.0.0.0.505.2892.2-1j5j1j1.8.0....0...1c.1.64.img.. 22.7.2220...0j0i67k1j0i8i30k1j0i24k1.0.W8vdGWFM2V0#imgrc=attGGb3u9uVmyM:

36 Lewis & Bridger, op. cit., 75.

37 Beverland, M.B. 2005. Crafting brand authenticity: The case of luxury wines. *Journal of Management Studies*, 42(5): 1 022.

38 Ibid., 1 007.

39 Lewis & Bridger, op. cit., 105.

40 Ibid., 78.

41 Personal communication with author, December 2012, Johannesburg.

42 Dunn, M.J. & Searle, R. 2010. Effect of manipulated prestige-car ownership on both sex attractiveness ratings. *British Journal of Psychology*, 101(1): 76.

43 Ibid., 77.

44 *Sarie Kos*, Winter 2018 edition, page 99.

CHAPTER 5

PERSONALITY

Richard Shambare

LEARNING OBJECTIVES

After reading this chapter, you should be able to:

·   define personality
·   explain the concept of African personality and how it fits in the wider personality discussion
·   describe the psychoanalysis theory of personality
·   list the five attributes of the Big 5 personality theory
·   explain how personality influences consumer behaviour
·   explain how *ubuntu*, as an African philosophy, affects consumers' personality.

Key terms		
Big 5	culture	personality theory
cardinal trait	customer	post-purchase
consumer	market segmentation	pre-purchase
consumer behaviour	OCEAN	trait
consumerism	personality	*ubuntu*

OPENING CASE STUDY

Sisters Jane and Joeleen are practically inseparable. They attended the same primary school, high school and university. They frequently buy the same type of clothing and shoes, and also wear the same hair styles. Many people struggle to tell them apart. Joeleen is the eldest in their family of five children.

Upon graduating with their BCom degrees, the sisters decide it is time they each bought a car. Jane buys a two-seater Mazda MX-5 after consulting her father and her brother, who both work as computer technicians. Joeleen opts for a double cab Mitsubishi bakkie after seeking advice from her other two sisters and her mother. Jane's consultation lasted one night and Joeleen's about two weeks.

How is it that these two sisters, who have bought similar items for most of their lives, suddenly begin to show differences in their decisions about buying a car?

5.1 INTRODUCTION

This chapter discusses the place and role of personality in consumer behaviour. Personality refers to specific internal differences between people, in other words differences that are not tangible/visible to the eye. This includes variations in patterns of thinking, mannerisms, habits and actions, as exhibited by individuals in their daily lives.[1]

Many of the differences, such as the manner in which consumers interact with one another, are really a manifestation of variations in consumers' personalities. For example, some people tend to be more outgoing than others and enjoy meeting new people, attending social gatherings and chatting to people they have not met before (socially confident individuals). Individuals that exhibit these behavioural characteristics (also known as personality traits) are usually classified as extroverts. In contrast, individuals with a tendency of being reserved (often referred to as shy) and who prefer spending time on their own, or only with a small friendship group, are often considered to be introverts. These differences in personality dispositions or personality traits (introversion vs extroversion) shape individuals' consumption processes. In simple terms, personality traits determine the manifestation of one's personality, which in turn shapes a wide array of behaviour, including consumer behaviours such as product choice, manner of consumption and complaint patterns.

To illustrate the personality–consumer behaviour connection, consider the consequences of people's disposition/nature of being either introverted or extroverted, which is referred to by psychologists as the personality trait of extraversion.[2] A person who scores high in extraversion on a personality test is considered to be an extrovert and the 'life of the party', whereas a person low in extraversion is less outgoing and may be considered an introvert. By nature, introverts are usually less expressive and tend to focus more on their inner thoughts and feelings.[3] As such, introverted consumers tend to be less confrontational. Extroverts, on the other hand, express their feelings and thoughts more openly. As such, the implication of this personality trait on consumer behaviour (for example, consumer complaint patterns) is that introverts will be less likely to express themselves verbally in purchasing situations or to return to a store to complain about a faulty product than extroverts. Introverts tend to opt for less confrontational complaint patterns or 'private complaint actions such as exiting or boycotting the firm brand and negative word-of-mouth' – specifically talking to people they know and feel comfortable with.[4] On the other hand, extroverts are more likely to exhibit public complaint patterns, for example the immediate confrontation of service staff upon experiencing poor service.

The influences of personality traits on consumer behaviour are innumerable. It is for this reason that marketers devote much attention to understanding personality and it is well-documented in the marketing literature.[5] However, it is important to note that most studies on consumer behaviour are drawn from Western-oriented conceptual frameworks, with African philosophies such as *ubuntu*, which form the foundation of much of the prevalent consumer behaviour in the South African marketplace, rarely being mentioned. It is against this background that the overarching purpose of this chapter is to sensitise readers to the following: (a) the relationship between personality and consumer behaviour; (b) African philosophies on personality, and (c) the use of African philosophies to both understand and explain a multitude of consumer behaviours in South Africa.

The balance of the chapter is therefore structured as follows. In the next section, personality is defined. Thereafter, various theories explaining the foundations of personality and their implications on consumer behaviour are presented.

5.2 PERSONALITY DEFINED

According to Albanese,[6] personality is that stable and consistent characteristic that defines a person – that single attribute that differentiates one individual from another. Others define personality as

- '[a] relatively stable organisation of a person's motivational dispositions arising from the interaction between biological drives and the social and physical environment'[7]
- 'the sum of all the physical, psychological and spiritual characteristics that influence the behaviour of an individual'[8]
- 'whatever it is that makes people who they are'.[9]

Personality therefore consists of those internal, personal, non-visible characteristics that not only distinguish people, but also determine their common and generalised patterns of behaviour.[10] It is that one element that can be used to classify individuals into a collective based upon their similarities, and can therefore be used as a way of organising and grouping consistencies in individuals' reactions to situations.[11] In marketing terms, this collection of individuals with similar behaviours is known as a market segment.

Figure 5.1 shows how the various social, physical and environmental characteristics culminate in personality, which in turn influences people's (consumers') behaviour patterns.

Personality is determined by the interplay of the physical, psychological, spiritual, social and environmental contexts within which an individual lives.[12] However, because it is intangible, it is difficult to measure. One approach is to use personality traits to explain behavioural patterns. For example, extroverted individuals are more expressive, which can be observed through their openness about their thoughts and feelings.

Behavioural patterns are useful in two dimensions:

- A collection of individuals possessing similar behavioural patterns can be grouped together to form a market segment (signified by the lower segment of Figure 5.1).[13] An example is a motorcycle club whose members are identified by their specific dress code. These members will often have similar interests, lead similar lifestyles and have similar motives and consumption patterns. It would not be surprising to find that many of them belong to similar professions.

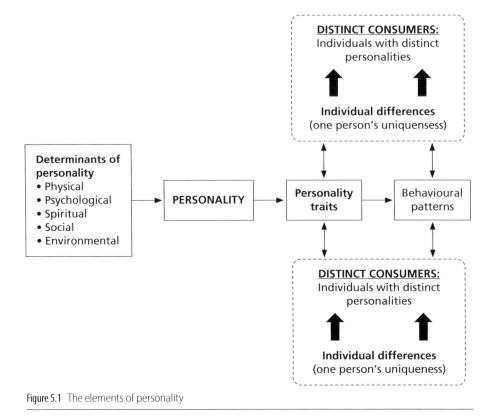

Figure 5.1 The elements of personality

- The individual differences accounted for by personality and behaviour tend to differ from one person to the next. This distinctiveness is the factor that makes an individual stand out as an independent consumer (signified by the upper section of Figure 5.1). To this effect, Opute[14] defines a consumer as 'individual with a distinctive personality'.

Personality therefore accounts for both differences and common behavioural patterns between consumers and is key to defining both individual 'consumers' and 'market segments'.

5.2.1 Why is personality important in the study of consumer behaviour?

Studies have indicated that people's behaviour remains relatively constant over time.[15] People tend to be creatures of habit and any change (including in behaviour) is difficult. Schreiber and Hausenblas[16] explain that 'the mere mention of this word [change] may cause some people to feel uneasy. We often find

ourselves resisting change, perhaps because of the perceived risk or fear associated with it'. Human behaviour therefore tends to be systematic and follow a
certain pattern. As such, it can be considered to be stable[17] and therefore measurable and predictable.[18]

To remain competitive, it is in a retailer's best interests to be able reliably
and accurately to measure, anticipate and predict the behaviour of its customers. Consumer behaviourists and marketing managers invest a great deal of
effort on research directed towards understanding the motives for, and drivers
of, consumption in order to decode consumer decision-making processes and
predict consumer choice behaviour.[19] This is integral to the marketing function
of any business for the following reasons:

It enables a business to design unique market offerings for specific market
segments in a way that reliably and accurately satisfies each segment.

The business is empowered to concentrate on particular market segments
rather than targeting the entire (i.e. unsegmented) market, hoping to appeal to
at least someone. This increases a business's marketing efficiency in that customers' needs are more easily satisfied, and satisfied customers are more likely
to become loyal customers.

Because consumer personality-based segments are stable enough to predict
variances in consumer choices, retailers can successfully employ different marketing strategies to appeal to each one.

There are three fundamental principles upon which contemporary marketing thought rests:[20]

- *Profit maximisation:* In order to secure its survival and growth, every business wants not only to make a profit but to make the most profit possible.
- *Market segmentation:* By specialising on marketing particular products to
  specific smaller groups of customers, retailers not only benefit from the
  associated economies of scale but also stand a better chance of retaining a
  particular group of customers by satisfying their needs.
- *Consumerism:* Customers will only accept and pay for goods or services
  that they want, and will only repurchase those with which they are satisfied. Retailers' responsiveness to consumer needs is highly correlated to
  profitability.

Also known as the marketing concept philosophy, Foxall explains is as follows:[21]

> … a philosophy of business organisation which has three major implications: firstly, the success
> of any firm depends above all on the consumer and what he or she is willing to accept and
> pay for; secondly, the firm must be aware of what the market wants well before production
> commences, and, in the case of highly technological industries, long before production is even
> planned; and thirdly, consumer wants must be continually monitored and measured so that,
> through product and market development, the firm keeps ahead of its competitors.

Table 5.1 summarises the three different phases of consumer behaviour and the
possible activities involved in them. These behaviours, positive and negative,
are influenced by personality.

Table 5.1 Phases of consumer behaviour (see also chapters 1 and 11)

Phases of consumer behaviour	Activities
Pre-purchase	Researching products, prices and retailers (also referred to as window shopping) Product trials, for example test driving a car
Product acquisition	The activities involved in the actual purchase of goods and services Complaining about bad service Selecting distribution channels Choosing the method of payment Impulsive purchases Compulsive shopping Shoplifting
Post-purchase	Fraudulently retuning products Recycling and re-using products Complaining Littering Claiming product warranty Hoarding Referrals

5.2.2   Personality as a predictor of behaviour

Although it would be easiest to assume that consumers are purely economic and will always seek to maximise their utility at the least financial cost possible, in reality the 'economic man' hardly exists and consumers rarely make economically rational decisions. This is because several factors other than financial considerations influence behaviour. Sociological and psychological influencers such as personality have proved to be more reliable when trying to understand consumer choice dynamics better.

An example of the immense power that socio-psychological factors have on consumer behaviour is the growing trend of the *skothane* culture among young South African consumers. *Skothane* revolves around the practice of showing off material possessions such as expensive designer clothing and jewellery ('bling bling'). Figure 5.1 depicts Scott Harney, a *skothane*

Figure 5.2   A *skothane* (Scott Harney)

cartoon, whose name was anglicised to rhyme with the word '*skothane*'. Scott Harney's posture as well as his choice of wardrobe – colourful and costly shirt, shoes and gold tooth – exemplifies the *skothane* way of life.

Another feature of *skothane* is the disregard for economic factors in favour of satisfying social and psychological needs. In *skothane* contests, consumers destroy their belongings

Figure 5.3 A *skothane* pouring custard on the ground to illustrate his economic freedom

and set fire to their cash, simply to make the point that 'they can afford to', 'they have' and 'they can do it'. Figure 5.3 shows a *skothane* pouring custard, considered to be a luxury grocery item, on the ground.

Skothaneism, among others, exemplifies that consumers are not always persuaded by reasons that might, at face value, appear to be practical, sensible and logical. In reality, it is usually not just one but multiple factors (psychological, economic, sociological and cultural) that influence behaviour.[22] Personality plays a big role in this.

In the next section, the various theories explaining the source of personality are discussed.

5.3 WHERE DOES PERSONALITY COME FROM AND HOW DOES IT DEVELOP?

This chapter highlights the following five personality theories: Allport's trait theory, Cattel's source theory and the five-factor (Big 5) model, which are discussed under trait theories, followed by Freud's psychoanalysis and the African perspective on personality.

5.3.1 Trait theories of personality

In simple terms, a personality trait (for example, being an optimist, motherly or an introvert) describes an individual's qualities and speaks directly to a pattern of behaviour, thought and emotion. As psychological qualities, traits are relatively stable and remain fairly constant; in other words, they do not change much across various situations.[23] Because of this consistency, researchers use trait theories to express assumptions and ideas of personality. Although there are numerous personality trait theories, this chapter focuses on the main three,[24] namely Allport's trait theory, Cattel's source theory and the five-factor (Big 5) model (see Figure 5.4).

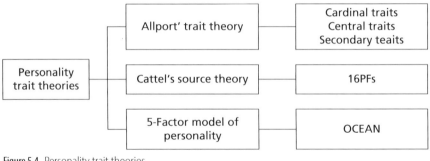

Figure 5.4 Personality trait theories

Allport's trait theory

According to Allport's trait theory, behaviour is influenced by people's experiences and what they value in life.[25] For instance, students who place a lot of value in achieving high marks will naturally work hard to ensure that they pass with flying colours. As such, the theory suggests that the best way to understand human behaviour is by studying the things that people love.

The theory identifies more than 16 000 traits which can be categorised into three main sub-groups:

* Cardinal traits
* Central traits
* Secondary traits.

Cardinal traits

A cardinal trait is one that directs most of the actions and behaviour of a person, for example greed, kindness, justice and equality. Cardinal traits motivate people and give them a sense of purpose in life; they often manifest over a long period of time, if not an entire lifetime. In other words, they act as guiding posts for human behaviour and actions. Often, an individual's life is influenced by only one cardinal trait. For instance, the late Nelson Mandela, former president of South Africa, was guided by the cardinal trait of justice – he thus devoted his life to the attainment of justice and equality for all South Africans, sacrificing 27 years of his life in prison in the fight for freedom and democracy.

APPLICATION BOX

Rate yourself[26]

Indicate the extent to which you agree or disagree with the following statements. These statements are designed to measure how you compare to Nelson Mandela in terms of the cardinal trait of justice.

* I often think about having a society that is just, fair and equal.
* I am deeply concerned when I see other people being treated unfairly.
* I would easily sell my expensive sneakers or clothes to buy clothes for the poor.

- I easily step into a fight when I see that someone is being beaten up.
- I am not afraid to speak the truth for justice.
- I am prepared to leave my partner or spouse to go and fight for my belief for justice.
- I would not accept a R5 million payoff to abandon my fight for justice.
- I am involved in voluntary work in my community.
- I would willingly sacrifice my life to pursue global peace and justice.

If you agree with most of the above-mentioned statements, chances are that you and Mr Mandela share the cardinal trait of justice. If not, there are other equally important cardinal traits. Below is a list of some notable South Africans and the cardinal traits that seem to have guided their lives:

- Thabo Mbeki (integrity)
- Steve Biko (equality)
- Desmond Tutu (justice and equality)
- Miriam Makeba (free spirit)
- Charlize Theron (excellence)
- Cassper Nyovest (wealth)

Central traits

Central traits are the building blocks of personality.[27] The best way to characterise them is to think of the descriptors that are often used in reference letters or testimonials (for example, Nyota is an *intelligent* young man or Becky is a *hard-working* person). Central traits are responsible for shaping most of our behaviour.

Central traits differ from cardinal traits in two ways: (1) they are observable in shorter spans of time, and (2) while an individual's behaviour is usually mostly influenced by a single cardinal trait, his or her personality is a function of the interplay of many central traits. Ultimately, it is personality that gives rise to cardinal traits and long-term behaviour.

Some examples of central traits include:

- intelligence
- shyness
- anxiety
- friendliness
- kindness.

Secondary traits

Secondary traits are circumstantial traits that appear less frequently and usually under certain situations. For example, Michelle may become nervous whenever she is asked to speak in front of her class, but when she is outside the classroom, she likes to talk and laugh a lot. Nervousness about speaking in public is therefore one of her secondary traits.

Table 5.2 presents a brief synopsis of some consumer behaviours associated with Allport's traits.

Table 5.2 Allport's traits applied to consumer behaviour

Allport's traits	Implications on consumer behaviour
Cardinal traits (for example, wealth creation)	Consumers whose central traits revolve around wealth creation tend to be very conscious about their expenditure. As such, these consumers tend to spend considerably longer periods of time planning purchases and selecting among the cheapest retailers and products.
Central traits (for example, honesty, being talkative, being observant)	Upon receiving extra change from a cashier at a supermarket, a consumer that can be described as having the central trait of honesty will only accept the change that rightly belongs to him or her and will insist on returning the rest to the cashier.
Secondary traits (for example, becoming impatient while waiting in a queue)	Individuals who exhibit impatience in stressful situations such as waiting in a bank queue often complain about the perceived poor service. At times, these consumers are sensitive and demand high levels of recognition.

Cattell's source traits

Prior to the 1940s, personality models were qualitative in nature with few, if any, mathematical approaches being used. This changed, however, in 1941 when Raymond Cattel applied factor analysis to reduce thousands of traits to only 16 (known as the 16PF).[28] This was a major breakthrough as researchers could now work with a relatively small number of personality traits, which enabled better and more precise measurement. Factor analysis also allowed for the manipulation of variables, something that was impossible in the old (non-mathematical) approaches.[29]

Table 5.3 shows how Cattell's 16 traits affect people's (consumers') behaviour. The main traits are presented in the left column and the implications of each in the right. Each main trait has two corresponding, but opposing, traits which define it. For example, 'openness to change' is one of the main traits, which is in turn defined by the two opposing traits, flexibility and attachment. Consumers tend to fall somewhere between these two extreme positions of either being willing to change their usual way of doing things, or absolutely not.

Table 5.3 Cattell's source theory and consumer behaviour

Personality trait	Implications/example of consumer behaviours
Abstractedness Imaginativeness vs practical	• In terms of abstractedness, practical consumers sometimes follow step-by-step guides in product use. They are systematic in their purchase and usage of products. • Imaginative consumers tend to be less systematic and often find new ways of using products other those stipulated by the manufacturer.

Personality trait	Implications/example of consumer behaviours
Apprehension Worried vs confident	• Some consumers are anxious. They rarely make purchase decisions on their own. These are worried consumers who rely on consultations and advice from friends and family. • More confident consumers will most likely do their own research and make their purchasing decisions independently from others.
Dominance Forceful vs submissive	• Behaviours associated with forceful individuals might include the tendency to complain and express their feelings verbally regarding bad customer service or unhappiness with a product. • A consumer who is more submissive might not be as vocal and forceful about a negative experience.
Emotional stability Calm vs highly strung	• Calm individuals are generally cool and collected. They are often easy to get along with and do not exhibit erratic behaviours. • Highly strung consumers are easily irritated and often complain more frequently.
Liveliness Spontaneous vs restrained	• Spontaneous consumers are free spirited. They are susceptible to peer pressure and, as such, may exhibit acts of consumer misbehaviour, for example vandalism. • Restrained consumers
Openness to change Flexible vs attached to the familiar	• Consumers who are highly attached to the familiar on the openness to change scale tend to have extreme loyalty to brands. • Those exhibiting the flexibility trait are more willing to try out new products and also to switch retailers.
Perfectionism Controlled vs undisciplined	• Undisciplined consumers are sometimes susceptible to binge consumption and compulsive buying behaviours. • Disciplined consumers will be less likely to engage in impulsive buying behaviour.
Privateness Discreet vs open	• Discreet individuals mind their own business. They are less likely to be conspicuous consumers. They also tend not to be consumers of expensive brands. • Those who are observed to be more open are usually seen to prefer conspicuous consumption. An example is this type of consumer is the *skothane* (see section 5.2.2).
Reasoning Abstract vs concrete	• Consumers who score low on reasoning (in other words, are more abstract), • Consumers who score high on reasoning (in other words, are more concrete) are methodical. They take considerably longer to make decisions.
Rule consciousness Conforming vs non-conforming	• Conforming consumers tend to abide by societal rules and norms. • Non-conforming consumers tend to be relatively younger and more rebellious. They may, for example, be involved in acts of misbehaviour such as shoplifting.

Personality trait	Implications/example of consumer behaviours
Self-reliance Self-sufficient vs dependent	• Self-sufficient consumers depend on their own knowledge and efforts versus that of others. They can be highly critical and particular about their preferred standards. • Dependent consumers
Sensitivity Tender-hearted vs tough-hearted	• Tender-hearted consumers are higher on sensitivity and • Tough-hearted consumers are lower on sensitivity and are less likely to be involved in consumer misbehaviour actions.
Social boldness Uninhibited vs shy	• Uninhibited consumers tend to show preference for conspicuous consumption. • Shy consumers are usually reserved and show preferences for private consumption patterns.
Tension Impatient vs relaxed	• Impatient consumers are often demanding of individual attention and are time conscious. • Relaxed consumers are more easy-going and less likely to make a fuss.
Vigilance Suspicious vs trusting	• Highly trusting consumers are less critical about others. They are more likely to believe retailers' claims. • Suspicious consumers tend to be mistrustful. They are known to conduct their own research on products and their use.
Warmth Outgoing vs reserved	• Outgoing consumers tend to seek out thrill-seeking experiences such as white water rafting and other outdoor activities. • Reserved consumers

Over and above reducing the number of traits, Cattell provided a standardised questionnaire to measure personality traits that resulted in greater flexibility and application of the 16PF, beyond just through trained psychologists.[30] Marketing was one of the disciplines, among many, that recognised the potential for standardised personality measures. Eventually, almost all personality trait theories relied on mathematical procedures to develop standardised questionnaires.[31]

One such theory is the five-factor model of personality, discussed next.

Five-factor model of personality

The five-factor model of personality (popularly known as the Big 5 model)[32] is one of the most widely used personality trait theories.[33] The Big 5 model was developed by Lewis Goldberg, who based his theory on Cattel's 16PF, reducing and simplifying the number of traits to five:

- Openness
- Conscientiousness
- Extroversion
- Agreeableness
- Neuroticism

For ease of remembering, the first letters of these five traits make up the mnemonic 'OCEAN'. Each of the five personality factors represents a range between two extremes. For instance, the factor 'conscientiousness' measures the extent to which people range between self-discipline and carelessness. Table 5.4 summarises the Big 5 factors and provides some applicable examples.

Table 5.4 The Big 5 model[34]

Factor	Definition	Examples
Openness to experience	A tendency to be free-spirited vs traditionalist	**HIGH:** imaginative, independent, creative
		LOW: practical, conforming, routine
Conscientiousness	A tendency to be self-disciplined vs careless	**HIGH:** organised, careful, disciplined
		LOW: disorganised, careless, impulsive
Extraversion	A tendency to be introverted vs extroverted	**HIGH:** sociable, fun-loving, affectionate
		LOW: retiring, sombre, reserved
Agreeableness	A tendency to be friendly vs self-centred	**HIGH:** soft-hearted, trusting, helpful
		LOW: ruthless, suspicious, uncooperative
Neuroticism	A tendency to be emotional vs calm and even-tempered	**HIGH:** anxious, insecure, self-pitying
		LOW: calm, secure, emotionally stable

Trait theories are the most common approach to explaining personality[35] for the following reasons:

- *Easy to use:* Traits are relatively easy to understand in that they mostly use simple, everyday language, for example 'friendly' or 'aggressive'. As such, traits are often self-explanatory.
- *Versatility and wide applicability:* Because of their simplicity, trait theories can be applied in various disciplines and settings with little modification and have gained prominence in psychology,[36] personology[37] and consumer behaviour, among others.[38]
- *Availability of measurement scales:* Due to the popularity of statistics and mathematical measures in psychology, most personality trait theories are almost always accompanied by measurement scales or questionnaires. Examples are Cattell's questionnaire,[39] the technology readiness index,[40] the Big 5 personality traits[41] and the Myers-Briggs Personality Inventory.[42]

DISCUSSION

The Big 5 traits

The Big 5 traits are openness to experience, conscientiousness, extraversion, agreeableness and neuroticism. Every individual exhibits some unique combination of these traits. For instance, one might have a tendency of being friendly while at the same time possessing a tendency of being introverted. People will behave differently depending on their particular personality, therefore within a retail context, it is important for sales staff to be prepared to deal with a wide array of customers whose behavioural tendencies will almost always be unpredictable.

Discussion questions
1. To what extent can the Big 5 model be of use in anticipating customers' behaviour?
2. Suppose you are the sales manager for a leading retail outlet in South Africa and responsible for training the salespeople in your organisation. One of the subject areas that you are to teach is the personality and behaviour of customers. Discuss the topics you would include in your training.
3. Do you think it would be necessary for the sales manager to alert sales personnel about the consequences of their own personalities when attending to customers?
4. Visit the website: https://my-personality-test.com/ and attempt the Big 5 personality test. Share your results with your friend. Do you and your friend agree with the results?

5.3.2   Psychoanalysis

Sigmund Freud, an Austrian medical doctor, is regarded as the father of psycho-analysis. At the core of psychoanalysis is the belief that behaviour is an outcome of wishes, desires and feelings – both conscious and unconscious. Unlike trait theorists, who are mostly interested in explaining behaviour, psychoanalysts attempt to establish the source of behaviour.[43]

Two important assumptions of psychoanalysis theory are as follows:
*   Personality is formed by an interplay of three elements: the id, ego and superego.
*   An individual's early childhood years (up until about the age of six years) shape personality.

Freud's structure of personality

The interaction of the id, ego and superego culminate in personality and behaviour.[44]

The id

The id is unconscious and impulsive. It is the most primitive component of personality that remains mostly unchanged throughout an individual's life. The id's components are biological, in other words, they are passed down from one generation to the next and will always remain as the unconscious part of an individual's personality.[45] According to Grieve et al.,[46] the three components of the id are:
*   libido – pleasure seeking
*   ego – life preservation
*   aggression – tendency to harm others.

The id is the first component of personality to develop within individuals; like-wise, personality of a new-born baby consists only of the id.[47] In essence, the id is all about pleasure maximisation, and is not affected or regulated by logic, reality and everyday social life. Actions such as stealing, sexual relations, eating, beating another person are all examples of the id.[48]

The ego

The ego represents the decision-making component of personality, and is moderated and governed by the external world. The ego tries to reason out socially acceptable ways of satisfying the id such that negative consequences are minimised. To this effect, the ego seeks to balance two opposing forces: (1) the avoidance of unpleasant stimuli or any painful experience, and (2) the maximisation of pleasure. The ego is believed to develop around the ages of three to five years of age and is largely shaped by societal and cultural values.

McLeod[49] explains that Freud used the analogy of a horse and its rider to represent the relationship between the id and the ego. The id can be thought of as being the horse – wild and powerful. However, the rider is the ego. The rider, through the use of various approaches, trains and tries to rein in the horse to control it and move it in a particular direction.

Figure 5.5 Id, ego and superego[50]

The superego

The third component of personality is the superego. This element is highly influenced by social and moral values and might influence a person even further than what the ego does. Shambare et al.[51] comment that the superego can be regarded as the 'internal representative of society that regulates right and wrong behaviour'. The superego achieves this in two ways: (1) it tries to steer the id away from purely pleasure-seeking behaviours while extending the influence of the ego towards moral virtues, and (2) it sensitises the ego to society's expectations. In terms of the horse and rider analogy, the superego would be the expectations of the rest of the herd and their riders.

Since the superego is the component that is most influenced/shaped by external forces, it is naturally the one most targeted by marketing efforts.[52] The superego tries to regulate behaviour to fall in line with societal expectations, so by manipulating public opinion, marketers are able to influence an individual consumer's superego indirectly, which in turn modifies his or her behaviour. An example is the endorsement of products by celebrities. Since celebrities tend to be highly regarded within society, it is relatively easy for them to convince people that product X is good for them too.

5.4 PERSONALITY: SOME AFRICAN PERSPECTIVES

The personality theories that have been discussed thus far are all Western oriented and were designed to address the contexts of the developed world. However, a vast majority of consumers in many African countries, including South Africa, do not necessarily subscribe to Western values, norms and ways of life. Since personality is shaped by societal and cultural contexts, existing theories, while useful for describing and explaining a multitude of consumer behaviours in South Africa, often suffer cross-cultural limitations.

Many young consumers in Africa devise creative ways to express their Africanness within a globalised world. For example, African couples are increasingly satisfying both their Western and African ambitions by hosting two wedding ceremonies – a traditional African ceremony, and a 'modern' ceremony dubbed the 'white wedding'. The traditional African wedding is usually a family gathering (see Figure 5.6) and involves *lobola* (bride price) negotiations. *Lobola* is a token sum of money payable by the groom to the bride's family[53] and confirms that marriage has taken place. The 'white wedding' is a perfectly organised, formal event (see Figure 5.7), including the exchange of vows and rings – a custom borrowed from the West.

Figure 5.6 A *lobola* wedding ceremony in South Africa

Figure 5.7 A 'white wedding' in South Africa

The dual-wedding practice, considered from Sigmund Freud's viewpoint, is an act of ego – a reasoned-out compromise with the id. This compromise exists at two levels:

- *Avoidance of unpleasant stimuli:* Consecrating a marriage through a *lobola* ceremony, as expected and accepted by the community, amounts to doing the 'right thing' in the African culture. It promotes an individual's continued acceptance within this world and the after-life and, more importantly, it avoids that individual being ostracised from society. Failure to pay *lobola* and not inviting friends and family to the *lobola* ceremony is thought of as an act of abomination; such behaviour is likely to anger the ancestors and will attract social sanction and reprimand.[54]

- *Maximisation of pleasure:* Hosting a more 'modern' and western idea of a wedding could be seen as satisfying the bride and groom's primitive ids, at a personal level in terms of pleasure seeking. The couple is able to dress up in what would be considered more modern wedding attire, exchange vows and express their love the 'modern' way, with a kiss and rings. By hosting a 'white wedding', the couple is able to satisfy and express some pleasurable desires such as declaring their love in public, which is frowned upon in certain African cultures. It also permits the couple to register their marriage officially with the Department of Home Affairs and receive a marriage certificate, which may allow other desires to be realised, such as the following:

- The bride being able to adopt the groom's surname on her identification documents.

* In the case of 'in community of property' marriages, the couple can pool their income, increasing their credit rating and buying power.

The inability of existing conceptual frameworks to explain dual weddings demonstrates the inadequacy of Euro-centric theories in understanding consumer behaviour in African terms.[55]

In Africa, it is not possible to divorce people's belief in ancestors from their behaviour. African culture and philosophy are therefore not only the foundation but also the building blocks of 'African personality'.[56] At the core of the African personality argument is the assumption that 'man [in this context referring to both male and female) is the priest of the universe'.[57] As a 'priest', each and every person strives for harmonious relations with self, others and the surrounding environment.

This 'priesthood of the universe' is embraced in the African philosophy of *ubuntu*. *Ubuntu* (also known as *unhu*) is an African behavioural trait and a moral principle that is best described as compassion for humanity.[58] Maintaining harmony within communal life thus allows a person to have *unhu* or personality.[59]

African people value communal interests (in other words, the wishes and desires of the community) over that of individuals, including their own personal aspirations. For instance, individuals often sacrifice on personal expenditure (for example, buying a less expensive car) in order to afford to send money home for the upkeep of the extended family. In today's contemporary language, this practice of being responsible for and maintaining the extended family is often referred to as paying 'black tax'.[60] By helping to take care of the family, an individual acquires *unhu* or personality and 'truly' becomes a member of the society.

The *unhu* philosophy means that African behavioural and cultural expectations are different from those of the West. An Afrocentric approach to studying personality will likely provide valuable insights into consumer behaviour in South Africa and other African countries.

5.4.1   Ubuntu and its implications for consumers' personality

As mentioned above, Western cultures are individualistic in nature, but the African viewpoint tends to lean towards collectivism.[61] A comparative analysis of the differences between these two approaches and their implications for personality and consumer behaviour are summarised in Table 5.5.

Recognising a business opportunity, many businesses have developed community-oriented product offerings to cater to the needs of African consumers.[64] For example, the following three (black tax) products have been specifically designed to cater for African consumers and their extended families:[65]

* FNB has a funeral plan that covers up to 21 individuals, catering to the needs of larger families.

Table 5.5 The implications of *ubuntu* in terms of personality and consumer behaviour[63]

Factor	Comparative analysis: Western vs ubuntu perspectives		Implication of *ubuntu* on personality	Possible effects of *ubuntu* on consumer behaviour
	Eurocentric perspectives (individualism)	Afrocentric perspectives (collectivism or *ubuntu*)		
Philosophy	First the individual, then the community: *We are because I am*	First the community, then the individual: *I am because we are*	• Agreeableness: high • Trusting • Humble	• Humble and well-behaved consumers • Fewer incidents of consumer misbehaviour
Group vs individual relations and socialisation	• A high regard for the individual elevates the importance of the individual above the community • Individual independence	• A high regard for the group elevates the importance of the community above the individual • Dependence on people	• Extraversion: high • Humble • Polite • Face-saving behaviours	• Very little, if any instances of complaints • Poor service can be tolerated • Purchase decisions are communal. No one person makes the final decision • Preference for packaged deals (for example, free emergency assistance for car breakdown included in car insurance)
Opinion	Group opinion does not matter	Strong communal pressure	• Openness to experience: low • Peer pressure	• Loyal to trusted brands • Tendency to resist new products/innovations
Duty of persons	Individual rights are paramount	Duty towards the community is emphasised	• Conscientiousness: high	• Price sensitive • Black tax • Preference for products that cover the entire family (for example, family funeral cover)
Values	Formality, independence, self-sufficiency	Friendliness, helpfulness, hospitality, patience, brotherhood	• Neuroticism: low • Disciplined • Emotionally stable	• When in public, a person must be on his or her best behaviour • Consumer misbehaviour not tolerated

- AVBOB funeral and insurance services offers free transportation of the deceased to anywhere in South Africa, allowing a family's already limited funds to go further.
- Standard Bank offers a loan for *lobola*, allowing access to a lump sum of money which might have otherwise never been accumulated through saving.

RESEARCH BOX 5.1

The concept of the 'priesthood of the universe' is an important aspect of African life. This philosophy encourages people to always be mindful of how their actions affect other people, the community and the environment in which they live. This concept is enshrined in numerous areas of African lives, including consumption. One specific marketing implication the 'priesthood of the universe' concept has is that it discourages people from engaging in argumentative encounters with other people. Instead, in a marketing context, it can be argued that this implication would mean that consumers tend to avoid conflict and less likely to complain about poor service or a faulty product.

Research tasks

Interview 2–4 elders within your community (for example, aunts, uncles, grandparents), using the following questions:

1. What is a person's responsibility to self, others and the environment within the community?
2. In which contexts should this responsibility be exercised?
3. Are there exceptions where this responsibility can be excused?
4. What happens to an individual who refuses to obey these communal imperatives?
5. How much influence do you feel the ancestors have influence over this life?

SUMMARY

The main focus of this chapter was the multidisciplinary nature of personality as a driver of human behaviour, including consumer behaviour, and how understanding personality allows marketers to anticipate consumer behaviour.

An underlying principle in the study of personality and consumer behaviour is the assumption that, all things being equal, human beings are creatures of habit. In other words, they rarely deviate from their accustomed routine and order of doing things. This means that their behaviour tends to be constant throughout their lifetime and therefore should be predicatable. Another important feature of personality is that it enables consumers to stand out as individuals, while at the same time being a part of a larger group sharing similar personalities.

The chapter demonstrated that African philosophies such as *ubuntu/unhu* are instrumental in shaping the personality of African consumers and therefore have the potential to uncover and explain much of the consumer behaviours prevalent in the African marketplace.

While consumer behaviour is complex, personality has been found to be most reliable factor in predicting it thus far and it is therefore used as the basis for much of the segmentation and differentiation in the marketplace.

SELF-ASSESSMENT QUESTIONS

1. By means of practical examples, explain how personality and consumer behaviour are related.
2. Give practical examples of how quantitative personality scales and questionnaires have influenced personality in consumer behaviour.
3. Discuss how Sigmund Freud's psychoanalysis theory differs from the personality trait theories.
4. Discuss the *ubuntu* viewpoint of personality. How is this viewpoint similar to or different from other Western personality theories?
5. Explain how businesses in South Africa are redesigning their product offerings to be able to capitalise on the *ubuntu* philosophy.

EXPERIENTIAL EXERCISE

Suppose you are the marketing manager at a popular retail store in South Africa. In the 15 years since you have been in this job, you have realised that there are certain acts of consumer behaviour that are more likely to be performed by specific consumer groups. For instance, analysis of your shop records indicate that young males are up to ten times more likely to be shoplifters than any other consumer group. Upon further investigation, you realise that personality can be used to predict consumer behaviour. How could you apply this knowledge in recruiting service personnel for your shop?

Discuss how you could go about differentiating or categorising customers using personality.

EXTRA RESOURCES

For further information on the concepts discussed in this chapter, watch the following videos:
- https://www.youtube.com/watch?v=Wa3t_OpW35E
- https://www.youtube.com/watch?v=7vFf5CS27-Y
- https://www.youtube.com/watch?v=pCceO_D4AIY

CASE STUDY 1

Is obesity an important issue in South Africa?

An investigation by the Medical Research Council in 2010 revealed that 20% of high school children in South Africa are overweight and 5% are obese[66]. The implication of these findings is that many south African children are at risk of suffering from chronic heart disease, diabetes and high blood pressure later on in life. In addition, research has revealed that a third of the women in South Africa are overweight, while just under a third of south African women are obese. Only 13% of the men in south Africa are regarded as obese[67]. These results are particularly shocking in a country where 29% of women do not get enough to eat and often go hungry. The question that needs to be asked is, 'Why are the majority of women in south Africa either overweight or obese?' The research carried out suggests that some of the underlying factors contributing to the obesity problem in South Africa include the following:

- 54% of consumers in South Africa feel that it is more important for food to be filling than healthy. This outcome is understandable in a country where many do not get enough to eat. 49% of consumers feel that they cannot afford healthy foods, while 79% see healthy food as more expensive.
- The majority of consumers do little, if any, exercise.

- Healthy food is seen by many consumers as not tasting good and not offering value for money.
- Many South African consumers do not believe the marketing hype around healthy food.

Discussion questions

1. Obesity is becoming a major problem among women in South Africa. Taking into account the four personality viewpoints discussed in this chapter, do some Internet research to describe the underlying personality factors that may be contributing to South African women's tendency toward obesity.
2. Comment on the implications of the research findings discussed in the case study for marketers and retailers.
3. The South African government is planning to introduce legislation to reduce the amount of salt and sugar in the food manufactured in south Africa. Do you think that this legislation will help to solve the obesity problem in South Africa? Use your Internet research findings to support your viewpoint.

CASE STUDY 2

Understanding big earners in South Africa[68]

Research in South Africa on the characteristics of people who earn more than R30 000 per month has revealed that the majority of these individuals are found in Gauteng (approximately 50%), 16% live in the Western Cape and 13% in KwaZulu-Natal, whilst the remainder are located in the other provinces in fairly even numbers. Approximately 90% of top earners live in metropolitan areas, with 33% of these located in security estates. This research also demonstrated that financial success is closely correlated with education, with many respondents having either an undergraduate or post graduate degree.

In addition, the majority of these individuals exhibited an entrepreneurial flair and they tended to save or invest 10% or more of their earnings. Approximately 37% of this segment is represented by black South Africans.

'Top enders' appear to be more conservative in terms of their financial investments.

In this segment, there is a distinct correlation between risk aversion and wealth. Most of the people in this group modified their purchasing and shopping behaviour in response to the recent recession and the financial turmoil currently experienced in the world. For example, these consumers now tend to shop around more, they have cut back on luxuries and they travel less. They also replace their cars less frequently than they did in the past. Most people belonging to this group regard marketing and advertising as a nuisance.

They prefer to get their information and advice from their highly developed networks and the internet.

Discussion questions

1. List five traits that you can identify from the text about the behaviour of Top Enders. Give reasons for choosing each of your identified traits.
2. Imagine that you are the marketing manager for a new luxury holiday estate on the North Coast and you want to target top enders in Gauteng in the hope of persuading them to purchase a holiday home in the new estate. Describe how you would promote your holiday resort to them, taking into account the information provided in the case study.

REFERENCES

1   Boshoff, C. 2017. *Principles of marketing*. Cape Town: Oxford University Press; Opute. 2018. Exploring personality, identity and self-concept among young consumers. *Young Consumer Behaviour: A Research Companion*, 79–97.
2   Goldberg, L.R. 1990. An alternative 'description of personality': The Big-Five factor structure. *Journal of Personality and Social Psychology*, 59(6): 1216–1229.
3   Cherry, K. 2018a. The Big Five personality traits. Available at: https://www.verywellmind.com/the-big-five-personality-dimensions-2795422 (accessed on 19 May 2018).
4   Kitapci, O. & Dortyol, I.T. 2015. Do personality types make consumers exhibit different complaint behaviours? *Journal of Marketing and Consumer Behaviour in Emerging Markets*, 2(2): 8.
5   Cherry, 2018a, op. cit.; Foxall, G.R. 1984. *Consumer behaviour: A practical guide*. New York: Routledge; Goldberg, op. cit.; Kitapci & Dortyol, op. cit.; Meyer, W.F., Moore, C. & Viljoen, H.G. 2013. *Personology: From individual to ecosystem*, 4th ed. Johannesburg: Heinemann; Shambare, R. 2012. *Predicting consumer preference for remote banking services in South Africa and Zimbabwe: The role of consumer perceptions versus personality variables*. D.Tech Business Administration, Business School, Tshwane University of Technology.
6   Albanese, P.J. 1993. Personality and consumer behaviour: An operational approach. *European Journal of Marketing*, 27(8): 28–37.
7   Foxall, op. cit., 57–58.
8   Grieve, K., Van Deventer, V. & Mojapelo-Batka, M. 2007. *A student's A-Z of psychology*. Claremont: Juta, 188.
9   Meyer et al., op. cit., 10.
10 Albanese, P.J. 1993. Personality and consumer behaviour: An operational approach. *European Journal of Marketing*, 27(8): 28–37.
11 Lamb et al., ibid.
12 Grieve et al., op. cit.
13 Azevedo, S., Pereira, M., Ferreira, J. & Pedroso, V. 2008. Consumer buying behaviour in fashion and retailing: Empirical evidencies. *MPRA*, 11908(3): 407–411; Kitapci & Dortyol, op. cit.
14 Opute, op. cit., 81.
15 Holm, A.C. 2010. Can your Myers-Briggs type change?/Neuroplasticity: The adaptable brain. Available at: http://www.annholm.net/2010/05/can-your-myers-briggs-type-changeneuroplasticity/ (accessed on 10 October 2018).
16 Schreiber, K. & Hausenblas, H. 2016. Why is change so hard? Available at: https://www.psychologytoday.com/us/blog/the-truth-about-exercise-addiction/201608/why-is-change-so-hard (accessed on 10 October 2018).
17 Kelly, M.P. & Barker, M. 2016. Why is changing health-related behaviour so difficult? *Public Health*, 136(Supplement C): 109–116; Schreiber & Hausenblas, ibid.
18 Foxall, op. cit.; Holm, op. cit.; Powell, G. 2014. Does consumer behavior change or is it constant? Available at: https://prorelevant.com/does-consumer-behavior-change-or-is-it-a-constant/ (accessed on 10 October 2018).
19 Shambare, 2012, op. cit.
20 Parasuraman & Colby, op. cit.
21 Shambare, 2012, op. cit.
22 Foxall, op. cit., 15.
23 Bettman, J.R., Johnson, E.J. & Payne, J.W. 1991. Consumer decision making. In Robertson, T.S. & Kassarjian, H.H. (Eds), *Handbook of Consumer Behaviour*. Upper Saddle River, NJ: Prentice Hall, 50–84; Shambare, 2012, op. cit.
24 Grieve et al., ibid.
25 Cherry, 2018a, op. cit.
26 Grieve et al., op. cit.
27 Adapted from ibid.
28 Ibid.
29 Cattel, H.E.P. & Mead, A.D. 2008. The Sixteen Personality Factor Questionnaire (16PF). In Boyle, G.J., Saklofske, D.H. & Matthews, G. (Eds), *The Sage Handbook of Personality Theory and Assessment: Personality Measurement and Testing* (volume 2). Thousand Oaks: SAGE.

30 Cherry, K. 2018b. Cattell's 16 personality factors. Available at: https://www.verywellmind.com/cattells-16-personality-factors-2795977?print (accessed on 15 October 2018).

31 Cattel & Mead, op. cit.

32 See Goldberg, op. cit.; Hofstede & McCrae, op. cit.; Holm, op. cit.; Opute, op. cit.; Parasuraman, op. cit.; Parasuraman & Colby, op. cit.

33 Goldberg, ibid.

34 Grieve et al., op. cit.; Hofstede & McCrae, op. cit.

35 Adapted from Grieve et al., ibid.

36 Cherry, 2018a, op. cit.

37 Grieve et al., op. cit.

38 Meyer et al., op. cit.

39 Shambare, 2012, op. cit.

40 Cherry, 2018b, op. cit.

41 Parasuraman, op. cit.

42 Hofstede & McCrae, op. cit.

43 Holm, op. cit.

44 Grieve et al., ibid.

45 McLeod, S.A. 2016. Id, ego, superego. Available at: https://www.simplypsychology.org/simplypsychology.org-psyche.pdf (accessed on 15 October 2018).

46 Grieve et al., op. cit.

47 Ibid.

48 McLeod, op. cit.

49 Grieve et al., op. cit.

50 McLeod, op. cit.

51 Methridge, C. 2017. The strange case of the id the ego and the superego jekyll and hyde as the unconscious mind. British Literature 1700-1900; A course blog. Online. Available: https://britlitsurvey2.wordpress.com/2017/05/02/the-strange-case-of-the-id-the-ego-and-the-superego-jekyll-and-hyde-as-the-unconscious-mind (Accessed 31 October 2018)

52 Shambare et al., op. cit., 320.

53 Ibid., 319.

54 Khumalo, T. 2015. Lobola app gives South African bride price. *DW Africa*. Available at: http://www.dw.com/en/lobola-app-gives-south-african-bride-price/a-18284800 (accessed on 15 October 2018).

55 Gelfand, M. 1970. Unhu – the personality of the Shona. *Studies in Comparative Religion*, 4(1).

56 Shambare, R. 2016. Consumer adoption of e-government in South Africa: Barriers, solutions, and implications. In *Handbook of research on consumerism and buying behavior in developing nations*. Hershey, PA: IGI Global.

57 Khoapa, B.A. 1980. *The African personality*. Geneva: United Nations University.

58 Ibid., 8.

59 Shambare, op. cit., 213.

60 Gelfand, op. cit.

61 Matubatuba, T. 2016. Black tax, ubuntu and the opportunity for brands. Available at: http://themediaonline.co.za/2016/05/black-tax-ubuntu-and-the-opportunity-for-brands/ (accessed on 15 October 2018).

62 Grieve et al., op. cit.

63 Adapted from Grieve et al., ibid., 203.

64 Matubatuba, op. cit.

65 Ibid.

66 Cloete, L., Mitchell, B., Morton, D. 2017. The role of obesity in the onset of type 2 diabetes mellitus. Nursing Standard. 31, 22, 59-69. Date of submission: 30 August 2016; date of acceptance: 16 September 2016.

67 Higgs, 2012. pp 27-29.

68 Adapted from Egan, P. 2011. New Light on Our Big Earners. Strategic Marketing, official publication of the Institute of Marketing Management (IMM), Issue 6, pp. 50—51. Reprinted by permission of the editor of Strategic Marketing, and author, Paul Egan.

CHAPTER 6

CONSUMER ATTITUDES

Mercy Mpinganjira

LEARNING OBJECTIVES

After reading this chapter, you should be able to:

- define what attitudes are and describe their characteristics
- describe the main components of attitudes
- discuss the relevance of attitudes during consumer decision making
- explain how attitudes are learnt
- describe the theoretical models that depict consumer attitudes and behaviour
- understand the predictive limitations of attitudes on consumer behaviour
- explain the methods used in measuring attitudes
- discuss strategies used to influence change in consumer attitudes
- discuss how marketing communication can be used to influence attitude formation and change.

Key terms

affective component of attitudes

attitude

attitude object

behavioural component of attitudes

cognitive component of attitudes

ego-defensive function of attitudes

elaboration likelihood model

multi-attribute attitude models

organisation-of-knowledge function of attitudes

single component attitude models

theory of planned behaviour

theory of reasoned action

tri-component model of attitudes

utilitarian function of attitudes

value-expressive function of attitudes

OPENING CASE STUDY

When asked to give a talk on skin care, Jane, a dermatologist, starts by asking a group of young women what they think about putting on make-up in general. Below are two of the responses she receives:

Jabu: To me I believe that wearing make-up is a waste of time and money. I do not wear make-up and why should I? I do not believe that women need any enhancements to their looks. The natural look appeals to me.

Vivian: I like make-up. I see it as part of personal grooming. I believe that I look better with my make-up than without it. This does not mean that I do it for other people. No, I do it for myself because of the way it makes me feel.

From the responses, what would you say about Jabu and Vivian's attitudes towards make-up?

6.1 INTRODUCTION

The term '**attitude**' is widely used to describe the way people feel, think or behave towards something, including products, other people, events and issues. Attitude is not tangible and as a result, one cannot directly observe it. One can, however, observe the effect of attitude from what people/consumers say and how they behave. For example, Jabu's response in the opening case study that she believes that the use of make-up is a waste of time and money shows that she has a negative attitude towards make-up. Vivian's response, on the other hand, shows that she has a positive attitude towards make-up and likes purchasing and wearing it.

Marketers take special interest in understanding consumer attitude. This is because attitude influences the way consumers respond to their products and services, including the decision to buy or not buy a product or service and whether or not to recommend it to others.

This chapter aims at providing a better understanding of attitudes and the way in which they affect consumer behaviour. It starts by defining attitudes and discussing their main characteristics, before examining their structural composition and main functions. The chapter then focuses on consumer attitude formation and how attitudes impact on consumer decisions and buying behaviour. This is followed by discussions on how marketers measure attitudes, strategies that can be used to change consumer attitudes, and how marketing communication is used to influence attitude formation and change. The chapter ends by highlighting the strategic marketing applications of attitudes.

6.2 DEFINING ATTITUDES

There are several definitions of attitudes available in literature. Here are two examples:
* 'The general and relatively enduring evaluations people have of all kinds of objects.'[1]
* 'A psychological tendency that is expressed by evaluating a particular entity with some degree of favour or disfavour.'[2]

However, the most commonly used definition of attitudes is by American psychologist Gordon Allport, who defined attitudes as 'a learned predisposition to respond in a consistently favourable or unfavourable manner with respect to a given object'.[3] Every part of Allport's definition highlights some of the main characteristics of attitudes, including the following:
* *Attitudes are object specific:* This means that attitudes are always directed towards something. An attitude object is thus anything tangible or intangible towards which a person can have an opinion. In assessing consumer attitudes, researchers ask questions that are object specific. For example, a consumer might be asked about his or her attitude towards Toyota cars, towards salespeople, towards a retailer such as Woolworths or towards the idea of eating out every day. The 'object' in the definition of attitudes thus needs to be interpreted broadly to refer to anything tangible or intangible

towards which a person can have an opinion. This includes people (including oneself), behaviour (for example, recycling, binge drinking), products, organisations, issues, events, advertisements and price.

* *Attitudes are learnt:* No-one is born with attitudes. They are learnt through personal experience with a given object, through reasoning about the object or through information received about the object. Family members often have a strong influence on consumer attitudes because of the important role that they play in the socialisation process of individuals. Peers and marketing communications also play an important role in shaping and influencing consumer attitudes. Sections 6.5 and 6.9 provide detailed discussions on factors that influence attitude formation and change respectively.

* *Attitudes are predispositions to respond:* This means that attitudes are characterised by a state of readiness and have a motivational quality to act or react in a particular way to given stimuli. The stimulus in this case refers to the 'object' towards which individuals may have an attitude. The action or reaction to the stimulus may be favourable (positive) or unfavourable (negative). A favourable attitude towards a brand is likely to propel a consumer towards buying the brand. An unfavourable attitude towards a brand, on the other hand, will discourage a consumer from buying the particular brand.

* *The response to attitude objects is consistent:* Attitudes tend to endure over time unless something happens or is done to change them. Since attitudes are enduring, marketers can expect customers who hold a positive attitude towards their products to keep on responding to their products favourably for some time. This response may include the decision to keep on buying or saying good things about the products. On the other hand, customers with a negative attitude towards the company's products will keep on responding negatively to those products unless something is done to change their attitudes. It is thus possible to infer a person's attitudes by observing his or her response towards attitude objects over time.

Other important characteristics of attitudes include the following:

* *Attitudes have valence (direction):* This refers to the fact that an attitude can be positive (favourable) or negative (unfavourable).[4] Attitudes can also be neutral. Some people, for example, have a negative attitude towards fast food, others have a positive attitude towards such food while others may be uncertain and have mixed feelings (neutral).

* *Attitudes have strength:* Attitude strength refers to the level of positivity or negativity that a consumer feels towards a particular object. In the example above, consumers holding a negative attitude may differ in how strongly they feel about fast food. Some may hold a very strong negative attitude because they have serious concerns about the healthiness of fast food, while the attitude of others may only be slightly negative because purchasing fast foods can be expensive in the long run.

Having defined attitudes, we now look at the main components of attitudes.

6.3 COMPONENTS OF ATTITUDES

Most researchers agree that attitudes have three components:
* Affective component
* Cognitive component
* Behavioural component

Each of these three components of attitudes is discussed in more detail below.

6.3.1 The affective component

This component is about the feelings people have towards attitude objects. These feelings are evaluative in nature. They are a response to a person's evaluation of an object. Affective response is used to assess consumers' all-encompassing favourable (positive) or unfavourable (negative) attitude towards certain objects. A consumer may, for example, say, 'I like Johannesburg' or 'I do not like Johannesburg'. Such statements are all encompassing as they do not tell the specifics of why or why not that person likes or dislikes the attitude object in question.

Table 6.1 provides examples of affective responses that people may have towards different attitude objects.

Table 6.1 Affective responses

Attitude object	Affective response
TV advert	Likeable or unlikeable Exciting or not exciting Disgusting or not disgusting
Restaurant	Pleasant or unpleasant Amazing or not amazing Relaxing or not relaxing
Stem cell research	Good or bad Desirable or undesirable Appropriate or inappropriate

The major advantage of using the affective component to understand attitudes is that it provides an overall evaluation of an object on favourability. It is thus easy for marketers to assess if customers have favourable feelings about their offering or not.

The disadvantage of using only this component is that by focusing on feelings only, marketers are not able to determine what is causing the customer's feelings. For example, if one were to ask customers about their feelings towards a TV advert, it might come out that many customers found the advert exciting. This information is, however, not helpful in determining *why*.

Consumers' overall feeling towards an attitude object is often a result of his or her feelings towards specific attributes of that attitude object. Thus, while marketers may be interested to know what customers feel about their products, it is also important for them to identify the factors that influence these feelings. This knowledge can help inform the development of effective marketing strategies to influence customers' feelings in a positive way. This need resulted in some researchers emphasising the need to go beyond the affective component when trying to understand attitude and to look at the cognitive component of attitudes as well.

6.3.2 The cognitive component

The **cognitive component of attitudes** is about a person's knowledge and perception towards attributes of an attitude object. This knowledge and these perceptions are expressed in the form of beliefs. For example, a consumer may perceive one brand of cars as safe to drive based on his or her knowledge that the cars fare well in car crash tests.

APPLICATION

Cognitive component of attitude

An individual's attitude can be inferred from his or her beliefs. Consider the following scenarios:

- After watching a TV show on modern farming methods that highlighted the common modern practice of using antibiotics in animal farming, Jane believes that organic farming is better for her health.

- Sizani believes that it is better to use a body lotions containing vitamin E because vitamin E helps improve moisture content and elasticity of the skin.

Discussion:

1. Comment on Jane's attitude towards organic foods.
2. Comment on Sizani's attitude towards body lotions containing vitamin E.

It is important to note that the beliefs that consumers have may or may not necessarily be based on correct or factual information relating to product attributes and/or benefits. However, irrespective of whether they are based on correct or incorrect information, what makes customers' beliefs important is that they influence buying behaviour. It is therefore to a company's benefit to supply the market continuously with correct information that reinforces positive beliefs about its products and to shape consumers' beliefs in a positive direction. In general, the more positive beliefs consumers have towards a product, the more favourable their attitude towards it is.

6.3.3   The behavioural component

Apart from the affective component and the cognitive component, attitudes can also be determined by looking at the **behavioural component**. This component is concerned with the consumer's intentions or likelihood to behave in a certain way with regard to an attitude object.[5] It is sometimes referred to as the conative component of attitudes. Under this component, attitude is inferred from the likelihood or tendency to accept or reject, approach or avoid, buy or not buy etc. a specific object. In consumer behavioural studies, intentions are central to explaining the behavioural component of attitude. Positive behavioural intention indicates a positive attitude towards an attitude object, while negative behavioural intentions indicate a negative attitude towards a specific object.

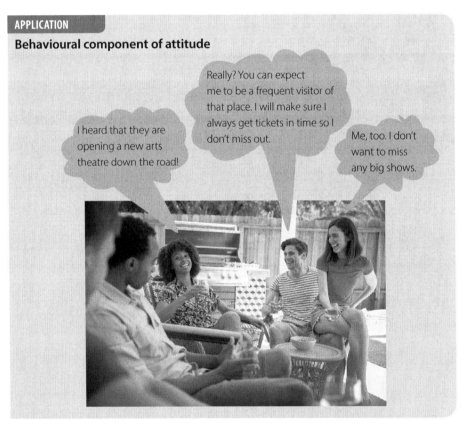

APPLICATION

Behavioural component of attitude

Consumer behavioural intentions are of great concern to marketers as they help in predicting how customers will act towards their company's products. Such information is particularly helpful in estimating the demand for products and planning production schedules. Being able to establish the number of people intending to watch a particular television programme, for example, can help a television station to decide whether to air the programme in the first place as well as to justify the programme scheduling.

6.4 MODELS OF ATTITUDES

Various models based on one or more of the three components of attitude (affective, cognitive and behavioural component) have been developed over the years by researchers in their quest to understand attitudes. The main difference between the models relates to both the number and also the nature of components that they emphasise in order to understand attitude. The models can be broadly grouped into single component, multi-attribute and tri-component models:

* *Single component models:* In general, the single-component attitude models measure attitudes as one-dimensional and consisting of the **affective component of attitudes** (the feelings people have towards attitude objects). Advocates of this model argue that attitude can be understood by simply examining the affect one has for or against an attitude object. General evaluative terms such as good or bad, poor or excellent, liked or disliked are commonly used when assessing attitude under a single component model.

* *Multi-attribute models:* Multi-attribute models portray consumer attitudes towards a product as a function of three components, namely (1) the attributes of the product, (2) beliefs about the attributes, and (3) the level of importance attached to the attributes or benefits associated with the attributes. Advocates of multi-attribute models contend that each product has several attributes that consumers consider during product evaluation. For example, a dentist may rate one brand of toothpaste better than another based on the following attributes: cavity protection capabilities, teeth-whitening capabilities, enamel-strengthening capabilities and bacteria-fighting capabilities. Multi-attribute models show that consumers have positive attitudes towards products that have more of the attributes that they regard as important. Consumers will therefore have negative attitudes towards products that have fewer of the attributes that they consider important. Multi-attribute models are thus compensatory in that the weakness of a brand in one attribute can be compensated by its strength in another.[6] Compensatory decisions are explained in more detail in Chapter 1.

APPLICATION

The multi-attribute model of attitude

Michael is a university student. His parents have given him R5 000 to buy a smartphone. The table below shows the attributes that Michael considers to be important as well as the level of importance attached to each attribute on a scale of 1 to 10, where 1 indicates the least important attribute and 10 indicates the most important attribute.

Michael has also rated his beliefs about each of the three brands of smartphones that he is considering to buy on a scale of 1 to 5, where 1 means that he believes the model does not fare well on the attribute and 5 that the brand fares very well.

Attribute	Importance	Beliefs about smartphone model		
		A	B	C
Price	3	5	4	4
Durability	4	5	5	5
Screen resolution	4	3	4	5
Battery life	5	5	5	5
Storage	3	4	3	2

Discussion:
1. Which attribute of a smart phone carries the most weight to Michael?
2. Which attribute has the least weight?
3. Based on multi-attribute scores, people have more of a positive attitude towards products that have more of the desired attributes. Which model of smartphone will Michael therefore have a more positive attitude towards? (Tip: multiply each belief score by the weight then add the total score in order to find the model with the highest overall score.)

- *Tri-component models:* The tri-component model is also commonly referred to as the ABC model of attitudes, where A represents the affective component, B represents the behavioural component and C represents the cognitive component. Advocates of the tri-component model maintain that consumers' attitudes towards a product cannot be determined by beliefs, feelings or behavioural intentions alone, but that all three of these components are interrelated and internally consistent. This means that if consumers have negative beliefs about a product, they will also have negative feelings towards it and their behavioural intentions will be negative as well. For example, if consumers believe that fatty foods are bad for their health, they will have negative feelings towards such foods and will avoid them. It also means that changes in one component will result in corresponding changes in the other components. For example, if a food product that used to be fried is now grilled instead and so lower in fat, consumers may now have positive feelings towards the product and their behavioural intentions will also be positive.

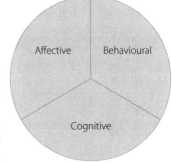

Figure 6.1 The tri-component model of attitudes[7]

6.5 FUNCTIONS OF ATTITUDES

Consumer attitudes serve four main functions: (1) the **utilitarian function**, (2) the **value-expressive function**, (3) the **ego-defensive function**, and (4) the **organisation-of-knowledge function**.

These four functions are based on the functional theory of attitudes developed by psychologist Daniel Katz.[8] The functional theory of attitudes shows that it is possible for different customers to have the same favourable attitude towards a product, yet for different reasons. This is because attitudes serve multiple functions which may differ from one person to the next:

- *Utilitarian function:* This function relates to the role of attitudes in directing consumers towards products that are rewarding and away from products that are not. For example, a consumer looking for medication that helps provide immediate relief from headaches will be attracted to familiar medicines or medicines that claim to fulfil this need. The consumer's attitude will direct him or her away from medications that will take a longer time to take effect.
- *Value-expressive function:* This function relates to the role of attitudes in directing consumers towards products that help them express their values in life. Consumers develop positive attitudes towards products that help communicate their value systems. For example, consumers who are environmentally conscious will have a negative attitude towards products that are damaging to the environment. This attitude will direct them away from such products and towards environmentally friendly products.

APPLICATION

Consistency of the tri-component model

Esther: For a long time I used to love high-heels.

Buntle: I never see you wearing them now.

Esther: Yes, I stopped

Buntle: But why? High-heels make you look like a lady!

Esther: I used to think like that too, but after reading an article in a health magazine on how high-heels can potentially damage your joints, I changed my mind. I don't like high-heels anymore. I believe flat or lower-heeled shoes are better for me and I plan to get rid of all the super high-heeled shoes in my wardrobe.

Buntle: Good luck. I love my high heels.

The favourable or unfavourable feeling towards the wearing of high-heeled shoes reflects the affective component of attitude. The cognitive component is reflected by the reasons for holding favourable or unfavourable opinions towards wearing high-heels, for example the fact that they make you look like a lady or they damage your joints respectively. The behavioural component is reflected by the wearing or not wearing of high-heels. In our example, Buntle may not have come across convincing articles on the dangers of wearing high-heels and therefore possesses no information that might change her feelings towards such shoes.

- *Ego-defensive function:* This function relates to the role of attitudes in directing consumers towards products that help protect their self-esteem. Marketing messages relating to personal care products, for example, often portray how the use of such products will help a consumer to protect his or her self-image or avoid social exclusion. For example, consumers may buy and use deodorant in order to avoid being associated with bad body odour.

- *Organisation-of-knowledge function:* This function relates to the 'need to know' that consumers have. It also relates to how attitudes help consumers to organise the vast amounts of information that they are exposed to as well as set up the basis on which to judge information. In this case, attitudes help consumers to pay attention to information about products that are of interest to them and to ignore information about products that are of no interest to them. However, even in cases where the consumer may be interested in gaining information about certain products, often the amount of information available is just too much to process. Consumers therefore develop beliefs about important attributes or benefits of products that help provide a frame of reference for evaluating information as well as new products.

Having discussed what attitudes are, as well as their composition and functions, we can move on to examine how attitudes develop. In other words, how does a consumer move from the point of having no attitude towards a given product or brand, to the point of having a positive or negative attitude towards it? This question is addressed in section 6.6.

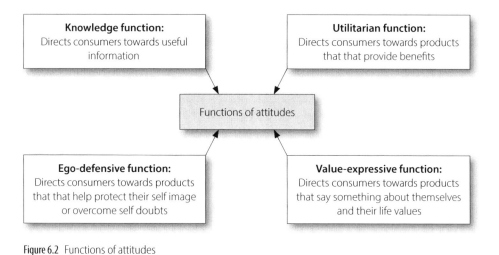

Figure 6.2 Functions of attitudes

6.6 THE FORMATION OF CONSUMER ATTITUDES

The fact is that no-one is born with attitudes. Attitudes are acquired (developed) over time as a person grows up. The definitions of attitudes discussed in section 6.2 capture the answer to the question of how attitudes are formed. According to Allport's definition,[9] attitudes are learnt. Section 6.6.1 looks at how attitudes

Functions of attitudes

Marketers often formulate marketing messages so as to appeal to the main attitude functions that the company feels its products properly serve.

James, a marketing management trainee at an advertising agency, is quite aware of this fact. His manager has asked him to come up with marketing messages that appeal to four different attitude functions. His proposal is captured in the proposed advertisements below.

Struggling with a smelly refrigerator? Baking soda can take that away

Veggie burger for the healthy you

Figure 6.3 Advertisement 1

Figure 6.4 Advertisement 2

Mouthwash. Hand on mouth. You don't have to cover your mouth when you want to have a private head-to-head chat with friends anymore.

Avoid single-use plastic shopping bags. They are bad for the environment. Demand re-usable, non-plastic shopping bags.

Figure 6.5 Advertisement 3

Figure 6.6 Advertisement 4

Discussion

Discuss the attitude function to which each of the advertisements is trying to appeal.

can be learnt, while section 6.6.2 considers various sources of influence on attitude formation.

6.6.1 How attitudes are learnt

People learn in different ways. Some of the major ways in which people learn include the following (see also Chapter 3):

- *Classical conditioning:* This is a learning process that takes place when an initially neutral stimulus is paired with either a positive or a negative stimulus, resulting in the formation of a similar response towards the previously neutral stimulus.[10] For example, when advertising a new product (that is unknown to the consumer), a marketer may pair it with something or someone who is known to have positive feelings towards such products, for example healthy foods, or a well-known or good-looking person, such as a rugby player. By so doing, they enhance the likelihood that the new product will elicit positive feelings through association. Marketers thus often make an effort to ensure that their products are associated with positive symbols and images. Learning through classical conditioning is related to the concept of stimulus generalisation. Stimulus generalisation is when one response is extended to a second stimulus that is associated with the first.[11] For example, studies show that consumers will often not hesitate to buy new products that are associated with brand names that they regard favourably. However, the reverse is also true: consumers will avoid new products that are associated with brand names that they have had negative experiences with.

* *Instrumental conditioning:* This is learning that takes place based on rewards and punishment for behaviour. It is common with low-involvement purchases, impulse purchases and trial purchases. For example, consider Salome, who buys a new type of dessert cream that she has not tasted before because her favourite brand is not in stock. After using the new dessert cream, Salome may develop a positive or a negative attitude towards it, depending on whether she liked it or not. Her evaluation will entail a comparison with her favourite product.

* *Observational learning:* This is the type of learning that occurs by observing others, thus acquiring possible responses through classical or instrumental conditioning. Norma may, for example, learn that binge drinking is bad for you by observing the negative effects that it has on her friends who do it. Children often learn by observing the behaviour of adults around them. Therefore, when they grow up, leave home and start making their own product choices, they are more likely to buy the same type of products and to demonstrate the same product consumption behaviour they were used to while at home.

* *Cognitive learning:* This is the type of learning that takes place as a result of carefully thinking about a problem and coming up with a decision or solution. It often entails searching for and processing information concerning a particular decision. For example, a mother who is looking for a private school to send her child to, may start searching for information on available private schools in her area and what differentiates them. Through this process, the mother will learn more about private schools and will be able to choose the best possible one for her child.

6.6.2 Sources of influence on consumer attitude formation

There are many possible sources of influence on the formation of consumer attitudes. The sources of influence can be categorised as follows:

* *Direct experience:* Marketers realise the importance of direct experience in influencing attitude formation. This is why they often strategise on how they can persuade consumers in the target group to try out a product. Free samples or coupons are often given out by companies with the primary purpose

of encouraging product trial. Once they have tried a new product, consumers evaluate it, resulting in positive or negative attitude formation. Attitudes formed in this way tend to be more resistant to change than those formed without direct experience.

* *The influence of social contacts:* Family, friends and peer groups all exert influence on the formation of a consumer's attitudes towards products. A child growing up in a family where the parents are health conscious and prefer to buy organic foods is likely to develop a negative attitude towards non-organic food products. This is because a family instils basic values and beliefs in its children through consumer socialisation. These values and beliefs later guide their response to products and situations. As children grow up, the circle of influence around them gets bigger and bigger. Later on, friends and peer groups start to play a greater role in influencing their attitudes. The need for social conformity may even result in changes in their basic values and beliefs, all of which may influence individuals' attitudes towards certain products.

* *The influence of marketing information and the media:* Companies spend a lot of money promoting their products with the aim of positively influencing consumer attitudes. The mass media, including newspapers, television and radio, are commonly used by companies as channels to reach consumers with information about their products. Many companies also use direct marketing through sales representatives, text messages and email advertising to reach customers, in an effort to persuade them to buy their products. Information coming from independent media sources is also highly influential in changing or strengthening consumers' attitudes towards a company or its products. Negative media publicity is often damaging to a company and its products, as customers often believe such information more readily than information coming from the company itself.

6.7 ATTITUDES AND BEHAVIOUR

One of the main reasons why the study of consumer attitudes is important is because of the influence that attitudes have on behaviour, especially in terms of the actual buying or consumption of products. The extent to which attitudes can help predict consumers' behaviour depends, however, on many other factors.

The focus of this section is on the factors that influence the likelihood of consumers' attitudes to predict their behaviour. The section also looks at some of the theoretical models that have been developed.

6.7.1 Factors impacting on the predictive power of attitudes on behaviour

The extent to which attitudes can accurately predict behaviour depends on a number of factors, including the following:

* *The strength of an attitude:* In general, the more strongly held an attitude is, the higher its predictive power on behaviour. The strength of an attitude depends on factors such as:
  – the level of the person's knowledge about the attitude object

- the source of his or her attitude in terms of former experience with a product
- the type of values associated with the attitude.

In general, the more knowledgeable a consumer is about a product or product attributes of interest, the stronger the influence his or her attitude will be in predicting behaviour. For example, an individual who knows a lot about the negative health effects of some preservatives used in food products will have strong negative attitudes towards using such preservatives and is unlikely to buy foods containing them. Attitudes formed as a result of personal experience with a product are better predictors of future behaviour than attitudes formed without personal experience. A customer who has found a product dissatisfying before, is unlikely to buy the same product in the future. On the other hand, an individual who has just been told about the product may want to check it out personally. In terms of values, it is important to note that some values that people hold are core to them, while others are not. Core values are deeply ingrained principles that strongly help guide behaviour, including consumption behaviour. For example, an individual may hold a negative attitude towards consumption of alcohol or pork due to religious values. Attitudes that are associated with core values have better predictive power on behaviour than those that are based on non-core values.

- *Situational factors:* Situational factors, including the degree of control a person has over his or her actual behaviour and changes in events, may affect the predictive power of attitudes on behaviour. In some situations, a person's ability to do what he or she plans to do is not fully under his or her personal control. For example, an individual may have a strong positive attitude towards pursuing a degree in marketing at a specific university. The actual behaviour (studying towards a degree in marketing at a chosen university) will, however, depend on whether the chosen university accepts the individual to enrol in its programme. In addition, translating attitudes into consumption often requires ability. A person may have positive attitude towards Mercedes-Benz cars, but never gets to buy one because of a lack of finances. Changes in events can also influence behaviour. For instance, Mary may have a negative attitude towards single-use plastic shopping bags, but may end up using one because she forgot to take along her reusable shopping bags when going to the supermarket. Stockouts (when a shop has no more stock of a particular product) may be another explanation for behaviours that are inconsistent with consumers' attitudes. Generally, it is not uncommon for consumers to buy alternative products when their preferred product or brand is not available.
- *Time frame:* The question here is how far into the future attitudes can help predict behaviour. In general, attitudes held at any point in time are better predictors of behaviour in the shorter term than in the longer term. For example, the extent to which a university marketing team can use attitude to predict the likelihood of high school students choosing to study at their university will increase if they direct their attitude questions to students completing their last year at high school rather than if they asked students in their first or second year of high school.

- *Specificity of attitudes:* This relates to how attitudes are measured and how specific the questions are in relation to the behaviour under prediction. In general, specific behaviours are better predicted by specific attitudes than general attitudes. For example, knowing an individual's attitude towards organ donation may not predict whether the person will or will not register as an organ donor. However, going a step further and measuring the person's attitude towards registering as an organ donor can help enhance the predictive ability of attitudes and behaviour in such cases.
- *Differences between expressed and held attitudes:* This also relates to how attitudes are measured. Often researchers rely on respondents' answers to specific questions in order to measure attitudes. This is called expressed attitudes. What consumers express through their answers to given questions may, however, not be a true reflection of their real attitudes, in other words, held attitudes. This is particularly true for topics that individuals consider sensitive or where they may feel the need to express what makes them 'fit in'. For example, an individual may express a negative attitude towards buying second-hand clothes, whilst in reality, he or she likes to visit secondhand shops to buy clothing. In such cases, the person's expressed attitudes will not be a good predictor of his or her behaviour.
- *Attitudes held by significant others:* Often a person's behaviour is influenced by the opinions and expectations of others, not just his or her own. Family, friends and society all have expectations about what is acceptable behaviour and what is not. A person's attitude may thus not accurately predict behaviour in cases where significant others have different attitudes and the individual in question feels the need to comply with the expectations of others. For example, a teenage girl may refrain from wearing mini-dresses just because her parents disapprove of them, not because she dislikes them.

6.7.2 Theories on consumer attitudes and behaviour

Various theories aimed at understanding the relationship between attitudes and behaviour have been developed over the years. These theories are helpful in understanding how attitudes influence behaviour. This section discusses two commonly cited theories, namely the theory of reasoned action and the theory of planned behaviour.

The theory of reasoned action

The **theory of reasoned action** was developed by Ajzen and Fishbein[12] in 1975 and later refined in 1980. Although its origins are in the field of social psychology, the theory is widely used in consumer behavioural studies. According to the theory, the most important determinant of behaviour is behavioural intention. This refers to an individual's readiness to perform a particular behaviour. According to the theory, behavioural intention is a function of a person's attitudes towards the behaviour and subjective norms. Subjective norms relate to the perceived influence of other people on a person's behaviour.

Ajzen and Fishbein defined attitude towards a behaviour as a person's general feeling of the favourableness or unfavourableness of that behaviour.[13] They also noted that a person's attitude towards a particular behaviour is a function of that person's salient beliefs (beliefs concerning consequences associated with the behaviour in question) that performing the behaviour will result in certain outcomes as well as the evaluation of the outcomes as desirable or not.[14] For example, Thembi may have favourable feelings towards enrolling in a healthy cooking club. Thembi's feelings may be a result of a belief that we are what we eat and eating healthily will make one healthy. In terms of his evaluation of the outcome, Thembi may regard gaining knowledge and skills on healthy cooking as a good thing.

A subjective norm highlights the influence of other people on a person's behaviour. It is defined as an individual's belief that certain other individuals approve or do not approve of his or her performance of the behaviour in question.[15] According to the theory, a subjective norm is itself considered to be a function of normative beliefs and a motivation to comply. Normative beliefs refer to an individual's belief that other people think that he or she should or should not perform the behaviour.[16] These other individuals are the people that the person in question considers to be important, for example his or her parents, colleagues, family doctor, spouse or other family members. If Thembi had, for example, grown up in a family that frowns upon unhealthy eating habits, he may feel that his family expects him to continue with their tradition of healthy eating even after leaving home.

While the theory of reasoned action has been widely used to predict consumer behaviour in many studies, it is not without limitations. Its major limitation relates to its failure to give adequate attention to the fact that behaviour is not always under the control of the individual. Thembi's intentions to join a healthy cooking club may, for example, not become reality if Thembi cannot afford it. In order to deal with this shortcoming in the theory of reasoned action, Ajzen proposed the theory of planned behaviour in 1985.

The theory of planned behaviour

The theory of planned behaviour is an extension of the theory of reasoned action. It differs from the theory of reasoned action in that it adds a component known as perceived behavioural control as a third factor (the other two factors being a person's attitudes towards the behaviour, and subjective norms) that influences behavioural intention. This factor was added in order to address the issue of behaviours that may not be under a person's voluntary control, for example as a result of a lack of skills, resources or opportunities to perform the behaviour. Perceived behavioural control is thus concerned with a perceived presence of factors that may facilitate or impede the performance of the behaviour of interest.[17] According to this theory, people are unlikely to develop strong behavioural intentions if they feel that they lack the opportunities or resources required to perform the behaviour. This is irrespective of the fact that they may have a positive attitude towards the behaviour as well as a strong belief that others would approve of the behaviour.

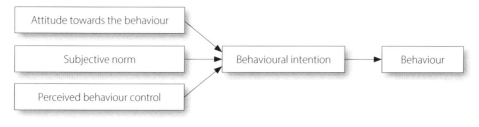

Figure 6.7 The theory of planned behaviour[18]

Establishing whether consumers hold positive or negative attitudes towards attitude objects requires that one is able to measure attitude. Section 6.8 looks at different ways to measure consumer attitude.

6.8 MEASURING ATTITUDES

Attitudes are one of the commonly measured constructs in consumer behaviour research. Attitudes can be determined by asking consumers to respond to specific questions or by observing their behaviour. Observational attitude research is commonly used in cases where consumers may be unwilling or unable to respond to questions, for example if the information is private or where the respondents are children. Nevertheless, asking consumers to respond to specific questions is the most commonly used method in measuring attitudes. Researchers make use of both qualitative and quantitative approaches in this regard.

6.8.1 The qualitative approach to measuring attitudes

Qualitative research is commonly used when a researcher wants to get an in-depth understanding of certain issues that is not possible through quantitative data collection methods. The questions are unstructured in nature, but are guided by a researcher's pre-determined objectives for the study, and further questions are often guided by a participant's responses. The information gathered through qualitative research is non-numerical in form. In-depth interviews and focus group discussions are two commonly used qualitative methods to collect data:

- *In-depth interviews* involve the collection of qualitative data through one-on-one discussions between a researcher and a willing participant, by means of open-ended questions that are organised in terms of an interview guide, which simply serves as a reminder to the researcher to attend to all the aspects of the investigation. The aim is to probe answers to questions to encourage participants to react spontaneously and so give deeper insight into their feelings, beliefs or behaviour. Usually, questions will not require simple yes or no responses. Examples of questions that may be asked during in-depth interviews include the following:
  - What do you think about going to Mauritius for Christmas this year?
  - How do you feel about a Christmas without family to share it with?
  - Who would you like to share your Christmas lunch with, and why?

- *Focus group discussions* involve the collection of qualitative data through discussions that are conducted with a group of selected individuals (usually between eight and 12 members). Similar procedures to those of in-depth interviews are used, in that an interview guide consisting of open-ended questions is developed beforehand. A trained moderator is used to guide the discussions. The advantage of focus group discussions is that the interaction that goes on between members of the group encourages a variety of views and responses that usually prompt additional responses from other members. As a result, large amounts of information can be obtained in a relatively short space of time, which is usually recorded with permission of the participants and transcribed later on. However, to encourage vibrant discussions, the participants should be compatible, for example not from contrasting socio-cultural backgrounds.

6.8.2   The quantitative approach to measuring attitudes

Quantitative research involves the collection of numerical data using structured questionnaires. Unlike qualitative research, quantitative research allows for easy collection of data from large numbers of respondents. Researchers using the quantitative approach to measure attitudes often do so using measurement scales. The three most commonly used scales in attitude research are:
- the Likert-type scale
- the semantic differential scale
- the rank-order scale.

The Likert-type scale

The Likert-type scale consists of a series of statements that respondents are requested to evaluate in terms of their level of agreement or disagreement. Although the Likert-type scale is technically a summated scale (in other words, it is the sum of a person's ratings for the statements used to measure attitude), the researcher has the option of treating each item in the scale as a separate attitude statement. Most studies make use of either a five or seven-point Likert-type scale when measuring attitude.

APPLICATION

The Likert-type scale: measuring attitude towards recycling at home

Mary would like to find out people's attitudes towards recycling at home. On her behalf:
- collect responses to the statements in the table below from each member of your class
- calculate the overall attitude of each class member by adding up each member's response points and dividing the total by the number of statement items
- calculate the overall attitude of the class by adding up the overall attitude of each class member and dividing it by the number of people in the class
- describe the class's overall attitude towards recycling at home.

Instructions

Please indicate your level of agreement or disagreement with each of the statements that follows by placing a cross in the appropriate box.

	Strongly disagree	Agree	Neither agree nor disagree	Disagree	Strongly agree
I believe that every home should be involved in recycling	1	2	3	4	5
Recycling by households is necessary	1	2	3	4	5
I like the idea of requiring every household to recycle	1	2	3	4	5

The semantic differential scale

The semantic differential scale is a rating scale composed of a continuum with polar-opposite descriptors. When using this scale, respondents are asked to indicate their feelings or beliefs about the attitude object by marking the appropriate point along the continuum. The most commonly used semantic scale has five or seven points along the continuum and shows only the two opposite descriptors of the scale. The major advantage of this scale in consumer behavioural studies is that it is easy to administer and can be used to compare different products, brands or companies along the same descriptors.

The application box below gives an example of a semantic differential scale and how it can be used to compare different product brands.

APPLICATION

The semantic differential scale: attitudes towards shopping for clothes online

Instructions

Form a group of eight people. Use the semantic differential scale below to do the following:

1. Calculate the score for each individual's attitude towards shopping for clothes online by adding the numerical value of the marked points and dividing the total score by the number of items. Every individual should respond to every one of the four item options.
2. Who has the most favourable and who has the most unfavourable attitude towards shopping for clothes online in the group?

	1	2	3	4	5	6	7	
Convenient	—	—	—	—	—	—	—	Not convenient
Time saving	—	—	—	—	—	—	—	Does not save enough time
Secure	—	—	—	—	—	—	—	Not secure
Good idea	—	—	—	—	—	—	—	Bad idea

The rank-order scale

The rank-order scale is a scale in which respondents are asked to rank given objects or ideas according to some specified criteria, for example levels of preference, importance or effectiveness. The order may represent a simple ordinal structure or a relative position. For example, customers may be asked to rank service providers such as restaurants according to the quality of service they provide. The one that provides the best service will be ranked 1, followed by 2 (the second-best option), until all the options have been ranked.

APPLICATION

The rank-order scale: shopping malls

Instructions

Ask a group of shoppers who have frequented two different shopping malls in the past three months. Label the malls as A and B and ask each shopper to rank them on a scale of 1 to 10 where 1 = does not meet the attribute, and 10 = best meets the attribute. Use the attributes below:
- Ease of accessibility
- Convenience
- Design appeal

Identify the shopping mall that each shopper has the most favourable attitude towards, based on a combination of the three attributes given.

6.9 CHANGING CONSUMER ATTITUDES

Although one of the main characteristics of attitudes is that they are consistent, this does not mean that they do not change. The ease with which attitudes change depends largely on their strength, with strongly held attitudes being more difficult to change. Changes in attitudes can be in any direction, from positive to negative or neutral and vice versa. Attitude change can take place before or after a purchase. Marketers are constantly looking for ways of influencing attitude change favourably towards their products.

This section discusses how marketers can influence changes in each of the three components of attitudes (affective, cognitive and behavioural component), with the ultimate aim of influencing consumers' overall attitudes towards a product or brand.

6.9.1   Changing the affective component of attitudes

Marketers can influence attitude change by using strategies that aim to influence the feelings or emotions of consumers towards a specific product or brand. Increased liking of a product positively influences the chances of a consumer purchasing that product. Some of the strategies commonly used to influence consumers' feelings include the following:
- *Influencing affect towards advertisements:* Research shows that the possibility of a consumer liking a product increases when he or she likes the advertisements used to promote it. Marketers often use advertisements to influence attitude change through classical conditioning. For example, by constantly pairing a brand of toothpaste with pictures of very white teeth, advertisers can influence consumers to like the toothpaste brand. Conversely, marketers can use advertising to influence people to refrain from buying some products. For

example, by constantly pairing cigarettes with damaged lungs, consumers can be encouraged to stop smoking. Well-liked celebrities may be used to endorse a product in an advertisement. Humour is also commonly used.

- *Associating the product or brand with special causes or events:* Marketers often highlight causes or special events that are sponsored by their company with the aim of positively influencing the public's attitude towards their products or brand. Examples are where the company provides care packages for orphanages, bursaries for under-privileged students or equipment for sports events such as football or golf tournaments.

6.9.2 Changing the cognitive component of attitudes

The cognitive component is often the most targeted in marketers' efforts to influence change. It involves peoples' knowledge and beliefs regarding the attitude object. Three common strategies may be used by marketers to change the cognitive component of attitude:

- *Changing customers' beliefs about the attributes of the product:* In order to be successful, marketers need to look critically at the beliefs being targeted to ensure that changes in the beliefs will result in positive product evaluation and thus persuade customers to buy the product. For example, some customers may be weary of buying a product that they consider to be high in fat. Marketers may want to change this negative belief into a positive one by emphasising that their food products contain 'good' fats. This may entail educating customers on the different types of fats commonly found in food products, such as saturated fats and unsaturated fats.
- *Changing the level of importance attached to the attributes of the product:* Sometimes customers have positive perceptions about a product based on attributes that do not exert much influence on their current buying decision. By changing the level of importance attached to the attribute, marketers can positively influence buying intentions. For example, research has shown that fibre aids in digestion and produces a feeling of fullness with fewer calories, thus reducing the risk of obesity. By emphasising these additional benefits in their breakfast cereals, marketers can increase the level of importance attached to the attribute of fibre and use it to encourage customers to buy their products. Marketers can also reduce the level of importance attached to attributes. For example, by emphasising a higher quality compared to competitors' low-priced products, marketers may diminish perceptions that their products are over-priced.
- *Adding new attributes:* Marketing messages depicting a product as 'new and improved' are meant to change customers' belief structures. For example, adverts for Omo washing powder may depict its new, enhanced formulation as being extra good at removing tough stains. This may help to position products more competitively. The more convinced consumers are about the benefits of the new attributes, the higher the likelihood of them changing their attitude towards the product to a more favourable one.

6.9.3   Changing the behavioural component of attitudes

Promotions such as free samples, coupons and reduced prices may encourage people to try a product they have not previously bought. Following product trial, consumers' attitudes towards products may become more favourable depending on whether they were satisfied or not.

Section 6.10 looks more closely at how marketing communication can be used to influence attitude change.

6.10 MARKETING COMMUNICATION AND CONSUMER ATTITUDES

Marketers continuously bombard consumers with marketing communication that is aimed at influencing positive consumer attitude formation or change. In order to do this effectively, marketing communication needs to be persuasive.

The focus of this section is on the factors that may affect how successful marketing communication efforts are in influencing positive attitude formation or change. The section discusses how factors relating to the source, the message, the medium and the receiver as the main elements in the communication process impact on attitude formation and change. This section also discusses the **elaboration likelihood model**, which is one of the most commonly used models in understanding the influence of communication on attitude.

6.10.1   Elements of the communication process

The communication process consists of the following key elements:

* The source
* The message
* The channel
* The receiver

The source

The source refers to the individuals used to communicate the message as well as the sponsors of the message. The ability of a source to influence attitude change largely depends on its credibility. Source credibility depends mainly on two factors, namely expertise and trustworthiness:

* *Expertise* relates to how knowledgeable the source is. In general, consumers find it easier to believe messages coming from someone they consider to be an expert than from someone they do not, or someone they do not know. For example, most consumers would find it easy to believe endorsements of oral hygiene products coming from a dentist, or a recommendation of an investment portfolio made by an experienced investment manager.
* The *trustworthiness* of a source relates to the perceived honesty and objectivity of that source. The credibility of a source is sometimes questioned if consumers believe that there is bias. A source may have expert knowledge on a product, but consumers may be unwilling to believe it because they perceive his or her ability to provide impartial information to be compromised.

Figure 6.8 Use of words and picture to convey a message

For example, a celebrity who is known to have been paid a large sum by a car manufacturing company to endorse its latest model may be less believable than a regular client. A salesperson selling insurance products may have expert knowledge, but consumers may be wary of this particular source because he or she stands to benefit from sales made. Consumers generally are known to find it easier to believe recommendations from non-marketing sources such as friends and family.

The message

The way in which the message is structured and conveyed has a significant impact on its level of persuasiveness and thus its ability to change consumer attitudes. Marketers need to pay special attention to the following:

- *The use of words and/or pictures in conveying the message:* The use of pictures is often regarded as highly effective in influencing an emotional response from targeted consumers. For example, advertisements aimed at promoting vaccinations show pictures of crying babies covered in small pox lying in hospital, as this is more persuasive than conveying the same message in words only. Unlike words, pictures are not, however, good at conveying factual information. Thus in most high-involvement purchase decisions where factual information is important for the consumer to make rational decisions, the use of words explaining the important attributes of a product and their benefits is likely to be more effective than the use of visuals only. Many marketing communication messages contain a combination of words and pictures in order to tap into the benefit of using each of these. The vividness with which words and/or pictures are conveyed also needs to be taken into consideration in designing a message that is likely to have a lot of impact on attitude change.

- *The type of appeal used in a message:* Different types of appeals can be used in marketing messages. These include rational appeals and emotional appeals:
  - *Rational appeals:* Communication messages with rational appeals are directed towards a person's cognitive ability to interpret the information. Such messages emphasise hard facts such as highlighting product attributes and associated benefits so that consumers can make an informed decision. This type of appeal is particularly effective in high-involvement purchase situations, for example choosing an investment product. Marketers of investment products may present their good past performance on returns on investment to support their claims that they will wisely invest customer's money.
  - *Emotional appeals:* Such messages put emphasis on stimulating sensory reactions such as feelings of affection, pleasure or guilt. Fear and humour are two commonly used methods to evoke emotions in marketing communications. Messages aimed at evoking fear typically show consumers the negative consequences of not changing their attitude or behaviour, for example a drunk driver involved in a terrible accident. Fear messages can also contain rational information to give people a reason to be scared, for example the latest statistics on deaths caused by drunk drivers. Humorous emotional appeals present messages that evoke feelings of fun. However, while humour helps to grab people's attention and is often highly memorable, it needs to be used with caution because people may differ in the way they interpret it.
- *Repetition:* Marketing messages are more effective at influencing attitude change when they are repeatedly brought to the attention of the target

Emotional appeal versus rational appeal ads

Text and drive – message can be 'Don't text and drive. It can cost you your life'

Use of non-plastic shopping bags – show message such as 'Plastic shopping bags release toxic chemicals into the soil. Help conserve the environment, use re-usable non-plastic shopping bags.

Figure 6.9 Emotional appeal (left) versus rational appeal (right)

market. This is because repetition helps to facilitate learning. Often people may not act on a message that they are exposed to for the first time for a variety of reasons, including unfamiliarity with the company or products being promoted, or a lack of interest in the particular product at that particular point in time. Multiple exposure to marketing messages from a company or about a product create familiarity, which helps to enhance trust. Repetition also helps to keep a message fresh in people's minds until they are ready to consider it or act on it.

The channel
Marketing communications can be conveyed using different types of media, including broadcast media such as television and radio, print media such as magazines and newspapers, and social media such as Facebook and Twitter. Marketers consider a number of factors when making media decisions, including:
- cost
- coverage
- nature of the product
- the characteristics of the target market.

Broadcast media are particularly effective for products requiring low-involvement purchase decisions, such as soft drinks that people buy routinely, as the message conveyed is often brief. Print media are effective for high-involvement, complex purchase decisions, such as buying a house, where lots of factual information is needed. Broadcast media are also commonly used where marketers want to influence attitude change by means of an emotional appeal using pictures and tone. For example, images of consumers at a party enjoying Coca-Cola aim to associate the product with having a good time.

The receiver
Several receiver characteristics are important and need to be taken into consideration in any communication effort aimed at influencing consumer attitudes. These include the following:
- *Consumers' level of knowledge about the attitude object:* Customers who are highly knowledgeable would need to be persuaded that certain critical product attributes were present before they would be convinced that a specific product or brand was good. For example, a nutritionist would find it easy to read food labels and make a personal judgement on the best brand, while an ordinary consumer would be more easily influenced by the nutritional claims made in marketing communication messages.
- *Consumers' current attitudes and how strong those attitudes are:* Customers with a neutral attitude towards a product are often easier to influence through marketing communication than those with a negative attitude.
- *Demographic characteristics:* Older, more experienced consumers may have developed fairly strong attitudes about certain products and brands over time, contrary to younger people who are newer to the market, have less established views and are therefore often easier to influence. This

explains why there are ethical concerns about marketing messages that target children. Research has shown that young people who are exposed to a lot of junk food advertisements will tend to consume more calories than those who are not.[19] This shows the significant influence that adverts can have on consumer behaviour.

6.10.2   The elaboration likelihood model

The elaboration likelihood model (ELM) was proposed by Petty and Cacioppo in the early 1980s.[20] These authors argue that while researchers may use a variety of models and variables, persuasion is the primary source of attitude formation and change. The model assumes that once consumers receive a message, they begin to process it according to two aspects: (1) their motivation, and (2) their ability to understand the information.

Petty and Cacioppo[21] identified several common motivational factors, including:

* the personal relevance of the information
* the specific consumer's innate need for cognition (some people enjoy critically analysing things)
* personal responsibility.

Some common factors that affect a person's ability to process a message include the following:

* Distractions such as noise may hamper a person's ability to consider a message properly.
* Repetition helps to reinforce a message and also improves a person's ability to process a message.
* Prior knowledge influences a person's level of familiarity with a message, which improves message-processing ability.
* A person's ability to process a message tends to be better when the message is presented in a way that is easy to understand.

Depending on these two aspects, one of the following two routes to persuasion will be followed:

* Central route to persuasion
* Peripheral route to persuasion

These are discussed in the sections that follow.

The central route to persuasion

According to the elaboration likelihood model, this route involves much logical consideration of the message received (high elaboration). Central processing of information takes place when the consumer is both motivated and has the ability to process the information received. This information is carefully scrutinised to determine its merits.

Any change in attitude will depend on the individual's cognitive responses to the arguments presented. The resulting alterations in attitude are resistant to change and are more successful predictors of behaviour. This route therefore dominates in the case of high-involvement purchase decisions.

The implication of this is that marketers need to pay a lot of attention to the quality of arguments presented in their communication messages, as this is what exerts a major influence on attitude change, especially in high-involvement purchase decisions.

The peripheral route to persuasion

This route does not involve extensive cognitive processing of information. It is taken when the consumer is not motivated to process information or does not have the ability to do so. In such cases, the consumer evaluates a message by relying on cues that are peripheral to the actual message.

Examples of common peripheral cues that consumers may use in evaluating marketing communication messages include the following:[22]

- Perceived credibility of the source
- Perceived attractiveness of the source
- Quality of the way in which the message is presented
- Use of a catchy slogan that contains the message

The implication of this is that marketers can play an important role in influencing changes in consumer attitudes by focusing on the content of the message as well as by looking at how the information is presented. For example, it is possible to influence consumer attitudes by using a popular spokesperson or by designing an interesting package for a product.

According to the model, attitude change under the peripheral route to persuasion tends to be relatively temporary, susceptible to change and less predictive of a consumer's eventual behaviour.[23]

RESEARCH BOX 6.1

Attitude research is important for a number of strategic reasons:

- *Attitudes help predict behaviour:* Research shows that consumers' intention to buy a brand helps explain actual buying behaviour. There is a relationship between the intention to buy (the behavioural component of attitude) and the actual behaviour. Through attitude research, marketers can predict demand for their products. This is important in planned production schedules so as to minimise the problem of stockouts or over-supply in the market.

- *Attitudes help explain behaviour:* An understanding of consumer attitudes is also helpful in explaining why consumers buy the brands that they normally do. For example, in cases where the brand is well established, satisfaction with a brand based on past purchase experience helps in forming a positive attitude towards the product. Thus apart from helping to predict future purchase behaviour, in such cases, attitudes help explain why consumers buy what they do.

- *Attitudes are a useful tool for market segmentation:* Market segmentation helps to divide a market into groups with similar needs or wants. Through attitude research, marketers may be able to determine the importance attached to different product attributes by different groups of consumers. Marketers can use this knowledge to decide which segments to target. Different bases are used to segment markets, including:

- *demographic segmentation:* dividing the market according to variables such as age, gender, level of education, race, income, etc.
- *geographic segmentation:* dividing the market on the basis of geographical location
- *benefit segmentation:* dividing the market by the product attributes sought by different groups of consumers

- *Attitudes help to guide new product development processes:* Through research, a company can establish the important attributes of a product from the consumers' perspective as well as the ideal levels of attribute performance. This information is important as it helps to determine the likelihood that a product will satisfy targeted consumers, and can therefore help in ensuring that newly developed products will satisfy consumers' needs and wants. Attitude research is also particularly useful in the concept-testing stage of new product development. It can assist a company to gauge if the market understands and values its ideals.

- *Attitudes help to evaluate the effectiveness of marketing strategies:* An understanding of consumer attitudes can, for example, help determine the effectiveness of a product positioning or repositioning strategy. This effectiveness is mainly a function of the needs of the target market, the product attributes that they consider important, and how they rate a company's products on those attributes, often in comparison to competing products. A favourable attitude towards a product indicates an effective positioning strategy.

- *Attitudes can also be used to help evaluate the effectiveness of marketing communication efforts:* Marketing communication efforts are often aimed at influencing positive attitude formation or change. Evaluation of consumer attitudes before and after exposure to a marketing communication campaign is a common marketing strategy used to assess the effectiveness of marketing communication.

SUMMARY

The study of attitudes is extremely important in understanding consumer behaviour. Attitudes can be defined as 'a learned predisposition to respond in a consistently favourable or unfavourable manner with respect to a given object'.[24] In consumer studies, the attitude object can be anything such as a specific product, a brand, a company or a type of behaviour. Attitudes serve a number of functions, including the utilitarian function, the value-expressive function, the ego-defensive function and the organisation-of-knowledge function. Attitudes consist of three main components: affective, cognitive and behavioural.

As a learnt predisposition, there are different sources of influence on consumer attitude formation. These include direct experience with a product and the influence of social contacts as well as the influence of marketing information and the media. Once formed, attitudes exert a great deal of influence on a consumer's actual buying behaviour. The theory of reasoned action and the theory of planned behaviour are two of the commonly cited theories that try to explain the relationship between attitudes and behaviour. The extent to which attitudes can be used to predict behaviour depends on a number of other factors, including how strongly an individual holds the attitude, situational factors such as the degree of control that the individual has over the actual behaviour, and changes in events that may make it necessary for the person to alter his or her behaviour, the time frame between development of attitudes and when the behaviour occurs, the specificity of attitudes, the similarity between expressed and held attitudes, and the influence of other people's attitudes, including family and friends.

Although attitudes are consistent and endure over time, marketers are constantly looking for ways in which they can influence favourable consumer attitude change towards their products and to strengthen existing positive attitudes in a very competitive market place. They do this by employing strategies aimed at influencing any of the three components of attitude. Marketing communication is the main tool used to influence attitude formation and change.

SELF-ASSESSMENT QUESTIONS

1. Define the term 'consumer attitudes'.
2. Briefly discuss the three main components of consumer attitudes.
3. Using examples, discuss the four main functions of consumer attitudes.
4. Using examples, discuss factors that influence the extent to which attitudes can help to predict consumer behaviour.
5. How can researchers measure consumer attitudes using qualitative and quantitative approaches?
6. Using examples, discuss what may influence the ability of the source of marketing messages to influence change in consumer attitudes.
7. Discuss four reasons why the study of consumer attitudes is of strategic importance in marketing.

EXPERIENTIAL EXERCISE

A survey was conducted a week after a group of men and women had been through a safe-driving programme. The results of the survey revealed that many of them had forgotten most of what was presented with one exception. All of them remembered vividly the images of Mike in tears after his three-year-old child was badly injured in an accident. The 'before' image was that of Mike enjoying a drive with his three-year-old son. The 'after' image showed that the car Mike was driving had collided head on with another car and his son was on life support while Mike had minor scratches. This was because Mike was wearing a seat belt while his son was playing on the backseat unbuckled.

Explain how you would use this information to mount another, more effective campaign directed against risky driving behaviours.

CASE STUDY 1

Attitudes towards online shopping

Increased accessibility and use of the internet in many parts of the world including South Africa has impressed on many retailers a need to start offering their products through the online channel. In South Africa, a number of mainstream big retailers as well as small ones have opened up online stores. Managers of these stores are tasked with the responsibility of growing the number of online shoppers.

Development of effective strategies requires a good understanding of consumer attitudes towards online shopping in general as well as towards specific online stores. Research shows that consumers' attitude towards online shopping have been changing over time. While in the early days many people had strong negative attitudes towards online shopping, today more people are accepting it. Research also shows, however, that there are still many consumers that are fearful of shopping online. Those who are skeptical of online shopping believe that it entails risk. Those who like the idea of online shopping believe that it is the modern way of shopping that needs to be embraced while managing the risks.

Discussion questions

1. No-one is born with attitudes. Discuss the possible factors that may contribute to some people having an unfavourable attitude towards online shopping in general.
2. If you were an online store manager, what would you do to influence consumers to have a positive attitude towards your store's online shopping facility?

CASE STUDY 2

Choosing a laptop

With many different brands of laptops available on the market, it is often difficult for some consumers to decide on the best one to buy. Esther is in this position and has asked her brother Keenly for advice on the main attributes to take into consideration. Keenly regards four factors as critical in evaluating laptops, namely screen resolution, portability, battery life and storage space. Assume that level of importance of each of the important attributes is measured on a five-point scale ranging from 1 = not important at all to 5 = extremely important and that Esther's ratings of four different brands of laptops are as indicated in the table below. Note that Esther regards screen resolution, portability and battery life as equally important.

	t (level of importance)	Laptop A	Laptop B	
Screen resolution	5	5	2	
Portability	5	3	3	
Battery life	5	5	4	
Storage space	4	5	3	

Discussion questions

Which brand of laptop, A or B, does Esther have a favourable attitude towards? Justify your answer.

1. The sales assistant at one of the retailing stores would like to influence Esther's attitude so that she can buy her recommended brand of laptop. Discuss how a good understanding of the theory of planned behaviour would help the sales person to influence Esther to develop a positive attitude towards the laptop brand that she recommends.

2. Discuss how the laptop manufacturers could influence attitude formation or change by focusing on:
   - the message source
   - the message itself
   - the medium used
   - the receiver.

ADDITIONAL RESOURCES

There are many video clips on consumer attitudes posted on YouTube. Conduct a Google search on the subject and watch some of the clips to get a better appreciation of how attitudes influence consumer behaviour. The following YouTube video clips are good examples:

- ABC of attitude: https://www.youtube.com/watch?v=Xn-_6emPzy4
- Multi-attribute attitude model: https://www.youtube.com/watch?v=AHrWMb8pgIE
- The link between attitude and behaviour: https://www.youtube.com/watch?v=7okBIVEgYKc
- SB London Research Panel: Untangling the consumer attitude gap: http://www.youtube.com/watch?v=khFrozKbH8w

REFERENCES

1. Horcajo, J., Brinol, P. & Petty, R. 2010. Consumer persuasion: Indirect change and implicit balance. *Psychology and Marketing*, 27(10): 938.
2. Eagly, A.H. & Chaiken, S. 1993. *The psychology of attitudes*. Fort Worth, TX: Harcourt Brace Jovanovich, 1.
3. Allport, G. 1935. Attitudes. In Murchinson, C. (Ed.), *A handbook of social psychology*. Worcester, Mass.: Clark University Press, 798.
4. Bizer,G., Larsen, J. & Petty, R. 2011. Exploring the valence-framing effects: Negative framing enhances attitude strength. *Political Psychology*, 32(1): 59–80.
5. Schiffman, L. & Wisenblit, J. 2015. *Consumer behaviour*, 11th ed. Boston: Peason Education, 147.
6. Assael, H. 1998. *Consumer behavior and marketing action*, 6th ed. Boston: Houghton Mifflin, 173.
7. Adapted from Rousseau, D. 2007. Buyer reality: Attitudes, learning and involvement. In Du Plessis, P. & Rousseau, G. (Eds), *Buyer behaviour: Understanding consumer psychology and marketing*. Cape Town: Oxford University Press, 196.
8. Katz, D. 1960. The functional approach to the study of attitudes. *Public Opinion Quarterly*, 24: 163–204.
9. Allport, op. cit.
10. Wells, V.K. 2014. Behavioural psychology, marketing and consumer behaviour: A literature review and future research agenda. *Journal of Marketing Management*, 30(11–12): 1120.
11. Do Vale, R.& Matos, P. 2015. The impact of copycat packaging strategies on the adoption of private labels. *Journal of Product & Brand Management*, 24(6): 648.

12 Fishbein, M. & Ajzen, I. 1975. *Belief, attitude, intention, and behaviour: An introduction to theory and research.* Reading, MA: Addison-Wesley.

13 Ibid., 6.

14 Ajzen, M. & Fishbein, M. 1980. *Understanding attitudes and predicting social behaviour.* Englewood Cliffs, NJ: Prentice-Hall, 65.

15 Ibid., 57.

16 Ibid., 73.

17 Ajzen, M. 1991. The theory of planned behaviour. *Organizational behaviour and human decision processes*, 50(2): 184.

18 Reprinted from Ajzen, ibid., 182 with permission from Elsevier.

19 Sky News. 2018. Young people who 'watch more junk food ads' consume 'thousands more calories'. Available at: https://news.sky.com/story/young-people-who-watch-more-junk-food-ads-consume-thousands-more-calories-11382365 (accessed on 17 August 2018).

20 Petty, R., Cacioppo, J. & Schumann, D. 1983. Central and peripheral routes to advertising effectiveness: The moderating role of involvement. *Journal of Consumer Research*, 10(2): 135–136.

21 Ibid.

22 Ibid.

23 Petty, R.E. & Cacioppo, J.T. 1986. *Communication and persuasion: Central and peripheral routes to attitude change.* New York: Springer-Verlag, 134.

24 Allport, op. cit., 810.

PART THREE
INTERNAL FACTORS

CHAPTER 7

SOCIAL CLASS, REFERENCE GROUPS AND THE DIFFUSION OF INNOVATIONS

Richard Shambare and Gift Donga

LEARNING OBJECTIVES

After reading this chapter, you should be able to:

- define social class
- discuss factors that influence a person's social standing in society
- explain the impact of social class on consumer behaviour in the market place
- describe different types of reference groups
- discuss factors that affect the influence of reference groups on consumer behaviour
- understand the concepts of diffusion and adoption of innovations
- explain factors that influence the diffusion of innovations in a market
- explain the innovation adoption process
- discuss the role of opinion leaders in influencing adoption and diffusion of innovation.

Key terms

adoption of innovation process	innovators	relative advantage
	invention	reference group
compatibility	laggards	social class
complexity	late-majority	social mobility
diffusion of innovation	observability	trialability
innovation	opinion leader	

A few years ago, the energy drink MoFaya was a non-entity. Both the company and the drink were unknown. MoFaya was mostly, if not only, found on the shelves of a few spaza shops and in a handful of gyms in Johannesburg's townships. However, today, things are different – MoFaya is a household brand within the South African growing energy drink market, rivaling the likes of Energade, Red Bull and Dragon.

The MoFaya brand slowly gained market share and is now distributed throughout the country in big supermarkets such as Pick n Pay. The popularity of the MoFaya brand skyrocketed after its endorsement by DJ Sbu – who also happens to be co-owner of the MoFaya Beverage Company. The company capitalised on his popularity and celebrity status to market MoFaya. A blitzkrieg of messages on Twitter, Facebook and various other social media platforms, showing DJ Sbu holding a can of MoFaya, spread the DJ Sbu-MoFaya message. It did not take long before many of DJ Sbu's fans and supporters became MoFaya consumers themselves.

Explain possible reasons why DJ Sbu's fans were keen to adopt MoFaya.

7.1 INTRODUCTION

Human beings are inherently social beings who belong to, and identify with, various types of social groups such as family, friendship, racial, religious, social class and many more. Social groups and group membership have a significant influence on consumer behaviour. Consider, for example, consumers belonging to a lower social-economic class group. Such consumers will tend to patronise shops that offer products and services at discounted prices because that is what most of them can afford. The interaction that takes place among members of social groups often influences attitudes and behaviours. For example, members of a virtual community such as TripAdviser may choose a particular hotel because other members have rated it highly.

This chapter focuses on social factors, specifically the influence of social class and reference groups on consumer behaviour. It also looks at diffusion of innovations in markets. The chapter starts by defining the concept of social class, before discussing the characteristics of the social class system, social class structures, measuring of social class and the marketing implications of social class. The chapter then looks at reference groups, discussing the different types, how they are used in marketing and factors that affect their influence. This is followed by discussions on diffusion of innovations, including characteristics of innovations and how they affect the diffusion process, the innovation adoption process and the influence of opinion leaders.

7.2 SOCIAL CLASS

Social classes are the hierarchical distinctions among groups of people within a society or country,[1] based on their socio-economic wellbeing and success. Members of a society with the most power and control over the means of production generally fall within the upper echelons of the social class framework. In contrast, those with little or no control over the means of production (i.e. the people that work for those in control) occupy the lower spectrum.

A social class is made up of people who are approximately equal in social status and community esteem. Members of the same social class tend to socialise regularly among themselves and share some behavioural norms. For example, sports such as tennis or golf tend to attract consumers from the middle to upper classes because they require specific and often costly equipment and premises, whereas soccer and rugby can be played in any local park so are more accessible to all classes. Social class is thus important because it influences the consumption behaviour of consumers.

7.2.1 Social class structure

The three main general categories used to divide people according to social class are upper, middle and lower class. These are then divided into upper upper class, lower upper class, upper middle class, middle class, working class, lower class and lower lower class (see Figure 7.1).[2]

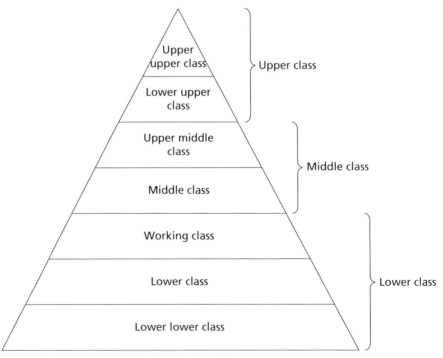

Figure 7.1 Hierarchical structure of social classes

The upper class

This is divided into the upper upper class and the lower upper class:

- *Upper upper class:* Membership of this social class is primarily determined through inheritance. Individuals belonging to this class tend to be those who have inherited their wealth and/or titles from their parents or relatives, for example the royal families. For instance, Mandla Mandela was considered to be within the upper upper class because of his stature as a chief in the Mandela clan of the Xhosa council.[3] His chieftaincy derives from his grandfather, Nelson Mandela, who was also a chief. Movement and mobility into and out of this social class is nearly impossible since the primary determinant is one's heritage or blood line. One of the few exceptions is marriage, as is the case with Meghan Markle, who one could consider to have formed part of the lower upper class, who became part of the British royal family. Through virtue of marriage to Prince Harry, the Duke of Sussex of the UK, Meghan's social standing migrated from lower upper class into the upper upper (royal) class, and she is now the Duchess of Sussex.

- *Lower upper class:* This is the lower segment of the upper class and movement into this and other classes is not as stringent. It consists mostly of the nouveau riche (newly rich). These individuals were not born rich and prior to their wealth would have not been considered to fall within the upper class. Generally speaking, the lower upper class would have made their wealth based on their individual actions, through their professions or business ventures. Examples of people falling into this class are industrialists, businesspeople, entrepreneurs, doctors, professors, corporate executives and church pastors, among many others.

The middle class

This is divided into the upper middle class and the middle class:

- *Upper middle class:* This social class falls in between the lower upper class and the middle class. It is constituted mainly of qualified professionals, most of them with university degrees and qualifications.

- *Middle class:* The middle class tends to be the largest social class (in terms of numbers). Consumers regarded as the middle class are often people occupying white collar jobs (for example, teachers, accountants and bank tellers). Certain blue collar workers, for instance, highly qualified artisans such as plumbers and electricians, can also be considered to be falling within the middle class.

The lower class

This is divided into the working class, the lower class and the lower lower class:

- *Lower class:* These are people whose standard of living is just above the poverty line. They are mostly unemployed or are occasional workers.

- *Lower lower class:* People falling within this class are most likely financially deprived (visibly poor) and rely on social welfare to meet their day-to-day needs.

- *Working class:* The working class mainly comprises mainly of average sala-ried workers. A majority of these are consumers who are employed in sectors that might not require specific qualifications, such as factory workers.

Countries and regions of the world differ significantly in the proportion of their populations belonging to different social classes. For example, in most developed countries such as the US, UK, Germany, France, Denmark, Norway, Australia, Canada etc., the majority of the adult population falls within the mid-dle social class. The class structure therefore takes on a diamond shape in that it is bigger in the middle and smaller on top and at the bottom.

On the other hand, the majority of the population in African countries, including South Africa, is in the lower class, with a small proportion of the population belonging to the upper class. As a result, the social class structure in Africa takes a pyramid shape. Figure 7.2 presents the diamond and pyramid shapes associated with distribution of population into lower, middle and upper class in developed versus African countries.

Social class membership is not fixed as people tend to move from one to another. Movement from lower to higher social classes, for example from mid-dle to upper, is known as upward social mobility and is more desirable than downward social mobility.

7.2.2 Measuring social class

While income can be used to measure financial status, it is not necessarily a trustworthy measure of social status. For example, in certain instances artisans may earn more than professionals, however this would not make them part of the so-called upper classes.

The following three approaches are better to measure social class: subjective, objective and the Living Standards Measure (LSM).

Subjective approach to measuring social class

This approach entails either asking individuals to estimate their own social class or asking knowledgeable key informants in a community, such as councillors

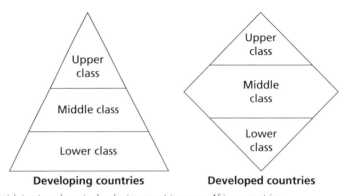

Figure 7.2   Social structure shape in developing countries versus African countries

and leaders of community civil society organisations, to evaluate the social standing of community members.

The practice of asking individuals to estimate their own social class is based on the understanding that most people are aware of their social standing in society. The result is thus a reflection of an individuals' self-image. The use of key informants means that a person's social class is determined by the image others have of the person.

The common shortfall associated with the subjective approach is that individuals may not indicate their actual position when asked about their social class. A person in the upper class may, for example, indicate middle class in order to avoid standing out. Similarly, key informants may rank some individuals as belonging to a higher class simply because such individuals project themselves as such.

Objective approach to measuring social class

This approach uses factual measures or descriptors of socio-economic status such as the following to classify individuals into different social classes:
- Income/wealth
- Occupation
- Education
- Place of residence

The key characteristic of the objective approach is that an external criterion is established. People are placed based on the extent to which they fit within the descriptors associated with a given class. For example, Credit Suisse in its Global Wealth Report, determines middle class as encompassing people whose net worth is between US$10 000 and US$100 000.[4] Using this criteria, South Africa's middle class in 2017 was estimated at 28,5% of the population.[5]

Classification of people based on occupation relies on the prestige which an occupation holds in society. For example, being an executive, manager or doctor is associated with more prestige than being a janitor, retail sales clerk or waiter, even though all may be vital to an economy. Education influences a person's skills and subsequently the type of job the person will occupy. Higher levels of education are generally associated with higher income and financial prosperity, so there is a link between level of education and place of residence. Individuals with a higher income can afford to live in more expensive residential areas, as well as bigger and nicer houses.

Living Standards Measure to measuring social class

Lamb, Hair, McDaniel et al. describe the Living Standards Measure (LSM) as follows:[6]

> The South African Advertising Research Foundation (SAARF) introduced a marketing research tool used to describe the South African consumer market, called the Living Standards Measure (LSM). LSM attempts to group similar people together and distinguishes between different groups of people in South Africa in terms of social class, or living standard, regardless of ethnicity, income or education. Instead of approaching social class from the point of view of

obvious demographic differences, the LSM quantifies the ownership of certain durable goods, access to services and the like, to provide a composite measure of social class. The LSM methodology is thus based on the premise that the consumption behaviour of South Africans is largely determined by their social class as measured by ownership of durable goods and consumption of services.

The LSM tool has been refined several times and now 10 LSM groups can be distinguished. The groups are referred to as LSM 1 to LSM 10, but to offer a more detailed description, LSM 7, 8, 9 and 20 are subdivided into low and high groups.[7]

People are classified into an LSM group based on 29 descriptors:[8] (1) access to hot running water from a geyser, (2) computer (desktop or laptop), (3) electric stove, (4) domestic worker(s) or helper(s) in household, (5) zero or one radio in the household, (6) flush toilet inside or outside the household, (7) motor vehicle in household, (8) washing machine, (9) refrigerator or combined fridge/freezer, (10) vacuum cleaner or floor polisher, (11) Pay TV subscription, (12) dishwasher, (13) three or more cellphones in the household, (14) two cell-phones in the household, (15) home security service, (16) free-standing deep freezer, (17) microwave oven, (18) rural dweller outside Gauteng or the Western Cape, (19) house, cluster house or town house, (20) DVD or Blu-ray player, (21) tumble dryer, (22) home theatre system, (23) home telephone (excluding cell-phones), (24) swimming pool, (25) tap water in house or on plot, (26) built-in kitchen sink, (27) TV set, (28) air conditioner (excluding fans), and (29) living in a metropolitan area.

The presence, or otherwise, of these variables for each respondent, is coded. A formula is then applied to yield a score for each respondent, the value of which determines his or her LSM group membership. LSM group 1 has the lowest living standard, whereas LSM group 10 has the highest living standard.

According to Boshoff, De Meyer-Heydenrych, Human et al.:

> LSM-related research is continuously conducted by the SAARF and made available to marketers. Such research provides greater insights about the demographics, media usage, lifestyle and preferences shared by the members of each LSM group. This information can be used by marketers to gain insight and understanding regarding consumer behaviour of members of each LSM group. This information can be used by marketers to gain an improved understanding of their target markets and to guide product development, media channel selection and segmentation.[9]

For instance, LSM research released at the end of 2014 indicated that LSM 1 generally comprises more females than males, aged 50 and older, residing in rural areas, and that the medium they are more readily exposed to is radio. In contrast, LSM 10 (high) comprises more males than females, aged 35 and older, residing in urban areas and having access to a wide range of media including commercial radio, television (often DSTV), print (for example, newspapers and magazines), cinema and outdoor advertising. They have also accessed the internet at least within the last seven days.[10]

The LSM segmentation system is unique to the South African market, with other tools existing in different parts of the world.

7.2.3   Application of social class in marketing and retailing

Social class can be used for different purposes, including the following:

- *As a means of market segmentation:* Social classes group people within a particular society into segments of consumers who share similar backgrounds, behaviours and lifestyles. As such, marketers consider members of a specific social class possessing similar values, psychographics (behavioural patterns) and occupations as being a distinct market segment.[11] Marketers therefore often target marketing communication and advertisements to consumers of a particular occupation,[12] for example engineers or teachers. Marketers also regularly develop products that are aimed at different customers in different social classes. For example, almost all of South Africa's Big Four banks (Absa, Nedbank, FNB and Standard Bank) offer accounts and account packages according to consumers' social class. At the lower end, there are 'student' types of account and at the other extreme, platinum or private banking.

- *As a predictor of consumer behaviour:* According to Lamb et al., '[l]ifestyle distinctions between the social classes are greater than the distinctions within a given class. The biggest gap in lifestyles is evident between the middle and lower classes. Different social classes have different buying and consumption patterns. Social class can also indicate where certain types of consumers will shop'.[13] For example, wealthy, upper-class consumers might shop at boutiques and frequent more expensive and exclusive restaurants, whereas middle class consumers will more regularly visit larger shopping centres. Consumers regularly purchase products and services that are associated with the social class to which they belong. Social class is therefore a reliable measure to predict consumer behaviour, such as which products and brands consumers are likely to purchase as well as which stores they are likely to visit.

The utility of social class is that over and above predicting various consumer actions, it also provides explanations as to why consumers conduct some of these actions. For example, some consumers may purchase goods and services with the main purpose of showing-off their social class, or to keep up with those in a higher social class than their own, also known as 'keeping up with Jones's'. This manifests itself mainly through conspicuous consumption – luxury products such as designer clothes and sports cars usually appeal to such consumers.

One reason for this is the link between social class and **social status**. Social status refers to the relative ranking of members of a social class in terms of wealth, power and prestige.[14] In this context, wealth refers to economic and financial assets. Power is the degree of personal choice and the influence that consumers have on others within the society. Lastly, prestige denotes that degree of recognition that consumers within a social class receive from others. From these three factors, marketers are able to deduce how members of a particular social class are likely to socialise, which stores they patronise, which goods and services they like to buy, how they pay for those goods, their holiday and travel destinations, type and quality of food chosen, and so on. Each individual, in the motive to maximise pleasure and minimise discomfort, will strive to maintain his or her own social status and, invariably, his or her social class. Naturally, this human instinct triggers various actions and decision-making processes on the part of consumers that are aimed at maintaining social class.[15]

Different social classes have different levels of exposure to different media types. For example, while in South Africa, middle- and upper-class consumers can be easily targeted by means of magazines and newspapers, lower-class consumers are more inclined to watch television and listen to the radio. Different social classes also prefer certain types of content to others. For example, businesspeople will most likely frequent business- and financial-related magazines and websites, whereas teachers will most likely frequent those with educational content. The marketer will therefore need to think strategically about where to place their marketing material in terms of which target market they would like to reach.

APPLICATION

Targeting the lower social class

While consumers in the lower social class have less income to spend, they have the same necessities, for example the need for food, clothing and housing.

Discussion questions

In small groups:

1. Discuss some of the strategies used by companies in your area to appeal to consumers in the lower social class in the following product categories:
   - Housing
   - Clothing
   - Food
   - Credit services
2. Do any of the strategies used by companies to target consumers in the lower social class pose ethical questions? Discuss.

As part of society and different social classes, individuals are constantly influenced by other people and using others as the basis for their consumption judgements and decisions. Such people form part of an individuals' reference group. Section 7.3 looks at reference groups and their influence on consumer behaviour.

7.3 REFERENCE GROUPS

A reference group is a set of individuals with whom others evaluate themselves for some direction towards developing their own knowledge, attitudes and/or behaviour. It is called a reference group because its members serve as a point of reference.[16] For instance, marketers often use celebrities to lend credibility to new products and services and help convince potential customers to purchase the new offerings. Let us imagine that you like running and your favourite athlete endorses some new running shoes. Chances of your purchasing those running shoes are high, as you would be inspired and would want to be a pro just like him or her.

Every consumer forms part of one group or another, such as a family group, church group, work group, friendship group etc. Group members influence each other's attitudes and consumption behaviours. For example, Lerato notices that everyone in her friendship group likes to wear a specific brand of make-up. Lerato will therefore most likely purchase the same brand of make-up as her friends. People are also likely to discuss certain purchases (for example, buying a new car) with others in their reference group in order to obtain their opinions and advice.

7.3.1 What constitutes a group?

Not every collection of individuals is a group. A group is established if its members have defined relationships (directly or indirectly) such that their behaviours depend on each other. Individuals will only stay in a group as long as the benefits that they get exceed the sacrifices that have to be made. In the case of a friendship group, some of these benefits might be moral guidance, emotional support, common activities and hobbies (such as playing a game of soccer or going to a mall together) and consumer socialisation. From a group perspective, consumer socialisation refers to members guiding each other in terms of purchase and consumption behaviour.[17]

A group may also simply be defined as two or more people who interact to accomplish either individual or common goals. The broad scope of this classification includes intimate groups, for example friends who spend a lot of time together and always go shopping together, as well as larger, more formal groups such as a neighbourhood watch. A reference group may not even be aware that it is acting as such. For example, a teenage boy may admire a specific football team and use this team as a reference point, without their ever having met.

From a consumer behaviour perspective, groups are important to marketers and retailers, since they influence the purchases made by individuals. For example, when a group of friends goes shopping, their purchases will most likely be influenced by each other.

7.3.2   Classification of groups

There are many ways in which to classify groups, such as frequency of contact, degree of formality and the nature of membership.[18]

Frequency of contact

The frequency of contact between members determines whether a group is primary or secondary.[19]

Primary groups are small intimate groups composed of people that share close personal relationships with each other, interact frequently and often communicate on a face-to-face basis. Examples are family members, close friends, classmates or neighbours. Members of primary groups value each other's opinions and feedback. Primary groups provide a strong sense of belonging as members exhibit a strong sense of cohesiveness and spontaneous interpersonal behaviour.

In contrast, secondary groups consist of people who interact only occasionally and their relationships are more impersonal. Secondary groups do not exhibit the same concern for fellow members and although face-to-face meetings may take place, communication efforts tend to be more through mass media (for example, members of a local library).

Members of primary groups tend to have a stronger influence over each other's attitude and behaviour as consumers than members of secondary groups. The critical differences between primary and secondary groups are therefore frequency or consistency of interactions and the perceived importance of the group to the individual.

Degree of formality

Another important classification of groups is according to their formality, that is, the degree to which the group structure, the group's purpose and the members' roles are defined. Where the group has a well-defined structure (for example, a formal membership list) and specific roles and levels of authority (for example, a president, treasurer and secretary), and definite goals (for example, to help the elderly or to address students' concerns), then it would be classified as **formal group**. The local chapter of one of the major South African political parties, with elected officers and members who meet regularly to discuss topics of civil interest, could be regarded as a formal group. In contrast, an **informal group** is loosely defined and may have no specified roles and goals. Meeting your neighbours over lunch once a month for a friendly exchange of news would be an example. Informal groups are based on regular interaction between group members, a common lifestyle or common interests.

From the consumer behaviour perspective, informal groups are a major target for marketers because their less defined structures provide a more conducive environment for information exchange and influence about consumption-related topics. For instance, Castle succeeded in marketing its lager to groups of friends by coining it 'the beer that brings friends together'. In their advertisements, they often put across a concept of friendship, fun and unity resulting from sharing their beer[20].

Figure 7.3 Group of friends enjoying beer together

Nature of membership

Sometimes, groups are classified by membership status. Membership groups are those where the key members recognise each other as being part of the group by virtue of a common bond, for example church groups, family and work organisations. Another example of a membership group is your high school's alumni association.

A **symbolic group** is a group of which an individual is not officially a member and/or to which he or she does not qualify to belong, but the individual acts like he or she is a member by adopting the group's clothing, attitudes, values and behaviour. An example is a man dressing in camouflage outfits, learning how to track animals and knowing how to survive in the bush, because he is interested in animal conversation.

7.3.3   Reference group influence

Consumers' decisions, behaviours, purchases and lifestyle are affected by three main types of influence, namely the normative influence, the value expressive influence and the informational influence:[21]

- **Normative influence** refers to the pressure exerted to conform to the norms and expectations of the group. Conformity in this case is important for social acceptance. An example is peer pressure, where in order to avoid social ridicule, a person does what others are doing. Normative influence can also often be seen in fashion choices. For example, Harley Davidson motorcycle riders dress similarly, often with the HOG (Harley Owners Group) symbol pertinently displayed on their jackets.
- **Value-expressive influence** takes place when an individual uses a reference group's values, norms and behaviours as a guide for his or her own actions. For example, a business student might dress like a prominent business executive she admires to enhance her image and aspirations.
- **Informational influence** occurs when the group provides the consumer with information that enables him or her to make a decision.[22] For example, a consumer may follow advice from friends about the most affordable and reliable fibre optic service provider to use. Opinion leaders may have more knowledge about and experience of certain product categories and consumers will therefore trust their feedback. Informational influence can also occur when a consumer observes a group's behaviour to infer characteristics about a product or brand that the members of the group use.[23] For example, a man might notice that all of his favourite soccer players wear the same brand of boots and will most likely conclude that this brand is of high quality and might improve performance.

The degree of influence that reference groups exert on consumers depends on following factors, among others:

- *Individual factors:* Individual factors such as personality traits, commitment to a group and level of confidence affect the degree of influence that reference groups exert on consumers. For example, some people regard social norms and values as important and readily conform. They are therefore more likely to be easily influenced by reference groups than people who are non-conforming. Similarly, the more committed a person is to a reference group, the more influence the group is likely to exert on him or her. A consumer's knowledge regarding products and services, resulting from information they may have as well as past experiences, affords them a sense of confidence when making purchasing decisions. The more confident a consumer is regarding a purchasing decision, the less likely he or she is to seek other people's advice, thus limiting the degree of influence reference groups may have on his or her purchasing decisions.
- *Reference group-related factors:* Reference group-related factors, including the extent to which a group is regarded as trustworthy, knowledgeable and attractive by an individual, can affect the degree of influence that the reference group is able to exert. For example, endorsement of spices and

ingredients is likely to be perceived as more credible coming from a chef than a person who does not cook. If consumers are concerned with getting the approval of consumer groups that they like or with which they strongly identify, such groups are likely to have a strong level of influence on the products or services that they buy.

- *Product-related factors:* Conspicuousness of the product and its importance to a given reference group determine the extent to which a consumer may be influenced to buy it. When buying conspicuous products such as designer watches or clothing, individuals are more prone to take into consideration the opinion of reference groups than when buying products that others are unlikely to notice. In terms of degree of importance, a Harley Davidson motorcycle and associated accessories would be highly important to have in order for a consumer to feel like part of the group.

7.3.3 Types of reference group

The three main types of reference group against which consumers evaluate their attitudes, behaviours and beliefs are as follows:[24]

- Aspirational reference groups
- Associative reference groups
- Dissociative reference groups

Aspirational reference groups

Aspirational reference groups are those groups that consumers admire and desire to be like, but of which they are not currently members. For example, a young student might be inspired by a detective who visited his school on career day and has decided to join the police force when he is finished studying. The student admires detectives and desires to be like them and form part of their group.

There are two types of aspirational reference groups:

- *Anticipatory aspirational reference groups:* This is one which a person intends to join at a future time.
- *Symbolic aspirational reference groups:* An individual does not form a part of such a group and is unlikely to join in the future. However, the individual nonetheless adopts the values, norms and patterns of behaviour similar to member of the group.

Associative reference groups

These are groups to which an individual automatically or essentially belongs, such as extended family groups, employee groups or school classes. The ethnic, gender, geographic and even the age groups to which a consumer belongs also constitute associative reference groups.

Even consumers who perceive themselves as individually minded, respond well to products that are linked to appropriate associative reference groups. However, when consumers misunderstand their position in a reference group, they tend to make poor consumption decisions. For example, if a person believes he is a skilled cyclist when in fact he is little more than a beginner, he may buy equipment or services unsuited to his capabilities.

Associative reference groups can also emerge from a brand, as is the case with fan clubs such as the Volkswagen club in South Africa. A **brand community** is a dedicated group of consumers with a designed set of relationships involving a specific brand and product use, for example HOG.[25]

Dissociative reference groups

Dissociative reference groups are groups with which the consumer does not wish to be associated. In this case, an individual views the values, attitudes and behaviours of the group to be inconsistent with his or her own, for example a street gang or a hunting party. However, it is important to note that dissociative reference groups are not always characterised by bad habits. For instance, some consumers may avoid using products associated with being 'elderly' or belonging to a lower social class.[26]

Marketing implications

The influence of the various groups has important implications for marketers and retailers in reaching certain markets, as follows:

- *Aspirational reference groups:* Having knowledge about their target consumers in terms of their aspirations and needs enables marketers and retailers to associate their product with relevant groups and to use the right spokespeople to represent them.[27] For example, many organisations use celebrities such as sports stars to endorse their products or communicate with the target market.
- *Associative reference groups:* Marketers can also classify and properly represent target consumers in ads by precisely reflecting the hairstyles, clothing, accessories and general conduct of their associative reference groups. For example, when marketers want to persuade young people to purchase the latest smartphone, they might use an advertisement depicting a group of young, trendy individuals who are all using the latest smartphone and showing how they enjoy the different features of the phone. The advertisement might be successful if the target market (young people) identify with the people in the advertisement, and therefore feel that this new smartphone is representative of their values and behaviours.
- *Dissociative reference groups:* Marketers and retailers should avoid using dissociative reference groups in their marketing efforts. For example, by revoking their endorsement when a celebrity commits a crime or demonstrates unpleasant behaviour, marketers ensure that their products are not associated with it. For example, major brands such as Nike and M-Net started revoking their endorsements and sponsorships as details of Oscar Pistorius' shooting of his girlfriend Reeva Steenkamp emerged.

One important marketing area that reference groups exert strong influence over is the diffusion of innovations, which is discussed in the next section.

7.4 DIFFUSION OF INNOVATION

In order for an organisation to remain competitive, it needs to be innovative in terms of its products and services. This is often manifested through introduction of new products or services to the market. Diffusion of innovation refers to the nature in which new products spread across the market and how the products are accepted by the target population or a group of consumers.

An innovation is not always an invention. An invention is defined as 'the creation of a product or a process for the first time'.[28] Some popular examples of inventions are the printing press, the wheel and the television. An innovation, on the other hand, is any thought, behaviour or thing that is new because it is distinctly different from the existing products on the market, and more importantly, is perceived as new by potential adopters and creates positive value.[29]

For all practical purposes, then, products, services, attributes, packages and ideas all amount to innovations if they are seen as being new and different by consumers, irrespective of actually being new, as long as they create value. Table 7.1 compares and contrasts an invention with an innovation.

Table 7.1 Invention versus innovation

Aspect	Invention	Innovation
Definition	Creating a product, device or process for the first time	The introduction of a modified or a better product that seeks to provide a better solution for existing market needs
Requirements	Knowledge, competence and financial aid	Technical knowledge, competence, knowledge about market needs
Perception of newness	Newness is objective because the product or service has never been seen or provided before in any form	Newness is subjective and the newness is defined by the potential adopter
Examples	Printing press, telephone, TV	Laser jet printer, new models of smartphones, digital cameras

Innovations introduce new ways of, or approaches to, consumption. For instance, mobile banking has largely altered how consumers interact with their banks (in other words, changed consumers' behaviour). Equally, the internet, through online shops such as Takealot.com, Zando and Bid or Buy, has introduced novel ways for South African consumers to purchase products, while websites such as OLX.co.za or gumtree.co.za have provided ways through which consumers can dispose of their unwanted products. It is for this reason that studying the adoption and diffusion of innovations forms an important part of the consumer behaviour discipline.

APPLICATION

Degrees of innovation

Try to recall new products that you have encountered in the past three years. As you reflect on these products, try to consider their varying degrees of innovation. For example, smartwatches such as the Samsung Galaxy Gear is more of an innovation than the new Black Label 1 litre beer bottle.

7.4.1 Types of innovation

Innovations can be arranged on a continuum from those requiring minor change in consumers' behaviour, to those that demand radical change.[30] For example, upgrading your printer to the latest version offered by the brand will require minimal change in your behaviour, as you are already familiar with this brand's printers. An example of an innovation which demands new behaviour is electronic commerce (e-commerce) or internet shopping. Online shopping has completely changed how consumers select, purchase and pay for products. Three typologies have been identified, namely:

* continuous,
* dynamically continuous, and
* discontinuous innovations.[31]

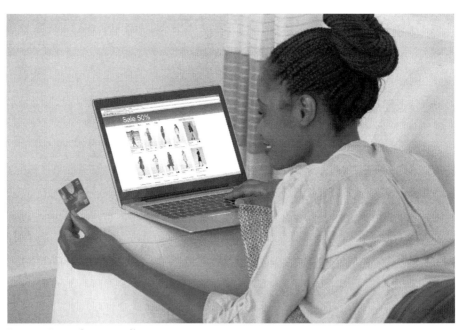

Figure 7.4 Types of innovation[31]

Behavioural change as depicted in Figure 7.4 refers to some alteration or modification in the consumers' actions, attitudes and/or beliefs if an innovation is adopted or utilised.[32] It is this that determines the complexity of an innovation.[33]

For example, switching to Coke Zero from regular Coke would require a far less substantial change in behaviour than attempting online shopping for the first time.

Continuous innovation

Continuous innovations represent 'improvements to existing products'.[34] Typically, continuous innovations are used in very similar ways to the products that preceded them. They do not introduce major changes to the dynamics of an industry as they involve modest enhancements of existing technologies or products.

This type of innovation has the least disruptive influence on consumers' established behaviour. An example would be herbal toothpaste. Most consumers are already familiar with how to use ordinary toothpaste and herbal toothpaste is used in the same way, so a move to herbal toothpaste would not change their usual oral hygiene routine.

Dynamically continuous innovation

A dynamically continuous innovation is a product that performs the same functions as the old product, but possesses numerous advantages, over and above better performance. In general, dynamically continuous innovations can perform the existing functions of the product considerably faster and more effectively, for example automatic teller machines (ATMs) and electric toothbrushes.

A characteristic feature of dynamically continuous innovations is that these products are modifications of existing products and these modifications will naturally affect the consumption behaviour of the consumer. In some instances, new products or processes also qualify as dynamically continuous innovations. For example, mobile app banking could be regarded as a new product.

The effort and behaviour change expected of consumers in utilising dynamically continuous innovations is moderate, as shown in Figure 7.2, because consumers will already be familiar with the product or service. Consumers will only need to come to grips with certain changes that have been in order to improve it.

Discontinuous innovation

Most of the innovations in the discontinuous innovations category are new products that rely on new technologies and inventions,[35] often demanding a significant change in consumers' behaviour (see Figure 7.2). The proper use of discontinuous innovations generally requires new experience, understanding and additional learning. These innovations are so new, that consumers sometimes find them very complex. Aeroplanes, microwave ovens and the internet were once discontinuous innovations which radically changed consumers' behaviour.

The continuity or discontinuity of an innovation is an important dimension as it is the basis on which the newness of the innovation can be determined. The following sections explain the diffusion (distribution) and adoption (acceptance) of the different types of innovation and, more specifically, how the type of innovation affects the rate of both among the target population.

7.4.2   Factors influencing diffusion of innovation

While the idea of stimulating consumers with innovative products seems appealing, convincing consumers actually to use these new innovations may be more challenging. For example, when hybrid corn was initially introduced as a new product, the rate at which it was adopted among many farmers was very slow. Despite promises of the hybrid corn providing yields about 20% higher than traditional corn, several farmers were reluctant to try it because a failed harvest could be devastating economically, including possible loss of their farm.[36]

Since it is not easy for consumers to accept new market offerings,[37] it is necessary for marketers to understand the underlying factors that influence potential adopters' innovation adoption decisions. Rogers[38] distinguishes four main elements: (1) the innovation itself and its attributes, (2) the social system, (3) the communication process, and (4) the timing. See Figure 7.5.

Innovation attributes

- Compatibility with the lifestyle values and norms of consumers
- Clear advantages
- Good visibility within society
- Simply defined use
- Easy to try out

Social system

- Positive attitude in relation to changes
- Positive attitude towards education and science
- High degree of homogeneity
- Higher compatibility with innovation

Innovation ——————— **DIFFUSION AND ADOPTION** ——————▶ **Successful adoption of innovation**

Communication

- Continuous communication between marketers, retailers and the innovation execution team
- Continuous communication by the retailers
- Communication outside the retailers among intermediaries, customers or consumer groups
- Precise communication channels
- Clear message

Time

- Appropriate timing of introducing the innovation to the market
- Accurate forecast of frequency of purchase

Figure 7.5 Elements of successful diffusion and adoption of innovation[39]

The innovation and its attributes

There are five attributes that will determine the success of the diffusion of an innovation, in other words the likelihood that diffusion will gain momentum and more people will adopt the innovation:[40]

- **Compatibility:** An innovation greatly corresponds to the lifestyle values and norms as well as consumers' existing skills and habits.
- **Relative advantage:** The innovation's benefit is clearly visible.
- **Complexity:** The innovation does not require exceptional skill to use.
- **Trialability:** An opportunity to test the innovation exists.
- **Observability:** The innovation is clearly detectible within a society.
- The innovation attributes are explained in the following section. Generally, innovations that are rated highly in several of the areas are most likely to diffuse quicker through the desired target market.[41]

Compatibility

The compatibility of a new innovation indicates how well suited a product is to a consumer's lifestyle, values and needs. Innovations that are perceived as incompatible are in most cases resisted. For example, if new sportswear was developed with an antibacterial finish that meant the clothes did not need to be washed after every exercise session, as convenient as this might seem on paper, athletes might dislike the idea of wearing 'sweaty' clothes repeatedly and so avoid the product. On the other hand, most South African consumers have steadfastly embraced the move from conventional cell-phones to smartphones as they regard them as more compatible with their needs.

Marketing implication: Marketers and retailers need to ensure that product characteristics conform to consumers' needs, values and lifestyle. Alternatively, they need to modify designs to add features that will enhance this. Rather than convincing consumers to adopt a novel product, they should offer consumers products they require and promote features that they need. Marketing plans should therefore centre around offering products that are compatible with the concerned target markets. In addition, it is not only a matter of the product but also the communication message which needs to reflect the sentiments of a novel product's compatibility.

Relative advantage

The relative advantage associated with a new innovation demonstrates its additional benefits over substitute products. Manufacturers and retailers in South Africa regularly check the extent to which their products compare with others in the market. An innovation that offers 'additional advantages for the consumer will most likely be adopted faster, since it helps consumers to satisfy their needs, resolve problems, or accomplish their goals'.[42]

There is no one single formula that defines a product's relative advantage. Any feature or attribute of a product which delivers additional benefits provides a relative advantage over other products or innovations. Table 7.2 gives some examples of the relative advantages of common everyday products.

Table 7.2 Examples of relative advantage

Product	Substitute product	Relative advantage of the product over substitute product
Gautrain	Metro (shosholoza) train	Faster Cleaner Keeps to schedule
NSFAS Online submission (application)	Manual NSFAS submission (application)	No queues Immediate feedback
App banking (online)	Branch banking	No queues Convenient
Email	Letters	Fast and convenient No need to visit the post office
Uber	Metered taxi	Cleaner cars Transparent fares Estimate of the fare beforehand Taxi comes to your location using GPS on your cellphone

Marketers often capitalise on the unique benefits presented by a product's relative advantage, advertising their products accordingly. For instance, Capitec bank uses the tagline '*skip the store and ATM queue*' for its banking app.[43] Although banking apps are not exclusive to Capitec, using the app presents a relative advantage over waiting in a queue at an automated teller machine (ATM) or inside a bank.

Similarly, Uber uses '*Your ride, on demand*' as its slogan (as shown in Table 7.2 and Figure 7.6) to emphasise its round-the-clock taxi service. Consumers can use their app to order a taxi ride wherever and whenever they want.

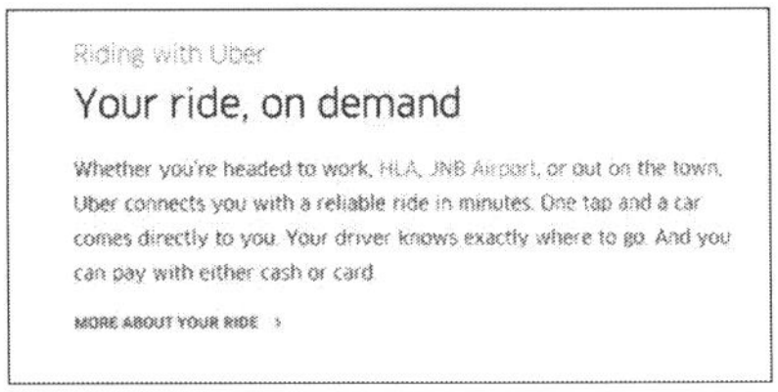

Marketing implication: If consumers do not perceive that an innovation has a relative advantage, marketers may need

Riding with Uber
Your ride, on demand

Whether you're headed to work, HLA, JNB Airport, or out on the town, Uber connects you with a reliable ride in minutes. One tap and a car comes directly to you. Your driver knows exactly where to go. And you can pay with either cash or card

MORE ABOUT YOUR RIDE ›

Figure 7.6 Relative advantage: Uber[44]

to add one by physically redesigning or reengineering the innovation. They also need to communicate and demonstrate the product's relative advantage to consumers who are not yet clear on it. For instance, mobile banking initially diffused slowly among South African consumers until financial service providers started using advertisements and social media posts to demonstrate its convenience and security.

Another way to communicate an innovation's advantage is through highly credible and visible opinion leaders. For example, South African national team and Kaizer Chiefs goal keeper, Itumeleng Khune, is Nike South Africa's brand ambassador.[45]

If consumers perceive a new product as costly, marketers can use special price-oriented sales promotions and provide guarantees or warrantees that make the product seem less expensive. For instance, in 2015, MTN South Africa slashed the price of its popular, own-branded Steppa 2 smartphone from R999 to R799 to entice more customers to buy the device.[46]

Figure 7.7 Consumers can find new features frustrating

Complexity

Complexity denotes the extent to which an innovation is perceived by consumers to be difficult and complicated to use or understand. Because individuals typically resist change and adjustment in behaviour patterns, the more complicated a product seems, the less likely the product will be adopted.

Complexity is related to the nature of the innovation:

- For continuous innovation (improvements to existing products), the degree of complexity is inversely related to the rate of adoption since the innovation is used in much the same manner as the products from which it originated.
- Innovations that are perceived as dynamically continuous (introducing a new, different or better technology) have a pronounced effect on consumers' behaviour patterns and as a result take longer to diffuse within the marketplace.
- When it was first introduced, the internet was an example of a discontinuous innovation, which at first might have been complex in terms of understanding how to use it.

Marketing implication: Marketers and retailers can reduce perceptions of complexity associated with a product in two fundamental ways: (1) by redesigning a product so that it becomes easier to use, or (2) by introducing a range of products that vary in complexity in terms of the number of attributes or features. In this case, consumers can select the product that they feel meets their needs in terms of what it can do (features and attributes) as well as the degree of complexity they are willing to cope with. Expert salespeople can also assist consumers who find the product complex.

Trialability

Trialability indicates the extent to which consumers are afforded the opportunity to try out new innovations prior to purchase. A trial provides consumers with a chance to evaluate the product's relative advantages and potential threats.[47] A classic example is trying out a new model of iPhone in an iStore before committing to its purchase. Several software firms offer restricted-use trials so that consumers can understand the products' features and associated benefits before buying. For instance, Avast is a popular internet security software firm, well-known for its value-for-money online antivirus protection service. By offering a new customer a 30 day free Avast antivirus trial, they are hoping those who sign up for the trial will end up becoming a customer.

Marketing implication: Marketers and retailers can stimulate trial through promotions. Free samples, for instance, encourage trial by consumers who might otherwise not consider the product, for example perfume testers and car test drives. In South Africa, when SatiSkin relaunched its brand, it placed tester units in-store to allow prospective customers to try its products prior to purchase.

Observability

Observability indicates the extent to which the outcomes of utilising a new product are evident to the target market. If consumers can see how others are benefitting from using it, the product is more likely to be successful and diffuse quicker. For example, Errol Arendz got his big breakthrough when Karin Barnard, wife of famous heart surgeon Dr Chris Barnard, wore one of his designs at a prestigious function.

Marketing implication: Observability of innovations can be enhanced by the use of distinctive packaging, styling and colour, or unique promotions. Distinctive packaging can also be used to convey the benefits of the product. Another method is associating a product with a well-known person (reference group), or using advertising that suggests that the consumer will be rewarded in terms of benefits and social acceptance. For example, car manufacturers such as BMW South Africa and Audi allow well-known South African celebrities to drive their cars. During advertisements, celebrities can be used to convey the benefits consumers will experience when using the specific product or service.

The communication process

Through the communication process, companies and customers get to share information. Careful selection of communication channels as well as the communication message itself are critical to ensuring that consumers not only get to know about an innovation, but that their interest is aroused and they want to try it, and that they eventually move over to purchasing the new product.

Organisations make use of marketing communication tools such as advertisements, sale simulation, direct marketing, personal selling and public relations to facilitate diffusion of an innovation. The success of an innovation is also stimulated by communication between opinion leaders and potential adopters. Opinion leaders are individuals who are knowledgeable about a product category and who might have used the new product or service. They are often consulted by family, friends and colleagues to provide advice about it.

The communication channel refers to the medium through which a marketing message is transmitted to its intended audience. Use of mass media such as radio and television tend to be more effective in creating awareness, while interpersonal channels such as personal selling and use of opinion leaders are effective in ensuring formation of positive attitudes and influencing positive action, including purchasing decisions.

The communication message is the content in the communication process. It should be clear and useful, and accurately convey the advantages and attributes of the innovation. It also needs to capture the attention of consumers and motivate them to purchase the new product. The following information related to the innovation should be considered when formulating the message:[48]

- The wishes and needs of consumers
- Benefits
- Exclusivity
- Durability
- Ease of use
- Relevance with regard to consumers' norms, values and skills

Time

This is how long it takes for the innovation to be adopted in the market. The extent to which a consumer moves from the product awareness stage to product purchase or rejection defines the time that a new product takes to diffuse through the market.[49]

The time taken by individuals to adopt an innovation is influenced by the following factors:[50]

- The **innovation adoption decision process** whereby an individual moves from initial awareness of a new product through to its adoption or rejection
- The characteristics of the target market
- The innovation's **rate of adoption** within the target market, frequently measured as the total number of members in a target market who have adopted the innovation in a given time period

These factors are discussed below.

The innovation adoption decision process

The innovation adoption decision process refers to the different actions and decisions that the consumer takes in the five-stage process of adoption.[51] These five stages consist of the following:

- *Knowledge stage:* This stage commences from the moment that a consumer is exposed to information about an innovation, pays attention to the innovation and get to know how it functions.[52] Knowledge of the innovation is facilitated mainly through mass media, however it can also be influenced by opinion leaders. In order for consumers to progress to the next stage in the innovation decision process, they need to be interested in the innovation, in the sense that it addresses their needs and they see the innovation as relevant.

- *Persuasion stage:* This is the stage where individuals develop a positive or negative attitude towards an innovation. During this stage, the consumer becomes more psychologically attached to the innovation and enthusiastically searches for information about it. The credibility of the source of information is crucial at this stage, since the consumer will only select those that are perceived as trustworthy.[53]
- *Decision stage:* This stage occurs when the consumer engages in activities that lead to the adoption or rejection of the innovation. Different strategies may be employed by marketers to facilitate positive decision making on the part of the consumer, including giving out free samples. Where limited trial is not possible or desired, consumers may rely on the experiences of those who have used the new product before deciding whether to adopt or reject the innovation, which they can do at any of the five stages of the process.
- *Implementation stage:* This stage occurs when the consumer starts using an innovation. Up to the implementation stage, the process has mainly been a mental exercise. Since the innovation will still be new to consumers, marketers and retailers need to be ready to address any questions that consumers may have as well as provide relevant information and after-sales service, in order to reduce cognitive dissonance. Cognitive dissonance refers to the immediate sense of uncertainty that a consumer experiences after a purchase, when nothing has occurred yet to ensure the individual that the product will perform as expected or that it is worth the money spent.[54]
- *Confirmation stage:* During this stage, individuals seek reinforcement for their innovation adoption decision. Consumers usually refer to previous innovation adoption decisions to obtain confirmation on whether their adoption decision was optimal or not. The confirmation stage is therefore a mechanism to double check that both the decision to purchase and the product itself meet their needs. Consumers may in fact reverse their decision to implement the innovation, or vice versa.

APPLICATION

1. List 10 products or items (for example, computers, cell phones, books) that are in your possession.
2. For each, indicate the type of innovation (continuous, dynamically continuous, and discontinuous).
3. Briefly explain how you became aware of each product and how you reached the decision to adopt the products, or first use the products.
4. Discuss and compare your answers with a friend.

The characteristics of the target market

Innovativeness refers to how quickly an individual adopts a new product or idea, compared to other consumers in the target market.[55] According to the diffusion of innovation model, there are five different adopter categories, summarised in Table 7.3.[56] Note that consumer characteristics within a particular category may vary, for example not all laggards have a small income and not all highly educated or high-income consumers are innovators.

Table 7.3 Characteristics of adopter categories as well as the percentage of the market they represent[57]

Adopter segment	Typical characteristics
Innovators (the first 2,5% to adopt the innovation)	Risk takers; financially stable; highly educated; use numerous, diverse information sources
Early adopters (the next 13,5% to adopt the innovation)	High social status (see section 7.2); strong opinion leaders; slightly above-average education level; more careful in adoption choices when compared to innovators
Early majority (next 34% to adopt the innovation)	Consider adoption of innovation after the innovators and early adopters; above average social status; seldom hold opinion leadership positions
Late majority (next 34% to adopt the innovation)	Doubt innovations; below-average social status; lower financial liquidity; limited opinion leadership
Laggards (last 16% to adopt the innovation)	Little to no opinion leadership; fear of debt; focuses more on 'traditions'; relatively low social status; low financial liquidity; family and close friends serve as information sources

Innovators form the smallest segment of the market (2,5%) and are the leaders in adopting new products. They are mostly risk takers, adventurous, typically highly educated and sociable. Marketers and retailers usually target these consumers first when they introduce an innovation. Individuals may not necessarily be innovators for all types of products, only certain categories, such as household technology or fashion. Individuals who are innovators for several products are referred to as **polymorphic**, while individuals who are innovators in a single product category are regarded as **monomorphic**.[58]

Communication messages directed at innovators should accentuate the newness of the product. Information should be factual and highlight the innovation's unique properties.

The *early adopters* form a slightly larger part of the market (13,5%) and tend to be role models for others, possess good social skills and act as opinion leaders, in other words those individuals who are known for their expertise and who usually garner respect within the larger social system. Early adopters utilise both interpersonal sources (people they interact, with such as friends and colleagues) and mass media (for example, newspapers, radio, magazines and television) as sources of information. Marketers and retailers who are introducing an innovation need to focus on early adopters by advertising and communicating through marketing channels that they frequently use. The adoption of an innovation by early adopters usually sets the trend for others who do not have access to the same information, or who prefer to obtain knowledge of an innovation from these early adopters rather than from advertising campaigns. Early adopters influence adoption decisions of the early majority, who constitute a sizeable portion of the market (34%).

Communication messages meant for early adopters need to be tailored to highlight the prestige that is associated with the innovation, accentuating its exclusiveness, not forgetting the norms and values that are considered acceptable by society. For example, particular premium luxury clothing brands would come to the fore with new fashion ideas that are available for those who are willing and eager to set the trend in their social network.

The *early majority* consists of consumers who wait until many of the early adopters have tried and like a new innovation before purchasing it.[59] The category consists of individuals who are quite thoughtful before purchasing new products, although they generally adopt innovative products shortly before the target population as a whole. The early majority constitutes about 34% of the buyers in the target market. They may have a great deal of contact with mass media, salespeople and opinion leaders (who are found in the early adopters group), but they are not opinion leaders themselves.[60]

Information aiming to reach the early majority should state the economic benefit of the innovation, also sharing the experiences of early adopters of the innovation.

The *late majority* constitutes a third of the target market (34%). These consumers tend to be cautious when assessing innovations, taking more time than normal in adopting the innovation, and are usually subject to some pressure from peers. As a result, these consumers tend to wait until the adoption of the innovation has reached a 'critical mass', thus the stage where the product has proven itself and is not considered new anymore, before they consider buying it. At this stage, they will be able to access a great deal of information regarding the product as well as other consumer's feedback regarding the product. Messages that are aimed at the late majority should indicate the economic benefits of the innovation and emphasise the possible loss that may be incurred due to late adoption of the innovation.

Laggards tend to be tradition bound and base their decisions on what happened in the past. Even though they constitute 16% of the target market, they are not a viable market for new products as they are inclined to be suspicious of products they are not familiar with and tend to stick with products they have used in the past, or for a long time. It is for this reason that they tend to purchase the innovation only once the rest of the target market has adopted it.

Information for this segment should emphasise the innovation's relationship with familiar lifestyle norms and disclose the extent of adoption and its potential relation to tradition. These consumers are generally reluctant to take any risks and only purchase products and services that have really stood the test of time.

Marketing implication: Marketers have to understand who innovators are, and how they can be reached through marketing communication and appropriate media. For an innovation to diffuse quickly, marketers need to recognise the importance of those consumer segments who are the first to buy a new product (innovators). Firstly, innovators adopt new products independently of the opinions of other people and are more likely to be receptive to information about new products, including marketing information. Secondly, by virtue of their experience with the innovation, innovators may also communicate information to other adopter categories, thus positively influencing innovation adoption. Innovators also have a considerable social influence further than their immediate groups, and are likely to be opinion leaders.

Rate of adoption

Rate of adoption refers to the relative speed with which consumers of a target market adopt a particular innovation. It is generally measured as the number of individuals who adopt an innovation in a given period.[61] The rate of adoption of innovation is related to the categories of adopters (innovators, early adopters, early majority, late majority, laggards) present in the market. The number of consumers that adopt an innovation changes in line with the stages through which new products pass from the time they are introduced in the market, also known as the product life cycle. Figure 7.8 shows how the diffusion of innovation progresses with time.

The stages of the product life cycle are as follows:

- *Introduction stage:* A product is introduced into the market, marking the beginning of a new product cycle. Since innovators are risk takers and looking for new products to try, they may be the only people aware of the new product at this stage. Recalling that the innovators represent only a

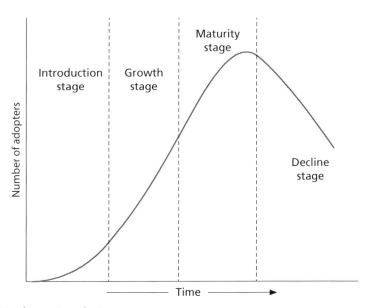

Figure 7.8 Rate of innovation adoption

small percentage of the population, the sales of the new product will be low. However, there is an advantage for the marketers in this situation, in that the new product does not yet have any competition.

- *Growth stage:* As the early adopters begin to adopt the product, sales begin to grow and profits usually start to follow, thus the product has entered the growth stage of the life cycle. Many of the early adopters willingly pass information about the product on to other people. Once the early adopters have tried and given their approval to a product, the early majority will begin to follow, thus causing the new product to enter a period of rapid growth. Competitors begin to enter the market and promotional efforts to stimulate secondary growth in demand begin.

- *Maturity stage:* The product is established and the aim for the manufacturer is now to maintain the market share they have built up. At this stage, sales and profit growth within a product category start to slow down. In addition, competition is at its highest within the product category, and competition from outside the category usually starts. This is also the stage characterised by adoption by the late majority consumers, who typically wait until they see the product being approved by others.

- *Decline stage:* Competition outside the product class may grow due to new and improved technology or changing consumer tastes. This will usually force a decline in the product category's sales and profits. The laggards will resist switching to new alternative products entering the market from competitors, and manufacturers who can still profitably serve this category will continue to do so. Eventually, even the laggards will switch to the new product, and the last companies producing the product will be forced to withdraw, thereby eliminating the product.

The social system

A social system can be seen as the physical, social or cultural environment to which people belong and within which they function. Social systems often affect the adoption of a particular innovation. Marketers may refer to these systems as market segments or target markets, which they can describe in terms of innovativeness and openness to innovation. The social system consists of individuals, groups and organisations, along with the factors associated with these, including cultural values, opinion leadership, modernity, physical distance and homophily within the groups:

- *Cultural values:* A person's cultural affiliation has a pertinent influence on his or her values, in other words the underlying reasons and motivations that direct behaviour. For example, a person might form part of a cultural group which tends to be individualistic, thus generally attending to personal needs and wants, as opposed to being collectivistic and therefore accommodating others' needs.[62] Individualism versus collectivism is an important influencing factor in terms of one's attitude towards innovation: in individualistic societies, individuals are more open to accept innovations, whereas in collectivistic societies, the mutual thoughts of others are considered before an

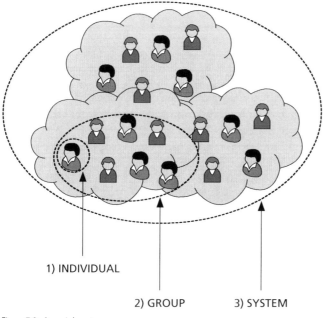

1) INDIVIDUAL

2) GROUP   3) SYSTEM

Figure 7.9 A social system

individual adopts an innovation. Consumers in individualistic cultures are therefore more likely to adopt new innovations, whereas those in collectivist cultures are more likely to adopt products with small improvements (incremental innovations). Chapter 8 explains this phenomenon in more detail.

- *Opinion leadership:* Individuals deemed to possess credibility, for instance experts in a field or trusted individuals such as parents, can have a substantial impact on the adoption and diffusion of new products. These individuals are considered to be opinion leaders, as they have the ability to influence the views of others. Opinion leaders could, for example, provide positive or negative information regarding a new product and seeing as their opinions are held in high regard by other consumers, they have the ability to influence the diffusion of an innovation. Opinion leaders influence others, but may also be influenced by others whom they trust and look up to in their social network.

- *Modernity:* Modernity is the extent to which consumers in the social system have positive attitudes toward change. Consumers in contemporary social systems highly regard science, technology and education, and are concerned with progress and change in the goods that are produced. Thus, the more modern the social system, the more receptive its consumers are to innovation.

- *Physical distance:* The diffusion of innovations tends to be faster when individuals in a social system are physically close to one another, because it is easier to share information and to learn from others. Conversely, an innovation tends to diffuse more slowly as the physical distance between consumers increases. Observability is an important determinant of adoption.[63] When consumers are physically closer together, for instance students living in the same dorm room at university, there is a greater chance that they will see each other's actions and exchange product information.

- *Homophily:* When consumers in the market are similar in terms of education, values, needs, income and other dimensions, diffusion tends to be quicker,[64] simply because people have similar interests and behaviour, and understand one another. In addition, similar people are likely to interact with one another and transmit information. This is called homophily and the target market is referred to as homophilious. In a heterophilious social system, on the other hand, where individuals are dissimilar, innovation diffusion will understandably be slower because consumers may have little common ground, for example different income groups that vastly influence the affordability of products, or differences in age that influence people's interest in the world around them. One of the problems associated with the diffusion of new products is that the consumers who are involved in the adoption process are usually diverse.

Marketing implication: Marketing efforts can influence resistance, adoption and diffusion by affecting the social system. For example, if members of a social system are heterophilious, marketers may need to use targeted communications that show the product's relevance to consumers' unique needs, values or norms, and may need to place the messages in specialised (target market specific) media.

SUMMARY

This chapter looked at the three related topics of social class, reference groups and diffusion of innovations. Social class refers to a status hierarchy used to classify individuals and groups of people within a society based mainly through social-economic success. Social class is accordingly ranked from low to high, with the higher classes associated with a higher level of prestige. In most African countries, there are more people in the lower social class than in the middle and upper class. Social class, among other things, affects the ability of consumers to afford products and services.

A reference group is: 'a set of individuals with whom one evaluates oneself for some direction towards developing one's own knowledge, attitudes, and/ or behaviour'.[65] There are three main types of reference group: aspirational, dissociative and associative. Reference groups exert normative, informational, value-expressive types of influence on individuals. The degree to which reference groups influence consumers depends on a number of factors including the susceptibility of an individual to being influenced, the attractiveness of a reference group to an individual and the level of conspicuousness of the products in question. Both social class and reference groups affect diffusion of innovations in a market. Diffusion of innovation refers to the way that new products spread across the market and how these are accepted by the target population/group of consumers. The rate at which diffusion of innovation takes place depends on factors associated with the innovation itself, including its degree of complexity, relative advantage, compatibility with consumer's needs, values and behaviour as well as trialability. Other factors that include the effectiveness of the communication strategy, the characteristics of the adopters and the social system.

ADDITIONAL RESOURCES

SELF-ASSESSMENT QUESTIONS

- Distinguish between an innovation and an invention and provide examples.
- Discuss the different adopter categories and their characteristics.
- Of which adopter group do university students usually form a part? Provide justification for your answer.
- Marketers and retailers are interested in social class and status for a number of reasons. Explain the applications of social class in marketing and retailing.
- Explain the number and type of social classes in South Africa.
- What are reference groups and why are they important in marketing?

Experiential exercise

Assume that you work for Samsung in South Africa and you have been tasked with the responsibility of promoting the adoption of the Samsung health app. The app helps individuals to track various aspects of their daily life that affect their health, including physical activities, nutrition, stress levels, heart rate, sleep etc.

Explain how you would determine the potential market segments that would be attracted by this app. How would you promote the app to attract customers from these market segments?

CASE STUDY 1

South Africa's Brothers for Life tackles men's involvement in HIV prevention[66]

Launched in 2009, Brothers for Life (BFL) is an ongoing South African health communication programme that promotes HIV testing, voluntary medical male circumcision (VMMC), male involvement in the prevention of mother-to-child transmission of HIV (PMTCT) and prevention of gender-based violence.

BFL uses a variety of innovative approaches to diffuse the principles of positive behaviour among South African males. For VMMC, BFL used the diffusion of innovations principles of observability and trialibility by interviewing men who underwent the VMMC procedure and publicising the interviews through a national TV and radio campaign. Through storytelling, BFL connected other men to the experiences of their peers and encouraged them to make a decision to go forward with the procedure. In support of these activities, BFL also created an SMS number that men and women could text to get answers to their questions about VMMC as well as directions to the nearest clinic. BFL successfully increased knowledge of VMMC from 8% in 2009 to 47% in 2012. Statistical data also shows BFL activities led to an increase in VMMC uptake.

In another example, BFL used the same principles to promote HIV testing by creating 1 000 Twitter accounts for World AIDS Day 2011 and recruiting HIV-positive volunteers to tweet about HIV stigma and promote HIV testing using the hashtag #HIVarmy. Within hours, the #HIVarmy hashtag was trending (being tagged at a greater rate than other tags) in South Africa and then globally. Local celebrities picked up the hashtag and joined the conversation. At midnight, all 1 000 accounts were terminated with the word 'deceased' displayed in the avatar. The last tweet warned South Africans that 1 000 of their fellow citizens die needlessly from AIDS-related causes daily.

The innovative Twitter campaign created a virtual social network, recruited opinion leaders and used a new communication channel to achieve diffusion of HIV testing and awareness messages.

Discussion questions

1. Provide examples of communication channels from the case study.
2. Do you think the local celebrities had significant influence on the trending of the #HIVarmy hashtag? Justify your answer.
3. Why do you think the hashtag #HIVarmy was an innovative Twitter campaign? Justify your answer.

CASE STUDY 2

Targeting South Africa's affluent market[67]

The South African affluent market, which consists of LSM 10 consumers, is a market segment that is currently growing, despite the difficult economic climate in the country.

This market segment is driven by consumers who purchase luxury items, either to demonstrate that they are on the way to success or to provide them with high-end experiences that set them apart from the rest. The affluent market in South Africa is characterised by four sub-segments:

1. The moneyed aristocracy, which consists of consumers who were born into wealthy families and who are confident living a luxurious lifestyle. These consumers prefer the classic, well-known brands.
2. The established business magnates, who represent consumers whose wealth is based on business success and their professional choices in life. These consumers value personal service, experiences and limited editions of luxury items.
3. The self-made riches, which is made up of consumers who are highly ambitious and who are constantly striving to achieve success. For these consumers, the acquisition of a luxury brand represents status.
4. The deluxe aspirers, which comprises consumers who need others to recognise the fact that they have made it in life. For these individuals, luxury items demonstrate their success.

Although this market segment is currently dominated by affluent whites, it is believed that within the next twenty to thirty years, this will change as black high-end consumers become the majority. For marketers targeting the black high-end consumer, this segment offers exciting prospects as these consumers see luxury brands as reflecting their status in society.

Discussion questions

Assume that you are the marketing manager for a tourism agency that targets the LSM 10 market in South Africa. The owner of the travel agency has just read about the four sub-segments in the LSM 10 market segment and he wants you to make recommendations on how the agency should utilise this knowledge in marketing to each of these sub-segments.

1. Discuss how you would approach this task.
2. Explain under which conditions you would:
   - Combine these sub-segments and market to the whole LSM 10 market segment.
   - Select only one sub-segment and target it with your marketing mix.
   - Have a separate marketing mix for each market sub-segment.
3. What would be your suggested promotional strategy for each of the sub-segments, taking into account the characteristics of each sub-segment given in the scenario?

ADDITIONAL RESOURCES

- Definition of social class: https://www.chegg.com/homework-help/definitions/social-class-49
- Marxism and social classes: https://www.youtube.com/watch?v=GEqCmPOOusU
- Social class and consumer behaviour: https://www.youtube.com/watch?v=0gJBpeMHo7s

REFERENCES

1   New World Encyclopedia. 2015. Social class. Available at: http://www.newworldencyclopedia. org/p/index.php?title=Social_class&oldid=991054 (accessed on 19 June 2018).
2   Hoyer, W., Macinnis, D. & Pieters, R. 2016. Consumer behaviour, 7th ed. Boston: Cengage Learning; Khan, S. 2011. *Marketing mix strategy adaptation: A retail organisation's response to the global economic downturn.* Doctoral dissertation. Cape Peninsula University of Technology; New World Encyclopedia, ibid.
3   Mabena, K. 2009. 'Mandla' tells court to use his real name. Available at: https://web.archive.org/ web/20090610205539/http://www.thetimes.co.za/News/Article.aspx?id=1014300 (accessed on 10 July 2018).
4   Credit Suisse. 2017. Global Wealth Report. Available at: https://www.credit-suisse.com/ corporate/en/articles/news-and-expertise/global-wealth-report-2017-201711.html (accessed on 29 September 2018).
5   Korhonen, M. 2018. FACTSHEET: Measuring South Africa's (black) middle class. Available at: https://africacheck.org/factsheets/factsheet-measuring-south-africas-black-middle-class/ (accessed on 5 October 2018).
6   Lamb, C.W., Hair, J.F., McDaniel, C., Boshoff, C., Terblanche, N., Elliott, R. & Klopper, HB. 2015. *Marketing*, 5th ed. Cape Town: Oxford University Press.
7   Haupt, P. 2017. The SAARF Universal Living Standards Measure (SU-LSM™): 12 years of continuous development. Available at: http://www.saarf.co.za/lsm/lsm-article.asp (accessed on 25 October 2018).
8   Ibid.
9   Boshoff, C., De Meyer-Heydenrych, C., Human, D., Maduku, D., Meintjes, C. & Nel, J. 2017. *Principles of marketing*. Cape Town: Oxford University Press, 48.
10 http://www.saarf.co.za
11 Schiffman, L. & Kanuk, L. 2017. *Consumer behaviour: Global and southern African perspectives*. Cape Town: Pearson Education.
12 Ibid.
13 Lamb et al., op. cit.
14 Schiffman & Kanuk, op. cit., 282.
15 Khan, op. cit.; New World Encyclopedia, op. cit.; Schiffman & Kanuk, op. cit.
16 Hoyer et al., op. cit., 298.
17 Mpinganjira, M. & Dos Santos, M.A.O. (Eds). 2013. *Consumer behaviour: South African psychology and marketing applications*. Cape Town: Oxford University Press.
18 Blackwell, R., Miniard, P. & Engel, J. 2006. *Consumer behaviour*, international student ed. Mason, OH: Thomson Higher Education, 717–718.
19 Hanna, N. & Wozniak, R. 2001. *Consumer behavior: An applied approach*. Upper Saddle River, NJ: Prentice Hall.
20 Allevents.in. 2017. Castle Lager – Nyama Fest. Available at: https://allevents.in/ndola/castle-lager-nyama-fest/1244198525690914 (accessed on 4 June 2018).
21 Blackwell et al., op. cit., 524.
22 Joubert, P. 2010. *Introduction to consumer behaviour*. Cape Town: Juta.
23 Ibid.
24 Hoyer et al., op. cit., 298.
25 Ibid., 299.
26 Mpinganjira & Dos Santos, op. cit.

27 Hoyer et al., op. cit., 299.
28 Grasty, T. 2017. The difference between 'invention' and 'innovation'. Available at: https://
   www.huffingtonpost.com/tom-grasty/technological-inventions-and-innovation_b_1397085.
   html (accessed on 3 June 2018); Ostherr, K. 1998. Review of artificial mythologies. *A Guide
   to Cultural Invention*, Fall 1998 http://www.findarticles.com/p/articles/mi_qa3709/is_199810/
   ai_n8821092.
29 Rogers, E.M. 2003. Diffusion of innovation, 5th ed. New York: Free Press.
30 Ibid., 407.
31 Adapted from Hawkins, D.I., Best, R.J. & Coney, K.A. 1995. *Consumer behavior: Implication
   for marketing strategy.* Chicago: Irwin, 477–481.
32 Ibid.
33 Robertson, T.S. 1967. The process of innovation and the diffusion of innovation. *Journal of
   Marketing*, 31 (January): 14–19; Shambare, R. 2012. Predicting consumer preference for remote
   banking services in South Africa and Zimbabwe: The role of consumer perceptions versus
   personality variables. D. Tech Business Administration, Business School, Tshwane University
   of Technology.
34 Shambare, ibid., 89.
35 Robertson, op. cit.; ibid.
36 Perner, L. 2018. Diffusion of innovation. Available at: https://www.consumerpsychologist.com/
   cb_Diffusion_of_Innovation.html (accessed on 9 May 2018).
37 Curran, J.M & Meuter, M.L. 2005. Self-service technology adoption: Comparing three
   technologies. *Journal of Services Marketing*, 19(2): 103–113. Available at:
   https://www.emeraldinsight.com/doi/abs/10.1108/08876040510591411 (accessed on 29 October
   2018); Rogers, op. cit.
38 Rogers, ibid., 36.
39 Adapted from Banytė, J. & Salickaitė, R. 2008. Successful diffusion and adoption of innovation
   as a means to increase competitiveness of enterprises. *Engineering Economics*, 56(1): 54.
40 Ibid., 51.
41 Blackwell et al., op. cit., 550.
42 Hoyer et al., op. cit., 417.
43 https://www.capitecbank.co.za
44 Uber.com. 2018. Riding with Uber. Available at: https://www.uber.com/en-ZA/cities/
   johannesburg/ (accessed on 31 January 2018).
45 http://www.diskifans.com
46 Mofokeng, P. 2015. MTN slashes Steppa 2 pricing. TechFinancials.co.za. Online: techfinancials.
   co.za/2015/06/03/mtn-slashes-steppa-2-pricing (Accessed: 31 October 2018).
47 Hoyer et al., op. cit., 419.
48 Banytė & Salickaitė, op. cit., 52.
49 Blackwell et al., op. cit., 552.
50 Rogers, op. cit., 20.
51 Ibid.
52 Blackwell et al., op. cit., 554.
53 Arnould, E.J., Price, L.L. & Zinkham, G.M. 2005. *Consumers*, 2nd international ed. Boston:
   McGraw-Hill, 40.
54 Babin, B. & Harris, E.G. 2013. *Consumer behaviour*, student ed. Mason, OH: South-Western
   Cengage Learning, 294.
55 Rogers, op. cit., 22.
56 Adapted from ibid.
57 Ibid.
58 Blackwell et al., op. cit., 554.
59 Du Plessis, P.J., Rousseau, G.G., Boshoff, C., Ehlers, L., Engelbrect, M., Joubert, R. & Saunders,
   S. 2010. *Buyer behaviour: Understanding consumer psychology and marketing*, 4th ed. Cape
   Town: Oxford University Press, 118.
60 Ibid.

61 Rogers, op. cit., 221.
62 Hoyer et al., op. cit., 382.
63 Rogers, op. cit.
64 Hoyer et al., op. cit., 423.
65 Ibid., 298.
66 Brothers for Life. 2012. #HIVarmy case study. Available at: http://worldsbestcasestudies.com/social/twitter/brothers-for-life-hivarmy-case-study/ (accessed on 5 June 2018).
67 Bouwer, C. 2012. SA's big spenders keep buying. *Strategic Marketing*, 3: 14–17. Reprinted by permission of the editor of *Strategic Marketing* and author, Cara Bouwer.

CHAPTER 8

CULTURAL AND SUB-CULTURAL INFLUENCES ON CONSUMER BEHAVIOUR

Bertha Jacobs and Tania Maree

LEARNING OBJECTIVES

After reading this chapter, you should be able to:

* define the concepts 'culture' and 'sub-culture'
* describe how variation in cultures can be explained
* differentiate between material and non-material culture
* describe the characteristics of culture
* define the concept values
* differentiate between terminal and instrumental cultural values
* describe the different value typologies
* discuss South African cultural values
* describe how sub-cultures are formed
* define counterculture and cultural jamming
* identify and describe sub-cultures that are evident in South Africa
* discuss the importance of culture and sub-culture in consumer decision making.

Key terms

acculturation	environment-oriented values	norms
Afrocentric	Eurocentric	other-oriented values
beliefs	instrumental values	self-oriented values
counterculture	ideology	sub-culture
culture	language	terminal values
enculturation	multicultural	values

OPENING CASE STUDY

Zandile, Lizelle, Anna and Karyska are four women born and raised in South Africa. All four are working together at a financial firm in Johannesburg. Zandile was born in the Eastern Cape and studied at the University of Cape Town. She is an avid soccer supporter of Ajax Cape Town and over weekends watches their games in full supporter's gear. When she got married, her fiancé had to pay *lobola* to her father. She had a traditional Xhosa wedding which was attended by her relatives, friends and nearby community.

Lizelle was raised in an Afrikaans suburb in Pretoria. She does Cross-Fit twice a week at a local gym; on Saturdays she watches rugby with her family and friends and afterwards they *braai*. She is a Christian and got married in a church. Her wedding was attended by a small group of close family and friends and she wore a white wedding dress.

Anna is a Jewish lady who grew up in the Northern suburbs of Johannesburg. Celebrating traditional Jewish holidays such as Passover, *Yom Kippur* (Day of Atonement) and *Rosh Hashanah* (Jewish New Year) with her family is very important to her. When she turned thirteen a *Bat Mitzvah* was held with her extended family and friends to celebrate her coming of age. On her Bat Mitzvah she received money in multiples of 18 as this is symbolic of giving *chai* or life in Jewish culture.

Karyska is a Hindu lady who relocated with her husband from Durban. Her wedding was attended by almost 700 guests. During her wedding ceremony her father relinquished his responsibility over her to her husband. An important part of the wedding ceremony was the seven steps (*saptapadi*) the couple had to step together in a northern direction to seal their marriage. In her pass-time, she and her family are passionate cricket supporters and watch matches on TV or attend them at stadiums.

Although all four women's nationality is the same, their cultures, religious denominations and lifestyles within the South African context are not. Their differences are reflected in their consumer behaviour. (*The descriptions of the four women were stereotyped for the purpose of the case study.*)

8.1 INTRODUCTION

Culture and **sub-culture** are *external influences* in the consumer decision-making process (see Chapter 1). This means that the culture or the sub-culture we belong to, in many ways affects our consumption behaviour. What brands we buy, how we dress, what we eat, which restaurants we patronise and how we spend our free-time are all influenced by our different cultures.

This chapter takes a closer look at how various aspects of culture influence consumers' consumption. In the end, consumers express their culture through their choice of food, clothing, interior decor, housing and technology. Consumers' cultivation in their various cultures and sub-cultures has an extremely strong effect on what products they buy, how they buy and why they buy. In this chapter, the nature of culture, the variation found between cultures and the characteristics of culture are explained in more detail. This chapter also explores the influence of cultural values, characteristics of values and different value typologies.

Sub-cultures and how they are formed and the different sub-cultures that are unique to South Africa are also covered. The chapter concludes with marketing and retail applications regarding culture and sub-cultures within the context of consumer behaviour and how culture can be included in market research studies.

8.2 CULTURE DEFINED

Culture can be defined as the knowledge, values, beliefs, habits, customs and language that are shared by a specific group of people in a larger society, and are socially transmitted and acquired through learning from others in the group.[1] Each society has a dominant or mainstream culture which distinguishes it from other societies as well as distinctive sub-cultures which deviate from the mainstream culture. Various factors may lead to a *common*

Figure 8.1 Culture include shared values, beliefs, and customs unique to a specific community or society which result in common behaviour.

culture, such as nationality, language, religion, ethnicity, education, profession, sex/gender, family, social class, life-style and organisational factors.[2] Even though culture is often referred to as a nation's personality, many nations are **multicultural**. For instance, South Africa consists of diversified ethnic, religious and sub-cultural groups with different values, beliefs, customs and languages. The sense of belonging to one cultural or sub-cultural group can override the association to another cultural or sub-cultural group. This was found in a study about Muslim female students, whose affiliation to their Islamic religion was more important to them than their nationality.[3]

Even though definite differences between cultures exist, there are also *universal communalities*. Culture provides us with a way to organise and categorise our thoughts about how to do things. Customs that are common to most cultures are gender role and age differentiation, courtship, etiquette, funeral and marriage rites, taboos, religious rituals and bodily adornment.[4] However, the way these customs are practised will differ from one culture to another. For example, in both Western and Eastern cultures people mourn the dead, but in most Western cultures, people mourn by wearing black, while in various Eastern cultures people mourn by wearing white. Another example is courtship before getting married. In Western society men and women have the freedom to choose whom they want to date and eventually marry, but in many Eastern cultures marriages are arranged by the parents.

Culture is the pattern of shared behaviour by members of a group who regularly interact with each other and therefore all cultural behaviour is underpinned by the same important concepts such as values, beliefs, norms, customs and language:

- **Values** are defined as organising principles that direct our behaviour.[5] Values relate to what people believe is important in their cultural context and live by it.

- **Beliefs** are opinions or convictions individuals hold about what is acceptable and true. A person can have countless beliefs about almost everything, but will only have a handful of values.
- **Norms** are the standards for appropriate and unappropriated behaviour set and maintained by a culture.[6] Norms can refer to parenting, proper dress, beauty standards, manners, and gender and age expectations. Although cultures have different ideas about what constitutes proper or improper behaviour, all cultures have norms.
- **Language** is the verbal (i.e. words, characters, symbols and speech) and nonverbal (i.e. gestures, hand signs and facial expression) way we communicate in our group. Part of language is the abstract meaning and symbolism of verbal and nonverbal communication that are unique to each culture.

These concepts will be discussed in more detail throughout the chapter.

Because of the shared characteristics and differences that exist within a country's culture, it has many useful applications for marketers, such as market segmentation (i.e. the division of a market of consumers into smaller groups of consumers with similar needs and wants) and marketing communication, product development and brand extension. To satisfy any target market's needs and wants, you need to understand their culture.

APPLICATION

Consumer behaviour and cultural universal life events

Despite differences between cultures, there are various universal aspects all cultures share that are also evident in consumer behaviour. Gift giving, courtship, birth, weddings, funerals, graduation and rites of passage are some of the cultural universal life events which occur across different cultures, but differ between cultures in terms of how they are practised.

Discussion questions

1. Think of your own culture and how your culture handles these life events: what is the dress code (think of colours and styles for men and women), what food is served, what are the protocols or rituals involved, and what does the ceremony entail? Think of different products and services that are consumed in these life events.
2. Share and compare different cultures' practice of these universal life events in your class.
3. How can marketers be sensitive to cultural practices when marketing products to certain cultural groups?

8.3 VARIATION IN CULTURE

Culture is a complex, dynamic construct and refers to a phenomenon that is constantly evolving. People who share a national culture also share common cultural features which distinguish them from other national cultures. Different aspects of culture can be used to explain and describe the variations between them. The next section explains why cultures vary by describing material and non-material culture, functional areas of culture, and dimensions of culture.

8.3.1 Material and non-material culture

Examining a culture's **material and non-material patterns** can explain variation across cultures. This refers to all the material possessions as well as the shared behaviour of members of a particular culture:

- *Material culture* refers to tangible products, also called artefacts. This includes clothing, tools, houses, furniture and utensils to make food. The climate combined with the natural resources and technology available will determine the type of products made by the cultural group. Consider how houses across South Africa are built with the different materials that are available in the surrounding environment. For example, clay houses with grass roofs and Ndebele houses decorated with colourful geometric shapes are found in the northern parts; there are sandstone houses built with wrap-around *stoeps* in the middle parts of the country; and Cape-Dutch houses are found in the Western Cape. Cultural groups in different parts of South Africa will use different material to build their houses, and they might also decorate their houses differently.
- *Non-material culture* relates to the intangible aspects of culture. It includes the shared understanding of values, beliefs, ideology, standards, customs, religion and symbolic meaning. Although non-material aspects of culture are not visible, they manifest in products, people's behaviour and their choices. The shared meanings are ingrained in the members and transferred into the products that they make.

The difference between material and non-material culture stems from whether the focus is on the item itself or on the idea that relates to the making or use of the item. For example, beaded Zulu love letters (material culture) are made by unmarried Zulu girls and given as symbols of their love during Zulu courtship rituals. The different geometric beaded patterns and colours have specific meanings to express how they feel about their loved one (non-material culture). This custom with the shared symbolic meaning is understood by all members of the Zulu culture. Another example is the hipster sub-culture that has been found in many urban areas since the mid-2000s. The ideology (non-material culture) of this sub-culture is free thinking, creativity, embracing differences, and being socially and environmentally aware. Hipsters' ideology is visible in the consumption of specific products or services (non-material culture). They might attend indie and alternative music festivals, get their clothing at vintage or thrift shops, buy organic and artisanal foods at markets, and try out craft beers and alternative restaurants.

8.3.2 Functional areas of culture

Another way to explain variation among cultures is the *three functional areas of culture* (i.e. ecology, social structure and ideology).[7] The three functional areas of culture relate to how individuals in society organise themselves into a cultural system to manage everyday life:

- *Ecology* refers to the way in which a society adapts to its immediate natural environment. Technology associated with a culture is used to shape, acquire and distribute resources. For instance, compare more traditional cultures where food is cultivated and then sold or exchanged on local farmers' markets, to post-modern cultures where food is processed in factories, packaged, distributed and sold in stores across the country. Using available natural resources to adapt to the physical and social environments forms part of cultural ecology.[8] Consider how people dress differently in warmer and colder areas in the country. For instance, South Africans living in areas with extreme winters (the Free State and Northern Cape), for example, would buy more thermal insulated clothing than those living in warmer areas with mild winters (e.g. KwaZulu-Natal). Think of how retailers stock products to suit consumers' needs in these different climates throughout South Africa.

- *Social structure* of a culture is the way people in a society maintain and organise social life. This reflects how roles, social order and structure are formed within a culture. In some cultures, multigenerational families are common, where grandparents, parents and their children live together in the same house. These extended families make decisions jointly, in contrast to some cultures where family units are much smaller, sometimes even just a single mom and her child (see Chapter 9). Other ways of organising social order are by distinguishing between gender, age, social, occupational and marital status categories. Clothing especially is used to differentiate between male and female, young and old, married or single, and rich and poor. For example married couples wearing wedding rings to denote their marital status. Consider how brands and retail outlets today use brands and store image to differentiate between social standing, age and gender.

- *Ideology* refers to the outlook or mindset of a culture. It consists of the shared values, beliefs and ideals that interlink members of a culture and characterise the cultural group.[9] Cultural ideology prescribes the standard that group members aspire to achieve and define what is important. For example, ideals of equality, what is good or beautiful, and success are shaped by the ideology of a culture. Consider the different beauty ideals in different cultures. Culture will prescribe what is beautiful and members will cover, accentuate or modify certain parts of their bodies according to the beauty ideal of their culture. Today, countless beauty products (for example, corsets, sunbeds, hair straighteners, teeth whitening and dieting products, etc.) are aimed specifically towards helping consumers achieve the beauty ideal of their culture.

8.3.3   Dimensions of culture

Hofstede's model of culture proposes four dimensions to explain the variability across cultures.[10] *Dimensions of culture* relate to how individuals within a society interact with each other, how we view ourselves in relation to others, and what we are or do in our society. The four dimensions of culture outlined by Hofstede's model of culture are as follows:

* *Power distance* refers to how inequalities of power are handled by a culture. Cultures with higher power distance are more accepting of hierarchical order and differences in social status and class, while cultures that exhibit a lower degree of power distance emphasise equality and informality, and attempt to equalise the distribution of power. Examples of countries characterised by a high degree of power distance include China and Malaysia. In contrast, Israel and Austria have lower power distance scores.[11]

* *Individualism versus collectivism* refers to the degree to which a society is interdependent; where 'I' is the focus as opposed to 'we'. Cultures with a strong emphasis on individualism view the individual as central and for them, aspects such as freedom, individual achievement, human rights and gender are important. To the contrary, in collectivistic cultures, the group is prominent and group-related values such as loyalty, community well-being and harmony, as well as personal belonging, are appreciated.[12] The *ubuntu* concept in Africa is typical of a collectivistic approach. Australia and America have high individualism scores and consumers may express their individualism through buying products that are limited editions or one of a kind, in contrast to collectivist countries of Colombia and Ecuador, where consumers would express their belonging to a group by buying similar products.

* *Masculinity versus femininity* are, in this context, not related to gender. Rather, a masculine culture is characterised by competitiveness, personal achievement and success. In contrast, feminine cultures are typically driven by caring for others and quality of life. Examples of masculine countries include Japan and Switzerland, and feminine countries include Sweden and Denmark. This may also be reflected in the products produced in these countries. For instance, Sweden and Denmark highly value motorcars with safety and protection features (for example, Volvo and Subaru) whereas motorcar brands from Japan promote robustness and durability (for example, Toyota Hilux bakkies).

* *Uncertainty avoidance* indicates the degree to which a culture feels intimidated by uncertainty or ambiguous situations. Measures may be taken to avoid or manage change, for example implementing organised religion, sumptuary laws (for example, clothing restrictions) or political restraints. Some countries (for example, Singapore and Jamaica) embrace change and unknown situations and have low uncertainty avoidance. In contrast, countries such as Portugal and Greece have a high occurrence of uncertainty avoidance and tend to have an aversion towards uncertainty and change.[13] Cultures with high uncertainty avoidance might approach new products with suspicion, while those scoring low on uncertainty avoidance might be more susceptible to new products.

DISCUSSION

The Hofstede dimension scores for South Africa[14] are:

- *Power distance:* The country rates 49 on the Hofstede index, which means that South Africans are generally accepting of hierarchical order.
- *Individualism versus collectivism:* A high score of 65 indicates that South Africa is overall an individualistic society.
- *Masculinity versus femininity:* South Africa scored 63 in this dimension, indicating that South Africa is a more masculine culture.
- *Uncertainty avoidance:* A score of 49 on the measure indicates that South Africans prefer to avoid ambiguity and change.

Discussion questions

In your group, discuss the scores South Africa received on the Hofstede dimensions.

1. Do you think these scores reflect the cultural dimensions of South Africa?
2. How would you approach introducing a brand from South Africa into cultural markets with high uncertainty avoidance?
3. How would the different cultural dimension scores influence the type of products consumers in South Africa buy? Give examples.

The abovementioned models are useful for marketers to identify the major cultural differences between countries. For retailers and marketers, it is important to understand the variations between one national culture and another so as to develop appropriate product and marketing strategies that will satisfy the needs and wants of those specific target markets. By addressing cultural differences when extending a marketing mix to a different culture, global marketers can develop a marketing mix suitable to the broad characteristics of the targeted culture.

8.4 CHARACTERISTICS OF CULTURE

Culture has different characteristics that describe how it functions in society:

- Culture satisfies needs.
- Culture is transmitted from one generation to the next.
- Culture is learnt.
- Culture guides behaviour.
- Culture is enduring yet dynamic.
- Culture is shared socially.

In the section that follows, we will look at these characteristics in more detail.

8.4.1 Culture satisfies needs

All societies have universal needs such as physiological needs (i.e. food, water and sleep) and complex social needs (i.e. belonging to a group, acceptance by others) (see Chapter 2). The ways in which specific societies choose to satisfy these needs differ. Culture provides a way to satisfy the needs of

Figure 8.2 One of the strongest human needs is to belong to or to be part of a group.

people by setting the direction and standards of how to behave appropriately. For example, eating habits (i.e. which food is eaten, how the food is prepared and how it is eaten). Consider how different cultures prepare and eat beef. Another example is how culture provides the appropriate dress codes for occasions such as graduations, formal dinners, weddings, funerals or going to work. Culture will continue as long as it satisfies the needs of the people who adhere to it. However, material and non-material culture can be modified to meet new or changing needs within a culture. For example, think about how traditional clothing, in various ethnic groups in South Africa, has been modified to facilitate more modern needs of dressing within these ethnic groups. A specific example is the African head-wrap (*Dhuku/iDhuku*). Traditionally, how the head-wrap was tied indicated if a woman was married, a widow, young or old. Nowadays, women no longer need to display their life stage so explicitly and rather wear it to indicate their cultural heritage or as a fashion statement.

8.4.2 Culture is transmitted from generation to generation

Culture is transferred from one generation to the next through two specific processes: enculturation and acculturation. **Enculturation** is learning how to act and behave according to the cultural expectations of one's own culture. During enculturation you learn from your parents, siblings, family and others in the cultural group.

Acculturation is the process of learning about a culture that is foreign to one's own culture. Acculturation occurs when people from two different cultures come into continuous first-hand contact, and a change in the cultural patterns of either or both groups takes place. For example, a South African child actively learning about the South African culture (what to eat, what to wear, etc.) is engaging in enculturation. When the same South African child learns about the

Figure 8.3 Culture is transmitted and learnt from others.

Japanese culture, he or she is learning through acculturation. During acculturation, the adoption of new customs is possible, for instance the child may start eating sushi or learning karate. Consider how globalisation has contributed to acculturation in South Africa and made it possible for consumers to buy products not traditional to the country.

8.4.3   Culture is learnt

Children acquire knowledge of culturally acceptable behaviour as they grow up. The knowledge is passed down from generation to generation. Three forms of cultural learning have been identified:[15]

* *Formal learning* is learning by instruction, for example children get taught acceptable behaviour from significant others such as parents, grandparents and older siblings as they grow up. Boys and girls are cultivated differently in many cultures in terms of what is expected of them in terms of how they should behave, dress, their chores and responsibilities etc.). Consider how toys for boys and girls differ.
* *Informal learning* occurs when children learn behaviour through imitating the actions of other people, for example young children often mimic the actions of their parents, older siblings or family. Culture-specific skills like cooking, weaving, braiding hair or dressing are generally learnt from watching others practise them.
* *Technical learning* occurs in schools where children learn from teachers what is expected of them and what is considered to be acceptable conduct. For example, punctuality is taught through structured classes at schools.

Consider how you would buy specific products or brands, such as breakfast cereal, or prepare a Sunday lunch in a specific manner, because you were cultivated to it by your parents.

8.4.4　Culture guides behaviour

The cultural values, beliefs and norms that are shared in a society guide culturally acceptable behaviour. These values, beliefs and norms dictate what is considered to be suitable and appropriate behaviour. Examples are table manners, etiquette, age and gender roles. Culture also dictates what non-verbal communication (such as gestures) is acceptable. For example, the sign symbolising 'okay' (that is, the rounded thumb and index finger) is generally acceptable in South Africa, yet it is the symbol for the 'evil eye' in some Middle-Eastern countries, and is considered to be a rude and offensive gesture in Greece.

Figure 8.4　Culture dictates what non-verbal communication (such as gestures) is acceptable.

8.4.5　Culture is enduring yet dynamic

Culture is learnt and shared from one generation to the next (it is enduring). This makes it resistant to change and relatively stable. People tend to hold on to what they know and are familiar with. However, culture is also dynamic as it is continually changing to adapt to the environment. Cultural change can occur gradually over time, or be more drastic due to current events such as war, technological innovation or globalisation. As a result, culture allows for shifts in values over time. Values that are considered outdated might even be dropped.

For example, a study conducted among young Africans in South Africa indicated that even though most ethnic groups still consider the practice of paying *lobola* important, there are some who believe that *lobola* is an outdated practice. In addition, acculturation allows for different cultures to 'mingle' and influence each other's behaviour. Also, consider how products from other countries have become popular in South Africa, like sushi, pizza, parka jackets and fur coats.

8.4.6　Culture is shared socially

In all cultures, there are shared ideas, values, beliefs, norms and customs. These shared elements link the members of a culture to each other. Sharing of common values, customs and experiences is facilitated through language. In addition, there are several institutions that promote cultural sharing processes:[16] the family, educational institutions, houses of worship, mass media and virtual communities. The family is considered to be the primary transmitter of enculturation and as such, plays a vital role in consumer socialisation (the process where children learn how to be consumers). Educational institutions also assist in the sharing of culture: history, patriotism and basic learning skills are shared through schools and other educational institutions. Houses of worship (for example, churches, synagogues, temples or mosques) assist in transmitting religious teachings and provide spiritual guidance and moral training.

Mass media is a major influence in sharing cultural ideology. Mass media provide and disseminate information about new trends, habits and even customs.

Popular media is furthermore recognised as a growing cultural learning tool and as such, many people believe that limiting their children's television viewing habits minimises the potential negative learning that may result from this medium. A relatively new vehicle for the sharing of culture is virtual communities. Social networks (for example, Facebook, Twitter, Tumblr, Pinterest, Instagram and Snapchat) enable people to share ideas, opinions and new trends quickly. It should be noted that the diversity of the South African population means that commonly shared values are fewer in the general population than those shared within sub-cultures. This means that shared values will be specific to the culture or sub-culture you identify with rather than to the general South African culture. (This is discussed in more detail later in this chapter.)

Figure 8.5 Social media has become popular to share ideas and opinions about products and services

8.5 CULTURAL VALUES ARE REFLECTED IN CONSUMPTION

Values are guiding principles that motivate and direct our thoughts and actions and can be held on a personal (individual) or cultural (group) level. Our values are socially learnt in our respective cultures and points out what we view as important. In the cultural sense, values are considered socially and individually desirable or worth striving for. This stems from an individual's need to belong and be accepted in their culture. As values are instilled into us from an early age, we want to achieve these goals and adhere to these values.

For example, the ideal of our culture of achieving success would be something someone would want to strive for. From a consumer behaviour perspective, our preferences, dislikes and product choices are shaped by our values. In other words, if you have strong and established economic values, it will be important to you to save money and time when shopping. You will typically be more price sensitive and seek out bargains and products that are value for money.

8.5.1 Characteristics of values

Values are so ingrained within a person that we tend to behave in accordance with those values without consciously thinking about them. Consider going clothes shopping. If your culture favours certain prints or styles, you may automatically be drawn to these in stores, even if you are not fully aware of it.

Values have the following characteristics:
• Values are *relatively stable* and are less subject to change. Values will serve as standards to which consumers are committed, so they will not easily

deviate from making decisions about products and services with which they are satisfied. For example, if certain health products provide you with the desired effects in your exercise regime, you will stick with them.

- Values are *energised forces* that serve as the basis for personal goals. For example, consumers will be motivated to buy specific brands or patronise specific restaurants.
- Values are *expressive*, and individuals are motivated to communicate their values to others. Through purchasing specific products, consumers display to others what is important to them. For instance, if it is essential to be seen as a successful professional, a man may splurge on an expensive, tailor-made suit.
- Values are *receptive* and shape the way we would like others to respond to us. For example, others may react with envy or delight towards certain products (for example, clothing brands, cars or cell phones), indicating that they are impressed or aspire to buy such products as well.

8.5.2   Typologies of cultural values

Cultural values represent important beliefs that underlie consumer behaviour. Three typologies are presented in this chapter to classify cultural values, namely: terminal and instrumental values; self-orientated and other-orientated values; and Schwartz's value theory.

8.5.2.1   Terminal and Instrumental values

Rokeach[17] proposed that our values determine that 'certain patterns of behaviour or end states are preferable to others'. This relates to what is desired as the outcome (terminal) and what is desirable (instrumental):[18]

- **Terminal values** refer to values that are associated with desired end-states or favoured states of being. In other words, they are those things in life we aspire to achieve, can work towards and are important outcomes for us, for example a comfortable life, respect, freedom, security and happiness.
- **Instrumental values** are those that suggest preferred modes of action or desirable behaviour whereby terminal values can be achieved. Desirable behaviour refers to the personal characteristics that are important within us, in other words the method we use to achieve our goals or objectives, for example independence, competence, competitiveness and honesty.

Marketers often utilise terminal or instrumental values in developing advertising material. When focusing on terminal values, an advertiser would typically stress the emotional benefits of the advertised brand (for example, advertisements for perfumes that show people in love – where love portrays the end state). Alternatively, rational, logical specifications and the features of the brand emphasise instrumental values, for example retailer advertisements that feature special deals that could result in money saving, and unique benefits of a product that will improve durability and increase the service life of a product.

8.5.2.2 Other-oriented versus self-oriented values

Values across cultures are commonly categorised as other-oriented or self-oriented.[19] The other-oriented or self-oriented values will determine how consumers will make decisions as well as what products and services they will prefer:

- **Other-oriented values** focus on the relationships between members of a society. Cultures with strong other-oriented values are sensitive to the expectations of others in the group and regard social acceptance, conformity, obedience and harmony as important to them.[20] Cultures with strong other-oriented values practice joint decision making, considering the opinions of family and friends. Consumers are more aware of buying products that will be acceptable for their family and friends. Decision making is collective, like in many Asian cultures where product and services are purchased to conform to the community.
- **Self-oriented values** refer to the way in which the individual approaches life and individual goals. Self-oriented or inner-directedness relate to non-conformity or individualism. Cultures with strong self-oriented values prioritise personal goals and are less concerned about the expectations of others.[21] In these cultures, the emphasis is on what will benefit the individual, rather than the group. Especially Western cultures are more self-oriented and will, for example, focus on material well-being. Consumer decision making is more concerned about how products will reflect an individual's achievement and contribute towards self-fulfilment and self-expression through uniqueness. Think of luxury brands, certain colours (for example, gold and platinum) or certain types of fabric (for example, wool and silk) that a consumer will buy to signify success or individualism.

8.5.2.3 Schwartz's values

Schwartz's value theory defines ten universal value types that are recognised across cultures. Each value type has a different motivational goal (i.e. what drives it or what outcome members want to achieve).

The ten value types are divided into four categories which indicate different motivational goals, namely (1) openness to change, (2) self-transcendence, (3) conservation, and (4) self-enhancement. Certain values are congruent (these are those that are adjacent, for example openness to change and self-transcendence), while others are in conflict with one another (contradicting values) (these are those that are opposite one another, for example openness to change and conservation). Congruent values involve similar types of behaviour to express those values, while contradicting values are expressed by contrasting behaviours.[22] It is important to note that values have intensity and can be strong or weak, which indicates the effort that a person will make to achieve the desired end state.

The four categories have the following corresponding value types, as explained in the following section.[23]

- Openness to change
  - *Hedonism* is related to pleasure, sensuous gratification and enjoyment of life. For cultures with high hedonistic values, the enjoyment of experiences, products and services are important.
  - *Stimulation* refers to having an exciting life, novelty and being daring. When this value is pertinent, a person will be motivated to experiment with different products and will require of retailers to offer a large product variety or experience-based consumption (for example Build-a-Bear)
  - *Self-direction* is related to creativity, independence and choosing one's own goals, thus not depending on others for advice and direction.
- Self-transcendence
  - *Universalism* includes being broad-minded, and having wisdom and a sense of equality (impartiality). The discovery of the truth or the search for knowledge is a motivational factor for these consumers.
  - *Benevolence* refers to honesty, helpfulness and loyalty. When this value is strong, convenience and comfortable shopping environments, as well as loyalty programmes and good service, will be important.
- Conservation
  - *Tradition* includes being humble, respectful and accepting one's original culture or religion. Having a meaningful life and being driven by spiritual aspects like modesty and nobility will be important to consumers within cultural groups who have strong traditional values.
  - *Conformity* is about complying with social expectations. The need for approval and social acceptance are important in these cultures. Consumers will, for example, dress for acceptance and to conform to the group, which is in contrast to persons with a strong self-direction, as discussed earlier.
  - *Security* involves maintaining the social order, having harmonious relationships, stability and safety. Consumers from cultures with strong conformity and security values may make product choices to enhance a feeling of unity within the group.
- Self-enhancement
  - *Power* refers to achieving social status, authority and wealth. The motivational goal is to be successful. Consumers will purchase luxury products or status brands to impress others or to signify their economic status.
  - *Achievement* includes being successful, ambitious and influential. Success is signified by buying status-bearing products to impress or influence others. Achievement and power are examples of congruent values that will be achieved through similar consumer behaviour.

8.5.3 South African cultural values

The South African society is defined by two major cultural outlooks, namely **Afrocentric** and **Eurocentric**. A gap exists between these two outlooks, and as the diverse cultures within the country indicate, there are marked differences in how people from each outlook approach life:

- *Afrocentric* refers to the African notion of collectivism, which is a shared and participative approach to life. The concept of *ubuntu* underlies Afrocentricity and it states that a person can only be a person through other people. It focuses on enjoying life as opposed to amassing riches, and the success of the individual is not considered to be as important as group acceptance and recognition. The concept of the self is seen as something 'outside', in relationship to the world around the person.
- *Eurocentric* refers to Westernised values (commonly originating from European cultures) that generally focus on individualism. An example of Westernised values is illustrated in the 'protestant work ethic', which refers to the values represented by thrift or frugality, hard work, discipline and independence. Thus, the achievements and performance of the individual are appreciated, and materialism, work ethic and individual success are deemed important. In this European-style approach, the self is seen as something 'inside', like a container of thoughts and strengths.[24]

It should be noted that the intermingling of diverse cultures in South Africa causes the changing of traditional values through acculturation. In addition, the exposure of people to Western values through mass media is thought to increase Westernisation. Traditional African values, for example, have adapted to some aspects of Western values, sometimes to the extent that traditional values are replaced. African youth is reported to be attracted to Western values because of the perceived economic prosperity associated with them.[25] Also look at the content in Research Box 8.1 on page 225 for examples of how Afrocentric and Eurocentric cultural outlooks have developed or merged in the South African market.

DISCUSSION

South Africa is known as the 'Rainbow Nation' for good reason: it has a diverse and colourful national culture, and contains many sub-cultures. South Africa's population is as interesting as it is diverse. The country's cultural diversity is wonderfully illustrated through the influences of its different ethnic tribes, with unique languages, traditional dress and food patterns. Just some of the different ethnic groups found in South Africa are Khoikhoi, San, Ndebele, Xhosa, Zulu, Tswana, Sotho and Venda.

In contrast, European influences from the Germans, Greek, Portuguese, British, French and Dutch are also captured in the national culture. With Nelson Mandela's inauguration in April 1994, he wore a Western three-piece suit (see this web site for images: https://www.enca.com/south-africa/throwback-to-nelson-mandelas-inauguration). Although Nelson Mandela was a Xhosa, he did not wear the traditional dress that men wear for special occasions, comprising of a white tunic, strands of beaded necklaces and an *ingcawa* (a white and black blanket) over the shoulders (https://theculturetrip.com/africa/south-africa/articles/an-introduction-to-south-african-traditional-dress/).

Discussion questions

1. Why do you think Nelson Mandela wore a Westernised suit for his inauguration?
2. Can you give an example of the different cultural influences on the clothing practices of South Africans?
3. How do you think Afrocentric and Eurocentric values influenced Nelson Mandela's choice?
4. Which other values, explained in section 8.5, may also have played a role in his decision making?
5. During Nelson Mandela's presidency, he regularly wore the Madiba shirt to various occasions (see this web site for the Madiba shirt story https://www.presidential.co.za/brands/presidential-shirt-1/products-story.html). Why do you think the Madiba shirt became such an important symbol of South Africa's unity and a popular product till today?

8.6 SUB-CULTURES

A **sub-culture** is a smaller distinctive group or segment of individuals within a broader society who shares the same pattern of behaviour. The term *'microculture'* is often used instead of sub-culture to define a smaller group within a larger culture that displays similar preferences and behaviour, but has its own distinct characteristics apart from the mainstream culture.[26] Members of a sub-culture or microculture will exhibit similar consumer behaviour such as buying the same brands, dressing alike, eating at the same restaurants or engaging in the same activities. For example, Comic Con is a sub-culture event attended by consumers who are fans of comic books fantasy and science fiction movies and art. In text above, the hipster sub-culture was also explained. Other examples would be Harley-Davidson motorcycle riders, or sport supporter clubs (for example, the Barmy Army cricket supporters with their distinct dress, mannerisms and songs).

A **counterculture** can be defined as a sub-culture that rejects societal norms and values and seeks alternative lifestyles.[27] Countercultures often openly challenge or reject the norms and values of the mainstream/dominant culture and are characterised by non-conformity to the dominant culture. Especially younger consumer groups are inclined to engage in countercultures because they are less invested in the dominant culture and often do not agree with the values, beliefs and norms of the dominant culture. For example, the hippies in the 1960s were opposed to the conventions of the time, like making war or using nuclear weapons; they rather followed an ideology of living in peace with others and in harmony with nature and spirituality. Another example is environmentalist or green consumers who are against the abuse of natural resources and hence demand eco-friendly or organic products, less packaging and fair-trade practices from retailers. An extreme form of counterculture is *cultural jamming*. This is a form of cultural resistance where consumers protest socially against any form of exploitation, destruction of nature or cruelty to animals, and sometimes engage in eco-terrorism like attacking animal breeding or testing facilities.[28]

8.6.1   Classification of sub-cultures

Members of sub-cultures have an already established connection or association with each other because of their shared interests, values, ideas and behaviour. Sub-cultures, therefore, form important 'natural' market segments that are often targeted by marketers for specific products or services. In addition, sub-cultures and countercultures are important consumer market segments because they represent consumers with new and emerging needs and wants, which will create opportunity for retailers to develop new products and services. Consider the hip hop sub-culture that started during the 1970s. With the hip hop sub-culture the need for unique street-style clothing, music, collectables and accessories emerged. Throughout its growth into the 80s and 90s, new clothing styles and ways to create the look developed with this sub-culture.

Even though sub-cultures share common characteristics with the mainstream or dominant culture, members of a sub-culture have unique traits that differentiate them from the larger population.[29] Again, consider the distinctive style of dress of members of the hip hop sub-culture. The style of dress originated from urban streetwear and includes elements of large baggy pants, bright colours, baseball caps, basketball sneakers and large gold chains. Although many of these dress elements were also worn by the mainstream culture, it was not styled in the same way, giving them a distinctive look.

Sub-cultures emerge through a common position, or mutual values and beliefs. Sub-cultures can be formed based on factors such as age, religion, geographic (location), lifestyle, activities or ideology. Figure 8.6 illustrates

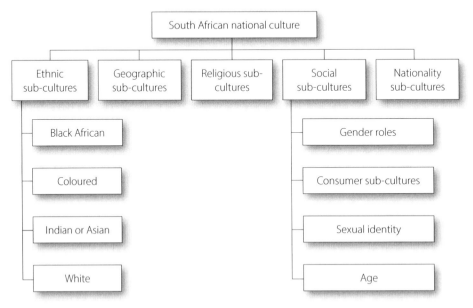

Figure 8.6 Factors used to classify sub-cultures in South Africa

the most common factors used to classify sub-cultures in South Africa, namely ethnicity, geographic location, religion, social factors and nationality. Each of these sub-cultures also has several subsets that are evident within the major sub-cultural grouping. These sub-cultures are discussed in more detail below.

8.6.1.1 Ethnic or population sub-cultures

The ethnic sub-culture of a society refers to the different ethnic or population groups within a country. In 2017, Statistics South Africa (Stats SA) estimated the mid-year population of South Africa at 56,52 million. In South Africa, four major ethnic or population groups exist: black African (45 656 400/80%), coloured (4 962 900/8,8%), Indian or Asian (1 409 100/2,5%) and white (4 493 500/8%). Figure 8.7 presents the ethnic population distribution in South Africa.

The black African population group is the most prevalent population group in the country, followed by the coloured and white population groups. The black African population therefore represents the largest market segment in South Africa. The black consumer segment comprises different ethnic groups (for example, Nguni, Sotho Tswana etc.) as well as various sub-cultures (for example, Born Frees, black upcoming professionals, Black Diamonds or the new comfort class, etc.; see Research Box 8.1). The upcoming black middle class has become a fast-growing and influential consumer group and is estimated to represent around six million of the population.[31] In 2012, the annual collective spending power of the black middle class within South Africa was estimated at R400 billion.[32]

Within the black African population group, further distinction based on tribal affiliation is made to form distinct black ethnic/tribal sub-cultures. The South

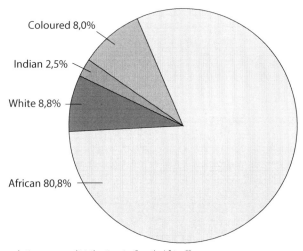

Figure 8.7 Ethnic population group distribution in South Africa[30]

African government information web site (http://www.info.gov.za/aboutsa/people.htm) refers to the following ethnic/tribal sub-groups within the black African population group:
- Nguni (including Zulu, Xhosa, Ndebele and Swazi people)
- Sotho-Tswana (southern, northern and western Sotho/Tswana groups)
- Tsonga
- Venda

The Khoi and San people also form part of the black African ethnic/tribal sub-cultures. The black African tribes are differentiated by variances in cultural practices as well as language (isiNdebele, isiXhosa, isiZulu, Sepedi, Sesotho, Setswana, Siswati, Tshivenda and Xitsonga).

8.6.1.2   Geographic sub-cultures

The geographic sub-cultures in South Africa are represented in different regional areas in the nine provinces in the country. Table 8.1 shows the percentage distribution of the total South African population across the nine provinces. The largest group of people live in Gauteng, followed by KwaZulu-Natal. The province with the smallest number of residents is the Northern Cape.

Following is a brief outline of the nine provinces and their respective populations (according to the South African Government Information[33] and Statistics South Africa, *Mid-year population estimates*[34]):
- *Eastern Cape:* This province is extremely diverse in terms of climate and landscape. It contains regions as varied as the dry Karoo and the forests of the Wild Coast. The major language group in the Eastern Cape is isiXhosa. About 11,5% of the total South African population reside in this province.
- *Free State:* Situated in the heart of the country, the Free State is characterised by farmlands, mountains, goldfields and towns scattered across its

Table 8.1 Population distribution across the provinces[36]

	% of total population	Population estimate
Eastern Cape	11,5	6 498 700
Free State	5,1	2 866 700
Gauteng	25,3	14 278 700
KwaZulu-Natal	19,6	11 074 800
Limpopo	10,2	5 778 400
Mpumalanga	7,9	4 444 200
Northern Cape	2,1	1 214 000
North West	6,8	3 856 200
Western Cape	11,5	6 510 300
Total	100	56 521 900

landscape.[35] Of the 5,1% of the total South African population living in the Free State, 64% speak Sesotho and 12% speak Afrikaans.

- *Gauteng:* Although this is the smallest province, it is the most densely populated one, being home to 25,3% of the total South African population. It is also known as the 'Place of Gold' or *Egoli*, and is referred to as the economic hub of the country. Gauteng boasts a more even spread of prominent language groups, with isiZulu- (22%), Afrikaans- (14%), Sesotho- (13%) and English- (13%) speaking people. Its high level of urbanisation allows for a diverse and almost cosmopolitan mix of people.

- *KwaZulu-Natal:* This province lies at the coast and is a popular vacation destination because of its warm year-round climate and welcoming beaches. IsiZulu is the most prominent language of KwaZulu-Natal. The province is also known as the 'Zulu Kingdom' and the Zulu cultural influence is characteristic of the province. It has also been influenced culturally by its relatively large Indian population. KwaZulu-Natal is the second most populated province, with 19,6% of the total South African population living there.

- *Limpopo:* This is the most northern part of South Africa and is also referred to as the Great North. It is named after the Limpopo River, which forms its northern border. Around half of the 10,2% total South African population living in Limpopo speak Sesotho (sa Leboa), followed by Xitsonga.

- *Mpumalanga:* This province is also known as 'The place where the sun rises'. It is situated to the east of the country and is a region that is extremely diverse geographically. It has mountains, valleys, waterfalls and forests, and is also known for its vibrant wildlife. Siswati and isiZulu are the most prominent languages spoken in Mpumalanga, influencing its cultural landscape.

- *Northern Cape:* This province is the largest in size but the least populated as only 2,1% of the total South African population lives there. The most dominant language groups are Afrikaans and Setswana. Its cultural heritage includes San rock art and it is home to the last remaining San people, who reside in the Kalahari.

- *North West:* The 'platinum province' is named for its platinum mining initiatives. It is a sunny and warm province, centrally located in the country. The most prominent language spoken in the North West province is Setswana.

- *Western Cape:* Home to the 'Mother City' (Cape Town), the Western Cape is a popular tourist destination and boasts a culturally diverse population. Afrikaans is the language group most represented in this province, followed by isiXhosa. About 11,5% of the total South African population reside there.

APPLICATION

Because of the diverse sub-cultures in South Africa, consumers' behaviour differs across regions. Marketers use information on the characteristics of the relevant population groups to customise their marketing messages for specific geographical areas.

8.6.1.3 Religious sub-cultures

The major religious sub-cultures found in South Africa are African traditional beliefs and religions that originated in Europe and Asia such as Christianity, Judaism, Islam, Hinduism and Buddhism. A Statistics SA Household Survey of 2015 reveals that most South Africans are Christians (86%) and most likely to live in Northern Cape (98,4%) and the Free State (97,7%). The second-largest group consists of people who follow ancestral, tribal, animist or other traditional religions (5,4%) and about 5,2% indicated they have no religious affiliation. Followers of Islam (1,9%) mostly reside in the Western Cape, Gauteng and KwaZulu-Natal. Hindus comprise about 0.9% of the South African population and about 3,3% of the population of KwaZulu-Natal. Only 0,2% of the South African population indicated to be Jewish and 0,4 undetermined or another religion.[37] Figure 8.8 provides a visual representation of this data. Religious sub-cultures have set values, beliefs and norms that manifest in different ritualistic behaviour such as wedding and funeral rites, celebrations and festivals, distinctive ways of dressing and eating. This has implications for consumer behaviour and marketing (see the discussion box below).

Discussion questions
1. Which rituals are prominent in your religion or one of which you are aware?
2. Describe two products that you feel are prominent in the religious festivals of your own religion or one of which you are aware. How are they usually marketed around the time of the festival?

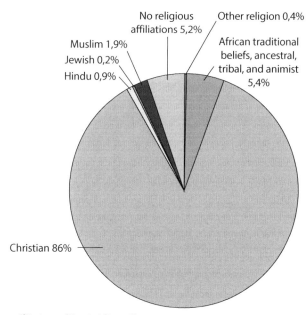

Figure 8.8 Religious affiliations of South Africans[38]

8.6.1.4 Social sub-cultures
Social sub-cultures can be formed based on various factors such as gender, age, sexual orientation, lifestyle, activities or technological interests.

Gender sub-cultures
Gender sub-cultures are natural market segments based on a categorisation of gender as male or female. Marketers often use gender sub-cultures for gender-specific products. In this way, for example, Nivea traditionally markets skin-care ranges aimed at women, but now also offers a line of skin-care products specifically formulated for men. Retail stores such as Truworths Man and Markham specifically target men. However, the roles of men and women in modern society have evolved. The traditional roles of 'husband who works' and 'stay-at-home mom' are no longer considered to be the norm. Modern women have careers and full-time occupations, make notable financial contributions towards their households, have more spending power, and enjoy more authority in terms of the household's financial decisions than traditionally was the

case. This makes them a viable and desired market segment for more than just cosmetics and household products. They are, for example, also targeted by financial institutions such as banks and investment companies, car merchants and travel companies.

Traditional male roles have also evolved because of women entering traditionally male-dominated careers. Men have become more involved in household tasks such as child rearing.[39] An outcome of this evolution is that men are now portrayed as fathers and as being involved in household activities in advertisements. In addition, the advent of the so-called 'metrosexual' (a modern man who cares about his physique and uses grooming products) has led to many beauty salons expanding their product and service ranges to target men who are looking for a bit of pampering. As men have become more interested in their appearance, they have also become more interested in fashion. In 2017, menswear contributed to 42% of the total South African retail industry value.[40] Consider the implications of changes in gender role expectations for new products and services.

Age sub-cultures

Consumers can be grouped according to their age. For example, a global teenage (thirteen to nineteen years of age) sub-culture exists. Members of this sub-culture have shared similarities across national cultural borders. In South Africa, approximately 9,5 million of the population can be classified as teenagers between 10 and 19 years.[41] This is a large segment and is targeted by companies as diverse as radio stations and clothing retailers.

Age sub-cultures contain generational groups or cohorts, which is the term used for people who grew up during a particular time period and who are characterised by shared life experiences, such as technological changes in their era and common trends in their lifetime. The generational cohorts are natural market segments with similar needs and wants as well as consumer behaviour. Consider how retailers adapt their store image and brands to acknowledge consumer age sub-cultures (compare Miladys or Truworths with YDE or Legit).

Marketers distinguish between the following active age sub-cultures:[42]

- *Seniors or the grey cohort (elderly people):* This generational cohort can be divided into three segments: young-old (65–74 years old), old (75–84 years old) and old-old (85 years and older). This cohort grew up in the Depression era and want value for their money and economic benefits. Seniors can also be divided into new-age elderly and traditional elderly. New-age elderly differ from their traditional counterparts for various reasons. For example, they perceive themselves to be younger than their actual age, they are financially secure, they have higher levels of life fulfilment and they are more innovative. Because of these characteristics, they are more likely to try out new products than their more traditional peers, allowing for marketers to target them as possible opinion leaders. However, seniors are a diverse group ranging from those who do not utilise modern technology to those who are well versed in new technology. Cyberseniors are experienced internet users, breaking the stereotype of elderly people being fearful of it.

- *Baby Boomers:* The Baby Boomers derived this label because of the many babies born after World War II. Boomers were born between 1945 and 1964, and represent a large and generally affluent market segment. They grew up in the 1950s and 1960s youth culture. In South Africa, this age group comprises approximately seven million people,[43] and they tend to buy for reasons of indulgence and to respond well to promotional messages that promote image building.[44]

- *Generation X:* Members of this generation were born between 1965 and 1980 and represent about 10 million people in South Africa.[45] Characterised as valuing personal freedom and striving for an enjoyable life, they grew up in an era with high divorce rates and often spent time alone as their parents were working. These factors may contribute to this generation's focus on strong family values and prioritising family before their careers. Other influential factors were the rock and pop music culture of the 1970s and 1980s, together with the anti-fashion statements of countercultures such as the punks and skinheads. Generation X consumers are technologically savvy and knowledgeable about the media and global events. They are therefore not easily taken in by advertising that aims to reach a mass market and does not differentiate between groups. To reach this segment, marketers must be believable and sincere in their approaches, and link their campaigns to the distinctive values of this generation.

- *Generation Y:* Born between 1981 and 1999, the members of this generation (also called the millennials) comprise more than fifteen million consumers in South Africa.[46] As one of the largest generational cohorts in the country, it is an important market segment. In addition, this group contains young people who are entry-level adult consumers and who will probably retain the brand preferences they build now for the rest of their lives. For these reasons, amongst others, this segment is valued by marketers of a variety of products. Generation Y consumers are technologically savvy and very connected. Sometimes referred to as the 'always on' generation, they are constantly in contact with their family and friends through different technologies. This generation is known to be optimistic and open to new experiences. As a result, they are innovators, who love to shop and are fashion drivers. Products such as new technologies and fashion are often aimed at them as they are likely to try out new things and distribute information about them, often through social media.

- *Generation Z:* Those born from the year 2000 onwards are the youngest consumer cohort. About 21 million people in South Africa belong to this cohort.[47] Members are very informed and grew up with computers, the internet, smart phones and advanced technology. Generation Z consumers are highly influential in their parents' buying decision making and often dictate what the family eat, where they eat and what activities they do. They are also called KIPPERS (kids influencing their parents' purchases). Using technology (for example, apps, the internet and digital advertisements as well as social media) is very important to reach this cohort. See techno-hippie in the research box under section 8.9.

Consumer sub-cultures

Consumer sub-cultures include brand and virtual sub-cultures.

- *Brand sub-cultures:* These are groups that are loyal to a particular brand. For example, sport supporters are known to be loyal to their preferred sports team brand. In South Africa, popular local soccer teams include the Vodacom-sponsored Kaizer Chiefs and Orlando Pirates. The popular motorcycle brand, Harley-Davidson, boasts a unique owners' club, the Harley Owners Group (HOG). This club has more than a million club members in South Africa and promotions are often run through its web site (http://www.harley-davidson-capetown.com/harley-owners-group).
- *Virtual sub-cultures:* These are communities that operate online, such as users of social media. Thus, users of Facebook can be classified as a virtual sub-culture. Virtual social communities are explored in more detail in Chapter 12.

Gay and lesbian sub-culture

The gay and lesbian sub-culture refers to the sizeable homosexually oriented sub-culture. The gay and lesbian population in South Africa totals around 4,9 million people (see Black Pinks in Research Box 8.1) Most members of this market have higher disposable incomes than the average consumer. The Lunchbox Media Gay Consumer Profile 2012 surveyed gay and lesbian consumers. The report highlights some important statistics that should be of interest to marketers and retailers:[48]

- Gay advertising is more likely to attract the attention of gay and lesbian consumers.
- Most of the respondents indicated that they would specifically support marketers that advertise in gay ('pink') media, for example mambaonline.com, the *Gay Pages* and *The Pink Tongue*.
- This sub-culture consists of early adopters, which means they are innovative in terms of trying out new brands.
- This is a brand-loyal consumer group who prefer it if brands identify with them.
- Half of the respondents indicated that they believe that they are ignored by mainstream advertisers and that gay people are not accurately portrayed in the media.
- Luxury brands are important to gay and lesbian consumers, and they make regular purchases online.

8.6.1.5   Nationality sub-cultures

Nationality sub-cultures refer to the ancestral origins of people and relate to their country of birth. South Africa is home to immigrants from all over the world. Some have been living in South Africa for many generations and identify themselves as South African, yet still have strong ties with their family's country of origin and cultural heritage. Examples include Greeks, Portuguese people, Eastern European Jews, Hungarians and German immigrants (and/or their descendants). South Africa also has a sizeable Asian population. The nationality

Figure 8.9 Cyber seniors are experienced internet users, breaking the stereotype of elderly people being fearful of technology.

sub-culture is often represented by owners of specialty stores who sell products (often food) that are particular to a foreign country, such as Chinese supermarkets and German grocers.

8.7 MARKETING AND RETAIL APPLICATIONS OF CULTURE AND SUB-CULTURE

From this chapter, it is evident that culture is an important external factor in groups' and individuals' consumer behaviour. Culture explains why some products and services appeal to some consumer groups and how consumers use products within their cultural context. If marketers and retailers understand cultural values, beliefs and customs they will have better insight into how best to position their products for their respective target markets.

Cultural values, for instance, influence product choice and dictate purchases or purchasing behaviour. Because different cultures and sub-cultures may attach different meanings to particular symbols and objects, marketers need to consider the unique interpretations of brand logos, advertising imagery and brand symbols when marketing to different cultural groups. Sensitivity and awareness of how and why consumers in different cultures act differently is important. For example, consumers with self-oriented values appreciate unique and prestigious products that indicate their individualism and they favour advertising that focuses on the needs and preferences of individuals. In contrast, cultures that value collectivism favour advertising that depicts groups.

Having insight into the customs and traditions of cultures is also important. Different sub-cultures display unique behaviours that are associated with their unique customs. Religious groups, for example, often need to adhere to dietary restrictions. Followers of Islam are restricted to halaal foods and Jewish consumers follow kosher dietary laws. Knowing about this culturally specific behaviour allows retailers to have sections that are dedicated to foods for unique groups. Customs associated with life events such as weddings, funerals, coming of age, graduation and birth also provide many opportunities to retailers to serve sub-cultural groups.

Understanding how factors such as age, gender, ethnicity, language, religion, geography and nationality influence members from different cultures and sub-cultures is highly important to formulate effective marketing strategies and to understand differences in consumers' behaviour in the market place. For example, teenagers and adults will adopt different products, which provides opportunity for the proper introduction of new products and services. Marketers and retailers in South Africa, a multicultural country with diversified consumers, especially need to cater for cultural differences to ensure that their marketing strategy is appealing to a particular culture and not offending anyone.

8.8   RESEARCHING CULTURE

Consumers' culture is more complex to measure than, for instance, consumers' demographic characteristics such as age, income, gender and population group. Straightforward questions like what is your age, gender etc. will suffice to measure these variables. However, culture is quite complex because of the variables (for example, values, beliefs, norms, customs, language and technology) that underlie it and which have to be considered. Also, culture is influenced by various factors such as historical events (for example, war, political elections and economic recessions), popular culture (for example, movies, music and entertainment) as well as globalisation (for example, technology, acculturation and immigration trends) that are not easy to predict.

Marketers doing market research and studying consumers' different cultures have to consider various factors in order to understand consumers' needs and wants. Techniques that are used to measure culture are content analysis, ethnographic fieldwork and value measurements,[49] briefly discussed in the following sections.

8.8.1   Content analysis

Content analysis is the study of written and visual material. It involves examining pictures and words, and describing them in order to understand the meaning and ideas behind them. This allows the researcher to draw narratives and conclusions.

Because the content of a society's media (for example, advertisements) reflects prevailing societal norms, content analysis is an effective way to measure changes in cultural values or differences between various cultures. For example, the content of advertisements today can be analysed and compared to the content of advertisements for similar products from previous decades in order to assess changes in the portrayal of women in advertising media. A content analysis study conducted on South African television commercials concluded that women were not often depicted as sex objects.[50] This result reflects the prevailing South African attitude of protecting women from sexual objectification and abuse, something that contributes to the uniqueness of the South African culture.

8.8.2 Ethnographic fieldwork

This technique is a qualitative research method (thus non-numerical) that entails the immersion of the researcher (actual participation and observation) in the culture under study. This immersion enables detailed observation of the actions, interaction, emotions and beliefs of members of a society, and results in compiling rich data about the study group. The researchers can infer the major values that underlie the behaviours of the society from this data.

8.8.3 Value measurements

Survey (quantitative) research methods can be used to collect data on the values of a society, usually through structured questionnaires that produce quantifiable data. These surveys often require consumers to rank order specific values based on importance. The Rokeach Value survey, for example, consists of eighteen terminal value items (such as a comfortable life and freedom) and eighteen instrumental value items (such as ambition and courageousness).[51] The results of such surveys are utilised by marketers to segment consumers based on their prominent value orientations.

When using these three methods to collect data in consumer behaviour studies, it is important to focus on the meaning of words and symbols in context because they can have different meanings in different languages and cultures. Other important aspects to consider are authority orientation, power distance, time perspective and the collectivistic versus individualistic approach of the culture under study (see section 8.9).[52]

8.9 INTERNATIONAL CROSS-CULTURAL MARKETING AND RETAIL STRATEGIES

As cultures vary in many ways, when marketing internationally, the retailer and/or the marketer needs to be aware of the cultural values and uniqueness of the targeted nation. One of the most obvious adaptations that may be necessary when expanding into a foreign country is language. A South African retailer wishing to expand into another country will need to consider converting marketing material and store displays into the dominant language spoken in the foreign market. In Africa, for example, Portuguese is the official language of Angola and Mozambique, French is spoken in Cameroon and Niger, and English and Swahili are the official languages in Kenya.[53]

Apart from the actual spoken language, the context of language is also important. Generally, collectivist societies tend to be high context, whereas individualistic nations tend to be low context in terms of language. In a low-context country such as America, communication is extremely clear, and words retain their context across various situations.[54] Low-context language means that there is no hidden meaning and that the words used reflect exactly what is meant. Information is exchanged explicitly. In contrast, in high-context cultures such as those in Asian countries, language is not explicit as the meanings of words vary depending on the parties speaking to one another, the circumstances and the place where the communication is taking place.

Other cultural influences also need to be considered when engaging in cross-cultural marketing. The dominant religious values in a country will influence the choice of marketing and retail strategies. For example, when opening a restaurant in a Muslim country, adhering to halaal laws and regulations will be important, while allowing different eating or buying sections for families and single people (for example, in MacDonald's) would be a wise retail layout strategy.[55]

Before entering a foreign market, a cross-cultural consumer analysis should be done. Apart from language and meaning differences, it is advisable to research the following across cultures:[56]

● marketing segmentation opportunities (for example, income, age, gender and other segmentation variables may vary widely),
● consumption patterns, perceived benefits, evaluative criteria (for example, the same product may be consumed in different ways across nations),
● family structure and socio-economic conditions (for example, the decision-makers in the family may have different roles in different countries), and
● research conditions and possibilities (for example, experienced researchers might not be available in that country).

Understanding the international consumer and his or her culture is essential, but so too is being aware of cultural dynamics when dealing with distributors, suppliers, governments and competitors in the foreign market. A company hoping to expand its business into a foreign country needs to ensure that it conducts proper research first, attending to all the aspects mentioned. Not everyone in a country is the same and sub-cultures exist within any nation. Small things such as a brand symbol or the colour used in packaging can mean different things in different countries. For example, in China, the colour red is a symbol of joy and festivities, whereas in many Western cultures, it is associated with danger.

RESEARCH BOX 8.1

Marketers need to use any available tools when defining their target markets. The Living Standards Measure (LSM) has been an invaluable segmentation tool for many years. However, Deon Chang[57] argues that it is not sufficient any more as there have been many socio-cultural changes since its inception. Technology has also had a major impact on society and segmenting people based on ownership of certain products is limiting. Flux Trends, led by Chang, proposes a new cultural profile of modern South Africans: one that includes aspects such as interests, cultural impact and spending power.

In *New Urban Tribes of South Africa*,[58] Chang gives an overview of twelve so-called tribes that are unique to South Africa. He identifies them as follows:

- *Diamond Chips:* The sons and daughters of the original Black Diamonds, they are characterised as world-aware free spirits who hold strong opinions. They are technologically sophisticated, fashionable and wealthy.
- *Faith-based Youth:* These young people hold strong beliefs based on the Bible, but they are not part of the traditional religious institutions of their parents. They rather opt for the Missional Church, which focuses on personal relationships.
- *Techno-hippies:* These people are described as geeks who are well versed in the latest techno-logical gadgets and platforms. They combine their 'tech savviness' with a preference for living green and supporting initiatives that aim to save the planet.
- *Empowerment Kugels:* These are the modern Black African version of the typical kugel: ladies of leisure with expensive lifestyles. They depend on their husbands, who are often prominent, well-off businessmen or politicians.
- *Domestic PAs:* A new interpretation of the domestic maid, the Domestic PA manages the home of her usually affluent employer (madam). She cooks, raises children and, in many cases, is responsible for the household grocery shopping, which provides her with considerable spend-ing and decision-making power.
- *Afrikaans Artistes:* These Afrikaans-speaking South Africans pursue creative arts (especially music), and are zealous in protecting and promoting their language and the Afrikaans culture.
- *Indo-Asians:* Consisting of Indian and Chinese people, the Indo-Asians are a small but economi-cally powerful group. They value family above all else and have a strong work ethic.
- *Black Pinks:* This group encompasses members of the black African gay community, who gener-ally have good jobs and enjoy spending money on travelling and socialising in trendy places. They are fashionable and brand conscious, and demand high quality.
- *Single Parent, Double Life:* These are young, single women who are juggling 20-something life and motherhood. Despite falling pregnant at a young age, they still follow their dreams and spend money on themselves. This lifestyle is made possible because their parents often take over their child-rearing responsibilities.
- *Bieber Brats:* Also referred to as Generation Z, this tribe consists of spoilt nine- to 12-year old chil-dren who are real digital citizens as a result of growing up with the internet and sophisticated technology. Despite their youth, they are consumer savvy and cultured in their tastes.
- *Lost Generation:* This tribe encompasses the disenchanted majority that has no employment, education or power. They desperately want to rise above their circumstances to the level where showy cars and high-end fashion would represent their desired status.
- *Rainbow Revolutionaries:* This group displays a broad sense of community. They are liberal, environ-mentally conscious and politically active. They tend to be well educated and socially aware.

SUMMARY

Consumer behaviour is influenced by the broader culture and sub-cultures of which the consumer is part. Culture is the set of beliefs, customs and values that are shared by members of a society. Children learn cultural customs and accept-able behaviours from their families as well as from institutions such as schools and the media. The major South African cultural values relate to Afrocentricity and Eurocentricity.

Within the broader South African national culture, several sub-cultures are found. Sub-cultures are generally based on ethnicity, geographic region, religion, social group and nationality. Within each sub-culture, smaller sub-sets often exist, such as gender, sexual identity and age, within the social sub-culture. Sub-cultural customs and rituals often dictate acceptable consumption behaviour and therefore enable marketers to target sub-cultures as market segments.

When planning to expand their business into foreign markets, companies need to consider variations across cultures, such as language. Furthermore, research needs to be conducted to determine how cultural differences may impact on marketing and retail decisions. Various techniques for measuring cultural values exist. Marketers use data collected in cultural studies to develop indexes of values. This allows them to plan their segmentation and promotional approaches based on prevailing cultural values. Differences between cultures and change in cultural values over time can also be measured using value measurement instruments.

SELF-ASSESSMENT QUESTIONS

1. How would you define culture?
2. What are the characteristics of culture?
3. Distinguish between terminal and instrumental cultural values.
4. Differentiate between other-, environment- and self-oriented values.
5. What is the difference between Afrocentricity and Eurocentricity in the South African context?
6. How would you define sub-culture? Provide an example.
7. Describe various sub-cultures that are present in South Africa.
8. How do you think sub-cultural behaviour is learnt?
9. Can you think of examples of countercultures in South Africa?
10. What do these countercultures wear, how do they live, what do they buy?
11. Why are sub-cultures and countercultures important to marketers?
12 Can you think of new products that were developed especially for a sub-culture or counterculture?

EXPERIENTIAL EXERCISE

Assume that you are product developer for a major South African food retailer with a diversified consumer market, ranging from international to local consumers. Through globalisation, certain food products are now available in South Africa. The original ways of preparing and using these products have become blurred. Typical South African food products like biltong and chutney are now available in Australia and the UK. Also, food from various countries is now available locally, like M&Ms (USA), stroopwaffels (Netherlands), pizzas (Italy), sushi (Japan), burritos (Mexico), etc.

To promote the food retailer's wide range of international and local food products, you must present ideas of fusion food to sell in the retailer's convenient food lines.

1.   What would you consider in your fusion food strategy?
2.   How would you market these products to different consumers?

CASE STUDY 1

Active wear for the Muslim market[59]

Ayesha is a 20-year student attending a South African university. The campus environment is a multicultural mix where students from various backgrounds interact. Muslim religion prescribes very specific dress practices for Muslim women. Even though the Muslim culture dictates collective behaviour and dress codes for its members, female Muslim students follow varied dress practices on campus.

Depending on the country, Muslim garments comprise of a *hijab* (a head scarf), an *abaya* (a long black dress combined with a head scarf or face veil), *niqab* (a face veil worn by some Muslims) and *burqa* (type of veil and covering that conceals the woman's entire body including the eyes). In some instances, Muslim female students combine their Muslim garments with fashionable clothing, wearing only the *hijab* with denim jeans and modest tops.

Although Ayesha can sometimes only wear a *hijab* with fashionable clothing to campus, her clothing should always be modest, appropriate and loose-fitting. On Fridays, a holy prayer day in the Islam religion, Ayesha usually wears an *abaya*.

Ayesha is a good athlete, but her religion does not allow her to wear active wear as it is usually revealing and tight fitting, and Muslim garments are not very practical for athletic practice.

Discussion questions

1. Which sub-cultures are evident from the case study about Ayesha?
2. How is acculturation evident from the case study?
3. Identify a terminal and an instrumental cultural value from the case study.
4. If you were a brand manager for a well-known active wear brand, what product lines could you include to reach religious sub-cultures? Think of the different Muslim garments and how this could translate to active wear products.
5. Why do you think retailers and marketers need to understand different cultures when positioning their products?

CASE STUDY 2

A substitute for breakfast

Garth has acquired a position as a product manager at Fusion Foods. Fusion Foods is a company that specialises in healthy, alternative food supplements. The company is launching an alternative to breakfast cereals called 'AM2PM' and Garth is managing this new line. The new product (AM2PM) will be manufactured and sold in the form of an 'on-the-go' cereal bar. It contains all the necessary vitamins and nutrients to sustain the consumer from the time of consumption (presumably in the morning or AM) until dinner time (in the evening or PM).

If it is used in conjunction with a healthy eating programme, AM2PM can also be marketed as a diet supplement to people who want to lose weight or who are on kilojoule-controlled regimens. It is suitable for vegetarians and has been approved as kosher and halaal.

The proposed flavours are mixed berries, peach and banana. There are two major possibilities for this product: being marketed as a breakfast alternative or as a weight-loss product. Its direct competitors include the Kellogg's Special K bar, the Nestlé Milo bar and various other breakfast alternatives available in supermarkets and health shops.

The promotional campaign envisioned for the AM2PM bar includes commercials on television (leading to maximum exposure), magazine advertisements (aimed at selected audiences) and outdoor billboard advertisements next to major highways around the largest cities in the country. Fusion Foods is aware of the diversity of the South African market and wishes to run its printed campaign in four languages to reach the major population groups in the country.

Discussion questions

1. Fusion Foods wants to advertise in four languages. Propose four languages that would be suitable. Base your answer on the ethnic profile of the country. Hint: You need to find information on language groups within the major ethnic groups.
2. Access the South African Audience Research Foundation web site at http://www.saarf.co.za and find the latest All Media and Products Study (AMPS) figures for magazines. Using these circulation figures and the information given in the case study, propose four magazines that would be suitable for advertising the new breakfast bar.
3. Advise Garth on specific consumer sub-cultures that would be suitable for this new product. Be practical and specific in your answer.
4. Garth is considering positioning the product in the slimmer's market, primarily focusing on female consumers. Provide guidelines to Garth on appropriate slogans that he could use in promoting AM2PM to the slimmer's market.

ADDITIONAL RESOURCES

Asante, M.K. 2010. Afrocentricity and the argument for civic commitment: Ideology and citizenship in a United States of Africa. *The Annals of the American Academy of Political and Social Science*, 632: 121–131.

South African History Online. People of South Africa: Origins, language, culture and identity. (http://www.sahistory.org.za/article/defining-culture-heritage-and-identity)

Visit the web sites of the following tourism organisations:

*   Eco Tourism South Africa (http://www.ectourism.co.za/experience_eastern_cape/2/Ten_Heritage_and_Cultural_Excursions)
*   Gauteng Tourism Authority (http://www.gauteng.net/)
*   Tourism KZN (http://www.zulu.org.za)
*   Limpopo Tourism and Parks Board (http://www.golimpopo.com/)
*   Mpumalanga Tourism and Parks Agency (http://www.mpumalanga.com/).

Visit the web site of The Harley Owner's Group (http://www.hdavidson.co.za/harley-owners-group).

Visit the fashion sub-cultures web site (https://www.highsnobiety.com/2016/05/30/african-fashion-subcultures/).

Visit the following web site to learn more about South African sub-cultures such as the youth subculture called Izikhothane, the Smarteez (a fashion sub-culture) and the Zef sub-culture associated with music groups such as Die Antwoord: https://www.houseofyork.co.za/article/south-africans-and-their-subcultures.

REFERENCES

1   Schaefer, R.T. 2001. *Sociology: A brief introduction*, 4th ed. New York: McGraw-Hill Higher Education, 65.
2   Usunier, J.C. & Lee, J.A. 2005. *Marketing across cultures*. London: Pearson Prentice-Hall, 11.
3   Albrecht, M., Jacobs, B. Retief, A. & Adamski, K. 2015. The role of important values and predominant identity in the dress practices of female Muslim students attending a South African university. *Clothing and Textile Research Journal*, 1–17.
4   Eicher, J.B. & Evenson, S.L. 2015. *The visible self: Global perspectives on dress, culture and society*. London: Bloomsbury, 36.
5   Kaiser, S.B. 1997. *The social psychology of clothing: Symbolic appearances in context*, 2nd ed. New York: Fairchild, 289.
6   Schaefer, op. cit.,72.
7   Solomon, M.R. 2011. *Consumer behavior: Buying, having, and being*, 9th ed. Upper Saddle River, NJ: Pearson Prentice-Hall, 569.
8   Kaiser, op. cit., 530.
9   Ibid., 51.
10 Gillespie, K. & Hennessey, H.D. 2011. *Global marketing*, 3rd ed. Mason, Ohio: South-Western Cengage Learning, 64.
11 Usunier & Lee, 62.
12 Ibid., 63.
13 Ibid.
14 Hofstede, G. 2012. National cultural dimensions. Available at: https://geerthofstede.com/culture-geert-hofstede-gert-jan-hofstede/6d-model-of-national-culture/ (accessed on 23 July 2018).
15 Brijball, S., Parumasur, S. & Roberts-Lombard, M. 2012. *Consumer behaviour*, 2nd ed. Claremont, Cape Town: Juta, 77.
16 Babin, B.J. & Harris, E.G. 2012. *Consumer behaviour*, student ed. Mason, Ohio: South-Western Cengage Learning, 165; Schiffman, L.G. & Wisenblit, J. 2015. *Consumer behavior*, 11th ed. Upper Saddle River, NJ: Pearson Prentice-Hall, 367.

17 Rokeach, M. 1973. *The nature of human values.* New York: Free Press, 5.
18 Du Plessis, P.J. & Rousseau, G.G. 2003. *Buyer behaviour: A multi-cultural approach to consumer decision-making in South Africa,* 3rd ed. Cape Town: Oxford University Press, 397–400.
19 Triandis, H.C. 1989. The self and social behavior in differing cultural contexts. *Psychological Review,* 96(3): 509–510.
20 Ibid., 510.
21 Ibid., 509–510.
22 Bardi, A. & Schwartz, S.H. 2010. Values and behavior: Strength and structure of relations. *Personality Social Psychology Bulletin,* 29(10): 1208.
23 Schwartz, S.H. 2012. An overview of the Schwartz theory of basic values. *Online Readings in Psychology and Culture,* 2(1). doi:10.9707/2307-0919.1116.
24 Brijball et al., op. cit., 83.
25 Soontiens, W. & De Jager, J.W. 2008. South African values: A reflection on its Western base. *African Journal of Business Management,* 2(12): 224.
26 Babin & Harris, op. cit., 177.
27 Schaefer, op. cit., 79.
28 Solomon, M.R. & Rabolt, N.J. 2004. *Consumer behavior in fashion.* Upper Saddle River, NJ: Pearson Prentice-Hall, 492.
29 Kardes, F.R., Cline, T.W. & Cronley, M.L. 2011. *Consumer behavior: Science and practice,* international ed. Mason, Ohio: South-Western Cengage Learning, 261.
30 Adapted from Statistics South Africa. 2017. *Mid-year population estimates.* Pretoria: Statistics South Africa, 2.
31 News24. 2018. Measuring the (black) middle class: What are the facts? Available at: http://www.news24.com/Analysis/measuring-the-black-middle-class-what-are-the-facts-20180307 (accessed on 5 July 2018).
32 News24, ibid.
33 South African Government Information. 2012. South Africa's people. Available at: http://www.info.gov.za/aboutsa/people.htm (accessed on 4 July 2018).
34 Statistics South Africa. 2017. *Mid-year population estimates.* Pretoria: Statistics South Africa. Available at: http://www.statssa.gov.za/publications/P0302/P03022017.pdf (accessed 4 July 2018).
35 South African Government Information, op. cit.
36 Statistics South Africa, 2017, op. cit.
37 Statistics South Africa. 2015. Household survey 2015. Available at: http://www.statssa.gov.za/publications/P0318/P03182015.pdf (accessed on 4 July 2018), 27.
38 Adapted from ibid.
39 Brijball et al., op. cit., 126.
40 Marketline. 2018. Apparel retail in South Africa. Marketline industry profile. Available at: http://www.advantage.marketline.com.uplib.idm.oclc.org (accessed 18 May 2018).
41 Statistics South Africa. 2016. Demographic profile of adolescents in South Africa. Available at: http://www.statssa.gov.za/publications/Report%2003-00-10/Report%2003-00-102016.pdf (accessed on 26 June 2018).
42 Hawkins, D.I. & Mothersbaugh, D.L. 2010. *Consumer behavior: Building marketing strategy,* 11th ed. New York: McGraw-Hill/Irwin, 124; Solomon, op. cit., 540.
43 Statistics South Africa, 2017, op. cit., 10.
44 Schiffman & Wisenblit, op. cit., 415.
45 Stats South Africa, 2017, op. cit.,10.
46 Ibid.
47 Ibid.
48 Lunchbox Media (LBM). 2012. LBM gay consumer profile 2012. Available at: http://themediaonline.co.za/2012/06/profile-of-south-africas-gay-consumers-revealed/ http://www.mambaonline.com/2012/06/18/sas-gay-consumer-revealed-in-new-report/ (accessed on 5 July 2018).

49 Peter, J.P. & Olson, J.C. 2008. *Consumer behavior and marketing strategy*, 8th ed. New York, NY: McGraw-Hill, 282–283.

50 Holtzhausen, T., Jordaan, Y. & North, E.J. 2011. The portrayal of women in South African television commercials. *Southern African Business Review*, 15(3): 178.

51 Kardes et al., op. cit., 281.

52 Du Plessis & Rousseau, op. cit., 408–409.

53 Wolfstone Translation. 2013. Official languages of the world. Available at: http://www.wolfestone.co.uk/official_languages.php (accessed on 5 July 2018).

54 Gillespie & Hennessey, op. cit., 73.

55 Hawkins & Mothersbaugh, op. cit., 99.

56 Schiffman and Wisenblit, op. cit., 437.

57 Chang, D. 2012. *New urban tribes of South Africa*. Johannesburg: Flux Trends and Pan Macmillan South Africa.

58 Ibid.

59 Albrecht et al., op. cit.

60 Coetzee & Maree. 2012.

CHAPTER 9

FAMILY AND HOUSEHOLD INFLUENCES ON CONSUMER BEHAVIOUR

Mercy Mpinganjira

LEARNING OBJECTIVES

After reading this chapter, you should be able to:

- discuss the difference between family and household
- explain the main functions of the family
- discuss changes in family and household structure, and their influence on consumer behaviour
- describe the key roles that members play in the family or household decision-making process
- discuss factors that affect the role played by different family members in household decision-making processes
- explain the major causes of conflict in family or household decision making
- identify the influence of family life cycle stages on family consumption activities
- discuss why it is important for marketers to understand family and household decision making.

Key terms

consumer socialisation	family	non-family household
extended family	household	nuclear family
family	family life cycle	
	household	

OPENING CASE STUDY

Having recently graduated from university and gotten his first job, John moves in with his older brother, Sipho. Three months into living with Sipho, John is getting increasingly unhappy. Things are not as he envisioned them to be. One day he decides to phone his mom and share what is causing his unhappiness. Their conversation went as follows:

Mom: Glad you called, my boy. How is life in the city?

John: I miss home. I am tired of doing all the household chores for Sipho, including shopping. He seems to enjoy giving orders on what needs to be done, but won't do any of it himself. He seems to be forgetting that I am also working.

Mom: Be good to your brother. Don't forget that he is older than you.

John: Mom, he is just three years older than I am and besides, we both have full-time jobs. What he is doing is not fair.

Mom: So what are you going to do about it?

John: I plan to have a talk with him so that we can divide the household chores. I don't mind doing the shopping and cooking. We can decide on the menu for the week and that will help us plan our shopping. However, he needs to help with cleaning the house and washing dishes.

Mom: You can share the cooking responsibilities as well. It's high time Sipho learnt to cook good meals.

John: (laughing) Yes, cooking is not really Sipho's thing. I am happy to teach him how to make a few good dishes, though. He told me that before I moved in, he used to eat a lot of junk food because he was too lazy to prepare meals for himself. He

likes having me here and does not want me to move out. He says that he loves eating home-cooked food every day.

Mom: Okay, my boy, all the best with the cooking lessons. Be patient with him as it is not always easy to teach an old dog new tricks.

9.1 INTRODUCTION

In the year 2016, the population of South Africa was estimated at 55.25 million.[1] In the same year, the number of households was projected at 16.6 million.[2] This means that the average household size within South Africa is 3.3 people. The majority of these households are family units. This shows that although marketers often look at consumers as individuals, many consumption-related activities may take place in the context of a group. The various members of these household groups often exert an influence on what is bought or consumed.

This chapter offers the reader an understanding of family and household influences on consumer behaviour. It starts by defining the terms 'family' and 'household', and then looks at the main functions of the family before examining changes that have taken place in family and household structures over the years. The chapter then considers family and household decision making, focusing on the roles played by the different members and on causes and management of conflict. The last part of the chapter looks at the family life cycle and its influence on consumption activities, before highlighting why it is of strategic importance for marketers to understand family and household decision making and its influence on consumer behaviour.

9.2 FAMILY AND HOUSEHOLD

The terms 'family' and 'household' are often used interchangeably in literature. However, their meanings differ.

9.2.1 What is a family?

The **family** is considered to be the basic social unit of society. It is traditionally defined as a group of persons related by blood, marriage or adoption, who function together for member security and perpetuation of the unit.[3] Family relations

Figure 9.1 A nuclear family

are brought about by blood ties, marital ties or adoption. Blood ties apply to biological relationships established by birth, while marital ties are relations by marriage and include the partners themselves as well as in-laws. Adopted children also form part of a family.

The two basic family types are the nuclear family and the extended family:

- **Nuclear family:** This is a family composed of a married couple and their children. Members of a nuclear family are thus no more than one generation apart. Changes in society, including high levels of divorce and a large number of couples choosing not to have children, have resulted in the increase in the number of families considered to be variations to the typical nuclear family. The two common variations include *married couples with no children* and *single parents with children*. Single-parent families can also be the result of the death of a spouse. Another term for nuclear family is immediate family.

- **Extended family:** Traditionally, this is a common type of family in Africa and in most other developing countries. It is a type of family that includes the nuclear family plus other relatives, such as grandparents, uncles, aunts, cousins, nieces, nephews and in-laws. A typical extended family is

Figure 9.2 Extended family

composed of more than two generations of family members. Just as with nuclear families, there are different variations of the typical extended family. One of these is the blended family created when two single parents get married and their two families are combined. The other is the polygamous family, where the father has more than one wife, each of whom may have children with the father. Step relatives thus form part of an extended family.

9.2.2 What is a household?

The term '**household**' refers to an individual or a group of people (who may be related or unrelated) occupying a single housing unit. A household is a basic buying and consumption unit in a society. Households are commonly divided into two groups:

- **Family households:** A family household is a group of people related by blood, marriage or adoption occupying a single household unit. As noted before, there are different types of family. When members of each type of family occupy a single housing unit, they form a family household, for example a nuclear family household or an extended family household. Family households may also have additional people living with them who are not related by blood to the family.
- **Non-family households:** These are households that do not comprise family members (relatives), for example housing units occupied by a single person or by friends who are house sharing.

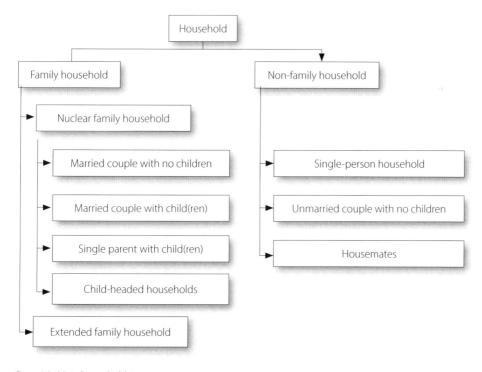

Figure 9.3 Main household types

Around the world, an average household unit consists of more than one person and the family household is the most common type of household. Members of a family have specific functions in relation to other members. Section 9.3 looks at the main functions of the family in relation to consumer behaviour.

9.3 MAIN FUNCTIONS OF THE FAMILY

The family plays a significant role with regard to consumer behaviour, including providing for the socialisation of members, ensuring the economic well-being of members and providing emotional support to members.[4]

9.3.1   Socialisation of members

Families play a critical role in the consumer socialisation process of members. The socialisation of children in particular is considered to be the central function of the family. **Consumer socialisation** refers to the way that consumers develop their abilities, approaches and understanding when they are in the marketplace.[5] Through consumer socialisation, people gain knowledge about products, services and markets, and this knowledge is useful during their decision-making processes.

Although the socialisation process is often discussed with reference to children, the process is in fact a life-long one. Consider the example of a mother asking her son about what features are important when buying a laptop computer. Through the consultation process, the mother acquires the knowledge needed to make the right purchase decision. Childhood, however, presents the family with the greatest opportunity to influence the socialisation process.[6] As children grow older, the influence of non-family forces, including friends and the media, increases and the family's influence may decrease accordingly.

Family members become socialised as consumers by means of direct consumer socialisation and indirect consumer socialisation:[7]

- *Direct socialisation* involves purposive teaching or sharing of information with the aim of passing on knowledge. For example, parents may engage in discussions with their children on a variety of consumption-related issues such as budgeting, how to evaluate different products and the best outlets at which to shop. The knowledge acquired through such discussions influences the attitudes of these children towards products as well as their consumption behaviours long after they have left home.
- *Indirect socialisation* occurs within a family, with children observing adults, who act as role models. Children learn a lot about consumer-related activities through their parents and may start to imitate them. The people being observed are often unaware that the child is learning something from their behaviour. Consider a child accompanying a parent on a shopping trip to a mall. Such trips provide children with the opportunity to learn things (such as where a particular shop is situated and what the shop sells) through observation. Children may also learn negotiating skills by observing their parents interacting with salespeople.

9.3.2 Economic well-being of members

Families provide for the economic well-being of members through the sharing of their resources. For example, families provide financial resources to their children and other dependants to enable them to meet the costs of living, including food, clothing, shelter, health care and education. While parents provide for their children economically until they are old enough to become financially independent, there is often a reversal of roles later in life. In most African families, adult children are expected to take on the responsibility of providing for their parents and other relatives.

Traditionally, the husband is the main economic provider for the family. However, changes in the family structure due to the devastating impact of HIV/AIDS in Africa have resulted in a growing number of child- and grandparent-headed households. In such families, children and grandparents respectively become the main economic providers. They often have limited income-earning abilities, resulting in many of these families living in poverty.

The growing number of women joining the workforce has also resulted in women contributing more financially. Pooling of resources from different members often helps to improve the purchasing power of the family. Families also contribute to the economic well-being of members through involvement in joint production activities. For example, it is not uncommon for people to employ relatives in family businesses or for members to volunteer their time and skills working in businesses owned by other family members. Research shows that children who grow up working in a family business often acquire skills that give them an advantage when establishing their own businesses later in life.[8] The family business thus acts as a nurturing ground for economic success later on.

In most rural communities, family members are jointly involved in cultivating the garden to ensure an adequate food supply for the home. Some of the produce may be sold to provide cash to meet other needs. In so doing, the family is economically providing for its members.

9.3.3 Emotional support of members

Providing emotional support is one of the primary functions of the family. This includes showing love and care to family members.[9] There are different ways in which members of a household can provide emotional support to each other, including the following:

- Respecting other members' feelings and choices
- Buying gifts for each other

Figure 9.4 Families provide emotional support.

- Verbal expressions of love (for example, complimenting members)
- Sticking together during difficult times

While the family has some fundamental functions, changes in its structure are having an impact in terms of the level of support individuals are able to give or get from their family members. Section 9.4 looks at some of the changes taking place in family and household structures, and the effects that these changes are having on consumer behaviour.

9.4 CHANGES IN FAMILY AND HOUSEHOLD STRUCTURE

The structure of families and households has undergone some significant changes over the years, such as average size, headship, age, ethnic diversity and social structure.

As families and households are the largest consuming units in society, these changes tend to have a significant impact on the marketing of goods and services.

9.4.1   The average size of families and households

The general trend in most countries, including developing countries, has been towards smaller family and household sizes.[10] Factors that may have contributed to this include the following:

- *Lower fertility rates:* Birth rates are declining. One of the reasons is that readily available birth control has made it easier for women to control the number of children they have, with many of them opting for fewer. Another is that women are more career oriented and choosing to have their children later in life (in their 30s and early 40s, instead of in their 20s) or not at all.

- *Rapid urbanisation:* Many people have been moving from rural areas to urban areas. This has meant, for most African families, a break from the extended rural family unit into smaller, often nuclear, family units.
- *Rising cost of living:* Many people are having to prioritise their obligations to their immediate families rather than their extended families.
- *Growth in divorce rates:* High levels of divorce have resulted in a higher number of household units of smaller sizes, as each partner gets a home of his or her own.
- *Delayed marriages:* Youth in urban areas often pursue further education to improve their employment opportunities and want a good start in their careers before getting married, which has resulted in the growth of single-person households.

The marketing implications of this have been enormous. For example, because family and household structures are getting smaller, there is an increased demand for smaller-sized packaged products. An increase in single parenthood has resulted in more people having to juggle work and home obligations,[11] leading to a higher demand for convenience foods (such as ready-to-eat meals) and domestic help (such as house cleaners, au pairs and nannies). The ability to afford these things has also increased because of the growing number of dual-income households.

However, breakdowns in extended family ties and high divorce rates have left some family members in an economically disadvantaged situation. Thus while the number of households may have increased, the purchasing power of some of them is not strong.

9.4.2   The headship of the family or household

In most African households, the father is traditionally the head of the household. However, a growth in the divorce rate has resulted in an increase in households headed by women. Other factors that have contributed a great deal to changes in household headship in South Africa and most other African countries are the HIV/AIDS epidemic and the structure of the labour market.

HIV/AIDS has resulted in a high growth in mortality rate, especially among people within economically active age groups. Often both the father and mother of a family pass away, leaving young children to look after themselves. The older children in such cases often take on the responsibility of looking after their younger siblings.[12] HIV/AIDS has thus resulted in an increase in child-headed households in many African countries. Such households are commonly characterised by high levels of poverty,[13] with many unable to afford even basic necessities such as food.

The labour market has also contributed greatly to changes in household structure in most African countries. Jobs tend to be more readily available in big cities and other urban areas than in rural areas. This results in an increase in rural-to-urban migration. In many rural communities, it is the men who move to the city, leaving their spouses and children at home. While the husband may still provide for the family, the result has been an increase in women-headed households in these areas.

9.4.3   The age of family or household members

In most Western countries, declining birth rates and growing life expectancy have resulted in an increase in households comprising elderly people. Aging households tend to have special demands, particularly in terms of health-related products and services.[14] However, many African countries have a relatively low life expectancy, especially in the light of the HIV/AIDS pandemic, which has resulted in a decline in aging households.

The HIV/AIDS pandemic in Africa has greatly affected people in the economically active age group of society. While most African countries have made progress in rolling out medication aimed at containing the disease, the economic costs have been high for many families. In most cases, the breadwinners are the ones who fall sick and become unable to provide for their families. Children and relatives also bear the brunt of the disease as some family members have to leave their occupations to take up the role of caregivers. In such cases, the income and therefore the purchasing power of the household suffers.

9.4.4   Growth in ethnic diversity of families and household

Increased migration of people owing to improvements in transportation services and the general impact of globalisation have resulted in a growth in multi-cultural communities in most urban areas around the world. People of different ethnic backgrounds and from different parts of the country, the continent and beyond are increasingly living within the same neighbourhoods and sometimes intermarrying. This has wide implications on the demand for products, as each ethnic group tends to have unique consumption patterns.[15]

Many food retailers are responding to this by stocking products that appeal to different ethnic groups. Targeting these groups may, however, demand adapting marketing approaches. It may even be necessary to use different languages in communications and on product packaging.

9.4.5   Changes in social structure

Changes in the family and household social structure affect the way in which people relate to each other and the roles that they take on. As indicated previously, the traditional African family is extended in nature. The disintegration of the extended family structure over time due to such factors as adoption of Western culture and movement of people to different places of work has reduced family members' sense of connectedness. High levels of individualism are also having an impact, especially in urban areas. Studies have found that many families in Western countries are becoming 'roommate families', where members structure their time and activities independently of each other.[16] It is not uncommon for each member to prepare his or her own food, have his or her own car and even buy groceries specifically for him- or herself.

In most families and households, there are usually well-defined roles for each member. In the traditional African family, the husband is the head of the household and is responsible for providing for his family economically, while the wife is responsible for the home and child rearing. However, an increase in education and work opportunities for women has resulted in more women taking up employment outside the home. Women are increasingly becoming responsible for their own economic well-being as well as that of their families. Most companies have recognised the growing market potential presented by the female market and some have developed products specifically targeted at this segment of the market. 1st for Women is an example of a South African company that specifically targets women with its products.

Figure 9.5 Changing domestic roles

As more women join the workforce, men are finding themselves in situations where they need to help with domestic chores. Many are taking on regular household duties, including shopping for groceries, taking care of children, cleaning the home and cooking for the family. As a result, marketers have started targeting marketing communication relating to household products at this group. Consider, for example, OMO adverts in South Africa, which put men at the centre of household chores.[17]

The next sections will focus more closely on issues relating to family and household decision making.

9.5 THE FAMILY OR HOUSEHOLD DECISION-MAKING PROCESS

Proper marketing research is often required in order to ensure that marketing strategies are based on the right information. This section starts by looking at research-related issues that must be kept in mind when trying to understand family and household decision making. We then look at the different roles that members of a family or household play in the decision-making process.

APPLICATION

Stimulating demand for a new children's sportswear brand
One of the major clothing retailers in the country has agreed to stock a famous sports celebrity's range of children's sportswear. As marketing manager, you have been tasked with the responsibility of overseeing the launch of the new clothing range and ensuring that it is the talk of town. You have also been asked to compile an integrated promotion strategy aimed at stimulating ongoing demand.

Discussion questions
1. Who in the family would you target your marketing messages at and why?
2. What kind of influence do you expect different family members to have in terms of deciding whether to buy the new range of children's sportswear or not?

9.5.1   Researching family or household decision making
The typical consumer decision-making process consists of five key stages (see also Chapter 1):
* Problem recognition
* Information search
* Evaluation of alternatives
* Purchase stage
* Post-purchase stage

Although individuals' and groups' consumer decisions are explained in terms of the same stages, decision making in a group context (as is the case with families and most households) is in many ways more complex than an in the individual consumer context (see also section 1.2.1). Marketing strategists who are trying to understand decision making in a family and household context need to bear this in mind. The main areas of difference are attributed to the following:
* Different family or household members are often directly or indirectly involved in the decision-making process. For example, the decision to buy a house may be taken jointly by a husband and wife. However, a couple with young children is likely to consider proximity to schools and whether there is an adequate-sized garden in which they can play. Thus, while the children may not get a direct say, their needs will have to be taken into consideration (as an external influence) in the buying decision-making process.
* The amount of influence that individual members exert on similar product decisions differs from family to family and from household to household. This is owing to the different decision-making styles that families or households may adopt. For example, in some families, children may be given the opportunity to have a say on the high school they would like to attend, while in other families, children may be expected to accept their parents' decision. In some families, the father may have the final say on major purchase decisions (patriarchal decisions), while in others the mother's opinions may carry more weight (matriarchal decisions). Sometimes, final decision making is shared equally by the spouses/partners (egalitarian decisions). Capturing

the amount of influence that different members have on specific product purchase situations increases the complexity of researching family and household decision making.

- It is normal to have different family or household members involved at different stages in the decision-making process. Consider Samantha's situation in the discussion box below. It is not always easy to identify exactly which stages are influenced by who. Despite this, it is often necessary for marketers to know the roles played by different people during the different stages of the buying process. Of critical importance is to know the sources of information that people use to make purchase decisions. Opinion leaders like Samantha's uncle (again this is an external influence) tend to exert a lot of influence on what is finally bought because of their perceived level of knowledge about the product in question.
- Family members who are involved in the decision-making process may evaluate the same product by considering different attributes. For example,

DISCUSSION

Samantha's new bicycle

Little Samantha asks her mother for a new bicycle because her old one broke while playing at Uncle Smith's house. When Samantha's mum goes to Uncle Smith's house to pick-up the broken bicycle, he advises her not to buy the same brand again because it was not durable. He recommends another brand.

The following weekend, Samantha and her parents go to a bicycle shop. Her mother asks for the brand recommended by Samantha's uncle and the salesperson shows them their range. Samantha chooses a pink bicycle and her father pays for it.

Samantha loves her new bicycle.

Figure 9.6 Samantha and her new bicycle

Discussion questions

1. Who initiated the idea of buying a new bicycle?
2. Who played a major role in influencing the specific brand of bicycle that the family ended up buying?
3. Uncle Smith indicated that the old bicycle was not durable. To which type of influence does this comment refer?
4. Who was responsible for paying for the bicycle?
5. Why is it so important to be aware of the different roles in the buying process?
6. Who finally produces evidence about the success of the purchase? Explain.

in deciding what to buy for school lunch boxes, most mothers may be more interested in food products that are nutritious. Children, on the other hand, may not like some of those foods and refuse to eat them.

- Since family members are economically responsible for each other, the consumption decisions of one member often have an influence on the other members. This is because availability of resources is often limited compared to the needs and wants that people have. A family decision to buy a new washing machine may mean that little Samantha will have to wait a while longer before she can get the bicycle that she wants. Complications like these make it difficult for researchers to understand fully the factors that affect consumption decisions on any single product. They therefore have to acknowledge and take into account other family or household members' contribution towards, and influence on, the consumption decisions.

All these factors make it harder for marketers to generalise how families or households make decisions. Researchers in this area tend to rely on observations and focus group discussions[18] because direct questioning often results in contradictory findings, with some members reporting things that are the complete opposite of what other members of the same family or household have said.[19]

RESEARCH BOX 9.1

Researchers have found that one of the best ways of trying to understand family and household decision making is to focus on the consumption process. The focus here is on identifying the parties involved in the consumption process. This is because in general, users of products tend to be more concerned about what will be bought, as they are the ones who are more closely involved in the use of the product. For example, a high tech washing machine purchased by the home owners, although their maid predominantly uses it to do the washing for the household demonstrates that the outcome of the purchase decision may not be very successful because the needs and skills of the user were not acknowledged. A good understanding of consumer roles thus enables marketers to target their marketing efforts accordingly in order to achieve the desired outcomes for their specific product. Section 9.5.2 looks more closely at the common decision-making roles played by members in family or household decision-making.

9.5.2   Family and household decision-making roles

Sharing of tasks is one important characteristic that makes a family or household function as a single cohesive unit. Members of a family share tasks such as shopping for the home, preparing meals, cleaning the house and taking care of the garden. When it comes to the consumer decision-making process, there are five commonly cited roles that members of a family or household fill:

- *Initiator:* This is the family member who identifies the need to buy a product and brings it to the attention of other family members. The role of initiator is commonly taken by product user.
- *Influencer:* This is the family member who provides important information about a product that influences the purchase decision of other family

members. Influencers are often more knowledgeable about the product category than other family or household members. They acquire the information by shopping around, reading product labels, or talking to friends or experts. The information provided by influencers is used to evaluate product alternatives and to decide on the final product to be bought. Influencers can also impact the buying decision through their actions. For example, a child who refuses to eat certain foods may affect a mother's decision on what to avoid when shopping. An older sister who is more knowledgeable on make-up can advise a younger sister on which brand is best.

- *Decider:* This is the family member who makes the final decision on whether or not to buy a product because he or she controls the finances or has the authority.[20] A mother may, for example, refuse to buy a cell phone for her teenage son although they can afford it and despite his constant pleas because she is convinced that the cell phone will be too much of a distraction.

- *Buyer:* This is the family member who makes the actual purchase. For physical products, this commonly involves going to the shop, paying for the product and ensuring that it is brought home. The role of a buyer is typically taken by adult members of the family or household, although children are sometimes sent by their parents to buy small items such as bread or sugar (then they are surrogate buyers). Children often engage in buying products related to their own consumption, for example snacks.

- *Consumer:* This is the family member who makes use of or consumes the purchased product. Many products bought in a family or household have multiple users or consumers, such as breakfast cereal, toiletries and furniture. The involvement of family members in other roles (as initiators, influencers, deciders and buyers) is often related to their involvement as users or consumers. For example, the member who enjoys bathing will influence the purchase of bubble bath.

The husband, wife and children are the major role-players in family decision making. Section 9.6 attends in more detail to the husband-wife influence, while section 9.7 considers the role of the children.

9.6 HUSBAND–WIFE INFLUENCE IN FAMILY DECISION MAKING

Marketers are often interested in knowing the amount of influence exerted by the husband or wife in the buying of their products. Researchers who study the dynamics of husband-and-wife decision making commonly classify purchases into four categories:

- *Husband-dominated decisions (patriarchal decisions):* Husbands have the most say in the buying decision process.
- *Wife-dominated decisions (matriarchal decisions):* Wives have the most say in the buying decision process.

- *Joint decisions (egalitarian decisions):* Both husbands and wives are actively involved in the buying decision process.
- *Autonomous decisions:* Decisions are made independently by either husbands or wives. This includes products that are not clearly dominated by either husbands or wives, nor commonly associated with joint decision making.

These categories also apply to same-sex marriages. Different families thus make their decisions in different ways.

APPLICATION

Relative influence of husband and wife in family decision making

The amount of influence exerted by husbands and wives in the buying decision-making process often varies from culture to culture.

Discussion questions

In groups of four, classify the products below into the following categories according to your traditional cultural context or what you have been accustomed to in your home:

- Husband-dominated buying decisions
- Wife-dominated buying decisions
- Joint decisions
- Autonomic decisions

Products:

- Food
- Kitchen appliances
- Living-room furniture
- Family car
- Groceries
- Life insurance
- Choice of holiday destination
- Luggage
- A restaurant for a family dining experience
- Children's toys
- Home maintenance products

A number of factors may determine the amount of influence exerted by husbands and/or wives in household decision making:

- *Role specialisation:* If the husband were a stay-at-home dad while the wife worked, he would be more involved in planning the children's after-school activities.
- *Age of the family:* Young couples would typically share most household decisions until they were confident to delegate certain decisions to the one or the other to save time.
- *Level of involvement:* A spouse would be more involved in certain household decisions that were of particular interest to him or her, or in which he

or she had more expertise. For example, financial decisions would be handled by the spouse who was a financial advisor and holiday destinations by the one who was a travel agent.

Section 9.7 discusses factors that affect the level of involvement of family and household members in buying decision making in more detail.

9.7 CHILDREN AND FAMILY DECISION MAKING

Children play an important role, directly or directly, in family or household buying decisions. From the moment children are born, families have a responsibility to provide for their needs. As they grow up, they start to exert a stronger direct influence on household buying decisions. This often starts when they make simple requests to their parents for specific products. These requests can be verbal or non-verbal, especially in the case of young children who are not yet talking. Babies and toddlers usually signal their preferences to their parents by pointing at things. If the parents do not provide the desired product, they may use their pester power by asking continuously until the parent gives in or throwing a temper tantrum in the middle of a store.

By the age of eight, many children start to receive pocket money from their parents or earn money for doing chores around the house. This money allows them to start making their own purchase decisions. By the time children reach their teen years, many of them are able to function relatively effectively as consumers, making their own product choices and performing the actual buying activity themselves.

Children are also increasingly playing a direct role in household purchasing decisions that do not involve their personal money. Studies have found that many young children tend to influence household purchase decisions involving products that are for their interests or their own use, such as their clothing.[21]

Figure 9.7 Children and family buying behaviour

As they get older, they also begin to exert a more direct influence on purchase decisions related to products that they do not use directly themselves. For example, most teenagers tend to be more knowledgeable than their parents about technological products such as cell phones and computers. Parents may therefore rely on them for their advice (input) regarding the purchase decision. Many teenagers like to comment positively or negatively on product choices made by their parents. For example, a teenage daughter may scorn her mother for patronising second-hand shops, which may influence her mother's future purchase decisions.

Time pressure on parents, especially when both of them are working, may result in teens becoming 'surrogate buyers'. This is when teens get directly involved in purchasing products, which entails making product or brand choices on behalf of the whole family.

Marketers have recognised the large potential of the children's market. Many directly target children with their marketing messages in order to nurture brand preferences, persuade them to buy their products or influence their parents to buy promoted products. Some companies sponsor child-related activities such as school events with the explicit aim of reaching the children's market by exposing them to certain brands. This practice has raised considerable ethical concerns. It is argued, for example, that it is not appropriate for companies to target children directly, seeing as they might not be mature enough to comprehend marketing messages properly. This is of even more concern with pre-teen children, as their cognitive abilities are not yet well developed. Hence marketers need to be careful in the way they craft their marketing programmes to avoid controversy.

DISCUSSION

Children's tactics to influence their parents

A number of tactics that children commonly use to influence their parents to buy products have been identified.[22] These include the use of pressure tactics, upward appeal, exchange tactics, coalition tactics, ingratiating tactics, rational persuasion, inspirational appeals and consultation tactics.[23] Based on Yukl and Falbe,[24] Wimalasiri[25] described each of these tactics, in the context of the child, as follows:

- *Pressure tactics:* The child makes demands, uses threats, or intimidation to persuade you to comply with his/her request.
- *Upwards appeal:* The child seeks to persuade you, saying that the request was approved or supported by an older member of the family, a teacher or even a family friend;
- *Exchange tactics:* The child makes an explicit or implicit promise to give you some sort of service such as washing the car, cleaning the house, or taking care of the baby, in return for a favour;
- *Coalition tactics:* The child seeks the aid of others to persuade you to comply with his/her request or uses the support of others as an argument for you to agree with him/her;
- *Ingratiating tactics:* The child seeks to get you in a good mood or think favorably of him or her before asking you to comply with a request;
- *Rational persuasion:* The child uses logical arguments and factual evidence to persuade you to agree with his/her request;

- *Inspiration appeals:* The child makes an emotional appeal or proposal that arouses enthusiasm by appealing to your values and ideals;
- *Consultation tactics:* The child seeks your involvement in making a decision.

Read more about these tactics in Wimalasiri, J.S. 2004. A cross-national study on children's purchasing behavior and parental response. *Journal of Consumer Marketing*, 21(4): 274–284 and/or Yukl, G. & Falbe, C.M. 1990. Influence tactics and objectives in upward, downward, and lateral influence attempts. *Journal of Applied Psychology*, 75(2): 132.

Discussion questions

1. Provide two practical illustrations of how each tactic can be used by a child to persuade his or her parents to buy specific products.
2. Describe to the class one of the tactics that you have personally used to influence a purchase decision in your home (or to prevent a purchase from being made).

9.8 FACTORS AFFECTING ROLES PLAYED BY MEMBERS IN THE FAMILY OR HOUSEHOLD, WITH REGARD TO BUYING DECISION MAKING

There are many factors that influence the roles that members play in family or household buying decision making, including the following:
- Role specialisation in the family
- Individualistic versus collective traits
- Time available for decision making
- The level of perceived risk associated with the purchase
- How authority is exercised within the family

These factors are discussed in more detail below.

9.8.1 Role specialisation in the family

The large number of activities and associated products that need to be bought in order to keep a family functioning make it necessary to have role specialisation.[26] Role specialisation affects the buying process in that the family member that is primarily responsible for an activity tends to dominate in buying products associated with that activity. For example, the member responsible for maintenance and upkeep will dominate in buying products such as spare lightbulbs and batteries, chlorine for the swimming pool, fertiliser for the garden etc.

Role specialisation between husbands and wives in most societies has tended to be closely associated with gender role orientation. However, the traditional view of husbands and wives having distinctly separate roles is being overthrown by a more modern view of responsibilities being shared between the two,[27] with no chores being associated with any particular gender.

9.8.2   Individualistic versus collective personality traits

Aside from being cultural traits (see more on this in Chapter 8), individualism and collectivism can also be associated with personality. Some people tend to have a more individualistic personality than others, therefore being inclined to exclude other people in their decision-making processes. For example, a young man with more individualistic traits is not likely to consider it important to consult his family when making a career choice. A young man with collectivist personality traits, however, most likely will.

These personality traits will also affect who is consulted when making purchasing decisions. In most collectivist African cultures, members of the extended family will play a role. For example, grandparents and/or uncles, aunts etc. may expect to be consulted when a family is deciding on whether to send a child to study at an overseas university. Individualistic families, however, may not see the need to discuss this with people outside the nuclear family.

9.8.3   Time available for decision making

Group decision making requires more time than autonomous decision making because deliberations have to take place before a final decision is made. As a result, autonomous decision making and one-member-dominated decision making are common when family or household members are pressured for time.

9.8.4   The level of perceived risk associated with the purchase

The buying of products is associated with different types and levels of risk. The common types of risk include the following:

- *Financial risk:* Generally, the more expensive a product is, the higher the financial risk associated with it.
- *Social risk:* The more visible a product is and the higher the need to make a public statement, the higher the social risk associated with the purchase situation becomes. The purchase of a dress to be worn to a wedding carries more social risk than the purchase of an everyday dress for work. Thus, the dress for the wedding may necessitate consultation with other members of the family or a close friend, while the dress for the office may be bought spontaneously.
- *Psychological risk:* This relates to the level of anxiety that a consumer is likely to experience if the wrong purchase decision is made. For example, a young mother is likely to feel a strong need to engage family members regarding her decision to employ a child-minder for her baby. In this case, the wrong decision could lead to feelings of deep regret and self-blame.
- *Performance risk:* There is a possibility that a product, such as a new washing machine, might not perform as expected or be as durable as was anticipated (therefore not lasting as long as it should, which will require premature replacement or costly repairs).

* *Safety risk:* There is a possibility that a product may not be safe to use, for example food bought from a street vendor may cause food poisoning, a slimming product that promises wonderful results may cause liver damage, or a cheap electrical appliance such as a desk lamp may cause a fire.
* *Security risk:* This is particularly relevant when buying items online or sharing personal information on social media.

Family or household purchase decisions carrying higher levels of risk are often associated with more member involvement. For example, buying a house poses a great deal of risk, therefore family members usually try to reduce it by considering the opinions of different role-players before making the final purchase decision. If friends recommend the school that is in the neighbourhood or how safe the area is, or maybe the quality of the services available, the decision will be made more confidently.

9.8.5   How authority is exercised by the family or household head

The extent to which children, in particular, play a role in family decision making largely depends on how authority is exercised within the family. Their participation tends to be low in families characterised by authoritarian rule of a particular parent. In such families, children are largely expected to abide by their parents' decisions. In families headed by non-authoritarian parents, children are often given the opportunity to express their views and desires.

Many members participating in a family or household decision-making process increases the likelihood of disagreements. Section 9.9 looks at the issue of conflict in family or household decision making.

9.9   CONFLICT IN FAMILY OR HOUSEHOLD DECISION MAKING

Conflict is a common phenomenon in family or household decision making, although most families or households work very hard to contain it and to reduce its effects.

Section 9.9.1 looks at the common causes of conflict and section 9.9.2 considers some of the ways in which families or households try to manage or resolve their differences.

9.9.1   Causes of conflict in family or household decision making

There are many possible causes of conflict in family or household decision making, which mostly relate to the following factors:

* *Differences in goals or values relating to what needs to be bought:* As a result of limited resources, most families or households have more needs and wants than their resources can deal with. Conflict often arises as differences emerge between family or household members on what needs to be prioritised. For example, the husband may plan on taking the family on an overseas trip for their Christmas holiday, while the wife may prefer to spend the money on renovating the family home.

Figure 9.8 Family conflict in purchase decision making

- *Differences in evaluations or perceptions relating to possible product alternatives:* Sometimes family or household members may agree on the general goal or value proposition, but disagree on specifics relating to the chosen product. For example, a parent may agree with her teenage daughter that she needs new shoes, but disagree with her decision to buy a particular style, colour or an expensive pair of branded shoes.
- *Differences in perceptions post-purchase:* Conflict in family decision making can also arise at the post-purchase stage. For example, the husband may buy tickets for an overseas trip without consulting the rest of the family first and they may have differing preferences, or the teenage daughter buys expensive branded shoes without first asking her mother.

9.9.2   Managing conflict in family or household decision making

Families or households use different strategies to reduce the possibility of conflict and to deal with conflict that occurs. The common strategies used in preventing or resolving conflict relating to consumer decision making include the following:

- *Reasoning:* This entails trying to convince the other members to agree to the purchase decision through the use of logical arguments. The teenage daughter may, for example, try to persuade her mother that she needs to buy an expensive brand of shoes on the basis that the shoes are durable and will last for a long time.
- *Bargaining:* This entails an explicit acknowledgement of the existence of conflict among family members, who then try to resolve it through compromising. For example, a mother may agree to buy the expensive pair of shoes for her daughter on condition that she will not ask for money for another pair of shoes before the next year.
- *Collecting more information on which to base a decision:* This is a commonly used strategy in conflicts that arise owing to a lack of sufficient knowledge on product attributes among members of the family. The new information gathered may convince family members of the merit of the purchase. Credible information sources are often sought in such cases to help evaluate alternative product choices.

- *Politicking:* This is commonly used when differences in the opinions of members are so extensive that they cannot be resolved easily. Members may use a variety of different strategies to win the favour of the other members or isolate the disagreeing members. For example, the husband may try to convince the children in the family to take an overseas vacation, leaving the mother isolated in her resistance. The mother may eventually accept the majority's decision, although this will probably be done grudgingly.
- *Asserting one's rights:* This is commonly used where agreement in a conflict is unlikely. The teenage daughter may, for example, insist on buying an expensive brand of shoes because she is paying with her own money. Thus, although the parents may not agree with her product choice, they may have no choice but to accept her decision since she has the right to spend her pocket money as she wishes.

Marketers can help in conflict management and resolution by providing as much information relating to their products as possible to enable consumers to make informed purchase decisions. Marketers also need to realise that families find themselves at different stages within the family life cycle and are likely to face different challenges when evaluating and choosing products. Section 9.10 explores the concept of the family life cycle and its impact on families'/households' buying decisions.

9.10 THE FAMILY LIFE CYCLE

Traditionally, the **family life cycle** refers to a series of relatively distinct stages through which individuals pass over time. As individuals move through these stages, their circumstances change and this tends to have a profound impact on their consumption activities. This section starts by outlining the stages in the family life cycle (see Figure 9.9) before looking at the changing circumstances often associated with each stage and their impact on consumption activities.

As mentioned previously, deviations from the traditional family life cycle are common these days, mainly as a result of high divorce rates and the large number of individuals who choose not to get married or have children, or who get married, but have no children. High divorce rates have also resulted in a growth in the number of single-parent families. There are also many individuals who do not get married, but have children out of wedlock. In South Africa and many African countries, a high death rate (particularly among individuals in the economically active age group) caused by the HIV/AIDS pandemic has resulted in a growing number of family households without parents, in other words with orphans only.

9.10.1   Stages in the family life cycle

As shown in Table 9.1, there are five basic stages in the traditional family life cycle. Alternative stages of the life cycle show that not all families will go through all five stages. For example, the family may not go through the parenthood and post-parenthood stages because they have decided not to have children.

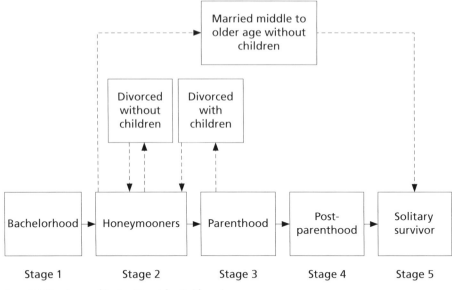

Figure 9.9 The stages of the traditional family life cycle

9.10.2   Family life cycle and consumption activities

As individuals move through the different stages of the family life cycle, they do not only get older but they also experience changes, for example in their financial situation, their interests and their social responsibilities. Below is a discussion on the common characteristics associated with each stage of the family life cycle and the effects of these characteristics on consumption activities:

* *Bachelorhood:* The majority of people in this stage are young, single men and women at the beginning of their working careers. Others may be older because they have decided to delay getting married or have not yet found the right person. Current levels of earnings of younger people in this stage tend to be lower in relation to their future earnings. However, they tend to have higher levels of discretionary income because of limited financial obligations. They often spend their money on rent, basic home furnishings, entertainment, personal clothing, transportation and even luxury items. Some may even buy their first car during this stage. Their purchase of food products is usually limited to small packet sizes. Consumption decision making is more individual and decisions are based on what they have learnt growing up in their homes.

* *Honeymooners:* As soon as two people decide to enter into a family relationship, consumption decision making tends to be more of a result of negotiations. Many find themselves in a situation where both spouses are working. The result is higher levels of disposable income than in the bachelorhood and parenthood stages. There tends to be an increase in the amount of money spent on durable home furnishing products, including lounge and bedroom furniture, television sets and home appliances.

Table 9.1 Stages in the family life cycle

Traditional, Western stages of the life cycle	Alternative stages of the life cycle
Bachelorhood: Consists of young single men and women ready to enter into marriage	*Bachelorhood:* Consists of young single men and women, who might delay entering into a permanent relationship to, for example, further their careers or improve their level of education.
Honeymooners: Consists of young married couples with no children	*Honeymooners/dedicatory stage:* Consists of recently married couples or partners, including of the same sex, in a more permanent relationship with no children
Parenthood: Consists of married couples with at least one child at home	*Parenthood:* Consists of a family headed by – • married couples or partners (also of the same sex) having at least one child in the home, or • singles (of either sex), either divorced or single due to death of a spouse or partner, having at least one child in the home, or • singles (of either sex), not married or in a permanent relationship, by choice, having at least one child in the home, or • singles, who might be a surviving young family member who takes care of other siblings after the death of one or both parents • a reconstructed couple after divorce, death or separation of a couple, including children from either or both partners/spouses
Post-parenthood: Consists of older married couples with no children living at home any more	*Post-parenthood:* Consists of older couples or singles with no children living at home any more
Solitary survivor: Consists of one surviving older spouse (widowhood)	*Solitary survivor:* Consists of one surviving older spouse (widowhood) or partner

- *Parenthood:* The arrival of a child brings with it many changes. Sometimes one partner, usually the wife, stops working in order to stay home and look after the child. In such cases, the family loses its double-income status. Even where the wife does not give up her job, the family faces growing pressure on its income directly related to costs associated with child rearing and probably day care. The family starts to spend money on products for children, including food and clothing. Family medical expenses also tend to rise.[28] The young family loses most of its free time and is hence not able to socialise much outside the home. As the child gets older and starts school, educational expenses increase. The parenthood stage is often broken down into three sub-stages, namely full nest 1, full nest 2 and full nest 3. The full nest 1 stage starts with the arrival of the first child and ends when the youngest child reaches school-going age at around six years old.[29] Full nest

2 includes families in which the youngest child is older than six years, while full nest 3 families are those with children still at home and the youngest being in the mid-teens.[30] The first full nest sub-stage (full nest 1) is therefore characterised by high pressure on family income and many families fail to accumulate any savings. As the family moves into the second and third full nest sub-stages, many of the partners who leave work to look after their young ones rejoin the workforce. Working partners also experience some career progression during this stage as they gain more experience. Thus despite the growth in education-related expenses, most families in second and third full nest sub-stages experience an improvement in their income situation. The parenthood stage in general is also characterised by an increase in the number of people having a direct influence on family decision making, particularly as the children grow up. Often, food and grocery shopping is done in bulk.

- *Post-parenthood:* This stage is also referred to as the 'empty nesters'. During this stage, many families are at their best financially. The children have all left the family home and the parents now have more time for their own interests. Spending on entertainment and the purchase of luxury items tends to increase. Most families have finished paying off their mortgages and other items bought on credit (for example, cars) by this time. Towards the end of this stage, most of them retire from paid employment and have more time to pursue personal hobbies or travel. However, for families that are not well prepared for retirement, the retirement years can be a financial struggle. The family no longer has steady income sources and sometimes starts to rely on its working children for support. Medical bills may become problematic.

APPLICATION

The family life cycle's influence on what families buy

The family life cycle exerts a great deal of influence on what families buy. Consider the scenario below:

Mary: I need to book a ticket for a family holiday to New York

Travel agent: When do you want to travel and do you have any special needs?

Mary: I have two small children, one aged five and the other two, so please book us on a direct flight.

- *Solitary survivor:* During the solitary survivor stage, many people are retired and have no steady source of income. Spending on medical bills starts to increase again as a result of age-related ailments. Some solitary survivors move to a smaller home or to a retirement village where they can receive specialist care as they get older. In most African families, surviving children and other members of the extended family take over full responsibility for looking after the elderly.

9.11 STRATEGIC MARKETING APPLICATIONS

A good understanding of family and household decision making and its influences on consumer behaviour is important for marketers in terms of the following:

- *Optimal market segmentation:* Market segmentation is an integral part of any marketing effort. It entails the division of a market into groups of customers with similar needs. Families or households consist of different types and find themselves at different stages in their life cycle. Each type and/or stage is associated with unique needs which significantly influence the nature and quantities of products demanded.

- *Forecast demand for different products:* Analysis of family or household consumption activities can help marketers to forecast the demand for their products. For example, changes in the family social structure in South Africa – in particular the fact that more women are joining the workforce – have resulted in an increased demand for ready-made food products and household devices that save time, as well as career clothing. The demand for childcare services is also on the increase. Some developed countries, including Australia and Britain, are experiencing an increase in life expectancy, which results in a high number of elderly people, which has led to an increase in the demand for products and services specifically catering for this market segment, including retirement villages and frail care homes.

- *Effective target marketing efforts:* Often, more than one person is involved in family or household decision making. Successful marketing efforts largely depend on knowing who is involved in purchase-related decisions as well as establishing what the stages are in the buying decision process and where the respective individuals exert an influence. For example, knowing that your company's products are male or female dominated in purchase decision making will enable the marketing team to design marketing communication campaigns that will reach the right segment of the market. Also, knowing that teenagers are brand conscious when purchasing sportswear will indicate how and where to post marketing material effectively.

- *Design products that appeal to members who are involved in family or household decision making:* When two or more people are involved in decision making, their individual evaluation frameworks for products may not be the same. Marketers therefore need to go beyond knowing who is involved in family or household decision making to understanding the product attributes that appeal to different individuals. Such information is also helpful in designing marketing communication messages that appeal to the different members.

- *Design appropriate strategies for their products:* Studies have shown that many parents take their younger children along when they go shopping. Many of these children make numerous requests aimed at getting their parents to buy them products they want, for example breakfast cereal. Equipped with this knowledge, most marketers with products targeted at young consumers (for example, sweets and toys) often demand retail shelf space that is easily accessible to young consumers.

SUMMARY

Every individual consumer is part of a family of some sort. Although the words 'family' and 'household' are often used interchangeably, they are not the same thing. A family is a group of persons related by blood, marriage or adoption that function together for member security and perpetuation of the unit.[31] A household, on the other hand, refers to an individual or a group of people, who may be related or unrelated, occupying a single housing unit.

Families have three basic functions towards their members: socialisation, economic well-being and emotional support. In most societies around the world, including South Africa, the family and household structure has undergone a number of significant changes. These changes relate to the average family or household size, the headship of families and households, the age of family or household members, growth in ethnic diversity of households of different ethnic backgrounds and changes in social structure.

Marketers are often interested in understanding the roles played by different members in the buying decision making of families or households. The dynamics of husband and wife decision making as well as the impact of the children are of particular interest. The role that members play in family decision making depends largely on role specialisation, the level of individualistic or collective personality traits prevalent in the members, the time available for decision making, the level of risk associated with the purchase, and how authority is exercised in the family or household.

Since family and household decision making often involves a number of role-players, conflict is common. Two major causes of conflict involve differences in (1) values relating to what needs to be bought, and (2) evaluation of products of interest. Reasoning, bargaining, collection of more information, politicking and asserting of one's rights are often used to resolve these disagreements.

Understanding the stages through which families move with time as depicted in the family life cycle is of great importance to marketers. From a more traditional perspective, the family life cycle consists of five basic stages and each stage is associated with unique characteristics in terms of income levels, age and family responsibilities, all of which exert a profound impact on the demand for different products and services.

Due to social changes, the stages of the family life cycle have changed over time to allow for recognition of same-sex partnerships, couples who never get married and often choose not to have children, and singles who have children but who choose to remain unmarried. Hence a study of family or household decision making is of strategic importance in marketing. It is helpful in ensuring optimal segmentation of the family and household market, forecasting demand for different products, ensuring that the right individuals are targeted and that the right images are portrayed in marketing material, designing products that are appealing to members involved in purchase decision making and designing appropriate placing strategies for products.

SELF-ASSESSMENT QUESTIONS

1. Discuss the difference between family and household.
2. Consumer socialisation is one of the primary functions of any family. Discuss the different ways in which the family performs this function.
3. Describe the different roles that members can play in family or household decision making.
4. Discuss the factors that may influence the extent to which different members influence family or household buying decision making.
5. Discuss the common tactics used by children to influence purchase decisions.
6. Conflict is common in household purchase decision making. Discuss the common strategies used by families to manage conflict.
7. Discuss the concept of the family life cycle and factors that are leading to its modification.
8. Why it is important for marketers to gain a good understanding of family and household decision making?

EXPERIENTIAL EXERCISE

You have recently been appointed as a travel consultant at a travel agency. Your responsibilities include holiday package development for retirees. Consider the following:

1. What factors would influence your development of holiday packages targeted at this market?
2. Which media platforms would you use to promote your holiday packages?

CASE STUDY 1

Looking after Nosipho

On the death of her mother when she was only eight years old, Nosipho went to live with her paternal grandmother, Ma Sithole, and her aunt, Ma Moyo, in a small village in Limpopo. At first, life in the village was hard for her and she missed Johannesburg, where she had lived with her mother. Life in Johannesburg was, according to her, much easier. School had not been far from home, whereas now she had to walk a long distance to get there. In the city, they had had electricity, so cooking had been done indoors on an electric stove. In the village, she had to learn to cook outdoors using wood. Her aunt, Ma Moyo, had been very instrumental in helping her adjust to life in the village.

Now, at the age of 18, Nosipho can look back with joy and thankfulness for the care she received from her grandmother and aunt over the years. She is a young lady of age and tomorrow she will be leaving the village for the first time since her mother's death to go back to Johannesburg, where she will be studying for a law degree at one of the universities.

While there is no immediate relative to look after Nosipho when she gets there, she is not worried because Ma Moyo has arranged for her to stay with the family of one of her own oldest and dearest friends. Ma Moyo had dropped out of school, but her friend had worked hard and was now employed as a nurse in a large hospital. Noshipho has been told that Ma Moyo's friend lives in a big house with her husband and two children. The family has offered one of their spare bedrooms to Nosipho and also to provide for her needs while she is studying.

Discussion questions

1. What kind of family does Ma Moyo's friend have in the city?
2. In what kind of family was Nosipho raised after her mother's death?
3. Identify and discuss the family functions played by Ma Sithole and Ma Moyo in this case.

CASE STUDY 2

Maureen's wedding!

Read the dialogue that follows:

Pam: We need to start preparing for Maureen's wedding. How many people is she planning to invite?

Mike: I am not sure, but one thing I do know is that she wants a guest list of no more than 50 people.

Mum: What? That will be impossible! This family is big and the whole village is looking forward to the occasion!

Pam: Mum, we cannot invite everyone. We plan to have the wedding reception at a five-star hotel and who is going to pay for so many people?

Mum: If that hotel is going to be too expensive, then you have to choose a more affordable place to host the reception. There is no way we are going to make the function exclusive to a few people.

Mike: Maureen will not be happy about this, mum. I don't know what you will do to convince her to open up her wedding celebration to hundreds!

Mum: Leave it to me, I will talk to Maureen.

Discussion questions

1. Conflict is common in family buying and consumption activities. Discuss four strategies that are often used to resolve it.
2. Which strategy would you recommend that Maureen's mother uses in trying to convince Maureen to open up her guest list to many more people?

ADDITIONAL RESOURCES

Go to Google Scholar or to your library and look for the articles listed below. They are intended to deepen your understanding of family and household decision making. Share your opinions on the issues investigated in the articles in class.

*   Broilo, P.L., Bertol, K.E., Espartel, L.B. & Basso, K. 2017. Young children's influence on family consumer behavior. *Qualitative Market Research: An International Journal*, 20(4): 452–468.
*   Iyer, P.P., Paswan, A.K. & Davari, A. 2016. Brands, love and family. *Journal of Product & Brand Management*, 25(1): 69–83.
*   Jeevananda, S. & Kumar, S. 2012. Degree of children influence on parents buying decision process. *European Journal of Business and Management*, 4(14): 49–57.
*   Singh, R. & Nayak, J.K. 2016. Parent–adolescent conflict and choice of conflict resolution strategy: Familial holiday planning. *International Journal of Conflict Management*, 27(1): 88–115.

REFERENCES

1   Statistics South Africa. 2017. *General household survey: Mid-year population estimates.* Pretoria: Statistics South Africa, 7.
2   Ibid., 8.

3   Rousseau, D. 2008. Reference groups and family decision making. In Du Plessis, P. & Rousseau, G. (Eds), *Buyer behaviour: Understanding consumer psychology and marketing*. Cape Town: Oxford Southern Africa, 71.

4   Basu, R. & Sondhi, N. 2014. Child socialization practices: Implications for retailers in emerging markets. *Journal of Retailing and Consumer Services*, 21(5): 798; Kim, J., Spangler, T.L. & Gutter, M.S. 2016. Extended families: Support, socialization, and stress. *Family and Consumer Sciences Research Journal*, 45(1): 104; Schiffman, L. & Wisenblit, J. 2015. *Consumer behaviour*, 11th ed. Boston: Pearson Education, 24423–246. [AQ: Are these page numbers correct? Should 24423 be either 244 or 223?]

5   Ward, S. 1980. Consumer socialization. In Kassarjian, H.H. & T. Robertson, T. (Eds), *Perspectives in consumer behavior*. Glenville: Scott Foresman, 382.

6   Ekström, K.M. 2015. Consumer socialization. In Cook, D.T. & Ryan, J.M.A. (Eds), *The Wiley Blackwell encyclopedia of consumption and consumer studies*. West Sussex, UK: John Wiley & Sons, 144.

7   Kim et al., 388; Arnould, E., Price, L. & Zinkhan, G. 2004. *Consumers*. Boston: McGrawHill/Irwin, 562.

8   Wang, D., Wang, L. & Chen, L. 2017. Unlocking the influence of family business exposure on entrepreneurial intentions. *International Entrepreneurship and Management Journal*, 58(7/8), 733.

9   Kornienko, O., Agadjanian, V., Menjívar, C. & Zotova, N. 2017. Financial and emotional support in close personal ties among Central Asian migrant women in Russia. *Social Networks*, 24 May, 53: 207.

10   United Nations. 2017. Population facts: Household size and composition around the world. Available at: http://www.un.org/en/development/desa/population/publications/pdf/popfacts/PopFacts_2017-2.pdf (accessed on 19 August 2018), 2.

11   Passias, E.J., Sayer, L. & Pepin, J.R. 2017. Who experiences leisure deficits? Mothers' marital status and leisure time. *Journal of Marriage and Family*, 79(4): 1001.

12   Newlin, M., Reynold, S. & Nombutho, M.M.W. 2016. Dealing with children from child-headed households in schools: Strategies for improving their academic performance. *Journal of Social Sciences*, 48(1–2): 51.

13   Ibid.

14   Mukherji, A., Roychoudhury, S., Ghosh, P. & Brown, S. 2016. Estimating health demand for an aging population: A flexible and robust Bayesian joint model. *Journal of Applied Econometrics*, 31(6): 1140.

15   Kim, S. & Iwashita, C. 2016. Cooking identity and food tourism: The case of Japanese udon noodles. *Tourism Recreation Research*, 41(1): 89.

16   Sheth, J., Mittal, B. & Newman, B. 1999. *Consumer behaviour: Consumer behaviour and beyond*. New York: Dryden Press, 575.

17   Bratt, M. 2017. The changing role of dads in ads. TheMediaOnline. Available at: http://themediaonline.co.za/2017/12/the-changing-role-of-dads-in-ads/ (accessed on 19 August 2018).

18   Rousseau, op. cit., 79.

19   Ibid.

20   Blackwell, R., Miniard, P. & Engel, J. 2001. *Consumer behaviour*, 9th ed. Fort Worth: Harcourt College, 365.

21   Calderon, J., Ayala, G.X., Elder, J.P., Belch, G.E., Castro, I.A., Weibel, N. & Pickrel, J. 2017. What happens when parents and children go grocery shopping? An observational study of latino dyads in Southern California, USA. *Health Education & Behavior*, 44(1): 5.

22   Wimalasiri, J.S. 2004. A cross-national study on children's purchasing behavior and parental response. *Journal of Consumer Marketing*, 21(4): 274–284.

23   Ibid., 276; Yukl, G. & Falbe, C.M. 1990. Influence tactics and objectives in upward, downward, and lateral influence attempts. *Journal of applied psychology*, 75(2): 133.

24   Yukl & Falbe, ibid.

25   Wimalasiri, op. cit., 276.

26 Kalmijn, M. & Monden, C.W. 2012. The division of labor and depressive symptoms at the couple level: Effects of equity or specialization? *Journal of Social and Personal Relationships*, 29(3): 358–374.

27 Ibid.

28 Fowles, D. 2016. Can you afford to have kids? Available at: http://financialplan.about.com/cs/familyfinances/a/CanYouAffordKid.htm (accessed on 19 August 2018).

29 Wilkie, W. 1994. *Consumer behavior*. New York: John Wiley & Sons, 195.

30 Ibid.

31 Rousseau, op. cit., 71.

CHAPTER 10

SITUATIONAL INFLUENCES ON CONSUMER BEHAVIOUR

Virimai Victor Mugobo and Alet Erasmus

LEARNING OBJECTIVES

After reading this chapter, you should be able to:

- understand the meaning and nature of a situation
- describe the situational factors that influence consumer behaviour
- explain the role of situational factors in consumer decision making
- discuss the relationship between situations and consumer behaviour
- understand how situations change
- discuss how marketers and retailers can apply situation-based marketing strategies in order to influence consumer behaviour
- discuss the challenge that marketers and retailers face when trying to manage situational factors.

Key terms

antecedent states	information	situation-based marketing strategy
atmospherics	processing	social environment
communication	mood	usage/consumption situation
situation	physical	
disposition situation	environment	
episodic state	purchase situation	
	segmentation	
	situation	

OPENING CASE STUDY

After completing his studies, Abel worked hard and has finally managed to secure a good job with great prospects. He is now preparing to propose to the girl of his dreams, who supported him through his studies and the teething years when he was entering the job market. He has made a reservation at an expensive upmarket restaurant for the occasion and has invited both sets of parents – who know all about his plans – to join them for dinner an hour later. He devoted a lot of hours and careful thought to choosing the perfect restaurant and although this will be the first time he has ever spent so much money on a single evening, he believes it will be well worth it.

10.1 INTRODUCTION

When consumers make decisions regarding the acquisition, consumption and disposition of various products and services, their choices will inevitably be influenced by the situation. Because the situation depends on multiple factors such as the occasion (for example, a birthday), time limitations, budgetary constraints or the desire to achieve specific task objectives, it is often difficult to predict a consumer's decisions beforehand, even if you know the person well. Consumers tend to behave differently depending on the circumstances.

Abel's experience in the opening case study highlights some of the concepts that are addressed in this chapter. He is facing what is probably going to be one of the most monumental events in his life. This explains why he spent a considerable amount of time contemplating the venue. Although the couple have several favourite restaurants, this is a special occasion and he wants it to be memorable. In his mind, this warrants the extra time and money spent.

10.2 WHAT IS A SITUATION?

A **situation** (context) refers to circumstances that are particular to a time and place that are not part of the knowledge framework of the consumer, or it pertains to the products that the consumer is interested in. Think about a consumer wanting to buy an ice cream: it can be purchased from an ice cream cart on the street or from the ice cream parlour in the shopping centre. The ice cream will be similar, as will the price, but the situation will differ significantly. A situation therefore arises as a result of factors over and above the characteristics of a person (the consumer) and the product or service that the consumer is paying for. Situational effects may be behavioural (for example, the consumer's demeanour at the particular time, such as demonstrating frustration when standing in a queue), experiential (for example, enjoying the shopping experience) or perceptual (for example, experiencing loneliness and feeling depressed although there are many people around in the crowd or in the queue in a store). A person who is irritated due to overcrowding in the store may leave without buying anything, even though his feeling towards the product has not changed. The situation therefore influences the way in which a consumer reacts.

Situational factors are independent of a consumer's established psychological characteristics and are temporary in nature.[1] A situation represents an influence in addition to the factors or characteristics that are normally associated with a person (consumer) or a product or a service. A retailer's acknowledgement that situational influences may have a pertinent influence on consumers' behaviour is crucial for an understanding and possible prediction of consumers' behaviour. For example, knowing that queuing may cause irritation can be resolved by providing additional pay points in a store during a sale or at peak times. Such knowledge then becomes an important input into the development of appropriate retail marketing and customer service strategies.

Situations can either support or inhibit consumers from achieving their purchase intentions.[2] For example, an individual may have planned to go on holiday during a particular period. An unexpected situation such as an illness or a death in the family may compel the individual to postpone the holiday or cancel it completely.

In the end, a consumer's decision-making process, consumption process, and the process of disposing of used and unused products will always occur in a context involving other factors. These factors include the following:

- Shopping environment
- Retailer's promotional materials and activities
- Salespeople
- Other people, such as peers and family
- Individual factors, such as the consumer's current physical and psychological condition
- Time of year, for example during a festive season or a severe winter

For instance, it would be inappropriate to advertise swimwear during winter or Christmas trees in May.

The behaviour of consumers changes from situation to situation, and some situations may lead to unexpected decisions. If retailers understand these situational factors, they may be able to find opportunities to serve their customers better than their competitors.

Situational factors may cause the buyer to shorten, lengthen or terminate the buying process. Therefore the effective analysis and appreciation of consumers' purchase, consumption and disposal situations facilitates the successful segmentation, targeting and positioning of products and services.

DISCUSSION

Situation-based retailing

Enock, an informal trader from Zimbabwe, deals in sculptures and other hand-made items. He imports his goods from Zimbabwe and Mozambique, and sells them to upmarket clients in Sandton, Johannesburg. During the 2010 FIFA World Cup™, Enock temporarily abandoned his usual merchandise to sell country-specific flags and soccer jerseys to mainly South African, Brazilian, British, Dutch and German supporters. He made thousands of rand.

The Soccer World Cup, one of the biggest global sporting events, attracted hundreds of thousands of spectators, and Enock found and took advantage of a ready and willing market. The soccer supporters were keen to buy any product that captured the mood. However, the World Cup was only a 30-day event, and Enock has since gone back to his usual trade in sculptures and hand-made goods.

Discussion questions

1. What situational factors motivated Enock to change the merchandise that he was offering for sale?
2. What are the potential benefits that Enock identified from the situation?
3. What challenges do retailers face when trying to offer merchandise that is situation specific?

The actual purchase of a particular product or service may be subject to various unanticipated situational factors, such as limited time, inadequate funds, the presence of other people and so on.[3] Belk[4] notes that situational factors refer to 'all those factors particular to a place and time of observation which do not follow from a knowledge of personal (intra-individual) and stimulus (choice alternative) attributes, and which have a demonstrable and systematic effect on current behaviour'. According to Anić and Radas,[5] situational factors can be defined as factors that are observed and relevant to a very specific place and time. Situational factors may thus be referred to as the immediate forces that do not come from within the person, or from the product or brand being marketed, but are specific to a situation that exists before, during and after a customer has made a purchase. These temporary forces stem from particular settings or conditions in which consumers find themselves, usually for a short period of time. The knowledge of situational influences on consumer behaviour is useful to retailers to understand and predict how consumers are most likely to behave in response to their offerings.

Many soccer supporters bought Enock's flags and soccer jerseys, not because it had been their long-term plan to do so, but mainly because of the atmosphere and the situation. They wanted to identify with their country, its team and also with their fellow supporters. The consumers were therefore in a mood centred around soccer and any product or service that captured this mood appealed to them.

10.3 TYPES OF SITUATION

There are four broad types of situation that confront consumers during the decision-making process: the communication situation, the purchase situation, the usage situation and the disposal situation. These may have varying impacts on the ultimate decision that the consumer makes with regards to the purchase of certain products and services[6]. (See Figure 10.1.)

10.3.1 The communication situation

The **communication situation** refers to the setting in which consumers are exposed to information from interpersonal or commercial sources that have an impact on their behaviour.[7] Consumers receive information at different times and in different contexts and places. The ability of the consumer to get the information, process it and act upon it depends on this setting.

Situational factors such as illness, thirst, hunger, lack of money, loneliness, the people present and the physical environment may support or inhibit the ability of the consumer to act upon the communication stimuli. If an advertisement for a person's favourite restaurant is being aired on television during a time when he or she is battling financially, that person is most likely to disregard it. A message delivered in a crowded and loud environment such as a nightclub is likely to go unnoticed or to be ignored by many potential customers simply because they cannot clearly decipher the message amidst the noise or they are not in the right mood to listen to it.

Figure 10.1 A positive purchase situation

On the other hand, a consumer will be much more attentive to advertisements that are aired during their favourite television programmes. Many consumers also value advice from their friends and family with regard to certain products and services.

10.3.2 The purchase situation

The **purchase situation** refers to the situation in which products or services are bought. Factors such as the people present, the store layout and design, the décor, the retailer's staffing levels, the store's **atmospherics** (or additional effects such as music), the behaviour and appearance of the store's salespeople and the location of the store may affect the purchase situation.[8] For example, a consumer can be persuaded to purchase a product by store displays or the advice of salespeople.

The purchase situation can also be affected by the consumer's mood: when in a positive mood, consumers deal with purchase decisions more easily and make decisions much faster.[9] How pleasurable it is may also be influenced by multiple other factors such as the amount of time available for the shopping trip, the weather conditions, the purpose of the purchase and the presence (or absence) of other people in the store.

Retailers and marketing managers can control some of these factors (for example, the store temperature, the convenience of store layout, size of fitting rooms or the number of salespeople on duty), but not every element. For example, it is beyond a retailer's control if a customer enters the store in a negative mood, if the customer's state of health is poor, if a customer has severe time constraints to deal with, or is hungry.

10.3.3   The usage situation

The **usage/consumption situation** refers to the context in which the product or service is used. When consumers buy different products and services, they do so in order to satisfy specific functional and emotional needs and wants. Many products are designed for use in specific circumstances, such as a home first-aid kit. The consumption situation can become the basis for the development and positioning of new products for specific consumer segments, such as special swimsuits for people who swim in extremely cold weather. The usage situation could also involve the presence and opinion of other people who might influence a consumer's product choice: a consumer would not want to be snubbed by others and might even want to impress them.[10]

10.3.4   The disposition situation

The **disposition situation** varies from situation to situation, which provides opportunities as well as challenges to retailers.

The method of disposing of products and their packaging is primarily influenced by factors such as:

* whether the packaging can be reused or not (for example, plastic containers can be used to store leftovers in the fridge)
* whether the packaging can be resold or not (for example, some packaging is returnable for a small fee)
* whether the product and/or packaging is harmless or not (for example, plastic straws are now considered extremely harmful to the environment and are even banned by many restaurants)
* the availability of time to dispose properly of items such glass bottles that can be recycled
* the place of disposal (when the place of disposal is not conveniently located, there is little chance that disposal will be done properly)
* the cost of disposal (if additional costs such as transport or the acquisition of special containers is required, proper disposal becomes a burden)
* the environmental awareness of the disposer (for example, some consumers are highly concerned about the ramifications of wasteful consumption and will make considerable effort to use packaging that can be recycled).

It is therefore imperative for retailers and marketers to be aware of, and to understand the factors that will influence the disposition of products and their packaging by consumers in order to develop alternative packaging that is less harmful to the environment and that is ethically sound. Proper disposal of unwanted products and recycling of useful products are matters that should be prioritised by retailers and encouraged among consumers to curb indiscriminate waste.

RESEARCH BOX 10.1

A report by the World Bank indicates that South Africa's daily production of trash is the 15th highest in the world. This equates to two kilograms per person per day, which puts South Africa at number 38 globally. Visit http://www.infrastructurene.ws/2016/08/17/how-much-rubbish-south-africans-dump-each-day/ or any other sources that explain the problems that are associated with pollution and environmental degradation.

Discuss the following among your friends:
1. How can you, as consumers, contribute personally to reduce the amount of waste created per person in our country per day?
2. How can you set an example in your household in terms of discrimination between waste and trash?
3. How does ocean acidification influence all of us, even inland?
4. How can the recycling of clothes be to the benefit of our natural resources?

10.4 SITUATIONAL CLASSIFICATIONS AND CHARACTERISTICS

Situations can be evaluated to anticipate consumers' behaviour in terms of five characteristics: physical features, social surroundings, temporal perspectives, task objectives and antecedent states (see Table 10.1). Every one of these factors may influence consumers' behaviour across the four situations highlighted above (sections 10.3.1–10.3.4).

Table 10.1 Situational classifications and characteristics

Situational characteristics	Examples of key features
Physical features	Store layout and design, store signage, size, colour, aromas, music, lighting
Social environment	People present; appearance and behaviour of salespeople
Temporal perspectives	Time of the day, time constraints, season and occasional states (for example, a promotional sale)
Task objectives	Plans, purpose of purchase and role of consumer
Antecedent states	Time, mood, occasional states (such as anxiousness, heath, hunger) and rituals

10.4.1 Physical features

The **physical environment** is composed of atmospherics that may influence consumers' judgement of the quality of service being offered by the retailer. The term 'atmospherics' refers to all the physical features in the retail environment, including the store layout and design, the décor, the ambience, aroma, sound and lighting to enhance the attractiveness and atmosphere of the environment.[11] Indications are that the physical attractiveness of a retail store significantly influences a consumer's choice of retailer, sometimes even more so than the merchandise offered.[12] Atmospherics may also influence a consumer's perception of the overall image of the business.[13]

The physical environment is composed of spatial elements and non-spatial elements. The spatial elements include physical features such as the structure and size of the store, location, and store and fitting room design and layout. Non-spatial elements include factors such as climatic conditions, noise levels, music, lighting and aroma. The section that follows discusses some of these factors.

Climatic conditions

The behaviour of consumers is influenced by prevailing weather conditions as well as the ambient temperature of the store itself.

Marketers and retailers are well aware of the type of products that will attract consumers' interest during winter, summer, autumn and spring. For example, jerseys, jackets and warm scarves are sought after in winter, whereas short-sleeved t-shirts, shorts and swimwear are popular in summer. Umbrellas may be in abundance in stores during winter time in the Cape, but they would be more in demand in summer in Gauteng. Certain types of food are also seasonal: think about soups in winter and ice cream in summer.

Notwithstanding the weather conditions or the season, in-store temperatures should always be comfortable. If a store is too hot or too cold, this could chase customers away.

Colour

Colour is a useful tool used in the retail industry to attract attention and to evoke consumers' emotions. For example, certain colours are regarded as being more suitable for the packaging of certain products.[14] Some colours are more effective than others in attracting the attention of consumers: think about pastel colours versus bright, intense colours on signage. Colours also symbolise different things in different cultures and settings, and many consumers associate certain colours with specific occasions.

For instance, the colours red and white are prominent on Valentine's Day, and many people in South Africa wear black when attending funerals. Green is usually associated with freshness and environmental friendliness, whereas the colour white is associated with purity and peace. Marketers often use bright colours such as red and yellow to create attractive window displays and to announce special sales promotions. Fashion trends may also create colour preferences during a particular season and therefore retailers have to act accordingly when they design promotional material or store and window displays. Colour is used for a variety of purposes in the retail industry, including attracting the attention of customers, affecting their moods and ensuring brand recall and memorability.[15]

Lighting

Lighting is viewed in terms of brightness, contrast, glare and sparkle. For example, tension can be created by brightness, and comfortable cosiness by lack of it (think about a candlelit dinner); a sense of negativity can be created by strong contrasts; a lively atmosphere can be created with glare and sparkle.[16]

In retail environments, lighting can be used to generate a suitable atmosphere, to draw attention to objects and to enhance visibility.[17] Hoyle[18] posits that the type and level of lighting has the potential to affect sales dramatically. The effect of lighting on consumers' willingness to shop, their willingness to spend more time in the store and in evoking consumers' moods and emotions can be skilfully manipulated for every retail context.[19]

Music

Retailers use background music to create a specific atmosphere in their stores. Mehrabian and Russell's model of pleasure-arousal-dominance (PAD) that was developed in 1974 and revisited recently, suggests that an environment can change an individual's mood and behaviour by modifying levels of pleasure, excitement and/or authority.[20] Research suggests that three qualities of music, namely temp, volume and genre, can influence consumers' buying behaviour in retail environments as follows:

- *Tempo:* Slow music causes customers to take their time over their meal and spend significantly more money on alcohol, while fast music reduces patrons' eating time.[21] The first scenario might be sought after for a sophisticated restaurant, while the second scenario would be ideal for a fast-food diner.
- *Volume:* Loud music decreases the total time spent in a store. While younger consumers tend to be more tolerant of louder music in the foreground, older consumers prefer background music.[22]
- *Genre:* The type of music being played in a store is one of the first things shoppers notice and retailers often select their music according to their target audience. Stores aimed at youth generally play music such as hip-hop, rap or house. With older customers, country or jazz music may be more suitable. In wine shops, for example, customers tend to spend more money when classical music is played; and although Christmas jingles may be mildly irritating when played in stores in October, they nevertheless encourage shoppers to think about gift shopping and when played during the holiday season, they increase sales of holiday-related goods. Retailers should therefore be aware of the music that their target market likes and should play happy selections in that genre in order to enhance consumers' shopping experience.[23]

Some retailers prefer not to play any music in their stores, reasoning that differing tastes may mean it will generally cause more harm than good. Ultimately, none of the characteristics of music are isolated and therefore the effect of music on consumers' purchase behaviour is not unrelated to other characteristics of the store. Nevertheless, music can play a part in attracting customers or discouraging them from shopping.

Aromas

Research indicates that a pleasant aroma creates feelings of joy and satisfaction.[24] However, the type of aroma should be suitable for the specific environment: while a subtle vanilla aroma was found to be powerful in terms of positively increasing consumers' emotions in a clothing store, other aromas might be totally unacceptable. In addition, there are gender differences in consumers' perception of aromas.[25]

Notably, in major shopping centres, fast food outlets are situated quite a distance from clothing retailers to prevent odours from clashing or creating negative impressions. It is also not coincidental that some fast food outlets and restaurants are located near the entrance.

Store layout

The impact of store layout on consumer behaviour has been widely researched. Store layouts may influence and determine how long consumers stay within the store, the merchandise to which they are exposed and the ease or difficulty they experience in finding what they want. The store layout also affects the flow of consumers within the store and may ultimately contribute to, or limit, crowding.

Figure 10.2 Store layout exposes the merchandise in the store to consumers and ensures the efficient flow of customers within the store.

Signs and displays

The major role of signs in the retail environment is to provide information to customers, such as where specific items may be found and prices. Some in-store signs and displays serve to let customers know about current promotions. Prominent and colourful in-store displays capture consumers' attention and may influence them to buy the products.

Figure 10.3 Consumers are most likely to pay attention to in-store displays that are attractive and eye-catching.

DISCUSSION

The influential role of in-store displays

Adam went to a new shopping centre in his neighbourhood to browse around, but particularly to purchase a new pair of designer jeans to wear to an important function the following weekend.

In one of the stores, a friendly, well-dressed salesperson assisted him in terms of the correct size and his preferred style.

At the entrance to the fitting room, he was attracted by a display of button-down shirts hanging from the wall in attractive colour combinations and because he was wearing a casual t-shirt, he grabbed two of them to try on with the jeans. The salesperson then handed him a belt to make sure the jeans sat properly before they measured the length of the trousers to do some hem adjustments for him. He was told that the belts were on promotion. The salesperson offered him something to drink while waiting for the tailor to do the measurements. Eventually, Adam left the store with a pair of jeans, two shirts and a belt, and went to the nearest coffee shop to celebrate his new outfits.

Discussion questions

1. What role did the salesperson play in Adam's decision to purchase more items than he initially planned to do?
2. What compelled him to consider shirts as well?
3. What convinced Adam to purchase the belt?

When Adam went to the store, his main mission was to purchase a pair of designer jeans. However, the situation in the retail store influenced his decision process rather dramatically. Adam's case illustrates the role of various factors within the retail environment in influencing consumers' behaviour. Factors such as the friendly assistance and support of the salesperson, attractive product displays, promotional offers and point-of-sale stimuli (such as refreshments) may ultimately influence the customer's decision to buy (or not to buy) certain products or services.

Adam was initially attracted by product displays and the prompt attention of the well-dressed salesperson, which made him more conscious about his own appearance and what type of shirt he would eventually want to wear with his new designer jeans. He had not even considered wearing a belt, or how it might influence the length of the trousers.

In-store sales and support personnel provide valuable information to customers before, during and after the purchase of goods and services. Because this service may be instrumental in influencing consumers to behave in one way or another, employees need to be adequately trained to deal with customers and must know the products well enough to answer queries and do demonstrations where necessary.

Point-of-sale stimuli refer to items that are strategically positioned to attract customers' attention and to influence their decision making. In grocery stores, popular point-of-sale merchandise items include beverages, sweets, newspapers, chocolates and magazines, which are not usually on consumers' shopping lists, but are bought on impulse at the till. In clothing retail stores, the point-of sale items may include accessories, small gifts and fashion magazines.

APPLICATION

In-store displays and consumer behaviour

1. Discuss the various physical environmental factors that retailers and marketers use in order to influence consumer behaviour in-store.
2. Are all unplanned purchases unnecessary purchases?
3. What role do in-store salespeople play in the consumer decision-making process?

10.4.2　Social environment

The **social environment** refers to interactions between people. The presence of other people before, during and after purchase may influence the current or future behaviour of an individual. This includes crowds, the people accompanying the consumer and the actions (or failure to act) of salespeople.

Crowding

Crowding refers to a situation in which the retail environment is too full of shoppers. When shoppers experience a feeling of being confined and claustrophobic, they tend to spend less time in the store, buying less, making quicker decisions and using less of the available information. This often leads to unsatisfactory purchases, unpleasant shopping experiences and a decline in the probability of revisiting the store.[26]

Hawkins et al.[27] argue that 'retailers must balance the expenses of having a larger store than required most of the time against the cost of dissatisfied customers during key shopping periods'. Many consumers will decide not to go into a supermarket when they realise that the queues at the checkout counters are long. They may choose to visit another store or to do their shopping at another time instead.[28] Underhill[29] refers to this as the 'butt-brush effect'. Some retail stores tend to be over-crowded during peak periods and in certain seasons. Such periods include, but are not limited to, early evenings during the rush hour, weekends (especially following pay day) and just before major holidays such as Christmas, Ramadan and so on. Retailers may therefore overcome the problem of over-crowding by having more checkout counters open, additional personnel on the floor and longer operating hours at these times.

RESEARCH BOX 10.2

Understanding the 'butt-brush effect'

Visit any crowded supermarket during peak hours. The purpose of your visit is to observe the behaviour of customers in a crowded retail environment.

Research task

* Observe at least five customers during peak hour from the time they enter a popular take-away fast food franchise until they leave with the food. Only observe one customer at a time (you can pretend to be waiting for someone).
* Record all of your observations, also attending to the behaviour of the assistants in the store.
* Analyse these observations. Write a two-page report on your findings and recommendations to the service provider's management suggesting how they can reduce crowding and improve customer service during peak hours.

Shopping partners

Shopping partners are people who accompany others to buy goods and services. Research indicates that close friends and relatives are trusted more than salespeople because it is believed that people who know you well will provide honest advice.[30] Trust refers to the perceived credibility of a person or company. Apart from providing advice, shopping partners may even make a decision on behalf of the consumer.

It is argued that the use of personal social networks to gather information is fundamental to consumers' purchasing behaviour and that it is so common that we seldom make a note of it. Friends and family in particular are consulted when people need to purchase something with which they are less familiar, a process referred to as *information passing*.[31] This phenomenon is associated with *relationship marketing* and suggests that consumers engage in interpersonal market behaviour due to personal, social and institutional influences. Through engagement with people they know, consumers simplify their buying and consumption tasks. It also helps to simplify information processing, reduce effort, decrease perceived risks, retain consistency in their reasoning about products and provide emotional relief. Such consultation forms part of the consumer socialisation process throughout life, which explains why it is an almost natural thing to do. Subsequently, it is worthwhile for marketers to take note of the influence of family, friends and peers in their marketing strategies and advertising campaigns.[32]

Admittedly, friends and family do not always possess the relevant product knowledge to conclude rational decisions (well-deliberated), but they are nevertheless trusted. The conversations that shopping partners have in the retail environment may influence them to make certain purchases that they might not have considered had they been shopping alone. This is called pester power.

Salespeople
Retailers employ salespeople to provide customer service within the store. The services offered by salespeople vary from store to store and may include activities such as the following:

- Making sales
- Indicating the location of specific merchandise
- Communicating prices to customers
- Providing product information
- Demonstrating products
- Dealing with customer enquiries and complaints

The actions of salespeople may have a profound influence, positive or negative, on the quality of service rendered by the retailer and the customer's overall perception of the store. In some instances, customers may walk away from a store when they feel that they have not been given adequate or proper attention, or they have received poor service.

Figure 10.4 A salesperson serving customers

However, many retailers have well-trained salespeople and invest in continual training for their employees to ensure that they offer excellent services to their clients. These salespeople are not only able to provide information, but they are also able to influence customers to buy from their stores. Ongoing training of staff members ensures that they stay up to date with contemporary customer service skills and techniques as well as product information.[33]

Research indicates that salespeople's emotional commitment in terms of their selling skills is influenced by how much they like their job as well as their sense of authority, and it will influence how long they will remain in their job. Therefore, it is worthwhile for retailers to invest in their salespeople and to empower them. It is common for consumers to patronise a store because they like the demeanour of the salespeople.[34]

10.4.3 Temporal perspective

As a situational influence, temporal perspective relates to the time taken to make a decision and the time required to make a purchase (including travelling time, waiting time in a store, and so on).[35] When experiencing time pressure, a consumer might, for example, limit the number of product alternatives that are considered or visit just a single store, maybe even the closest one.

The influence of the time factor on consumer behaviour is two dimensional, influencing firstly *when* consumers make certain decisions (for example, during specific times of the day, week, month or year) and secondly *how* decisions are made (what kind of food to eat or when to enter a restaurant).

APPLICATION

The influence of time on consumption behaviour

Every week day, Amy travels between her home in Pretoria and work in Johannesburg on the Gautrain instead of going by car, to save time. When she arrives at Rosebank station, which is within five minutes' walking distance from her office, she goes to the same restaurant on the corner and orders a cappuccino and a croissant. While enjoying her breakfast, she reflects on the previous day and plans her activities for the day ahead. This has been her routine for the past six months and has become a habit that she treasures before the frantic rush of her working day commences.

Discussion questions

1. How does time influence your consumption of certain goods and services?
2. What kind of opportunities does time provide to retailers to develop and market goods and services?
3. Identify and describe any five products that are related to time shortage.

As seen above, Amy's work day begins with breakfast at a cosy restaurant near her office. The people at the restaurant would be surprised if she walked into the restaurant one morning and ordered a burger, which is more the norm for lunch or dinner, instead of her usual croissant. They would be equally surprised if she ordered a beer, which is not appropriate at that time of day, to go with it.

Certain products and services are consumed more during specific times of the year than at other times of the year. For instance, umbrellas and raincoats are popular during the rainy season and many people go away on vacation during school holidays. Similarly, many products are associated with specific occasions, such as red roses for Valentine's Day and hot cross buns for Easter. Pre-Christmas shopping often differs in style, content and place from shopping done at other times of the year.

The amount of time consumers have available may influence their decision-making process. Sometimes consumers have all day to browse and to think about a purchase, consider all available alternatives and make an informed decision. However, in other cases, consumers may have 15 minutes before an appointment and may thus be compelled to make almost impromptu decisions. If a consumer wins a cash prize at the till and must choose an item on the spot, he or she may be influenced more by the time pressure to grab whatever is at hand than by what he or she really needs.

Some choices are made not because they are the best option, but because they are the most appropriate decision from a chronological (sequential or time) perspective, for example choosing a microwave meal rather than fresh ingredients because there is no time to cook.

A consumer with limited time does not have the luxury of carrying out a comprehensive search and evaluation of the different options available. However, the internet now provides consumers with a platform from which to search for products and services online instead of visiting stores in person, which saves time and money – even if they eventually go to a physical brick-and-mortar store to purchase the product. Nowadays, multiple retailers offer omni-channel retailing to optimise consumers' experiences. For example Woolworths, Pick n Pay and Truworths offer online shopping services in addition to physical retail stores.

10.4.4 Task objectives

Consumers generally purchase goods and services for a specific purpose, to perform a specific function. Clothes, for example, can be merely functional (such as a protective uniform/apron), but due to design, brand and aesthetical properties, they could also be worn to display status, to enhance your image, to boost self-image. A consumer may buy a jersey for protection against the cold, or may purchase a branded one to gain the admiration of friends. School uniforms are designed to create a sense of unity among pupils by reducing elements that may identify different socio-economic levels and portraying the image of the school. Task objectives refer to the reason why a consumption activity is occurring in a particular situation.

Plans and purpose

Consumers may buy goods and services to fulfil a certain plan, purpose or role. They have to make certain choices and consumption decisions in order to realise these plans. For example, a family may want to buy a new car in two years' time and so may decide to create a separate savings account, depositing money into that account every month and cutting down on unnecessary expenditure. The decision to save thus influences their current consumption choices as their main objective is to buy a new car in the future.

The purpose refers to the reason why the consumption activity is occurring. Consumers buy goods and services for a specific purpose, for example a chair that will be comfortable in the living room or one for the beach. They may also buy goods for themselves, or for others (as a gift), or on behalf of others (as a surrogate buyer). There are some special occasions that influence consumers to buy specific products and services, for example pumpkins to carve for Halloween or evening dresses to wear to the matric dance.

It may be the norm in a particular community for people to bring certain presents or gifts with them when attending specific functions or occasions. This is especially true for ceremonies and rituals such as weddings or birthdays. Consumers will need to consider the person receiving the gift as well as the purpose of the gift. For example, a wedding present would be very different to a birthday present for a four-year-old.[36] Sharing gifts is a collective act that links and connects people and is a powerful way to create feelings of solidarity and bonding.[37]

While the purpose of certain products may be clear, for example buying a heater for winter, the function and purpose of gift giving, sharing and commodity exchange are vague. Certain gifts, or giving money to someone, may be regarded as an insult or a bribe. Sometimes, the purpose of a purchase may be some form of exchange, for example Christmas presents.

Role
An individual's role can differ vastly when purchasing products and that would influence the consumer decision process as well as the factors considered. For example, a middle-aged woman may hold different roles in different situations. She may be a wife, a mother, a manager at work, a choir leader at church, a member of the school governing body and so on. When she buys products and services for her family, she is playing the role of wife and mother, and she is, to a large extent, motivated by the desire to ensure that her family is well cared for. When thinking about products, other people's needs are considered more than her own. However, when she is at work, she plays a completely different role as a manager and her main objective is to achieve the company's goals and objectives. When acting on behalf of her company, or as an institutional buyer, she is supposed to prioritise the company's needs and profitability rather than personal preferences.[38]

10.4.5   Antecedent states
Antecedent states also influence the behaviour of consumers when they buy, consume and dispose of products and services. Antecedent states are consumers' temporary moods and episodic states (discussed below), which are influenced by perception, evaluation and the consumer's acceptance of the external environment. They encompass a consumer's physical or psychological state immediately before his or her current state of action.[39]

Mood
The consumer's **mood** before, during and after consumption can play a role in influencing his or her behaviour. A mood is an emotional state that can be a catalyst in consumer decision making. Consumers buy different products and

services depending on their mood. When some consumers are excited, they express this positive mood by engaging in activities such as going out with friends for a meal, organising parties, spoiling themselves with clothes or simply by spending their money. Mood and emotions have been found to play a mediating role between consumers' understanding and actual behaviour in a retail setting. When in a good mood, consumers may purchase things or participate in activities on the spur of the moment.[40]

Marketers and retailers will try to create an appropriate 'in-store mood' to positively influence consumer decision making. This can be done with music, decor and store design, and also through customer service personnel (see section 10.4.1). For example, many supermarkets change their music depending on the time of the day, playing laidback styles in the morning and up-tempo songs during rush hour and early evening.

Episodic states

An **episodic state** is a temporary state that may influence a consumer's decision to behave in one way or another. An episodic state can also be referred to as a momentary condition and includes feeling lonely, sick, tired, angry, being in possession of extra money, having no money at all and so on. For example, a consumer who is unwell may decide to go to the nearest pharmacy to buy some medication or visit a local doctor for treatment. The consumer would not have sought this service if he or she had not been feeling ill. Similarly, an individual who has some extra money may decide to treat him- or herself, or others to a nice meal because he or she can afford it. On the contrary, a person who is experiencing financial difficulties is likely to spend money only on necessities.

Episodic states and moods can influence whether or not consumers buy, where they buy, what they buy and how much they buy. An understanding of episodic states and consumers' moods can help retailers and marketers to predict consumers' product or service preferences more accurately.[41]

Ritual situations

Rook[42] defines a ritual as:

> a type of expressive, symbolic activity constructed of multiple behaviors that occur in a fixed, episodic sequence, and that tend to be repeated over time. Ritual behavior is dramatically scripted and acted out and is performed with formality, seriousness, and inner intensity.

The behaviour of a consumer during a particular situation may be influenced by his or her desire to observe a certain ritual. A ritual situation can thus be referred to as a social occasion that triggers a set of interrelated behaviours that occur in a structured format and that have symbolic meaning. Key to a ritual is that it is a focused activity.[43]

Many societies observe certain rituals during ceremonies such as the birth of a child, death, birthdays, weddings, graduations, the purchase of a new home, reunions, the beginning of a new year, and so on. Mostly these rituals are associated with certain products. Retailers optimise these customs as an ideal opportunity to develop and market new products, for example special costumes for Halloween or chocolates for Valentine's Day. Certain stores have registries where brides can set aside items that guests can select as a present for their bridal shower or as a wedding gift.

Rituals and consumer behaviour

The observance of a particular ritual may demand that certain products and services be purchased. For example, two people who are about to get married may purchase items such as a wedding gown, wedding rings and a wedding cake. In the Xhosa culture, a boy who has just been circumcised is supposed to have a completely new wardrobe as this symbolises his initiation into manhood. Also, products such as blankets, traditional beer (**umqhomboti**), snuff and other artefacts are associated with certain traditional African ceremonies. The people who observe these rituals are therefore required to buy these items.

Discussion questions

1. Choose three rituals that are common in your community or culture. Explain the purpose of each and identify specific products and services that are associated with them.
2. How influential are these rituals on the consumption of the identified products and services?
3. How pertinent are rituals in modern times? Discuss.

10.5 DEVELOPING SITUATION-BASED MARKETING STRATEGIES

In view of the fact that consumers' emotions, attitudes and behaviour may be influenced by various situational factors, it is essential for marketers and retailers to design and develop appropriate **situation-based marketing strategies** to improve customer satisfaction and loyalty.

The ability to develop effective situation-based strategies can provide a retailer with a competitive advantage. However, many situational factors occur randomly, which makes it difficult for retailers and marketers to predict their occurrence and ascertain their impact on consumer behaviour. The five-step process of developing situation-based marketing strategies is set out in Figure 10.5.

10.5.1 Identify usage situations

The first stage in the process of developing a situation-based marketing strategy is to identify the various situations that may involve the use or consumption of specific products and services. This tends to differ across societies and cultures, therefore an in-depth understanding of the cultural environment is necessary. For example, the consumption of alcohol at ceremonies such as weddings and parties is accepted in some cultures but is taboo in others. Some tribes in the Eastern Cape use traditional beer to soothe their ancestors, whilst for others, beer is simply a beverage.

Retailers can use consumer forums, observational techniques, focus group discussions, surveys, interviews and secondary data to obtain information about usage situations from salespeople and consumers.

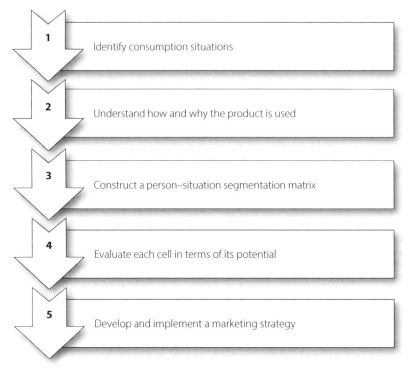

1 Identify consumption situations

2 Understand how and why the product is used

3 Construct a person–situation segmentation matrix

4 Evaluate each cell in terms of its potential

5 Develop and implement a marketing strategy

Figure 10.5 The five-step process of developing situation-specific marketing strategies

10.5.2   Understand how and why the product is used

Different individuals may use the same product, but for different purposes. It is therefore important as part of the development of situation-based marketing strategies to establish how individuals use or consume certain products and the reason for that usage or consumption. Marketers and retailers also need to understand the benefits that consumers seek when they consume certain products in specific situations. For instance, "wet wipes" (moist towelettes) were originally designed to clean babies during a nappy change, but are now also used for removing make-up, cleaning jewellery and for general personal hygiene, particularly where clean running water may not be readily available.

This information can also be obtained using consumer forums, observational techniques, focus group discussions, surveys, interviews and secondary data, so that retailers and marketers can properly promote their products.

10.5.3   Construct a person–situation segmentation matrix

The world is made up of billions of buyers with their own sets of needs and behaviour. **Segmentation** aims to match groups together and is essentially the identification of subsets of buyers within a market who share similar needs and demonstrate similar buyer behaviour.[44] Kotler & Armstrong[45] explain that market segmentation is the process of dividing a market into distinct groups with distinct needs, characteristics or behaviour that might require separate products or marketing mixes.

The person–situation segmentation matrix segments the market by combining data from multiple sources to create a holistic view of the interaction of a person (user) with an object in a certain situation (location context). An understanding of what the different situation segments should be is fundamental to its success. Table 10.2 highlights a person–situation segmentation matrix for potential users of a gym.

Table 10.2 Person–situation segmentation matrix for potential users of a gym

Gym service use situation	Young children	Teenagers	Young adults	Middle-aged adults	Older citizens
Routine exercises	Healthy lifestyle	Healthy lifestyle	Healthy lifestyle	Healthy lifestyle	Healthy lifestyle and long life
Recreation	Socialisation with parents	Socialisation with parents and friends	Socialisation with friends	Socialisation with friends	Socialisation
Competitive sporting		Fitness	Fitness	Fitness	Socialisation
Doctor's prescription	Rehabilitation	Rehabilitation	Rehabilitation and fitness	Rehabilitation and fitness	Rehabilitation and fitness

The person–situation segmentation matrix is an effective tool for identifying opportunities, segmenting and targeting specific markets, and positioning a retailer's products and services. For example, an individual intending to start a gym service could use the above matrix to establish the segments to target and the benefits that these segments may anticipate from the service provider. The matrix can also be used to compare the company's offering against competitors' products by putting them side by side in the matrix and comparing them in terms of their ability to meet market needs, quality, the possibility of entering new markets, pricing, and so on.

10.5.4 Evaluate each cell in terms of its potential

The steps in the evaluation process are as follows:
- Rank cells in terms of market share.
- Identify important benefits sought in each cell of the matrix.
- Figure out where your competitors are located in the matrix.
- Position your product in the matrix and determine how well you are meeting the need relative to your competitors.
- Identify opportunities based on segment size, needs and competitive advantage of your product or service.

10.5.5   Develop and implement a marketing strategy

Retailers are in business to make a profit through the provision of appropriate products and services that will satisfy customer requirements. After evaluating each option/cell to identify its profit potential, the retailer should only offer those products and services that have sufficient and sustainable profit potential in the long run. For example, when a gym (see Table 10.2) considers the needs of young children, the fact that it could draw more adults who could socialise with their children might open up multiple viable opportunities such as healthy refreshments and clothing items that could attract even more clients. The identified products and services must also be realistic, available or have the capability to be produced or sourced at competitive cost prices.

RESEARCH BOX 10.3

A tailor-made marketing strategy

Visit any coffee shop/restaurant during mid-morning or lunch time.

Research task

1. Interview at least five people who are busy working on their computers to establish why they chose to work in that environment. Do not extend the conversation to more than three minutes.
2. Record all of their responses.
3. Analyse these responses. Write a two-page report on your findings and make recommendations to the restaurant management. Your recommendations should focus on how the restaurant/coffee shop can develop a tailor-made marketing strategy in order to attract even more working people to their establishment

The development of situation-based marketing strategies should also acknowledge the relevance of the key areas below.

Physical evidence

The retailer needs to ensure that the environment in which goods and services are exchanged is attractive and fit for the purpose. The retail environment should support and/or enhance the image that the retailer needs to create in the minds of its customers. The equipment, buildings, furniture and other physical effects in and around the store all play a crucial role in creating a lasting impression and can also influence the behaviour of consumers. For example, consumers do not expect the interior of a discount store to be the same as an upmarket specialty store. However, when a retailer is situated in an upmarket mall, consumers would have certain expectations about the quality of the physical environment and related amenities such as rest rooms.[46] If even the parking area is not convenient, the retailer will be affected. Therefore retailers have to take a holistic view of the physical/structural elements that might influence their image.

Customer service training

This chapter has highlighted the importance of salespeople in the provision of services to consumers. For any retailer to be able to stay ahead of its competitors and to offer excellent customer services, it is essential that it have a dedicated, motivated and well-trained sales force. Organisations should therefore ensure that they implement ongoing training programmes to empower old and new employees and encourage them to be "walking billboards" for the company.

Apart from sales personnel's knowledge about the company and its products, they should be friendly, supportive and neatly dressed. Some researchers are of the opinion that employees are probably the most valuable asset of the food service industry.[47] In many retailers, the front-line staff determine the quality of the service delivered[48] because they create the first impression of the store/restaurant when customers enter.[49] Furthermore, their appearance strongly influences how customers evaluate their shopping experience.[50]

Environmental scanning and awareness

Retailers must constantly scan the environment for opportunities and threats that may impact on their business. This is because environmental changes and developments may influence consumers' behaviour, often unexpectedly. For example, when there are warnings of a pending water shortage, consumers may start stockpiling bottled water, as happened in early 2018 with the drought conditions in Cape Town. If a winter is not as cold as anticipated, the sales of heaters and electric blankets may be lower than expected and therefore retailers may have to have promotional sales to get rid of extra stock before summer arrives. Retailers also need to acknowledge social and sports events, holidays and other cultural developments to demonstrate that they understand their customers' needs. Such factors may also provide viable opportunities for the business, for example considering what children will need for the start of a new school year. While not all retailers are stockists of school uniforms, they could invest in stationery, sports equipment, lunch boxes, leisure wear and other related products.

RESEARCH BOX 10.4

Develop a marketing strategy

Consider any popular product or service of your choice.

Research task

1. Indicate the reason why consumers buy that product. Talk to a few consumers in order to obtain this information.
2. Construct a person–situation segmentation matrix for the product or service.
3. Recommend any marketing strategies that a retailer of the product or service could use in order to stay competitive.

SUMMARY

This chapter focused on the situational/contextual influences on consumer behaviour. Consumers' decisions to buy products and services are influenced by multiple factors, including the situations that exist before, during and after the product or service has been purchased.

The four situations that may influence a consumer's purchase behaviour are communication (in which the consumer receives information), purchase (when the consumer actually buys the product or service), usage (the environment in which the consumer uses or consumes the product or service) and disposition (the way in which consumers dispose of products or their packaging after use). The disposition situation has attracted much attention in recent years due to concern about excessive waste and environmental degradation. This presents manufacturers and retailers with various opportunities and challenges in terms of the quality of packaging, ease of disposition, ability to recycle, environmental impact, and so on. Retailers need to identify the key features of four of these situations in order to develop appropriate, competitive and sustainable situation-based marketing strategies for their products and services.

The social environment also impacts on consumer behaviour. This includes aspects such as crowding, shopping partners, the influence of salespeople and temporal factors (what to buy, and when to buy). Equally important is personal influences such as antecedent states (mood, emotions, and episodic states).

SELF-ASSESSMENT QUESTIONS

1. Using practical examples, explain a situation in terms of consumer decision making.
2. Name three situational factors and explain why retailers need to appreciate their influence on consumers' behaviour in a retail store.
3. Explain how antecedent states may influence patrons' behaviour in an upmarket restaurant.
4. Discuss how a grocery retailer could use atmospherics to create an unforgettable shopping experience for its customers.
5. Explain how temporal factors may influence consumers' behaviour in a clothing retail store.
6. Imagine that you are about to buy a new bicycle. Describe the communication, purchasing, consumption and disposition situations related to this purchase and explain the key factors that bicycle retailers need to consider when they develop their marketing strategies.
7. You are the manager of a popular supermarket in a crowded central business district. The supermarket tends to be over-crowded during peak hours and weekends. Describe the strategies that you would implement to overcome crowding. Is crowding good or bad for customers? Support your answer with valid reasons.
8. Why are retailers and manufactures concerned with how consumers dispose of their products and/or product packaging? In your answer, highlight the opportunities and challenges that the disposition brings to retailers and manufacturers.

EXPERIENTIAL EXERCISE

The disposition situation has become particularly important in recent years due to concern about excessive waste and environmental degradation. Form groups of five and plan a strategy to reduce the waste of packaging materials at sports events in your community that would excite, rather than frustrate, the spectators. Think of something that will focus on the re-use of materials or alternative ways to present the food and drinks, rather than simply supplying more rubbish bins. Report your strategies to the class and identify the three best, most practical and executable strategies.

Seasonal buying for competitiveness

Founded more than five decades ago, Rege Holdings is a South African registered retailer operating more than 50 luxury clothing stores across the country. Using its Rege Lifestyle brand, the company markets imported luxury clothing, targeting the middle-to-upper classes. During the past decade, the company has recorded phenomenal profits, largely as a result of the emerging black middle class that is fighting to find its place in a changing society.

Speaking at the company's 2012 annual stakeholders' meeting, Rege Holdings' CEO, Mr Gallant Fletcher, hinted that much of the company's success hinges on its ability to align its merchandise to the natural seasons in the environment. 'Rege Lifestyle will have the right product for you for that particular time of the year,' he claimed. Achieving the one-billion-rand net profit mark in 2012 was a major milestone for Rege Lifestyle and the company is geared for further growth.

In order to respond to changing customer preferences and trends, many fashion retailers have mastered the technique of developing new fashion designs extremely quickly to capture the current trends in the market and to align with customers' seasonal expectations and preferences. This concept of 'fast fashion' allows retailers to introduce new merchandise efficiently, thereby providing customers with product variety and choice throughout the year.

Fast fashion also ensures that clothing retailers do not stock fads and move in line or even ahead of fashion trends. In a press interview after the launch of its ladies' summer-wear merchandise, the marketing director of Rege Lifestyle, Mr Courtney Dakadzo, pointed out the importance of matching clothing lines to the appropriate seasons in the year as a marketing strategy to increase sales.

In the fashion and leisure clothing industry, the timing of the design, production and presentation of new merchandise to the customer is critical in creating a sustainable competitive advantage. It is important for retailers to manage their lead times efficiently and effectively to coincide with the seasons and fashion trends in the environment. (A lead time is the time from manufacturing until the merchandise appears in-store.) Many producers of fashion clothing have as many as six selling seasons and may produce up to eight lines for each season, making the timing decision complicated and risky.

The other challenge is that seasons vary across different markets and, coupled with changing customer tastes and preferences, accelerating competition and the short fashion cycle, seasonal buying becomes a complicated activity for many retailers. However, Rege Lifestyle has mastered this concept and the company is poised for market dominance.

Discussion questions

1. What are the major challenges that retailers face when they engage in seasonal buying? How can these challenges be overcome?
2. Is the concept of 'fast fashion' an effective long-term marketing strategy for Rege Lifestyle? Give valid reasons to justify your answer.
3. Is there any future in marketing merchandise that sells throughout the year, considering the emerging tendency for customers to prefer seasonal products? Motivate your answer.

Experiential retailing

Traditional retailers in brick-and-mortar stores are facing huge competition from alternative retail formats such as online shopping and have therefore had to adopt novel ways to make the existing stores more attractive and viable. Experiential retailing, where consumers are lured into the stores by innovative displays, interesting activities and entertaining ideas, has become one alternative to survive in a competitive environment.

The important characteristic of experiential retailing is that it attracts attention and changes frequently so that consumers do not know what to expect when next they enter a particular store. Stores can be partly experiential, for example having a section in the store where customers are exposed to interesting activities. They can also be entirely experiential, for example the Cape Union Mart display of sporting merchandise, where consumers can actually experience the bitterly cold circumstances associated with mountain hiking so that they can choose appropriate clothing, or try out certain activities.[51]

Discussion questions

1. What are the major challenges that brick-and-mortar retailers face in terms of the services that they are offering in modern times?
2. How can an interesting environment/context contribute to drawing more consumers to a store?
3. How would you revamp a supermarket to make the shopping encounter more exciting?

REFERENCES

1 Dubois, B. &, Laurent, G. 1996. The functions of luxury: A situational approach to excursionism. *Advances in Consumer Research*, 23: 470–477.
2 Gardner, P & Van der Steel, M. 1984. The consumer's mood: An important situational variable. *NA – Advances in Consumer Research*, 11: 525–529.
3 Hemat, H. &Yuksel, U. 2014. The effect of situational factors on cross-cultural consumer risk-taking. *Advances in Consumer Research*, 42: 786–786; Xie, G., Boush, D.M. & Boerstler, C.N. 2007. Consumer response to marketplace deception: Implication of the persuasion knowledge model. *Advances in Consumer Research*, 34: 406–410.
4 Belk, R.W. 1974. An exploratory assessment of situational effects in buyer behaviour. *Journal of Marketing Research*, 11(May): 157.
5 Ani´c, I. & Radas, S. 2006. The impact of situational factors on purchasing outcomes in the Croatian hypermarket retailer. *Ekonomski Pregled*, 57(11): 730–752.
6 Hawkins, I., Best, R.J. & Coney, K.A. 2010. *Consumer behavior: Building marketing strategy*, 8th ed. New York: Irwin/McGraw Hill. Reprinted by permission of McGraw Hill Education.
7 Hansen, F. 2001. Advertising and communication effects in low-involvement situations, with special emphasis on emotional effects and effects upon attitudes towards the message. *European Advances in Consumer Research*, 5: 290–292; Park, C.W. & Bahr, W.J. 1980. A situational analysis of communication effect: A new product purchase by mail order. *Advances in Consumer Research*, 07: 650–654.
8 Lin, C. & Lin, C.L. 2017. The influence of service employees' nonverbal communication on customer-employee rapport in the service encounter. *Journal of Service Management*, 28, 1:107–132; Hedrick, N., Oppewal, H. & Beverland, M. 2006. Store atmosphere effects on customer perceptions of the retail salesperson. *Asia-Pacific Advances in Consumer Research*, 7: 96–97; Lam, S.Y. 2001. The effects of store environment on shopping behaviors: A critical review. *NA – Advances in Consumer Research*, 28: 190–197.
9 Blythe, J. 2013. *Consumer behaviour*, 3rd ed. London: SAGE, 106.
10 Johnston, M.L. & Conroy, D.M. 2008. Place attachment: The social dimensions of the retail environment and the need for further exploration. *NA – Advances in Consumer Research*, 35: 381–386.
11 Spence, C., Puccinell, N.M., Grewa, D. & Roggevee, A.L. 2014. Store atmospherics: A multisensory perspective. *Psychology and Marketing*, 31(7): 472–488; Petermans, A. & Van

Cleempoel, K. 2009. Retail design and the experiential economy: Where are we (going)? *Design Principles and Practices: An International Journal*, 3. Available at: http://hdl.handle.net/1942/13265 (accessed on 26 August 2018).

12 Gilmore, R., Margulis, W. & Rauch, RA. 2001. Consumer's attitude and retailers' images in creating store choice: A study of two different sides of the same story. *International Journal of Value-Based Management*, 14: 205–221; Scott, N., Laws, E. & Boksberger, P. 2010. The marketing of hospitality and leisure experiences. *Journal of Hospitality Marketing & Management*, 18(2-3): 99–110.

13 Eroglu, S.A., Machleit, K.A. & Davis, L.M. 2001. Atmospheric qualities of online retailing: A conceptual model and implications. *Journal of Business Research*, 54: 177–184.

14 Jobber, D. 2001. *Principles & practice of marketing*, 3rd ed. London: McGraw-Hill, 74–75.

15 Aslam, M.M. 2006. Are you selling the right colour? A cross-cultural review of colour as a marketing cue. *Journal of Marketing Communications*, 12(1): 15–30.

16 Clusters, P.J.M, De Kort, Y.A.W, IJsselsteijn, W.A. & De Kruiff, M.E. 2010. Lighting in retail environments: Atmosphere perception in the real world. *Lighting Research Technology*, 42: 331–343.

17 Ibid.

18 Hoyle D. 2003. Chain store age. *Journal of Marketing*, 79(8): 149.

19 Quartier, K., Van Cleempoel, K. & Christiaans, H. 2008. Retail design: Lighting as an atmospheric tool, creating experiences which influence consumers' mood and behaviour in commercial spaces. Undisciplined! Proceedings of the Design Research Society Conference 2008. Sheffield, UK. July. Available at: http://shura.shu.ac.uk/496/1/fulltext.pdf (accessed on 26 August 2018).

20 Bakker, I., Van der Voordt, T., Vink, P. & De Boon, J. 2014. Pleasure, arousal, dominance: Mehrabian and Russell revisited. *Curriculum Psychology*. Available at: https://www.levenswerken.eu/flash/pleasure_arousal_dominance.pdf_ (accessed on 19 September 2018).

21 Caldwell, C. & Hibbert, S.A. 1999. Play that one again: The effect of music tempo on consumer behaviour in a restaurant. *E-European Advances in Consumer Research*, 4: 58–62.

22 Yalch, R. & Spangenberg, E. 1990. Effects of store music on shopping behavior. *Journal of Consumer Marketing*, 7(2): 55–63.

23 Broekemier, G., Marquardt, R. & Gentry, J.W. 2008. An exploration of happy/sad and liked/disliked music effects on shopping intentions in a women's clothing store service setting. *Journal of Services Marketing*, 22(1): 64.

24 Morrison, M., Gana, S., Dubelaar, C. & Oppewala, H. 2011. In-store music and aroma influences on shopper behavior and satisfaction. *Journal of Business Research*, 64(6): 558–564.

25 Spangenberg, E.R., Sprotta, D.E., Grohmann, B. & Tracy, D.L. 2006. Gender-congruent ambient scent influences on approach and avoidance behaviors in a retail store. *Journal of Business Research*, 59(12): 1281.

26 Chien, S. & Lin, Y. 2015. The effects of the service environment on perceived waiting time and emotions. *Human Factors and Ergonomics in Manufacturing & Service Industries*, 25(3): 319–328; Hensley, R. & Sulek, J. 2007. Customer satisfaction with waits in multi-stage services. *Managing Service Quality: An International Journal*, 17(2): 152–173.

27 Hawkins, D., Mothersbaugh, D. & Best, R. 2006. *Consumer behaviour*, 10th ed. New York: Mcgraw-Hill College, 491.

28 Saravanan, K., Vinayak, D. & Seok, L.H. 2014. Increasing sales by managing congestion in self-service environments: Evidence from a field experiment. Available at: https://ssrn.com/abstract=2523680 (accessed on 26 August 2018).

29 Underhill, P. 1999. *Why we buy: The science of shopping*. New York: Simon and Schuster, 117.

30 Guo, S., Wang, M. & Leskovec, J. 2011. The role of social networks in online shopping: Information passing, price of trust, and consumer choice. Proceedings of the 12th ACM conference on Electronic commerce (EC '11), 5–9 June, San Jose, California, USA. Available at: https://dl.acm.org/citation.cfm?id=1993574 (accessed on 26 August 2018).

31 Ibid.

32 Sheth, J.N. & Parvatiyar, A. 1995. Relationship marketing in consumer markets: Antecedents and consequences. *Journal of the Academy of Marketing Science*, 23(4): 255–271.

33 Pan, Y. & Zinkhan, G.M. 2006. Determinants of retail patronage: A meta-analytical perspective. *Journal of Retailing*, 82(3): 229–243.

34 Simintiras, A., Watkins, A., Ifie, K. & Georgakas, G. 2012. Individual and contextual influences on the affective commitment of retail salespeople. *Journal of Marketing Management*, 28: 11–12.

35 Hawkins et al., 2010, op. cit., 553.

36 Belk, R. 2010. Sharing. *Journal of Consumer Research*, 36(5): 715.

37 Ibid., 717.

38 Mudambi, S. 2002. Branding importance in business-to-business markets: Three buyer clusters. *Industrial Marketing Management*, 31(6): 525–533.

39 Sheth & Parvatiyar, ibid.; Oliver, R.L. 1980. A cognitive model of the antecedents and consequences of satisfaction decisions. *Journal of Marketing Research*, 17(4): 460–469.

40 Fiore, A.M. & Kim, J. 2007. An integrative framework capturing experiential and utilitarian shopping experience. *International Journal of Retail and Distribution Management*, 35(6): 421.

41 Ellis, H.C., Thomas, R.L., McFarland, A.D. & Lane, J.W. 1985. Emotional mood states and retrieval in episodic memory. *Journal of Experimental Psychology: Learning, Memory, and Cognition*, 11(2): 363–370.

42 Rook, D. 1985. The ritual dimension of consumer behaviour. *Journal of Consumer Research*, 12: 252.

43 Rossano, M.J. 2009. Ritual behaviour and the origins of modern cognition. *Cambridge Archaeological Journal*, June, 19(2): 243–256.

44 Füller, J. & Matzler, K. 2008. Customer delight and market segmentation: An application of the three-factor theory of customer satisfaction on life style groups. *Tourism Management*, 29(1): 116–126.

45 Kotler & Armstrong (2005: 54)

46 Grace, D. & O'Cass, A. 2005. An examination of the antecedents of repatronage intentions across different retail store formats. *Journal of Retailing and Consumer Services*, 12(4): 227–243.

47 Niu, H. 2010. Investigating the effects of self-efficacy on foodservice industry employees' career commitment. *International Journal of Hospitality Management*, 29: 743–750.

48 Johns, N., Chan, A. & Yeung, H. 2003. The impact of Chinese culture on service predisposition. *The Service Industries Journal*, 23(5):107–122.

49 Hui, C.H., Chiu, W.C.K., Yu, P.L.H., Cheng, K. & Tse, H.H.M. 2007. The effect of service climate and the effective leadership behaviour of supervisors on frontline employee service quality: A multi-level analysis. *Journal of Occupational and Organizational Psychology*, 80(1): 151–172.

50 Ryu, K. & Han, H. 2010. Influence of physical environment on disconfirmation, customer satisfaction, and customer loyalty for first-time and repeat customers in upscale restaurants. Available at: http://scholarworks.umass.edu/refereed/CHRIE_2010/Wednesday/13 (accessed on 19 September 2018).

51 https://www.google.co.za/search?q=Cape+Union+Mart+experiential+store+Sandton&tbm=isch &tbo=u&source=univ&sa=X&ved=2ahUKEwiC2_uM6cbdAhVrJcAKHWJtAb4QsAR6BAgDEAE &biw=1024&bih=666

PART FOUR
COMPLEXITIES OF THE CONSUMER DECISION-MAKING PROCESS

CHAPTER 11

MARKET SEGMENTATION FROM A SOUTH AFRICAN PERSPECTIVE

Mercy Mpinganjira

LEARNING OBJECTIVES

After reading this chapter, you should be able to:

- define and describe market segmentation
- explain why market segmentation is important
- discuss the key steps in market segmentation
- describe the different bases for market segmentation
- discuss the criteria for effective market segmentation
- critique the different market targeting strategies
- describe the process of perceptual mapping.

Key terms

concentrated targeting strategy	market segmentation	target market
differentiated targeting strategy	perceptual map	undifferentiated mass targeting strategy
	product positioning	
marketing mix	product repositioning	

OPENING CASE STUDY

After graduating with a degree in hospitality, Esther and her sister Bontle decided to start a catering company called E&B Fusion Caterers. The plan was to target the corporate clients in their city, providing catering services. After a year in operation, the two sisters realised that their targeted market was not responding well to their niche-marketing approach. Their revenues were significantly lower than projected, as bookings were much lower than anticipated. Acknowledging their lack of marketing expertise, they appointed Nomsa, an experienced marketing consultant, to help in developing a comprehensive marketing plan for their catering company.

Nomsa's first task involved an analysis of the company's current and potential customers and their needs. The analysis showed that while E&B Fusion Caterers targeted corporate clients, there was another big potential market that the sisters could easily tap into – the home functions market. She noted that there were similarities in terms of needs in the different groups, including the need for tasty and high-quality food. She also noted, however, that there were some important factors that made them significantly different. Some of the differences emanated from the fact that corporate customers were less price sensitive than the home market customers. Orders from home market customers were mainly to cater for family functions such as birthday parties and family get-togethers. Such functions were commonly held over weekends and were associated with a large number of attendees and thus large orders. On the other hand, corporate functions would usually occur during the week and most of them involved small numbers of people.

Based on the analysis, Nomsa recommended that E&B Fusion Caterers move away from its niche-marketing approach to a multi-segment marketing approach. This would entail developing different marketing programmes for each group of customers. For example, Nomsa recommended that the company implement different menus and tariff rates for corporate and home markets. While development of different marketing programmes for different customer groups was going to add to the marketing costs of E&B Fusion Caterers, Nomsa reasoned that the company was going to be able to grow its sales and consequently its profits significantly as its differentiated marketing programmes would target the needs of each customer group better. The ability to meet customer needs better would result in increased customer satisfaction and, in turn, increased opportunities for repeat business.

11.1 INTRODUCTION

The marketing concept suggests that the key to organisational success lies in identifying and satisfying customer needs and wants and doing it so as to create better customer value than competitors.[1] Customers are, however, not the same. They have varied needs and wants, which makes it difficult for companies to come up with offers that appeal to everyone. In order to deal with this problem, marketers often divide customers into groups, also known as market segments, based on similarities in their needs and wants. They then decide on the market segment or segments that they will target and how best to appeal to them.

This chapter aims at providing a better understanding of the processes of market segmentation, targeting of consumer markets and product positioning from a South African perspective. It starts by defining market segmentation, why it is important, common bases for market segmentation, the key steps in market segmentation and the criteria for effective market segmentation. It then looks at the selection of target markets by focusing on targeting options. This is followed by discussions on positioning, focusing in particular on the different bases available, the use of perceptual maps and the issue of repositioning. The chapter concludes with a discussion on researching market segmentation, targeting and positioning.

11.2 WHAT IS MARKET SEGMENTATION?

Market segmentation is one of the fundamental concepts in marketing. It refers to the process of dividing a market into smaller and distinct groups of consumers with similar needs or other characteristics that make them respond in a similar way to marketing efforts. Effective market segmentation is critical for business success. This is because market segmentation is in essence about gaining a better understanding of a particular market segment's consumer needs and wants. Without this understanding, it is difficult for any company to come up with suitable marketing offers. Take, for example, a product such as a television: at the basic level, people want a television to be able to watch TV programmes and movies. The choice of television may, however, be influenced by many other needs or want-related factors, including status, size or a particular brand that has a good reputation.

APPLICATION
Different needs and wants

Example of different product needs:
Two women enter the same cell phone store, where they are both offered many different options in different price ranges.

The older lady tells the shop assistant that she is looking for a phone that will enable her to receive and make calls as well as take photos. She is not concerned with other features. She then asks the assistant to recommend the best model on the basis of low price, ease of operation as well as the features specified.

The young lady asks the same assistant for a cell phone that will enable her to make and receive calls, but also to surf the internet easily, to manage her diary and to record videos. Price is not much of an issue to her.

In this example, it is clear that the two ladies are shopping for the same product (a cell phone), however their wants and needs differ greatly and they will therefore most likely purchase different products (different brands with different capabilities).

11.3 STRATEGIC IMPORTANCE OF MARKET SEGMENTATION

Market segmentation is important in that it helps provide a basis for the following:
- Selecting a target market or markets
- Designing appropriate marketing mix strategies

- Differentiating products
- Identifying opportunities and threats in a market
- Allocating resources

11.3.1   Selecting a target market or markets

Market segmentation is about identifying consumers with similar needs and characteristics (based, for example, on income level, age, location, education etc.) in a market. Through the segmentation process, a company is thus able to understand differences in consumers' needs between and within different groups. The process also allows a company to understand other factors relating to the different customer groups, including the size of different segments that will indicate how viable it would be for a company to proceed with a particular idea. This information is necessary in order for a company to make an informed choice on which market segments to target and which ones to avoid. For example, a company may decide not to target certain market segments because they are too small or because it is difficult to come up with marketing strategies that will appeal to them.

11.3.2   Designing appropriate marketing mix strategies

By allowing companies to group consumers according to pertinent similarities (for example, age, location or education level), market segmentation makes it easy for companies to come up with appropriate marketing mix strategies that would appeal to targeted customers. **Marketing mix** refers to the different choices companies make in the process of bringing their products and/or services to the market. A typical marketing mix is made up of what is known as the 4Ps of marketing: product, price, promotion and place. Market segmentation thus enables companies to apply the marketing concept more easily and to improve their chances of having satisfied customers.

11.3.3   Differentiating products

Most companies operate in markets that are characterised by stiff competition. It thus becomes necessary for a company to differentiate its offer (products and/or services) from that of its competitors. Through market segmentation, a company is not only able to make an informed choice on which markets to target, but also on what marketing mix strategies it should develop for that market. It is also better able to look at how the newly developed marketing mix strategies will differentiate it from competitors in a way that increases the offer's attractiveness to targeted customers.

11.3.4   Identifying opportunities and threats in a market

Market segmentation allows a company to identify new product opportunities, because when analysing consumers' needs and wants, it is possible to identify gaps in the market and to develop products that can successfully meet those needs and wants. The success of Woolworths Foods in South Africa is founded on its ability to identify a distinct market segment in the food retail sector, namely the health- and environmentally conscious consumer. Many of these consumers are willing to pay higher than the average price for products because they value healthy and environmentally friendly foods highly. This segment of the market has also been growing rapidly due to increased wealth in the middle and upper social classes in the country. New entrants often find it difficult to compete with Woolworths Foods as it has an established reputation as a leader in this food market. In the same vein, marketing segmentation helps companies to identify threats in a market. For example, the market entry of a company that offers specialised products or services that appeal to unique customer needs, can result in existing companies losing some of their customers.

11.3.5   Allocating resources

Few companies have the resources needed to offer different products to all market segments as well as to ensure adequate allocation of resourcing to all marketing activities associated with each segment.[2] The analyses associated with marketing segmentation enable companies to identify market segments with great potential. This information is useful in making decisions about resource allocation. Often, more resources are allocated to key consumer groups and key marketing activities that will help position a company well in relation to customer needs.

11.4 COMMON BASES FOR MARKET SEGMENTATION

Markets can be segmented on the basis of different factors. The choice of a segmentation base is critical because an inappropriate segmentation strategy can lead to lost sales and profit opportunities.[3] The common segmentation bases that companies often use to target consumer markets include the following:
* Geographic
* Demographic
* Use-related
* Psychographic
* Geo-demographic
* Living Standards Measure (LSM)

These common bases are discussed in more detail below.

11.4.1 Geographic segmentation

Geographic segmentation involves dividing up the market according to physical location. For example, markets can be divided based on suburb, city, province, country or world region, such as Africa, Europe or Asia. Markets can also be divided geographically into rural, semi-urban and urban areas, or by climatic area such as tropical areas or semi-arid areas.

Geographical segmentation is particularly useful where there are clear differences between the needs of consumers from different geographical locations. Consider, for example, the fact that most rural areas in Africa do not have electricity. The demand for electrical appliances is thus likely to be lower in rural areas than in urban ones. It would thus make sense for companies that sell electrical products to put more emphasis on and expand product ranges in stores in urban areas.

The significant differences in needs and consumption habits that often exist between people from different countries or regions of the world make geographical segmentation one of the most popular segmentation bases of multi-national firms. Such companies may even alter their products, promotion, pricing and placement strategies to meet the unique needs of targeted geographical units.

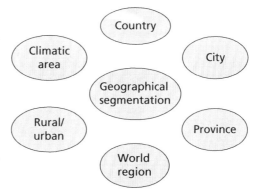

Figure 11.1 Some parameters of geographical segmentation

11.4.2 Demographic segmentation

Demographic segmentation is the most commonly used basis for segmenting consumer markets. It involves the division of markets based on demographic variables such as age, gender, ethnic or racial background, income, education level, occupation and even stage in the family life cycle. The popularity of demographic segmentation is mainly a result of the fact that it is often readily available in most countries.

The following different demographic variables may be used in segmenting consumer markets in South Africa:

- *Age:* Consumer needs and wants inevitably change with age. Companies can thus develop products targeting only specific age groups, or they can develop different products and marketing strategies for consumers in different age groups. For example, financial advisors often target 'high risk, high return' investment products to younger investors. This is owing to the fact that older investors (40 years plus) tend to be wary of taking high-risk investments at such a late age.[4] Many of them are more concerned with preserving their investments, while younger investors are more interested in growing their assets significantly and are thus concerned about possible risks.
- *Gender:* Gender is a common segmentation variable for companies operating in markets such as clothing, cosmetics, hairdressing, toiletries and magazines. As more women in South Africa join the workforce, many companies, including those dealing in products that were not traditionally targeted at women, such as motor cycles, house maintenance and gardening tools, have seen the growing market potential of this segment. Many have come up with products that they position to appeal specifically to the female market. For example, 1st for Women Insurance is a company that started in 2004 after a gap was identified in the market for short-term insurance products that cater for the unique needs of women.[5] Advertisements and promotional material therefore depict women and their unique characteristics, needs and preferences.

- *Ethnic or racial group:* South Africa is an ethnically and racially diverse country. This is why it is referred to as the Rainbow Nation. Research shows that people from different ethnic and racial groups tend to have distinct product preferences that distinguish them from other groups.[6] For example, Indians in South Africa are commonly associated with highly spiced foods, such as curries.[7] Black Like Me is one of the South African brands that has successfully targeted a market segmented along racial lines with ranges of products that are specifically targeted at the black population.
- *Income, education level and occupation:* Although these are separate demographic variables, they are closely related. For example, it is easy for educated people to enter into occupations that produce high-level incomes.[8] In general, a person's level of income is a good indicator of what he or she can afford. Marketers therefore often segment markets based on income level and design products that are priced differently so as to appeal to different income groups. Consider products such as Rolex watches and Lamborghini cars, which are clearly targeted at the wealthy members of society. In the same vein, the Edcon group of companies targets different income groups through different stores, namely the discount division that serves middle to lower income markets through Jet, Jet Mart and Legit, while Edgars, Prato and Red Square target higher-income consumers.

APPLICATION

Target income group

Indicate the main target market in terms of income group for each of the following retail chains in South Africa:

- Pep Stores
- Checkers
- Truworths
- Queens Park
- Ackermans
- Identity
- Woolworths

- *Family life cycle stage:* This involves dividing a market into different groups based on the life cycle stage that people are in. Family life cycle is a composite variable based on marital status, presence of children, relative age and employment status. The different life cycle stages are discussed in Chapter 9. Life cycle segmentation is based on the premise that as people pass through the different stages of the life cycle, their need for products changes. For example, the parenthood stage is widely associated with pressure on family time and income due to the need to accommodate dependents in the family, which influences expenditure on home entertainment, restaurants, cars, holidays and even food.

11.4.3 Use-related segmentation

Use-related segmentation divides the market into groups on the basis of usage rate as well as usage situation:

* *Usage rate:* Customers, including potential customers, can be divided into groups such as heavy, medium, low, non- or ex-users of a product. Different marketing programmes can thus be developed to appeal to consumers in the different segments. For example, a company may be interested in identifying the heavy users of its products because these consumers bring in the most sales revenue to the company. Some researchers have noted that it is not unusual in some industries to have 20% of customers responsible for up to 80% of their company sales.[9] A company may thus want to treat these customers in a special way to retain their business. Relationship marketing is often used by companies to maintain a sizeable segment of loyal customers. For example, many retailers in South Africa have loyalty programmes that reward customers who patronise their stores and encourage them to return. Apart from heavy users of a product, most marketers also pay special attention to non-users, with the aim of finding ways of appealing to these consumers so that they can try the company's products and become users, allowing the company to grow its customer base.

PicknPay: Smart Shopper

The PnP SmartShopper loyalty programme rewards customers for buying at PnP stores. Visit the PnP web site and then answer the following:

1. How do customers earn points through the SmartShopper programme?
2. How do you feel PnP could improve on the programme so as to add more value to shareholders, while at the same time retaining customers?

* *Usage situation:* Special situations or occasions often influence consumers in terms of what they purchase or consume. Consider the following statements:
* 'Whenever it is Mother's Day, I make sure I take my mother out to a nice restaurant for dinner.'
* 'I always buy my wife beautiful flowers on her birthday.'
* 'I wonder what I should cook today as I have important visitors coming.'
* 'We offer different packages for business and vacation travellers.'

All of these statements illustrate the importance of usage situation or occasion in determining what consumers buy. Products can thus be promoted to appeal to consumers in specific situations. For example, travel companies, especially those offering holiday packages, often promote their services aggressively just before major holidays, knowing that many people are on the look-out for new places to visit during such times.

11.4.4   Psychographic segmentation

While geographic, demographic and use-related variables are commonly used to segment markets, some marketers feel that these variables do not say much about what goes on in consumers' minds and what distinguishes one group from another. They thus advocate the use of psychographic segmentation, which is a basis to tap into consumers' way of thinking. Psychographic segmentation involves dividing a market into groups based on personality, motives and lifestyles:[10]

- *Personality:* Personality reflects a person's traits, capturing how one thinks, feels and behaves.[11] Research shows that choice of products is closely linked to people's personalities. This is why companies work hard to enhance the appeal of their brands by matching them closely to their targeted market's personalities. They do this by giving their brands personality traits. Some of the brand personality dimensions that are commonly used by marketers include the following:[12]
  - Sincerity
  - Excitement
  - Competence
  - Sophistication
  - Ruggedness

Each brand personality dimension is reflected by a number of facets. For example, honesty and wholesomeness are qualities related more to the sincerity dimension, while intelligence and success are related to the competence dimension. It can be said, for example, that marketers of organic food products

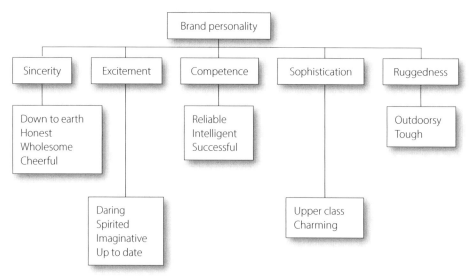

Figure 11.2 Dimensions of brand personality[13]

appeal more to consumers who value wholesomeness in the sincerity dimension of brand personality. Amusement parks appeal more to consumers who value exciting and/or daring traits under the excitement dimension.

* *Motives:* Consumers can also be divided into groups according to why they buy particular products. Different consumers may buy the same product but for varying reasons. For example, one consumer may buy a Mercedes Benz because he or she is looking for a reliable car, while another may view it as a status symbol. One consumer may buy bicarbonate of soda as a cooking ingredient, while another may buy the same product for the purposes of removing bad odours in the refrigerator or as an insecticide in the garden.
* *Lifestyle:* Lifestyle segmentation involves dividing people according to their interests. These interests normally determine how these people spend their time and/or money, for example which magazines they buy, which restaurants they patronise, how they travel, the types of vacations they take, participation in sports, etc. Marketers who are interested in lifestyle segments try to appeal to consumers based on their hobbies and activities. For example, manufactures of men's jeans can appeal to men who love to be outdoors or to business leaders.

11.4.5 Geo-demographic segmentation

Geo-demographic segmentation involves combining geographic and demographic variables in segmenting a market. For example, a company may decide to target working women (demographic) who are located in South Africa's major cities (geographic). Geo-demographic segmentation is sometimes used where there is a close relationship between where a person lives and his or her socio-economic status, as measured by income, education level or occupation. For example, in South Africa, it is more likely that there is a larger concentration of low-income consumers in the townships than in the suburbs. In the same vein, certain suburbs in the city are home to higher-income families than other suburbs and as such, the stores in those suburbs would be distinctly different in terms of the products that they have on offer and their price range.

11.4.6 The Living Standards Measure

The Living Standards Measure (LSM) was developed by the South African Advertising Research Foundation as a basis for segmenting the country's population into groups based on standard of living. The measure divides the population into ten distinct groups ranging from the lowest standard of living, LSM 1, to the highest, LSM 10. Markets are divided into different groups based on degree of urbanisation and people's wealth, as measured by ownership of certain assets[14] such as a car, a personal computer, a dishwashing machine and an electric stove. In making the calculation, a weighting is assigned to each variable included in the measure.[15]

Section 11.5 looks at the key steps in the market segmentation process.

11.5 KEY STEPS IN MARKET SEGMENTATION

The market segmentation process consists of a number of key steps:

- *Step 1: Identify a market.* This will depend on the market a company is operating in or wants to enter. For example, a small business may want to enter the clothing retail market and can further narrow down the market by looking at the shoe market or children's clothing.
- *Step 2: Identify the different potential needs of the consumers in the market.* When considering the shoe market, a number of factors may influence people's choice of footwear. For example, some consumers may be more concerned with shoes that will make a fashion statement, while others may be more concerned with affordability or durability. The people responsible for the market segmentation process need to list as many potential needs as they can identify.
- *Step 3: Select the basis for segmenting the market.* At this stage, the marketer needs to decide on the specific segmentation basis or bases that will be used to divide the market based in terms of the needs that were identified. Those most commonly used by South African companies include geographic, demographic, use-related, psychographic and geo-demographic segmentation as well as the LSM.
- *Step 4: Select the segmentation descriptors.* Each segmentation basis is associated with a number of descriptors. Just as in step three, the marketer needs to decide on the segmentation descriptor that best divides the market into groups based on clear customer differences. Age and income levels are examples of descriptors that may be used to segment the shoe market based on demographic characteristics.
- *Step 5: Profile and analyse each market segment.* Of concern at this stage, is the need to understand the specific needs and wants of each market segment, and to determine its attractiveness to the company. The analysis will thus include the following:
  - Identification of the critical factors that will persuade consumers to buy the product
  - Determination of each segment size to decide whether it is viable or not
  - Expected growth rate and profit potential
  An analysis of competitors in each segment is also necessary for the company to check its competitive advantage in the different market segments.
- *Step 6: Select the market segment to target.* This is the final stage in the segmentation process. It is advisable for companies to target market segments with high sales and profit potential as well as those where they can deliver competitively on consumer needs and wants.

Section 11.6 looks at the criteria for effective market segmentation in more detail.

11.6 CRITERIA FOR EFFECTIVE MARKET SEGMENTATION

There are many ways of segmenting a market. However, there are some critical conditions against which to check the robustness of any approach. In order to be considered effective, market segmentation generally needs to result in segments that meet four important criteria:

- *Measurability:* Marketers need to be able to measure the size of each market segment. Some market segmentation variables, such as age, gender and number of people living in a particular location, are relatively easy to measure. There are, however, other variables such as those relating to lifestyle and personality as well as motives, that are not easily measurable. Companies need to find ways of estimating the size of segments when dealing with such variables. One way of doing this, is through market research where a representative sample of the population is asked to respond to questions relating to their lifestyle, personality or buying motives. Findings from such studies can be extrapolated to the wider population.
- *Substantiality:* Irrespective of the basis chosen to segment a market, it is important that the resulting segment or segments be large enough for a company to target profitably. Although substantiality often goes with having a large number of customers, it is not always so. In some markets, for example the private banking market segment in South Africa, the number of individual customers may not be as great, but the profitability potential of the market is often much higher than that of the non-private banking segment. In looking at substantiality, it is wise for marketers to have a long-term view of the market and to check for the stability of segments over time. For example, if the population size of a smaller town has been shrinking for some time, it might not be wise to venture into the town with a novel product.
- *Accessibility:* In order to be effective, the market segmentation process needs to result in segments that marketers can reach using a customised marketing mix. Market segments may be inaccessible for a variety of reasons. For example, a company may find that it needs a licence in order to operate in a particular market, something which may not be easy to obtain. In some cases, the cost of reaching certain segments may be too high, making it not worthwhile to go for them.
- *Responsiveness:* The purpose of market segmentation is to identify consumer groups that need to be reached with a particular marketing mix in order to ensure consumer satisfaction. Thus, unless the consumer groups that were identified are homogenous within, and heterogeneous without, the primary purpose of segmentation will not be realised. Homogenous within means that potential customers in one segment have similar needs and buying behaviour. Heterogeneous without means that consumers in one group have needs and exhibit buying behaviours that differ from consumers in other market segments. Lack of clear differences between different customer groups makes the development of different marketing mixes targeted at each segment unjustifiable.

In any market, an effective market segmentation process is likely to result in a number of segments that meet the four critical criteria. Having segmented a market, a company has to make the choice in terms of selecting one or more markets in which to operate. The primary issue at this stage is to decide how many segments to go for and how to target them in terms of their marketing mix offerings.

11.7 SELECTING TARGET MARKETS

A **target market** can be defined as a group of consumers that a company has decided to aim its marketing efforts towards.[16] There are three main strategies that a company can use in targeting markets:
* Undifferentiated mass targeting strategy
* Differentiated targeting strategy
* Concentrated targeting strategy

This section looks at each of the three main targeting strategies in more detail.

11.7.1   Undifferentiated mass targeting strategy
The **undifferentiated mass targeting strategy** involves targeting the whole market with one marketing mix. A business adopting the undifferentiated targeting strategy uses a mass marketing approach to marketing. This strategy is commonly taken where the following situations exist:
* There are no significant differences in consumer characteristics that impact on their buying behaviour.
* There may be differences in consumers' needs, but the cost of developing separate marketing mixes for the different groups of customers in order to meet each group's exact needs far outweighs the expected gains.
* The company is the first to enter a market and there are no competitors to worry about.
* The product being marketed is largely an undifferentiated commodity, for example sugar, toothbrushes, toilet paper or batteries.

One of the main advantages of an undifferentiated targeting strategy is that it is associated with low cost.[17] This is because a company using this strategy only needs to develop one product. This allows it to mass-produce a product and thus push down production costs through the achievement of economies of scale. Marketing costs are also kept down as the company can use the same promotional, distribution and pricing strategies for its product.

One of the disadvantages of using an undifferentiated strategy is that it makes the company less focused on unique consumer needs, which is likely to result in failure to achieve high levels of customer satisfaction.

11.7.2   Differentiated targeting strategy
The **differentiated targeting strategy** is also commonly referred to as the multi-segment strategy. It entails the targeting of two or more distinct market segments and the development of a distinct marketing mix for each segment.

The main advantage of using a differentiated targeting strategy is that it enables the company in question to make more sales through its ability to appeal to more consumers in different market segments. A differentiated targeting strategy enables the company to satisfy different groups of customers better than through an undifferentiated strategy. This strategy also allows the company to better manage market risks. For example, when one segment is going through a difficult time for some reason, the company can survive by concentrating its efforts on other market segments. In 2018, the listeriosis outbreak in South Africa caused manufacturers to withdraw certain types of processed meats from the market.[18] In order to survive, the manufacturers therefore needed to focus on the promotion and sales of other products in their manufacturing plants.

The main disadvantages of a differentiated strategy relate to high costs and the possibility of cannibalism. Cannibalism refers to a situation where the sales of one product reduce the sales of another product.[19] For example, when technology companies such as Apple and Samsung introduce new versions of cell phones or tablets, the different versions end up in competition with each other. If the incremental value of introducing new products and adding new versions of a product is not properly assessed, a company may not benefit much. Thus, instead of a differentiated strategy helping to increase sales by appealing to more consumers, some of the existing customers in a segment may switch to the new products.

The specific costs that are likely to go up with the adoption of this strategy include the following:
- *Research costs:* Success with a multi-segment approach depends on a good understanding of differences between consumer segments. The company needs to monitor development in the different market segments continually to ensure the distinctness in market offering. The costs associated with this are likely to increase as more markets are served.
- *Product development and production costs:* In order to meet the needs of different groups of consumers, a differentiated targeting strategy requires that different products be developed and produced for the different customer groups or that modifications be made to existing products in order to cater for different needs. As the number of products that are developed and produced or modified increases, so, too, do the related costs that the company has to contend with. In general, the ability of a company to benefit from economies of scale decreases because smaller quantities of each product need to be produced for each segment.

• *Management costs:* As the number of segments targeted increases, so do the number of decisions that the company has to make. Planning and co-ordination of the different marketing mixes also require more time and resources from a management perspective.
• *Promotion and distribution costs:* A company using a differentiated targeting strategy needs to find ways of reaching different consumers. This often entails the development of different communication messages and the use of different media, resulting in an increase in promotional costs. In other cases, different distribution channels may be required to reach different consumer segments effectively. The development and maintenance of different channels further add to the costs.

To be successful, a company using a differentiated strategy needs to monitor its costs against sales and profits carefully. It also needs to ensure that it is able to take actions that can enhance the distinctiveness of its offering in each market segment without damaging its image.

11.7.3   Concentrated targeting strategy

With a **concentrated targeting strategy**, a company selects one particular segment of a market in which to operate and develops a marketing mix to target that segment exclusively. This strategy is commonly used by companies that want to portray an exclusive image as well as those with limited resources. For example, by targeting high-income customers, companies such as Porsche, Rolex and Louis Vuitton are able to maintain an exclusive, prestigious image in their respective markets. However, many small and medium-sized companies also practise concentrated targeting as a result of limited resources. For them, it makes good business sense to concentrate on a small segment of the market and to serve it well instead of stretching their resources too thinly over many customers.

One of the major advantages of a concentrated targeting strategy is that it enables a company to develop a strong position in the market.[20] The company hence gains recognition as a specialist. A concentrated strategy also allows a company to gain in-depth knowledge of its market/s, increasing its chances of developing an appealing marketing mix.

The main disadvantage of this strategy is that it entails high levels of risk. A company using this strategy is relying on a single market segment, which is like putting all of its eggs in one basket. Any adverse changes in the market will significantly impact on the profitability of the company, if not its survival. For example, imagine what would have happened if the car manufacturer Ford, had only produced one car model, namely the Ford Kuga. The Ford Kuga brand suffered from negative publicity after some of its cars were considered to have fire risks.[21] This was after a number of Ford Kuga owners reported that their cars had gone up in flames.[22] Ford had to recall those versions of the affected model.

Choosing a targeting strategy

There are many factors that any company needs to consider before it can choose its market targeting strategy. From the discussions on targeting strategy so far and referring to Figure 11.3, identify these critical factors. Justify your answers.

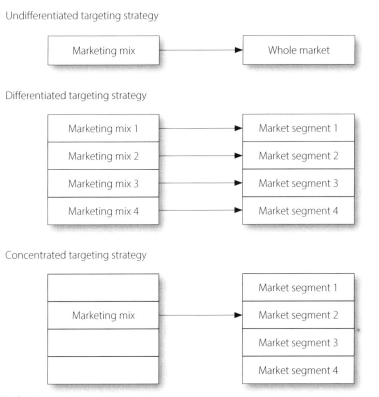

Figure 11.3 Market targeting strategies

Having chosen the market segment or segments to target, a company needs to decide on the position that it wants to occupy in the chosen market. Section 11.8 looks at this concept of positioning in more detail.

11.8 POSITIONING

Products occupy specific positions in the minds of consumers. For example, many people in South Africa associate Woolworths Foods with healthy food. This is the position that the brand occupies in the minds of customers.

In general, a product's position is about image and perceptions consumers hold about a product in relation to competing products, brands or retailers. Marketers do not like to leave the positioning of their products in the minds of customers to chance. They thus carefully plan the position they want their products to occupy and develop a marketing mix that supports the planned position.

APPLICATION

What comes to mind?

In groups of four, discuss what comes to mind when you hear the following names:

* Checkers
* Shoprite
* Jet
* Johannesburg
* Sandton Mall
* China.
* Zimbabwe

In planning **product positioning**, marketers are concerned with differentiating their products from those of competitors in such a way that their products have a competitive advantage over others in the market. Section 11.8.1 looks at the common bases that are used by companies to position their products in the marketplace so as to differentiate them from competitors' offerings. Section 11.8.2 then discusses the use of perceptual mapping in product positioning.

11.8.1 Bases used in positioning products

Products can be positioned in a market based on a number of different factors, including the following:

* *Product features:* Product features relate to the make-up of a product. Car manufacturers, for example, like to mention features such as airbags, GPS navigation systems and anti-locking brakes as some of the selling points for their cars. This is based on their understanding of consumer needs. 'Enrichment with calcium' is sometimes used to sell toothpaste on the market. The presence or lack of what are considered to be important product features can cause a consumer to have a positive or negative perception of one brand and not of another.

* *Product benefits:* Product benefits are closely related to product features, in that most benefits are the result of a product feature. When positioning using product benefits, the emphasis is not on what features the product has, but on what the consumer gains by using a particular product. For example, in the case of a car, the presence of airbags is often favoured by customers as they are designed to protect drivers and passengers during accidents. Anti-locking brakes are designed to increase driver control of a vehicle during an emergency situation, maintaining vehicle stability as well as directional control.[23] A GPS navigation system helps drivers know where they are and

provides turn-by-turn directions on how to reach particular destinations. Sophisticated navigation systems are also able to guide drivers to the nearest ATM, service station, hospital and police station. Thus, instead of emphasising technical features such as anti-locking brakes, which many customers may not understand, the emphasis would be on the benefits associated with the feature. A company that markets toothpaste would emphasise the toothpaste's benefits, such as its teeth-whitening ability and the prevention of tooth decay.

- *Product user:* Product-user positioning entails associating a product with a type of user or the personality of the user. For example, anyone buying Johnson's Baby Shampoo knows that the product is designed for infants. Companies selling cosmetic products often offer ranges for different skin types, for example sensitive skin, dry skin or oily skin.
- *Product use:* Positioning on the basis of use entails associating a product with specific occasions or circumstances. For example, champagne is positioned as a product for celebrations. The 'For Dummies' series of instruction books is targeted at people who are completely new to certain topics and would like to learn from sources that do not assume any prior knowledge.[24]
- *Competitors:* A product can also be positioned directly against or away from a competitor. An example of positioning directly against a competitor is where a pharmaceutical company claims that its pain-relief medicine provides faster relief than any other over-the-counter options. Many universities also like to position themselves against competitors. Using the QS world rankings or the Times Higher Education World University Rankings, universities are able to sell themselves based on their reputations.
- *Place of origin:* Some companies emphasise the country of origin to differentiate their products from competitors'. For example, companies may use 'Made in South Africa' to appeal to consumers who want to support local manufacturers as this helps in job creation. Audi South Africa uses its German connection to appeal to customers, as Germany is associated with excellence in engineering. Their advertisements often carry the German slogan, *Vorsprung durch Technik* ('advancement through technology).

11.8.2 Use of perceptual maps

A **perceptual map** is a graphical representation of the location that a product occupies in the mind of customers. Perceptual maps are used to aid in the proper positioning of products. Often a perceptual map is presented as a two-dimensional graph with a vertical and horizontal axis, thus allowing for the comparison of products on two attributes. It is, however, possible to use more than two dimensions in perceptual mapping and thus allow for products to be analysed using more than two attributes.

In general, the process of perceptual mapping involves three main steps:

- *Step 1: Identifying the important attributes* associated with a product category. Often companies will try to identify the important attributes by asking customers to indicate the factors that they consider important in choosing a particular product category. For example, a university may ask final-year high school students to list factors that they consider important in deciding at which university they would like to study. This will result in a number of variables that can be ranked in order of importance to then be used in perceptual mapping.

- *Step 2:* The second step is to ask consumers to indicate their *rating of the attributes of a specific product or brand.* Often marketers include competitors' offerings in perceptual mapping. This information reveals consumers' perceptions regarding each product in terms of certain attributes.
- *Step 3:* Consumers' perceptions regarding each product are then *plotted* on a perceptual map.

Figure 11.4 presents an example of a perceptual map. The example uses two attributes (tooth-whitening ability and decay-prevention ability) to check how different brands, labelled brand A, brand B and brand C, are perceived by customers. According to the graph, brand A and brand B are rated low on both attributes, while brand C is rated high on decay-prevention capability, but low on tooth-whitening capability.

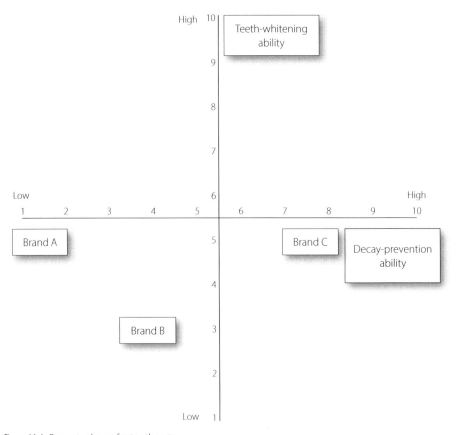

Figure 11.4 Perceptual map for toothpaste

Perceptual mapping is useful for a number of reasons, including the following:

- It enables companies to identify the important attributes that consumers look for when purchasing a product. This knowledge can be used by a company in its product design or improvement initiatives. The information is also useful in designing consumer communication programs to avoid communication of irrelevant information.
- It enables a company to know how consumers perceive its products in relation to competitors' offerings in the market, to establish how it is faring in the market in general as well as to identify who its close competitors are.
- It enables companies to identify gaps in the market, which is useful in making market-entry decisions. A company not wanting to position itself directly against certain competitors can get an idea on how to avoid them.

Effective positioning requires that companies continue monitoring the relevance of their strategies to customers. Changes in the market or in company conditions can make it necessary for a company to change its positioning strategy. Section 11.9 looks briefly at the concept of repositioning.

11.9 REPOSITIONING

Product repositioning refers to marketing efforts aimed at changing consumers' perceptions and impressions about a product or brand, for reasons that may include the following:

- *Errors in the way a product or brand is currently positioned:* Existing ways to create the desired image are not always successful. When a brand or product fails to occupy a desired position in the mind of customers, it becomes necessary to make corrections through re-positioning.
- *Trying to appeal to changing consumer needs and wants:* Customer needs and wants are not static – they change with time and circumstances. For example, as more and more consumers become aware of the dangers of environmental degradation, some companies are using this to their advantage by promoting information relating to their company's responsiveness towards environmental causes. This is done in order to influence customers' perceptions positively.
- *Targeting new customers:* Some products may have an appeal beyond a single market segment. A company that was initially targeting one or only a few market segments may want to reposition itself in order to appeal to new target markets and expand its market share.
- *Managing competition:* As a company operates in a market, new competitors often enter the market and old competitors may change their positioning strategy. This may create a need for repositioning, especially if the competitors' positioning strategy results in the loss of a company's distinctive identity in the market.

Therefore, while a company is positioning its brands and products in the market, or repositioning them, competitors are doing the same, which complicates the process and requires continual revision of existing strategies.

11.10 RESEARCHING MARKET SEGMENTATION, TARGETING AND POSITIONING

The effectiveness of market segmentation, targeting and positioning largely depends on a good understanding of the market. Market research plays a significant role in ensuring this understanding. Of much concern to marketers is understanding consumer needs, finding the right basis for segmenting a market, obtaining recent statistical evidence on segment size (if possible), acquiring information to assist in assessing the viability of different market segments, and finding out about customers' perceptions and impressions about a company and its products. Secondary research as well as primary research can be used to bring about this understanding.

11.10.1   Secondary research

Private organisations as well as government departments and agencies collect a great deal of information that can be useful in the processes of market segmentation, targeting and product positioning. For example, through Statistics South Africa, a company can obtain information on the demographic profile of people in different parts of the country, including gender ratios, number of people in different age groups and levels of education. This information can be used inter alia in assessing the size of different segments.

APPLICATION

Secondary sources of information for segmentation, targeting and positioning

Using the knowledge you have acquired on market segmentation, targeting and product positioning, discuss five possible sources of secondary information that a company can use to assist with customer segmentation in a particular geographical area. For each source, give an example of the kind of information you are likely to get as well as how you can use the information in the segmentation, targeting and positioning processes.

11.10.2   Primary research

This involves the collection of data for the first time to be used for the specific objectives relating to the problem at hand. The most commonly used data collection techniques in primary research are surveys and observation research. Survey research involves questioning of respondents by the researcher and assistants in order to obtain responses on set questions.

Observation research involves collection of data without direct interaction or questioning of participants by data collectors. For example, an artist planning the location of his or her studio may use observation research to decide on alternative locations by observing differences in the number of people who attend art exhibitions in different locations within close proximity of the area where he considers opening his studio. By observing attendance levels, it is possible to make inferences about locations that attract the largest number of people interested in the arts.

SUMMARY

This chapter has examined one of the fundamental concepts in marketing, namely market segmentation. Market segmentation refers to the process of dividing a market into smaller and distinct groups of customers with similar needs or other characteristics that make them respond in a similar way to marketing efforts. Market segmentation is important because it helps provide the basis for selecting target markets effectively, designing appropriate marketing mix strategies, differentiating products, identifying opportunities and threats in a market, and allocating resources.

Markets can be segmented on the basis of a number of factors. The common segmentation bases include geographic segmentation, demographic segmentation, use-related segmentation and psychographic segmentation. Sometimes two or more segmentation bases are combined to provide a basis for segmentation. Geo-demographic segmentation and the LSM are examples of such bases.

The key steps in the market segmentation process include identifying a market segment, identifying the needs of the consumers in the market, selecting the basis for segmenting the market, selecting the segmentation descriptors, establishing the profile of each market segment and selecting the market segments to target. In selecting target markets, a company can choose from three main strategies, namely the undifferentiated mass targeting strategy, the differentiated targeting strategy and the concentrated targeting strategy. The criteria for effective selection of a target market include the fact that market segments need to be measurable, substantial, accessible and responsive.

After choosing a market segment or segments to target, a company needs to decide how it is going to position itself in those markets. Perceptual maps are commonly used in deciding on a positioning strategy. In general, products can be positioned in a market based on a number of different factors, including product features, product benefits, product user, product use, competitors and place of origin. Errors in positioning as well as changes in market or company conditions often necessitate the repositioning of companies in the marketplace. To a large extent, the effectiveness of market segmentation, targeting and positioning depends on a good understanding of the market. Market research can be used to collect the necessary information so as to ensure that segmentation, targeting and positioning decisions are made on an informed basis.

SELF-ASSESSMENT QUESTIONS

1. Define market segmentation and discuss why it is an important part of marketing.
2. Using three different segmentation bases, discuss how you could segment the retail banking market.
3. Explain the common market targeting strategies.
4. What are the common bases used in positioning products?
5. Why is differentiation an important aspect of positioning?
6. Describe the steps involved in perceptual mapping.
7. Describe repositioning and the factors that influence a brand's decision to reposition.

EXPERIENTIAL EXERCISE

You have been employed as a manager of a small private game reserve in the Eastern Cape. The reserve is stocked with the Big Five game species. About 80 per cent of the visitors to your reserve are foreigners, mainly from Europe and North America. You would like to grow business by targeting more local visitors. This requires identifying suitable local customer segments and developing marketing strategies to target them.

1. What segments of the local customer market would you most likely target and why?
2. What kind of marketing strategies would you use to target the chosen market segment? Consider some of the elements of the marketing mix, including product, price and promotion.

CASE STUDY 1

ElectroCity

ElectroCity is a big international company specialising in the retail of high-end electronic home appliances. The company is considering entering the South African market. It views South Africa as a gateway into the rest of southern Africa. Its plan is to start operations in Johannesburg by opening at least five retail outlets in strategic locations. After Johannesburg, it plans to move to all of the provincial capitals of the country, and then to expand into the rest of southern Africa.

Owing to a lack of high levels of familiarity with Africa, the marketing director of ElectroCity, James, has decided to use a local marketing consulting company to advise on the best strategies to employ in entering the South African market and expanding to other southern African countries. Shaun, the lead local marketing consultant working on the project, wants James to describe the typical customer targeted by ElectroCity in its operations overseas to him. After some deliberation, James likes the idea of using the LSM in describing a typical target customer for the company in South Africa as well as in the other targeted African countries.

Discussion questions

1. What is your understanding of the LSM?
2. Do some research on LSM groups. Based on findings in your research, which LSM group would you advise ElectroCity to target in South Africa and why?
3. Why would segmenting the market using the LSM be beneficial for ElectroCity?

CASE STUDY 2

Market segmentation in small business

Last year, Mpho decided to attend a workshop about marketing for small businesses, organised by the local chamber of commerce. This decision came after she noticed that her business profits were dropping, despite the fact that most of her customers provided positive feedback on the quality of services offered by her dental practice.

At the workshop, Mpho picked up a number of marketing concepts, including the concept of market segmentation. Ruth, the facilitator of the workshop, spent a lot of time explaining the need for small business owners to appreciate the fact that while all customers are important, some may be more important to the business than others because of the contribution that they make towards business profits. She challenged the business owners to do a customer profile analysis and to identify the most profitable groups of customers for their companies.

After the workshop, Mpho decided to do the analysis and check if this was also true of her practice. She first segmented the market into two groups: upfront paying customers and health insurance customers. She further subdivided the insured customers by type of insurer. After analysing payment trends, she noticed that levels of bad debts were higher for customers associated with two of the five health insurance cover providers that she normally dealt with at her practice Based on this information, Mpho decided to refine her service offer. She specifically decided to limit the number of insurers accepted for claims by her practice. Customers covered by insurers associated with a lot of bad debts were to be served only if they were willing to pay cash and claim later from their insurance companies themselves. She noticed that by so doing, her business profits were in line with her budgeted estimates.

Discussion questions

1. What do you understand by target marketing?
2. What kind of market targeting strategy is Mpho practising?
3. What are the advantages and disadvantages associated with Mpho's chosen market targeting strategy?

Additional resources

Reading through the websites of companies that target some of their products at a specific group of customers may give you an inside perspective on how they describe their typical customers and why they target them. Here are examples of sites you can visit for this purpose:

1. ProfMed: http://www.profmed.co.za/
2. FNBBank: ttps://www.fnb.co.za/youth-and-student-accounts/
3. The Fry Family Food Co: https://www.fryfamilyfood.com/za/

View the following video clips for more information on some of the concepts discussed in this chapter:

- Understanding customer segmentation and profiling: https://www.youtube.com/watch?v=MEXmmHtKQzQ
- Types of market segmentation: behavioral and psychographic: https://www.youtube.com/watch?v=zumYa-gC0BI

REFERENCES

1   Hult, G.T.M., & Ketchen, D.J. 2017. Disruptive marketing strategy. *AMS Review*, 7(1/2), 21; Frambach, R.T., Fiss, P.C. & Ingenbleek, P.T. 2016. How important is customer orientation for firm performance? A fuzzy set analysis of orientations, strategies, and environments. *Journal of Business Research*, 69(4): 1429.

2   Dibb, S. & Simkin, L. 1996. *The market segmentation workbook: Target marketing for marketing managers*. New York: Routledge, 10.

3   Asiedu, E. 2016. A study of use and impact of market segmentation practices on bank performance. With special reference to commercial banks in Colombia. *Journal of Business and Financial Affairs*, 5(162): 267.

4   McCarthy, E. 2009. Time for another look at client risk tolerance. *Journal of Financial Planning*, 22(2): 23.

5   1st for Women. 2017. Company profile. Available at: https://www.firstforwomen.co.za/about-us/ (accessed on 20 July 2018).

6   Cui, G. & Choudhury, P. 2015. Effective strategies for ethnic segmentation and marketing. Proceedings of the 1998 Multicultural Marketing Conference. Springer, Cham, 354.

7   South Africa Tours and Travel.com. 2005–2012. Indian Cuisine in South Africa – taste it! Available at: http://www.south-africa-tours-and-travel.com/indian-cuisine.html (accessed on 21 July 2018).

8   Diep, F. 2015. Does more education make people wealthier? Available at: https://psmag.com/education/links-between-education-and-wealth (accessed on 20 July 2018).

9   Jeffery, M., Anfield, J., Riitters, T. & Rzymski, C. 2017. B&K Distributors: Calculating return on investment for a web-based customer portal. *Kellogg School of Management Cases*, 2. Available at: http://www.emeraldinsight.com/doi/abs/10.1108/case.kellogg.2016.000031 (accessed on 20 July 2018).

10 Hutchison, T., Macy, A. & Allen, P. 2009. *Record label marketing*. Burlington: Elsevier, 9.

11 Bazzani, C., Caputo, V., Nayga Jr, R.M., & Canavari, M. 2017. Revisiting consumers' valuation for local versus organic food using a non-hypothetical choice experiment: Does personality matter? *Food Quality and Preference*, 62: 144–154.

12 Aaker, J. 1997. Dimension of brand personality. *Journal of Marketing Research*, 34(3): 356.

13 Ibid. Republished with permission of American Marketing Association; permission conveyed through Copyright Clearance Center, Inc.

14 South African Audience Research Foundation. 2017. Living Standards Measure. Available at: http://www.saarf.co.za/lsm/lsms.asp (accessed 20 July 2018); Eighty20. n.d. LSM calculator. Available at: http:/www.eighty20.co.za/lsm-calculator/ (accessed on 20 July 2018).

15 Ibid.

16 Boone, L. & Kurtz, D. 2013. *Contemporary marketing*. Mason, OH: South-Western Cengage Learning, 44.

17 Lamb, C., Hair, J., McDaniel, C., Boshoff, C., Terblanche, N., Elliot, R. & Klopper, H. 2015. *Marketing*, 5th SA ed. Cape Town: Oxford University Press, 222.

18 Africa News Agency. 2018. #Listeriosis: Enterprise and Rainbow chicken issued with recall notices. Available at: https://www.iol.co.za/news/south-africa/gauteng/listeriosis-enterprise-and-rainbow-chicken-issued-with-recall-notices-13590086 (accessed on 3 August 2018).

19 Mortimer, G. 2016. How Kmart ate Target: A story of retail cannibalism. *The Conversation*, (31). Available at: http://eprints.qut.edu.au/95880/2/95880.pdf (accessed on 20 July 2018).

20 Lamb et al., op. cit.

21 Smyth, M. 2018. Ford Kuga at risk of fire once again. *Business Day*, 29 March. Available at: https://www.businesslive.co.za/bd/life/motoring/2018-03-29-ford-kuga-at-risk-of-fire-once-again/ (accessed on 20 July 2018).

22 Theron-Weperner. 2017. Burning Luga issue: Big business lessons from Ford's management failures- expert. Available at: https://www.biznews.com/thought-leaders/2017/01/27/kuga-ford-kuga/ (accessed 20 July 2018).

23 Aly, A.A., Zeidan, E.S., Hamed, A. & Salem, F. 2011. An antilock-braking systems (ABS) control: A technical review. *Intelligent Control and Automation*, 2(3): 186–195.

24 Graham, R. 2016. Dummies for dummies: Happy 25th birthday to the perfect guides for when all you know is that you know nothing. Available at: http://www.slate.com/articles/arts/books/2016/04/the_history_and_delights_of_the_for_dummies_how_to_books.html (accessed on 20 July 2018).

CHAPTER 12

COMMUNICATING WITH CONSUMERS

Tania Maree and Lené Ehlers

LEARNING OBJECTIVES

After reading this chapter, you should be able to:

- explain the changing consumer and the implication for marketing communication
- explain the marketing mix
- discuss the relevance of marketing communication in the marketing mix
- describe the elements in the communication model
- differentiate between traditional, alternative and new digital communication media
- explain internet and mobile marketing
- distinguish between the various forms of social media
- describe the consumer decision-making process and how it relates to marketing communications
- explain how marketing communication is researched
- discuss marketing and retail applications.

Key terms

alternative media	price	promotion
distribution	product	traditional media
digital marketing		

OPENING CASE STUDY[1]

On 7 October 2017, the beauty brand Dove tweeted the following: 'An image we recently posted on Facebook missed the mark in representing women of colour thoughtfully. We deeply regret the offence it caused.'

The apology came in response to a social media backlash that started when makeup artist and online beauty product retailer Naomi Leann Blake@NaytheMua posted images of a body wash advertisement that showed a black woman taking off her shirt to reveal a white woman underneath. What Dove intended to say with the advertisement was that Dove Body Wash is beneficial for every skin type but instead the message came across as a racial insult that had Facebook users who saw the advertisement up in arms. One user said it conveyed a message 'that the Black Woman is dirty and once you use Dove soap, you'll be clean and white'.

The reaction to the campaign could have been avoided if Dove had realised that in the connected world the consumer has the power when it comes to interpreting and sharing the marketing communication messages from brands and companies. Sound consumer insight and a customer-centric mind set should thus guide the formulation and sending of messages. Marketing and marketing communication is 'just a shot in the dark' without the necessary consumer insights.

In the digital age, consumers rely on one another for information on brands. They share information about brands, good and bad, in a blink of an eye with their social networks and brands need to be aware of the power of consumer-to-consumer communication. Brands thus have to keep up with the ever-changing consumer landscape and realise that it is not a case of influencing and persuading consumers by means of one-way marketing communication anymore. It is rather a case of turning consumers into 'active media of communications' and harnessing the power of the connected consumer.

12.1 INTRODUCTION

Marketing communication is an essential part of the marketing mix and entails the use of a variety of tools and functions that in the traditional sense, form part of a planned effort to deliver a specific message to promote a brand and organisation. Connected consumers have, however, changed the traditional way of marketing communication forever. These consumers are digital savvy and use a variety of devices such as tablets, e-readers, smartphones, laptops etc. to connect to the internet in order to interact with digital content. They live a digital life and embrace technology, from social networks to smartphones to intelligent appliances.

Consumers are no longer passive receivers of marketing communication messages aimed at them, instead they are part of the process, active media of communications, as illustrated by the opening case study. The power has shifted from companies to consumers and they therefore demand more; they want to participate, not just listen. Customer-centric communication is needed where companies and brands work 'with' the consumer to create customised communication offerings that will be beneficial to both marketers and consumers. The chapter will thus start with a background discussion on the changing consumer before it continues with an explanation of the place of communication in the marketing mix and the communication process. Traditional and digital communication media are then explained and the link between consumer decision making and marketing communication is elaborated on. The chapter concludes with an explanation of research and marketing communications.

12.2   The changing consumer

It is essential to think of customers as individuals and not a faceless group or just a source of data. This means that it is important for leaders to see the big picture, to innovate and look ahead. In the future, it will be this perspective, not technology alone, that will ensure that an organisation is more able meet challenges.[2]

Technology has changed, and continues to change, the world as we know it, and has had an overwhelming impact on marketing and marketing communication practices globally. New trends such as omnichannel marketing are challenging marketers to think and act differently when planning and executing marketing and marketing communication strategies. Consumers and companies interact with each other through multiple channels that include, inter alia, websites, mobile apps, physical and online stores, social media etc. These interactions can take place by means of multiple digital devices, including smartphones, tablets and computers. These interactions need to be consistent and seamless across all channels (hence the term omnichannel marketing). Consumer connectivity has shifted the power (the power to influence and/or the power of being in control) from organisations to the consumer and even more so to the social group. Consumers are quick to share stories about brands, good or bad, and are not afraid to do so as the communication power now lies with them and their social networks. This is a world where the influence of social networks is strong and where consumers trust random conversations about brands more than the messages from targeted advertising campaigns.

Consumer trust is thus in the 'f-factor' (friends, family, fans and followers), rather than in marketing communications. Consumers are not influenced by marketing communication campaigns as the only source of information anymore and instead seek out and listen to those that they regard as the authority and expert on a topic or brand. Strangers on social media are now seen as the experts and consumers will rather get advice from them and trust them more that they do advertising. People thus use technologies to get the things they need from each other instead of from companies.[3]

Companies cannot afford to ignore this phenomenon as consumers are continuously turning to their social networks for referrals before they purchase an item. In South Africa, 71% of consumers are more likely to purchase an item based on a referral from friends or family members forming part of their social network and 15% of consumers first learnt about a product that they were initially not aware of from discussions with their social networks. In South Africa, the 13 million Facebook users, 8 million on YouTube, 7.4 million on Twitter, 4,6 million on LinkedIn and approximately 2,7 million on Instagram, will continuously be exposed to reviews and complaints posted by friends, family and peers that will play a role in their purchasing decisions.[4] It is thus clear that in this technologically driven world, the connected consumer guides the design and planning of marketing communications. These 'new evolved' consumers should not be seen as passive receivers of marketing communication messages, but should instead be treated as active participants, seekers and contributors by companies and brands wishing to build a trustful relationship with them. They should be treated more like partners in the communication process than a receiver. They should be considered peers and friends of the brand if the brand wants them to regard the brand as being genuine and trustworthy.[5]

The consumer decision process is essentially a result of consumers' psychological processes, where consumers' perceived gains and losses influence their behaviour. The opening case study is a good example of a 'loss' felt by the consumer due to a perceived insensitive message. Companies therefore need to make sure that they lessen the impact of negative thoughts or negative communication messages from the consumer by engaging the consumer in meaningful and positive conversations about the brand. Nando's has done this successfully by means of their brand communities (discussed in section 12.6.3.2)

It is clear from the discussion above that the new 'typology' of customer in the 21st century dramatically influences the marketing and marketing communications efforts of companies as they are more empowered, internet savvy and have greater access to information in a digital world. They thus have more choices and rely more on peer reviews, website information and internet searches and comparisons when making decisions about products, brands and retailers. They also have the ability to create content online and influence each other positively or negatively. Marketers therefore need to optimise the power of digital marketing as it presents opportunities for them to engage in one-to-one communication with consumers. It also allows them to personalise conversations by means of multiple communication vehicles and platforms.[6] The digital marketing communication vehicles and platforms together with traditional media will be discussed further in section 12.6. It is, however, important to explain the marketing mix first, in order to understand the role and relevance of marketing communication in the overall marketing strategy of a company. The next section will address this.

12.3 THE MARKETING MIX AND COMMUNICATION

The marketing mix of an organisation is made up of the four Ps:
• Product
• Price
• Place (distribution)
• Promotion

In a traditional sense, these elements are combined into a marketing strategy that the organisation uses to inform the consumer about the offering and to persuade the consumer into action. Typically, a consumer wants a *product* to satisfy a particular need, and becomes aware of the product through advertising or some other form of message (*promotion*) from the organisation. The product is made available to the consumer at a particular *price* at outlets (*place or distribution*). Technological acceleration and the unstoppable nature of it have, however, changed consumers and their behaviours. Marketers cannot afford to be indifferent to these changes and how they have influenced the traditional marketing mix. Some of the most influential changes will be highlighted as part of the discussion of each of the elements of the marketing mix in the following sections.

12.3.1 Product
A **product** can be defined as a bundle of need-satisfying features that can be exchanged for a price. Products consist of both tangible and intangible

elements. Tangible aspects include the brand, packaging and quality indicators. Intangible attributes include aspects such as the style of the product and its image as well as the reputation of the manufacturer.[7] The attributes of the product combine to create an integrated offering that is aimed at satisfying the needs of the consumer.

In the digital age, the consumer becomes part of the product development phase by means of co-creation, which is a process where parties (for example, consumers, researchers, product development teams, designers, consultants etc.) join forces to learn from each other, share information and, as a result, create value. This process unites consumers into a single unit that interacts with the brand through participation in its development.[8]

Consumers can be part of a co-design process to change existing products or design new products or packaging etc. Consumers can also be part of a research project where brands monitor social conversations and use the insights either to add to the existing product mix or to improve products, packaging or ingredients etc. Increasingly, prominent brands such as Nivea use consumers as valuable sources of innovation. Nivea developed their Black and White deodorant as one that protects clothing from deodorant stains based on insights gained from monitoring social conversation and an online co-creation study.[9]

12.3.2 Price

Product **price**, simply put, is the selling value of a product and also represents the level of profitability of the product. Prices communicate meaning to consumers; psychologically, price may signify value as consumers tend to equate high prices with high quality. Organisations need to be aware of the perceived value that consumers hold towards the product. If the value is not perceived to be worthy of the price, consumers are not likely to buy the product at the set price.

Retailers often differentiate themselves from competitors by positioning their store as a discount store, signifying lower prices for everyday products such as milk, bread and sugar, and even clothing. Digitisation has, however, led to significant changes in how companies determine prices. Consumers' behavioural changes, such as consulting more sources online to compare prices and having access to 'free' digital products, have forced companies to rethink their pricing strategies and to apply new pricing models.

An example of such a change is the introduction of *freemiums*, where basic services are offered for free and consumers then pay a fee if they want to use the upgraded premium version. Spotify is a digital music, podcast and video streaming service that gives consumers access to millions of songs and other content from artists all over the world. They offer the basic functions such as playing music for free, but if a consumer wants more features, they then have to pay a subscription fee per month. Spotify premium features include, for example, playing any song, any time, on any device; downloading of music for offline listening; amazing sound quality and uninterrupted music, thus no advertisements in between songs. Spotify launched in South Africa in March 2018.

12.3.3   Place (distribution)

Product **distribution** encompasses all the channels that can be followed to bring the product from manufacturer to the final consumer. Apart from referring to the place where the product is available to the consumer, distribution also incorporates the activities that move the product there.[10] Through the distribution process, organisations aim to provide the right product to the target market at the right place, at the right time and also at the right price. Thus distribution may be seen as the glue that brings all of the elements of the marketing mix together.

Online channels and continued digitalisation have also affected the distribution models of manufacturing companies, service delivering firms and retailers. Retailers, for example, have to use various on- and offline channels to reach the consumer. Yuppiechef, traditionally an online retailer, has now opened its first physical store in the Western Cape. According to co-founder Andrew Smith, they believe the future of retailing is omnichannel – a combination of physical stores and e-commerce.[11]

12.3.4   Promotion

Promotion refers to all marketing communication.

The terms 'marketing communication mix' and 'promotional mix' are often used interchangeably. They are all the media, actions and materials that may be employed to reach a target audience with the aim of affecting their behaviour, attitudes and/or perceptions. The objectives of marketing communications range from creating awareness to persuading consumers to buy the organisation's offerings. Co-ordinating all promotional efforts is referred to as integrated marketing communication (IMC) and it allows for synergy across all messages sent by the organisation.[12]

Rapid technological developments and the changing business landscape have influenced the traditional marketing communication mix and its integration. Marketers face many new communication challenges due to changes in consumer behaviour as a result of technology and digitisation. Consumers are not passive receivers of communication messages sent through traditional media anymore; instead, they now actively seek information during various stages of their purchase journey using search engines, mobile browsers, blogs and brand websites, to name a few. Digitisation has not only led to new challenges in capturing the attention of the multitasking consumer but has also created new opportunities for marketers to communicate with the consumer at each stage of their purchase journey. Marketers now have a bigger mix to choose from and this has presented them with more communication possibilities in order to reach consumers and achieve their communication objectives. To develop a truly integrated marketing communication program, it is necessary to adopt a customer-centric viewpoint and understand how a consumer uses and processes communication during the decision journey.[13]

The following tools form part of the promotion element of the marketing mix. These tools combine to form the promotional or marketing communication mix:[14]

- *Advertising* encompasses all non-personal forms of communication transferred through media that are paid for by identified sponsors. Media can include traditional media, for example newspapers and television, as well as new digital media, for example social media. Traditional and new media will be discussed in more detail in section 12.6.1. The main aims of advertising are to gain the attention of the audience and to inform or even educate the consumer about the organisation's offerings. It aspires to persuade consumers to purchase the product and to serve as a reminder of the organisation's offerings, and is usually used in combination with other promotional tools. Checkers, for example, used television advertising as well as printed advertisements in magazines and newspapers to launch their Little Shop Mini Collectables sales promotion. Shoprite Holdings, of which Checkers forms a part, was the top spender on advertising in 2016 with a total amount of R1 512 522 344.[15]

- *Public relations* refers to the activities involved in managing the relationships between the organisation and its constituent groups (internal and external stakeholders). Maintaining goodwill and positive perceptions towards the organisation is achieved through communication. Many companies foster goodwill by engaging in social responsibility programmes. Cause-related marketing sometimes forms part of the public relations activities of a company. KFC's 'Add Hope' campaign is an example, where R2 from every meal purchased is donated to 'the fight against hunger'. The Add Hope initiative has raised over R378 million in the fight against hunger in the six years it has been running.[16]

- *Sales promotions* are aimed at eliciting an immediate response, such as persuading a consumer to try out the product or to purchase it. Tools such as free samples, coupons and discounts are used in an attempt to lower purchase risk. Retailers often use sales promotions to encourage shoppers to visit their stores. Checkers' Little Shop Mini Collectables is an example of a sales promotion campaign by a retailer. Checkers 'shrunk' some of South Africa's most recognisable brands and used them as part of a fun, exciting and educational promotion. Shoppers were rewarded with a free Little Shop Mini for every R150 spent in-store. What started as a promotion aimed at children and inspiring young South African entrepreneurs, ended in a 'craze' as people of all ages became obsessed with the miniature grocery items, swapping them on Facebook and posting pictures on Instagram.

- *Personal selling* is the face-to-face (personal) process whereby a salesperson attempts to identify the potential buyer's needs and preferences, and then to sell a suitable product or service to the prospect. A typical example is the salesperson in a Volkswagen dealership who establishes the needs of the potential buyer and then attempts to persuade him or her to purchase the vehicle that seems most suitable in terms of his or her needs. South African brands such as Justine and Amway only use personal sellers in the form of consultants to make their products available to the end-consumer.

- *Direct marketing* uses various advertising media to elicit an interactive response from the target audience. Since it requires direct responses to a promotional offering, direct marketing enables measurement of responses, thereby providing a good indication of the effectiveness of the campaign. Direct marketing includes telesales, which are popular with insurance and financial institutions, and email or 'spam' mail. The Protection of Personal Information (POPI) act makes it mandatory to ask for consent before engaging in direct marketing activities and prohibits the 'selling' of a person's private information to a third party. The POPI act will thus have far-reaching consequences for the direct marketing industry of South Africa.[17]
- *Sponsorship and events marketing* involves an organisation providing support (usually financial) to another person, organisation or event, but the organisation requires exposure of its brand in return. Red Bull is well known for its focus on sponsorships as part of its marketing strategy. The sponsorships of extreme sporting events, for example 'Red Bull King of the Air' kitesurfing event, is an integral part of the organisation's brand building efforts. Red Bull has also combined 'public relations' and sponsorship with the 'Red Bull Wings for Life World Run' event where hundreds of thousands of people participate on the same day, at the same time, all over the world to raise money for a charitable cause. The idea is to 'run for those who can't' and the money raised is then donated to the investigation of spinal cord injuries.[18] Red Bull uses digital channels, such as RED Bull TV, to make sure that consumers can watch all the events from Red Bull on demand on various devices like smartphones, Amazon Kindle Fire, computers, tablets and smart TVs. The brand thus ensures that it connects with the consumer constantly by loading fresh content daily and providing it free of charge.[19]

Figure 12.1 Screenshot of Red Bull Wings for Life World Run Event on Red Bull TV

12.3.5 Digital marketing as part of the promotional mix

Digital marketing is an umbrella term used to describe the use of digital technologies to promote brands and increase sales. It helps to create demand by utilising the power of the interconnected, interactive web. The American Marketing Institution describes it as processes made possible by digital technologies to create, communicate and deliver value to customers and other stakeholders. The digital environment provides new ways to reach and communicate with consumers and has unlocked many new digital tools and tactics such as search, content, affiliate, video, social media, email and mobile marketing. Digital marketing will be discussed further in section 12.6.3.

12.4 THE COMMUNICATION PROCESS

Communication is a process in which a message is sent from a source or sender through a communication channel to a target receiver. Four aspects are present,[20] namely:
- information in the form of a message (for example, a new product is being launched)
- people, who are the intended audience of the information (for example, the target consumers)
- format, where the most appropriate way to send the message is selected (for example, a television commercial)
- time, which refers to the correct time at or during which to convey the information (for example, during prime time on television).

Communication ranges from merely conveying simple information to developing and executing complex messages containing a great deal of information. Marketers and retailers, using the many tools available to them, aim to convey the correct information about their organisations to the correct target audiences to obtain positive responses. The communication model makes it easier to understand this process.[21]

Figure 12.2 indicates the flow as well as the elements of the communication process, namely the sender, the channel (medium), the receiver, feedback and noise. The sender develops a particular message, which is transmitted through a channel (or medium) to the intended receiver (in marketing communication, the consumer). Feedback occurs back to the sender in the form of some sort of response. The communication may be hampered or influenced by various factors outside of the intended communication. These factors are referred to as noise.

The digital environment has changed the ways of communication and thus also the interpretation of the elements of traditional communication processes, as mentioned before. An important aspect setting the digital world apart from the traditional is the ease with which consumers can share information, not only with close friends but also with an extended network. They can post reviews, comment on websites and get the necessary information they seek from consumers all over the world. Thus more a case of communication from consumer-to-firm, consumer-to-consumer and consumer-about-firm than only firm-to-consumer as indicated by the traditional communication process.[22]

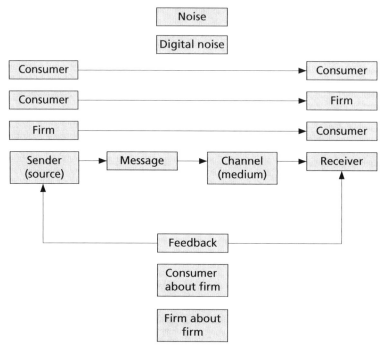

Figure 12.2 The communication process in a digital world

Although the consumer's communication behaviour has changed in a digital world, the basic elements of the communication process remain the same. Each of these elements will now be discussed in detail.

12.4.1 The sender

The sender (source) in marketing communication is the originator of the product message. The sender creates a message that is intended for a particular receiver. Creating the message is also referred to as encoding. The sender uses various tools to encode the message, such as words and images that are carefully chosen to be appropriate for the specific audience (receiver). The aim of the sender is that the receiver will decode or interpret the message in the manner intended by the sender.

In marketing communication, the sender is often a multifaceted construct. Often, it consists of the originator or sponsor (organisation) as well as the spokesperson (persona) that effectively represents the organisation within the actual message.[23] For example, in a personal selling situation, the sponsor (an organisation, for example BMW) is represented by the salesperson (spokesperson). In advertising, the sponsor is typically identified by symbols or slogans used in the advertisement (for example, the BMW logo in a magazine advertisement) and the brand can be represented by a spokesperson (for example, the driver of the BMW in the advertisement). In a traditional sense, the communication process starts with the organisation sending a marketing message to the consumer to influence and persuade the consumer, thus firm-to-consumer communication. In a digital world, consumers are quick to share information on their social networking sites about anything they want, including products and brands. Communication, in this instance, is thus from consumer-to-consumer. Consumers also write online reviews (consumer-about-firm communication) and they comment on companies' websites and blogs (consumer-to-firm communication). BMW has therefore also included social media marketing as part of their marketing communication strategy. The brand's efforts have paid off as they have broken through the ten million mark for followers on Instagram. This places them in the position of being the most successful automotive brand on Instagram worldwide.[24]

For the sender to be deemed a reliable source and therefore for the message to be seen as believable, source credibility is important. Credibility refers to the extent to which the sender is perceived to be knowledgeable about what is being communicated. If the organisation can ensure that the source of the message is deemed credible, the chances that the message will be successful are good. Source credibility consists of the trustworthiness and attractiveness of the sender as well as the expertise of the sender.[25]

If receivers have a lot of confidence in the sender, the source is considered to be trustworthy. Attractiveness refers to the appeal of the sender and includes the extent to which the receiver can identify with the source. Advertisers often feature celebrities in advertising as they appeal to many people and are considered to be attractive in various ways. Expertise is related to the knowledge that the sender has in terms of the communication topic. Traditionally, a salesperson who displayed extensive knowledge in answering questions about the product would have been seen as an expert and thus a credible source delivering a believable message. Connectivity has, however, changed that, and consumers will now consult more sources before being convinced of the 'expertise' of the source. The digital world has therefore created new challenges for marketers and brands to send messages that are seen as credible. The access to digital channels allows consumers to voice their opinion through likes, give recommendations through feedback and product reviews, and engage in interactive conversations with marketers throughout their purchase journey.[26] Conversations online is seen as electronic word of mouth (eWOM) and is regarded as one of the most influential information sources for the digital consumer.[27]

A 'one size fits all' approach in sending messages is therefore not enough and marketers need to be more customer-centric and follow a more personalised approach in communicating with the consumer (their target market). They have to understand the information needs of the consumer during every step of the purchase journey to design messages that will break through the clutter and appeal to the consumer. They also have to realise that the consumer is part of the conversation and a creator of content, not just a receiver of messages.

12.4.2   The message

The message relays the information that the sender wants to transmit to the target audience. The message can contain words, pictures and symbols that will combine into an information 'package' aimed at the receiver. Messages can contain verbal and/or non-verbal elements.[28] Verbal messages contain spoken or written information, whereas non-verbal communication includes visual aspects.

Marketing communication often contains both verbal and non-verbal messages in one communication piece. For example, the verbal message, when using traditional media such as a magazine advertisement for a retailer, will be the information presented in words (such as price specials). The non-verbal message will be incorporated in the retailer's logo and the pictures of the products featured in the advertisement. In marketing communication, tools such as personal selling, the appearance and attitude of the salesperson communicate a clear non-verbal message to the potential client. For example, the salespeople at a Mercedes-Benz dealership are well dressed and well groomed, which conveys a silent message about the style of the brand.

In the digital environment, marketers are able to design and deliver personalised messages and content to consumers using various digital channels. In creating content that appeals to consumers, marketers can start conversations about their brands that will be shared across social networks. Content marketing has therefore become much more important in recent years. Content marketing is defined by the Content Marketing Institute as targeted method that specific means to attract and maintain a specific audience.[29] It is thus more a case of creating interesting and meaningful content and matching the content (information or entertainment or both) to consumers' information needs at whichever stage in the buying journey they are in,[30] than it is the sending of a one-sided message. The message is still part of the content, but by making it part of meaningful content, it becomes more relevant and its ability to break through the clutter and catch the attention of the consumer increases.

The structure and the presentation (execution) of the message still play an important role in its eventual success. Design and appeal need to be considered:
* *Message designs:* This aspect includes resonance; positive or negative message framing; one- or two-sided messages, and presentation order. Resonance refers to word play that conveys double meanings that are often humorous. Positive framing occurs when the consumer is reminded of the product benefits to be gained, whereas negative framing alerts the consumer to the benefits lost by not choosing the product. A one-sided message claims exclusivity of the brand, while a two-sided message acknowledges competing brands. In terms of presentation order, research shows that points that are conveyed first as well as last in a particular message tend to be remembered better.[31]

- *Message appeals:* These refer to the cues used in the message that attract the attention of the target audience and also aim to influence or persuade the audience. Message appeals can be broadly divided into rational and emotional appeals. Rational appeals aim to convey logical, rational information. Emotional appeals focus on conveying the message by eliciting an emotional response from the target audience. An example of a rational appeal is when the salesperson focuses on the technical specifications of the product, thus factual information. A salesperson who is appealing to the prospective consumer's ego motives is using an emotional appeal. Fear and humour are popular emotional advertising appeals used by advertisers, often with great success.

12.4.3 The medium

The medium (channel) is the vehicle that transmits the message to the receiver. There are various media types available to marketers to enable effective communication of their messages. Communication media, digital and traditional, used in marketing and retail communication are discussed in more detail in Section 12.6. It is important that the product, the message and the medium chosen for the communication are compatible.[32] For example, advertising in-store promotions of a sportswear retailer in a magazine targeted at young mothers would be less suitable than advertising in a sports magazine aimed at sport lovers.

12.4.4 The receiver

The receiver (or target audience) of a message is the specific group of consumers that the communication is intended to reach. It must be remembered that target audiences are exactly that: a target for the message. The assumption cannot be made that the receivers will always decode the message as it was intended.[33] The opening case is a perfect illustration where receivers decoded the brand message differently from the intended message (see the opening case study). When the receiver decodes the message, he or she interprets it in some way, attaching meaning to what it contains.

Decoding is influenced by the knowledge, experience, emotions and attitudes of the receivers. As the receivers have their own personalities, preferences and interests, the message may not always be interpreted as intended. Consumers are also using different media sources and devices to get the information they seek and thus are active seekers and not passive receivers. This contributes to multitasking behaviour and lack of attention. Barriers to communication may therefore exist that could cause the message to be misinterpreted.[34] Barriers include the following:

- *Selective exposure:* Consumers choose what they perceive, for example they may switch channels to avoid having to watch television adverts. Netflix and Apple TV have altered television viewing behaviour. Consumers can now select when they want to watch their favourite programmes without the interruption of advertisements. Consumers can also apply AdBlock on the internet and choose to 'opt out' from email marketing. Marketers should therefore create content that the consumer will seek out and share. The MTN night shift campaign is an example of a television advertisement combined with Facebook and a YouTube campaign that captured the attention of South African consumers. By taking a well-known song and pairing it with how ordinary people survive the night shift, MTN created a campaign that resonated with consumers, resulting in 2 804 083 million views on YouTube.[35]

- *Psychological noise:* This refers to factors such as distracting thoughts or inattention that can impair the consumer's ability to notice a stimulus. For example, if you are daydreaming about scoring a winning goal in a soccer game, you will not be paying attention to a radio advertisement. Marketers can overcome this barrier by repeated exposure (repeating the advertisement often), using contrasts (such as surprising outcomes) and also by using alternate forms of advertising, such as mobile or internet advertising, focused on individual consumer needs.

12.4.5   Feedback

Feedback is the receiver's response to the message. In personal selling, for example, the desired response would be the consumer's decision to buy. Feedback allows the sender to establish whether the message was received as intended. Personal selling allows for immediate feedback, but this is not possible with all forms of promotion. How an advertisement affects sales, for example, cannot be measured directly. However, there are several types of research methods that may be used to gauge advertising effectiveness. These are discussed in section 12.8.

The digital environment has also altered the traditional view of 'feedback'. Digital channels have enabled consumers to immediately voice their opinions in the form of, for example, online reviews and social conversations. Digital technologies allow marketers to track these conversations and make informed decisions about future communications. Feedback thus becomes more 'immediate' in the digital environment.

12.4.6   Noise

Noise includes all stimuli that may cause disruptions in the communication process. For example, competing messages (also referred to as 'clutter') battle for the attention of the audience. Noise detracts attention from the message and therefore may dilute its impact. Because most noise factors cannot be controlled by the marketer, messages must be carefully designed and planned for optimum attention-attracting capabilities.

Digital technology has also created new challenges for marketers by 'contributing' to the noise in the form of various digital devices and media. Consumers can now easily switch between devices, for example turning to their mobile phones or laptops to search for information, purchase online or contribute content to their social media networking sites, while they are watching a programme on television. They are thus constantly in a mode of multitasking and in a state of inattention. Marketers have to break through this 'digital noise' when trying to communicate with the connected consumer. Consumer intelligence gained from data gathered on online behaviour can be used to personalise the message and create relevant content as mentioned above.

12.4.7 Illustration of the elements of communication

The elements of the communication process are clearly illustrated in Figure 12.3. The sender is Tiger Brands (their Doom brand). The brand is sending a message that it kills flies effectively. Visuals (the 'eye view' of the fly seeing and spying on personal information) and a verbal message ('the fly on the wall sees too much, kill it') is used to convey the message that Doom can be used to get rid of unwanted and annoying intruders like flies. It fits with the product description on the Tiger Brands website, namely 'Nobody likes to have their home visited by creepy-crawlies or embarrassing bugs. To help you keep your space pest free, Doom uses advanced active ingredients to ensure you are protected'.[36] The medium used to send the message is traditional print in the form of newspapers and magazines. The 'receiver' is all consumers experiencing a fly problem and who want to get rid of

Figure 12.3 Print advertisement of Doom: the fly on the wall[37]

these unwanted intruders. Feedback could be in the form of online reviews of the product, conversations about the brand or the advertisement etc.

12.5 COMMUNICATING WITH THE ONLINE CONSUMER

The basic communication model works well when explaining traditional media. In the context of the digital environment, however, the process is not as straightforward. Owing to the interactive nature of the internet, online communication usually entails a constant two-way flow of information. Interactive technologies enable interactions between the organisation and the consumer, but also a myriad of other people. This is because the consumer looking for a product may interact with the organisation's website, but also with users of the product via social networking sites and other social media to get more information. Since social media are strongly associated with word of mouth (WOM), the opinions of the consumer's contacts may influence the eventual buying decision even more than the organisation's communication efforts.

The impact of WOM influence is increased when the credibility of the message source is high (as with any source of information). Electronic WOM (also referred to as word of mouse, or eWOM) is defined as the exchange of knowledge between online consumers.[38] This has a direct influence on consumer brand loyalty, as the eWOM message is sent by a consumer who has experience of the product under discussion and may therefore impact the decision making of other consumers (see also Chapter 15).

Organisations need to be aware of the interpersonal nature of online communication and the different sources of information that are available to the online consumer almost instantaneously. Marketers that wish to communicate with the online consumer should use an integrated digital marketing communication approach that is executed across multiple digital platforms. A well-designed website that provides the consumer with relevant information is just one of the elements of such an approach. By also providing review or rating functions for online products, marketers address the human need to belong (we like to know what others think). This is thus a valuable addition to a website that enables consumers to view other consumers' opinions that they value because of their impartial nature.[39] It also provides instant feedback to marketers that can be used in redesigning their marketing mixes. The online shopping site takealot.com features a review option for the products sold through the website. This allows users to comment and rate products, thereby providing eWOM that many users find useful.

Research has shown that both traditional as well as social media communication strongly influence brand equity (the value of the brand). Traditional communication tends to have a stronger impact on brand awareness than social media. Conversely, social media communication impacts more on brand image because this is the avenue through which user comments about products and brands are shared, which is more credible than information coming from a brand manager or even salesperson who wishes to promote sales.[40] It is advisable for marketers to ensure synergy between traditional and social media communication in order to maximise the overall effect on brand equity. Reaching the online consumer effectively is therefore as much a function of traditional communication as communicating through new media.

APPLICATION

The communication process applied

Consol started airing a television commercial in January 2017 to communicate the message 'the best things come in glass'. The advert tells the story of a little girl in the park that fills her empty glass jar with 'the sounds of the park'. Her purpose is to capture each moment in the park by catching the sounds and experiences. These memories are then shared with her blind grandmother at home. Consol wants to show that glass jars do not just preserve food, they also preserve memories, precious moments and good feelings.[41] The advertisement can be watched at https://www.facebook.com/pg/ConsolGlass/videos/?ref=page_internal.

Discussion questions

Access the link provided above. Identify the elements of the communication process (the sender, message, channel, receiver, feedback, noise) in the advertisement.

Suggest ways in which Consol can communicate this message to the online consumer.

12.6 COMMUNICATION MEDIA

Targeting communication at consumers during every phase of their decision-making journey is the main aim of marketers when planning the message and executing it through various communication channels.

Communication media or channels can be classified into personal and non-personal categories. Personal channels are those that feature face-to-face interaction such as personal selling and word of mouth (WOM). Non-personal channels have no personal contact and are referred to as mass media. Mass media include traditional advertising media, alternative media and digital media. Consumers are increasingly using digital channels in their purchasing decision journey. This has created more opportunities for marketers to interact with them.

The idea of 'media' has broadened and can potentially include any digital touchpoint, such as using a mobile phone, playing a video game, watching a video, walking past an electronic billboard, engaging in social media activities, reading or writing a blog, and so on. Media planning has therefore become more complicated as consumers have access to more media, are spending more time with them and are consuming them simultaneously. Marketers and organisations need to broaden their thinking and create patterns of interactions with consumers using whatever channel or combination of channels necessary to reach consumers on their own terms.[42] The different channels available to create these interactions are discussed next.

12.6.1 Traditional media

Traditional media are also referred to as major advertising media, and include print and broadcast media.

Print media

Print media include newspapers, magazines and promotional brochures or leaflets. Newspapers have the advantages of high coverage, low costs and timeliness, as they are considered to be current. Disadvantages are poor printing quality and selective reader exposure, since not everyone reads newspapers.

In contrast, magazines have high printing quality and good segmentation potential as magazines tend to be focused on specific audiences, for example women or special interest groups. However, magazines lack flexibility due to long lead times and advertising costs are quite high.

Online sites such as Netwerk24 and News24 provide access to the news in a digital format 24 hours a day. Daily newspapers and magazines (for example, YOU) can also be accessed anytime and on any device via their e-format.

South African consumers still tend to use traditional formats, although more and more are adopting digital technologies (refer to the discussion box below).

Broadcast media

Broadcast media include television, radio and cinema. Television remains one of the most prominent advertising media and has the major advantages of high coverage and reach as well as the ability to incorporate both sound and visuals, which engages the consumer more easily. This allows for a great deal of creativity. On the downside, television commercials imply high costs in terms of production as well as low selectivity as a result of broad audiences. Owing to its popularity as an advertising medium, there are large volumes of clutter (competing messages) and also limited attention from viewers.[43] In South Africa, the most popular television channel (based on weekly adult viewership) is SABC1.[44]

Radio is a medium that is low in costs and is extremely flexible. It also has the potential of segmented audiences, specifically when focusing on local audiences. Drawbacks of radio advertising include clutter, the short time span of advertisements and low attention-grabbing ability as a result of limited creativity options. According to the Broadcast Research Council of South Africa (BRCSA), the most popular radio stations in South Africa during 2017 were Ukhozi FM, followed by Umhlobo Wenene (UWFM).[45] Consumers can also listen to these radio stations on any device via livestreaming (at Ukhozifm.co.za and Umhlobofm.co.za respectively).

South African broadcasting is in the process of a digital migration from analogue to digital. The International Telecommunications Union (ITU) has set June 2019 as the deadline for countries to have implemented digital migration. This process allows users to experience the benefits of clearer picture and sound as well as more channels. Dual illumination is a period during which both old analogue and new digital signals will co-exist. Consumers who still watch terrestrial services like SABC and e.tv have time to get the set-top boxes that they will need once the analogue services are switched off. MultiChoice has reacted by launching a GOtv platform in South Africa, which offers 12 channels for R99/month or a cheaper two-channel package for R49/quarter, which is a fraction of the cost of installing the full DStv package (prices relevant to the date of launch of the GOtv platform). Users will also get access to free-to-air content from the SABC and e.tv and community broadcasters if their GOtv subscription is paid up.[46]

Figure 12.4 The logo of Ukhozi FM

12.6.2   Alternative media

Alternative media include out-of-home and on-the-go media such as billboards and transit advertising (for example, taxi and bus advertising) as well as digital billboards and displays.[48] These media are continuously evolving and marketers are constantly looking for innovative ways to utilise them. In some suburbs,

South Africans' access to media[47]

The South African Audience Foundation (SAARF) launched its All Media and Product Survey (AMPS) in 1975 and has provided the much-used-and-relied-upon audience segmentation tool the LSM or Living Standards Measure. The Marketing Research Foundation (MRF) replaced SAARF and is working on a replacement for AMPS called MAPS survey. According to Greg Garden (MRF director): 'The goal of MAPS is to create consumer-centric research to track and understand daily consumer behaviour, decision making and consumption. The research results will be primarily used to deepen consumer understanding for target marketing, and as the basis for the planning of media space and time'. The Broadcast Research Council of South Africa (BRC) was established in 2015, with their role being 'to commission and oversee the delivery of radio and television audience measurement research for broadcasters, as well as the advertising and marketing industry'. They publish the establishment survey (ES) results quarterly to report on measurements.

The following data is based on the 'last AMPS results ever' of 2016:

- Print as a whole declined from 2015 to 2016, with the average readership down from 62,3% to 61,0%. Magazines' readership remained stable, however newspapers' readership declined, indicating a downward spiral for this medium.
- Television viewership remained stable at 91,8% from 2015 to 2016 with the traditional TV set still being the preferred device; only 1,4% of viewers consume this medium online or over their cell phones.
- Radio also remained stable, with 35 018 million listeners aged 15+. Listening over cell phones was showing an upward trend, with 41,7% listening on phones via radio listening apps such as FM Radio South Africa, and 4,5% listening online via a website or other app. Websites included the radio stations' own websites, for example http://www.kfm.co.za (where you can listen 'live' to KFM) or radio websites, for example http://www.radio-south-africa.co.za. Only 0,2% listened on DStv's audio channels.
- Exposure on bus shelters increased from 26.9% to 28.2%, while advertising on litter bins went down from 41,5% to 40,2%. Street pole advertising declined from 62,4% to 60,8%.
- Cell phone access in 2016 was 88,9% with the highest access for LSM 8–10 at 96,1%, followed by LSM 5–7 at 89,5% and LSM 1–4 at 79,7%.

Discussion questions

1. Bearing in mind the features of the traditional advertising media as well as the above-mentioned figures, which media would you choose if you wanted to reach a large part of the general South African population? Motivate your answer.
2. If you wanted to create a more personalised message using traditional media to launch a new ladies' perfume, and keeping in mind the above statistics, what would you do?
3. Access the website of the Broadcast Research Council of South Africa at http://www.brcsa.org and look at the Establishment Survey Results for October 2017 (http://www.brcsa.org.za/establishment-survey-full-year-release-october-2017/). Compare the results with the AMPS results above. Were there any changes from 2016–2017? Provide your viewpoints on the media habits of the South African consumer.
4. Choose two traditional media and create a complete profile of the demographics for that media based on the Establishment Survey Results for October 2017. What advice would you give to a South African retailer who wants to use traditional media to communicate to consumers between 25 and 34 years of age? Motivate your answer based on your demographic profile.

even the walls surrounding people's homes on busy streets are now utilised as billboards.

According to Koenderman,[49] the exposure of South African adults to outdoor media is high: 95,4% across all categories of out-of-home media. The accessibility of these media to the general public makes them attractive media to use for advertising.

12.6.3   Digital marketing

Digital marketing is an umbrella term used to describe communication via all digital channels, devices and platforms, online or not. Technically speaking, television, radio and digital billboards are also part of digital marketing as they are regarded as digital channels.

Digital marketing does not limit usage to the internet. If you download an app on your mobile phone using the internet, but thereafter it works independently using mobile technologies, it is still considered to be digital media. A mobile campaign, where digital marketers use SMS texts, is created using the technology of the internet, however after it has been sent, the receiver (consumer) does not need an internet connection to receive it.

Internet marketing, or online marketing as it is also called, is an important subset of digital marketing, since the majority of digital marketing falls within its scope (see section 12.6.3.1). In the digital environment, consumers have access to more media than ever before. Internet use has grown and mobile technology has created a lifestyle that revolves around mobile connectivity. The web has offered marketers opportunities to communicate instantly with consumers and has also allowed the consumer to reply. Consumers can now connect with brands through numerous new media channels that are often outside the control of the marketer. For example, in 2010 Greenpeace 'hijacked' Nestlé digitally by encouraging their supporters to swarm the company's Facebook page and to change their Facebook profile pictures to include tampered-with, anti-Nestlé logos, like 'Killer' instead of 'Kit Kat'(https://www.greenpeace.org/archive-international/en/campaigns/climate-change/kitkat/). (For more information on the Nestlé example, refer to the following article: https://www.cnet.com/news/nestle-mess-shows-sticky-side-of-facebook-pages/; and for more information regarding 'hijacked media', refer to the following link: https://www.mckinsey.com/business-functions/marketing-and-sales/our-insights/beyond-paid-media-marketings-new-vocabulary.

By understanding the main digital marketing communication options available today and using them in the various stages of the decision-making process, marketers have a better chance of connecting with the consumer and building better relationships. The next part of the discussion will focus on the internet, social media marketing and mobile marketing.

Internet

The internet is a globally interconnected computerised networking infrastructure that enables computers worldwide to communicate with each other.[50] The terms 'internet' and 'web' are often used interchangeably. The world wide web (www), which was established in the early 1990s, started out as a collection of internet sites with little functionality or constancy, and has since evolved into a truly interactive platform that enables transacting, information-sharing and communication, called Web 2.0.[51] It is the communication functionality of the modern web that is of particular interest to marketers. It can not only be used to provide product information but also to customise communication and transactional offerings.

E-business is the conducting of business activities via the web and includes all of the various activities associated with online transacting, promotion and distribution.[52] The term 'e-commerce' is often used interchangeably with the terms 'online shopping' or 'internet shopping' (see Chapter 15). 'E-retailing' or 'e-tailing' is related to e-commerce as it represents the virtual 'storefront' of the organisation. Retailers are increasingly using websites in addition to their physical stores to sell to consumers, aiming for their on- and offline channels to offer a unified experience. The seamless integration of on- and offline channels is called omnichannel retailing.

Yuppiechef is a perfect example of a South African omnichannel retailer. They have added physical stores to their retail channel mix and made changes to the brand to give customers a unified experience whichever channel (online store or physical store) they choose. The .com has been dropped from the logo and brand colours have been adjusted to suit a physical environment. To keep the digital interface alive in-store, online customer reviews have been integrated into price labels, and all products have QR codes to enable customers to access additional product information. If a customer scans the QR code in the physical store it leads directly to product pages online. Customers can make a more informed decision in the physical store based on the experience of others through customer reviews, as well as the in-depth product information available on Yuppiechef.com. They also have the option to purchase online (click) and collect in the physical store, or they can buy something that is not available when they are in the store and take delivery at their home or office.[53]

The internet has led to numerous digital marketing communication options that include, inter alia, websites, search marketing and social media marketing.

Websites are at the 'heart' of successful digital marketing. Companies use it as a 'shop window' for consumers to find out more about them.[54] If used correctly, a website has the ability to communicate all the elements of the marketing communication mix (advertising, public relations, sales promotions, personal selling, direct marketing, and sponsorships and events). A website should be designed in such a way that it is visually attractive and easy to use, and be able to achieve the highest ranking on the search engine results page. Websites can also be used for live broadcasting as in the case of radio channels and brands' own TV channels, such as Red Bull TV. An example of a website that uses all the elements of the marketing communication mix is that of Pick n Pay (http://www.picknpay.co.za/home). Pick n Pay uses advertising in the form of moving banner advertisements (typical graphical advertisements displayed on a website) and floating advertisements (a type of rich media advertisement that appears superimposed over the requested website's content) to advertise specials and promotions. Their current sales promotions are prominently displayed and consumers can access all their competitions via their competitions link. They also provide information on their sponsored events (sponsorship and events link), for example their women's walk. There is an invitation to subscribe to their mailing list and newsletter (direct marketing), and numerous public relations activities, for example the Nelson Mandela food drive community upliftment project, are advertised. Detailed information about the project and how one could become involved is given if one clicks on the advertisement. Pick n Pay also offers online shopping assistance (personal selling) in the form of a link that directs you to an email query platform. Other websites, for example Yuppiechef.com, offer a live chat option (using a live chat widget) that can provide immediate assistance with your online query.

Search marketing is a process of driving consumers to your website by using various tactics. Search engine optimisation (SEO) is the tactic used to enhance a website to achieve the highest ranking on the search engine results pages. Google uses 200 different factors in its algorithm to determine relevance and ranking.[55] Search engines are the primary method for most internet users to find the information they seek. The major commercial search engines like Google, Bing and Yahoo! direct most of the web traffic to the various websites. Search engines provide targeted traffic to a website, thus people looking for whatever the website offers. Users use search queries (words typed into the search box) to find what they are looking for. Search engines uses technology to 'crawl' the web and build an index to provide users with a ranked list of the most relevant websites based on the keywords entered into the search engine. If a search engine cannot find a site then that site will not generate any traffic. SEO is thus a marketing discipline whose focus is to grow visibility in organic (non-paid) search engine results by means of technical and creative elements used to drive traffic to a website.

Search advertising, also known as pay-per-click advertising, is a method to advertise your business on the results page of a search engine. The advertisers then pay for every click on their advertisement.

Online advertising is found on websites, emails and social media networks, and comes in the following forms:[56]

- *Display advertisements:* These are the boxes that appear on distinct sections (specifically reserved for paid advertising) of websites. Traditional banner advertisements, appearing at the top of a website, would be an example.
- *Pop-ups:* These are display areas, usually in the form of a small window, that appears in the foreground of a visual interface. They can be used for invitations to subscribe to newsletters, to ask consumers to 'like us on Facebook', for communicating special deals and for any other 'call-to-action' advertisements. Technology used to block pop-up advertisements has, however, influenced the popularity of using them in marketing campaigns.
- *Interstitial advertisements:* These are full-page advertisements that can appear in front of a destined website. They can interrupt a user while he

or she is waiting for a website to load. As mentioned previously, a user can activate AdBlock plus, a browser extension that removes all intrusive advertisements from browser experiences. Marketers therefore have to be smarter in their planning and how they allocate their marketing budget in order to make sure they reach their intended target market with the intended message.

APPLICATION

South African Pricecheck Tech and E-commerce Awards 2018[57]

The winners of some of the PriceCheck Tech and E-commerce 2018 awards were as follows:

- Best mobile shopping experience: Travelstart (runners-up: Takealot and Spree)
- The best niche shopping experience: Spree (runners-up: NetFlorist and Yuppiechef)
- People's choice award: Takealot (runners-up: OneDayOnly and Bidorbuy)

Discussion questions

1. Access the websites nominated for the best mobile shopping experience (https://www.travel-start.co.za/; https://www.takealot.com/; https://www.spree.co.za/). Evaluate them and explain why you think they were selected and why Travelstart won. Make suggestions to the runners-up as to how they might perform better in future.
2. Visit the websites nominated for best niche shopping experience. Look at the different forms of online advertising used and comment on the effectiveness and the 'personalisation' of the message.
3. Why do you think Takealot won the people's choice? Do you agree with this?

Social media

Social media is defined as 'an umbrella term for web-based software and services that allow users to come together online and exchange, discuss, communicate and participate in any form of social interaction'.[58] Marketers can communicate to consumers using their own social media channels, for example twitter, or they can pay for advertisements on social media networking sites like Facebook or apps like Snapchat.

A good example of how a brand uses social media is BMW. BMW has about 19 million fans on their main Facebook page.[59] The 'fans' are entertained with daily updates featuring images of its cars. Links are also provided to photo albums, car reviews, YouTube clips etc. BMW also has 10 million Instagram followers, which clearly illustrates the brand's commitment to social media. The brand regards Instagram as more than just another digital communication channel, using it to share the BMW brand lifestyle with its followers. The brand also encourages individual fans to share their involvement and enthusiasm for BMW by posting photos under the hashtag #bmwrepost.[60] The brand was also the first to create a 3D augmented reality (AR) kind of a product. BMW partnered with Snapchat to launch the BMW X2. They used advertisements on Snapchat that link to the AR version of the new car. Consumers can now see how products will look in the real world before they buy them. Snapchat users can also play around and customise the AR version of the car. They can make changes to the colour and move it around to view it from different perspectives.[61]

Table 12.1 presents general social media channels.

Table 12.1 Social media channels[62]

Social media channel	Description	Examples
Social bookmarking	Enables users to bookmark (save) and access their preferred websites or links online	https://getpocket.com/
Social media submission sites	Offer a platform for their users to submit content of interest to the broader community	http://www.digg.com
Discussion forums and sites	Users can start and participate in online discussions across a range of general or specific topics	https://www.reddit.com/
Video sharing sites	Online video consumption is a growing phenomenon as it is easy for anyone to upload and share videos on sites like YouTube	http://www.youtube.com http://www.vimeo.com
Rating and review sites	Companies, products, films, books, music etc. can be rated or reviewed on such sites	http://www.reviewcentre.com
Blogs and podcasts	These enable self-expression and sharing of personal opinions using a web-based journal-like platform. Podcasts are digital versions of blogs and feature videos, wikis, etc.	http://www.blogger.com http://www.podcast.com
Micro-blogging	A mini-blog; the user is limited in terms of the number of characters that may be used to express him- or herself	http://www.twitter.com
Wikis	Collections of web pages to which anyone can add information or on which anyone can collaborate	http://www.wikipedia.org
Social network sites	Sites that allow users to interact with a network of selected people, for example Facebook, Google+ and LinkedIn	http://www.facebook.com https://linkedin.com
Image sharing	Consumers love sharing visuals online such as photos, images, art and funny pictures. Instagram is a visually oriented social platform that allows you to post photos and short videos	http://www.instagram.com http://pinterest.com
Mobile sites	Mobile messaging and chatting platforms allow users to communicate with each other instantly. They can use text, video or voice to share information with each other	http://whatsapp.com http://wechat.com

Of particular importance to marketers are social networking sites (SNS), as these contain communities of users that influence each other as reference groups. Three of the popular SNSs are Facebook, LinkedIn and Google+. Users of social networking are increasingly accessing the networks using mobile technologies through their smart phones and tablets (for example, the Apple iPad).[63] As these users are online and in touch virtually all day long, the sphere of influence of social networking cannot be ignored. Mobile applications such as Instagram and WhatsApp enable users to communicate constantly and to share information, visually or via text and/or voice, almost instantly. Social sharing has also led to the phenomenon of 'going viral', defined by the Urban Dictionary as 'an image, video or link that spreads rapidly through a population by being frequently shared by groups of people'.[64] Marketers are always trying to create 'viral content', but in reality it is very difficult to 'master the art of going viral' since most things go viral coincidentally.

Video marketing and brand communities are also important elements in any digital campaign. Video can have a strong emotional effect on viewers and is considered the ideal tool for experiential marketing, where consumers can become 'part' of the video and identify with the actors. According to a survey by the Interactive Advertising Bureau (IAB), South Africa registered the second highest year-on-year growth in video consumption on smartphones globally.[65] Video marketing is therefore increasing in popularity to reach and engage with target markets. Live videos are used on brands' Facebook pages. These give authenticity to a brand as they are not scripted, but rather a live portrayal of the 'real and authentic' side of a brand. An example would be the 'live tour' video on Dunkin Donut's Facebook page, accessible at https://www.facebook.com/DunkinDonutsUS/videos/our-first-ever-live-tour/10154465505323238/. Brands can also use video to entertain (for example, the BMW video with Ethan Hunt from Mission Impossible, available at https://www.facebook.com/BMW/videos/10156624991962269/), to provide information (for example, an infotainment video providing product information and entertainment simultaneously, such as Nike Airmax, available at https://vimeo.com/192130017) or be used in brand storytelling. Dove, for example, uses 'real people to tell their stories'. They found a real father wishing to see his child and used his story as part of a campaign for their product range for men, linking the story to the healing, reuniting power of soap. The video can be accessed through the following link: https://www.youtube.com/watch?v=47WWytrYtDw&feature=youtube

Brand communities are groups of like-minded consumers who identify with a brand and share traits such as traditions and a sense of moral responsibility. Consumers organise into these communities to share experiences about brands.[66] Brands use this as part of their digital marketing strategy in order to connect with consumers on a more personal level. Nando's is a much-loved South African brand who has successfully created an online community where people can interact with the brand and with each other. The interaction is mostly tailored to Twitter and the brand is quick to respond with their typical humorous approach. They frequently post photos and retweet pictures of people at their restaurants. They are thus able to build a more personalised relationship with their consumers by making them feel special and connected.[67]

12.6.3.3   Mobile marketing

In South Africa, there are about 29 million smartphone users, 21 million of which use the internet mostly from their smartphones.[68] Mobile devices therefore need to be an important consideration in any marketing strategy. The Mobile Marketing Association defines mobile marketing as 'a set of practices that enables organisations to communicate and engage with their audience in an interactive and relevant manner through any mobile device or network'.[69]

Mobile engagement should be the focus of marketers, not just in terms of sending one-way messages via SMS marketing but also through the creation of content that reaches consumers at exactly the right time, place and mood and generates memorable touchpoints that encourage a favourable reaction to the intended message.

The various channels used as part of mobile marketing include mobile messaging channels such as SMS and MMS, and instant messaging (IM) like WeChat and Whatsapp; and QR codes (3D barcodes that compress complex information into an image that can then be decoded using a mobile phone). Online social networks have also extended their presence to mobile phones and some, for example Instagram, were created specifically for mobile devices.

Mobile devices also allow consumers to access information about companies and brands anywhere and at any time. They are thus able to search for information and compare prices during any stage of the decision journey. They can also use their mobile phones to complete the transaction through the use of the mobile web. Apps and music are some of the most popular items bought through mobile devices. The device and its interface as well as the context of exploring can influence a mobile shopper's behaviour and marketers need to take note of factors like ease of use, speed, visuals etc. that can impact on the experience of the mobile user.[70]

DISCUSSION

Popular social networking sites[71]

According to the Social Media Landscape study conducted in 2017, Facebook is still the most popular social networking site (SNS), with 16 million South Africans using it (up from 14 million in 2016). A total of 14 million of these users access it via their cell phones or tablets. Twitter continues to grow at a slow rate in South Africa, with users increasing from 7.7 million in 2016 to 8 million in 2017. The previous fastest growing app in South Africa, Instagram, has also slowed down with only 3.8 million users in 2017 as opposed to the 3.5 million in 2016. The professional network LinkedIn, has grown to 6.1 million users.

Figure 12.5   The logos of popular social networking sites

The platform most used for marketing purposes by South Africa's top brands was Facebook. Twitter, LinkedIn and Instagram grew in popularity, while YouTube lagged slightly behind. Declines were reported for Pinterest, Google+, WeChat, WhatsApp and Snapchat.

The lesson learnt from the survey is that widespread consumer adoption of a platform, as in the case of Whatsapp, does not necessarily mean that it will be a popular choice among brands as a communication platform.

Discussion questions
1. Access the Facebook website (http://www.facebook.com). Describe its main aim.
2. Access the LinkedIn website (http://www.linkedin.com). Create a profile if you do not already have one. Using the e-mail functionality, establish how many of your e-mail contacts are on LinkedIn.
3. Access the Twitter website (http://www.twitter.com). What are the major trends currently taking off in South Africa? And worldwide?
4. What are the major trends regarding Instagram usage in South Africa? And worldwide?

12.7 THE CONSUMER DECISION-MAKING PROCESS AND MARKETING COMMUNICATIONS

Figure 12.6 presents the link between the consumer decision-making process and marketing communications.

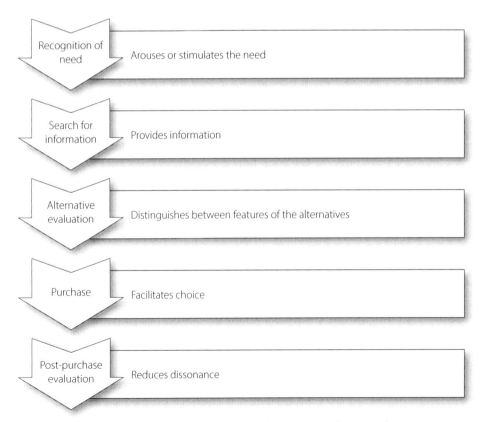

Figure 12.6 The link between marketing communication and the consumer decision-making process

As indicated by Figure 12.6, marketing communications play a role in every step of the consumer decision-making process. Digital technologies allow consumers to access information about a brand at anytime, anywhere and on multiple devices. They can also do it during any stage of the consumer decision-making journey. Marketers therefore need to understand consumers' information needs and also the media that might be more appropriate for any specific stage.

In the first step, where a consumer recognises a need and starts thinking about potential products or services that might satisfy it, appropriate media might be location-targeted mobile apps and advertisements, where technology (geofencing) is used to send information to consumers when they are near a business. Starbucks, for example, targets consumers that gave permission (opt-in) to receive relevant messages based on age, gender, interests and their location. Paid search advertisements triggered by proximity keyword searches could also be successful.

In the initial brand consideration stage (part of the first step), brands need to be visible if they want the consumer to consider them. Search engine optimisation and paid search ads as well as targeted display ads and Facebook posts, tweets and retweets, high visibility in traditional media and appearances in user-generated content like blogs and reviews might be appropriate.

During the search for information stage, consumers will actively look for more information about the brands that are now being considered as a possibility to fulfil their needs. Consumers will increase their search for information on the considered brands. This will lead to search engine queries, visits to outlets, and online (through social networking sites, for example) and offline (in person) queries to friends and family. Appropriate options for firms and brands to provide more information at this stage would be persuasive messages (messages to convince consumers that the product or service will benefit them by fulfilling their needs) in informative advertisements, YouTube videos, blogs and websites. During the information search stage and the alternative evaluation stage, consumers might want credible evidence to substantiate the brand's claims and might look at reviews, testimonials, Facebook posts, or to other 'experts' like celebrities or influencers via blogs and tweets. It is thus important for the brand to have continuously generated credible and positive reviews and endorsements through their own media as well as through shared media like social media if it wants to be the preferred brand choice (alternative).

When making the final decision (purchase stage), consumers might be more influenced by the emotional benefits and social appeal of the brand. Traditional advertising and celebrity tweets, YouTube brand videos, Facebook pages or posts and blogs might be effective in communicating this to the consumer.

Repeat purchases will only happen if the consumer is satisfied after the purchase. Brands therefore need ongoing communication to convince the consumer that the decision was the right one. The last stage is thus the post-purchase evaluation stage. During the post-purchase evaluation stage, post purchase communication in the form of emails, targeted traditional advertising, social media reinforcement through Twitter and Facebook pages as well as tracking of online reviews might be appropriate modes for firms to communicate and build relationships to reduce cognitive dissonance. Consumers might also want to share their experiences and marketers can provide platforms like Facebook likes, Instagram comments and retweets to address the need for sharing. To encourage 'brand love', marketers can connect with consumers through Twitter hashtag events, Facebook pages, brand communities and inspirational content on websites and blogs.[72]

12.8 RESEARCHING MARKETING COMMUNICATIONS

As investing in marketing communications is often quite expensive, it is wise to try to predict the effectiveness of a particular planned action. Advertising research is an important part of testing communication effectiveness. Measuring advertising effectiveness entails three aspects:[73]

* Pre-testing
* Pilot testing (in the market)
* Post-testing

Pre-testing aims to test the advertisement before it is placed and includes the following:

* Communication tests measure whether the advertisement says what was intended.
* Dummy magazines are 'fake' magazines that contain editorial pieces, typical advertisements and also the advertisement that is to be tested. Respondents participating in the pre-testing research study will evaluate these dummy magazines.
* Theatre tests flight commercials to gauge the reaction of the audience in a controlled setting.
* Thought listings are used to determine the thoughts that are elicited by an advertisement.
* Attitude change studies entail exposure to the test advertisement as well as others. Measurements are taken before and after exposure to determine if attitudes have been changed.
* Physiological measures track physical changes in the respondent, for example an eye camera can track what the respondent looks at first in the advertisement.

In pilot testing (also referred to as test marketing), the planned advertisement is tested in a controlled setting to measure reactions and purchase intent.[74] It usually takes an experimental form, as two versions of an advertisement can be run and reactions compared.

Post-testing of advertisements attempts to establish message effectiveness after the advertisement has been aired or published. Post-testing tracking methods include recall-and-recognition tests, awareness and attitude tracking, and behaviour-based measures such as tracking sales or the increase in traffic to a website after a product was advertised.[75]

There are several organisations that research social media. In South Africa, IAB South Africa (formerly known as the Digital Media and Marketing Association (DMMA)) is one of the most prominent. According to its website (https://www.iabsa.net/), the organisation is an independent, voluntary, non-profit association 'focused on growing and sustaining a vibrant and profitable digital industry within South Africa'. For its effective measures (EM) reports, it relies on local website market data collected through an on-page tag. Visitors browsing its sites trigger tracking calls to EM. Cookies (information that a website stores on your hard disk as a reminder of your preferences when using a particular site) are then retrieved and the detailed information about the page view is recorded into its collection servers. According to the February 2018 effective report, the top three sites visited were news24.com, gumtree.co.za and iol.co.za.[76]

Marketing research company, Nielsen, has also launched Nielsen Digital Ad Ratings (DAR) in South Africa. It is a measurement tool that provides gross rating points (GRPS), a measure of advertising impact, for digital campaigns across smartphones, tablets and computers. Advertisers, media houses and publishers are now able to establish maximum reach across all digital campaigns.[77]

12.9 MARKETING AND RETAIL APPLICATIONS

Marketing communication is an integral part of every marketing strategy. Marketers have a wide range of media available to reach their target audiences. Digital marketing, in particular social media marketing, has grown in importance and use for marketing and retailing. Social media have many applications for organisations. Social networking sites (SNS), in particular, have many avenues suitable to marketing and retailing.

Advertising using social networking sites can be effective as the organisation can focus on advertising messages based on people's profiles and interests.[78] Creating a profile for the organisation or even for its primary brands allows consumers to become 'fans' or 'followers' of a brand, which will impact on the reputation of the organisation. Many organisations also have 'share links' on their websites to enable consumers to post what they find interesting on their social networks. Social media make it possible for an organisation to find its brand advocates (people who are expressive brand supporters) and to 'reward' them with great content that they will share. In this way, the organisation is actually stimulating WOM and opinion leadership.

By being involved in micro-blogging (for example, Twitter), an organisation can keep its eye on trends and movements in the digital world. The organisation can raise its online profile by providing interesting content and links to useful information. This is also a quick way to establish whether good or bad comments are being posted to a large audience: an organisation can check its 'mentions' (it is possible to search for the company name on Twitter and track what is being said) and respond swiftly if negative situations occur.

Providing links to the organisation's website on social networking sites enables a broader scope of exposure. These SNS links can be communicated via traditional advertising channels as well as on product packaging. It makes it convenient for the consumer to link to the organisation's digital storefront.

Technological disruptions have affected the retail industry not only in how they communicate with the consumer but also in how they provide 'experiences' to consumers in an online or physical retail environment. Artificial intelligence and virtual reality technology, among others, have led to the move from traditional advertising to more experiential marketing and an omnichannel focus. Behaviour like showrooming (visiting a physical store to browse and try out a product, but purchasing online from any store that offers the product at a lower price) and webrooming (searching online but completing the purchase in a bricks-and-mortar store where the product can be touched and tested) has also forced retailers to rethink traditional ways of doing things.

South Africa is still falling behind in providing true omnichannel experiences, with some local retailers having the view that mass adoption of digital and mobile retail offerings will still take some time to become mainstream.[79] Other retailers such as Spree and Yuppiechef are, however, proactive in embracing the digital environment and the opportunities it presents. Spree won the Digital Innovator Award of the CXA (Customer Experience Africa Awards) in 2017 for its launch of the first image-searching shopping feature that identifies clothing or footwear seen in photos and images and then finds something similar for its users.[80] Yuppiechef, a well-known and loved e-commerce retailer, has opened its first physical store as part of its omnichannel strategy (also see section 12.6.3.1 above). They have now provided a space where people can browse in the store and can purchase online in the store and have it delivered at home. Through their 'genius bar', consumers can connect with the online store to manage their delivery, registry and wrapping preferences and continue with their seamless omnichannel journey.[81]

APPLICATION

Instagram[82]

Top Instagrammers with a huge following can make money on the photo-sharing platform. Trendsetters are treated as trusted experts whose opinions are respected. Brands partner with these 'influencers' by means of sponsored posts to communicate a trusted message to the 'follower' audience.

Influencer marketing is still a relatively new trend in South Africa, but is increasing in popularity among brands. Influencers that are 'non-celebrities' are seen as trustworthy and authentic, and consumers 'buy into' their lifestyle, making it a perfect platform for brands to connect with consumers.

Discussion questions
- Search for the 'influencers' with the largest number of followers in South Africa. Which brands need to partner with these influencers?
- Suggest other social media marketing strategies for these brands.

RESEARCH BOX 12.1

The opinions of others are important to consumers when making purchasing decisions. The increased use of social networking sites has empowered consumers with more information and as a result has led to changes in consumer behaviour when searching for information.

Consumer buying decisions form a significant part of social conversations on popular social networking sites Facebook and Twitter, for example. A South African study confirmed that these sites had a significant influence on the probability of purchasing specific mobile phone brands.[83] The study also found that Twitter's credibility had a stronger influence on the probability intent than Facebook, and that Twitter was perceived to be more credible than Facebook. This could have implications for eWOM messages in the sense that a Twitter eWOM message will be more powerful than a Facebook one. A possible explanation could be the influence of opinion leaders on Twitter. Consumers only follow or retweet messages from people they want to imitate.

SUMMARY

Marketing communications are an integral part of marketing and retail strategy. It is important to reach the target consumer with a message that will provide the meaning intended by the company. With the advent of the technological age, the consumer landscape has changed and with it the way marketing communication has been practised in the traditional sense.

Various tools exist that can be used to reach the target audience with a brand message. These tools can also be referred to as the elements of the promotional mix, which include advertising, public relations, sales promotions, personal selling, direct marketing, sponsorship and events marketing, and digital marketing.

The marketing communication process entails the development of a message by the sender. The message is sent through an appropriate channel to the receiver, who decodes the message. Feedback is then provided to the sender. The process may be hindered by noise or competitive stimuli. The process, in light of the changing connected consumer, should not be viewed as a simple linear process anymore, as the digital environment has changed consumers' information seeking and sharing behaviour. The importance of communicating with the online consumer and the influences that affect the online consumer therefore need to be considered in companies' marketing strategies. Various channels or media exist that may be used to communicate with the target audience, namely traditional (for example, print and broadcast media channels), alternative (for example, outdoor and moving media and displays) and digital marketing (for example, internet, social media and mobile marketing). Prominent new media channels, as part of digital marketing, include the social networking sites, which are growing more and more influential in the modern marketplace.

Marketing communications play an important role at various levels in the consumer decision-making process. The effectiveness of marketing communications needs to be evaluated and several research methods may be used to achieve this. The application of marketing in a retail environment also needs to take into account digital disruptions and retailers need to adapt to this environment.

SELF-ASSESSMENT QUESTIONS

1. Discuss the promotional element of the marketing mix.
2. Discuss the elements of the communication model and explain how the traditional view of the process has changed.
3. Explain how companies and brands need to communicate to the online consumer.
4. Explain the difference between traditional media and new digital channels available to marketers.
5. Explain the different digital marketing communication options provided by the internet.
6. Define social media.
7. Explain the difference between social media marketing and mobile marketing.
8. Explain how the communication needs of the consumer might differ for the various stages of the consumer decision-making process and recommend the appropriate media to use at each stage.
9. Explain what a physical store can do to communicate to a consumer and create an experience to convince the consumer to complete the purchase in the store rather than online.

EXPERIENTIAL EXERCISE

1. Make suggestions to a smartphone manufacturer as to how it could use social media marketing and mobile marketing to introduce a new, affordable smartphone to the teen market in South Africa.
2. Use your knowledge of the decision-making process and communication to advise a skincare brand on which media is effective to connect with the consumer through each stage of the purchasing journey.

CASE STUDY 1

Facebook data taken without consent

Consumers had long suspected and were relatively aware of the fact that the information they provided on social media was utilised for targeted advertising. Yet in March 2018, the news that the data of millions of Facebook users had been taken and used without their consent, shocked the world.

The incident involved the voter profiling company Cambridge Analytics in America, which offered users money to take a personality quiz through an app called 'thisisyourdigitallife'. The app 'scraped' information from the Facebook profiles of 270 000 users who took the quiz as well as detailed information from their friends' profiles. In the end, the profiles of about 50 million people were accessed. Cambridge Analytics was able to extract the following psychographic information from Facebook posts: fair-mindedness, conscientiousness, political views, self-disclosure, 'sensational interests' like militarism (weapons, affiliations) and violent occultism (drugs, black magic), intellectual activities (music, travel interests), credulousness (the paranormal, aliens) and wholesome interests (camping, gardening, hiking). This information could then be used to predict where and how a politician should focus his or her campaigning, for example what to say to appeal to certain groups of people. People were appalled and words like 'psychological manipulation of the worst kind' were uttered.[84]

As a result of this, a movement called #Deletefacebook has gained momentum. Even the WhatsApp co-founder Brian Acton shared his voice and told everyone to delete their social networking account from their digital life. The pressure on Facebook is increasing as different government agencies are on a hunt for the truth. Financially, the company has lost more than $50 billion in market valuation.[85]

This could have implications for South Africans active on Facebook as well. What prevents any data company pulling the same trick to influence people anywhere in the world?

Discussion questions

1. Do you think 'deleting Facebook' is the answer to protecting personal information? What is your suggestion in this regard?
2. Marketers' focus in the digital environment is on 'personalising' messages to connect with the 'attention deficit' consumer. How do you think this scandal will affect this focus?
3. Access your Facebook account. Are there any 'personalised' marketing messages? Analyse them in terms of how 'spot on' they were in targeting you.
4. Visit any brand's Facebook page and evaluate it based on its 'effectiveness' in getting 'likes'.
5. If you were a brand manager, what would be your 'new' plan to personalise messages if you could not use personal information anymore to engage with consumers? How would you do your job effectively while still respecting their right to privacy?

CASE STUDY 2

Samsung – South Africa's most popular electronic brand

Samsung is a well-known and loved brand. It was voted SA's best-loved electronic brand and best cellphone brand at the Sunday Times Top Brand Awards in 2017. Samsung is recognised as a leader in the market not only because its devices closely match the needs of consumers but also because of their approach to marketing and marketing communication.[86]

Samsung's approach when it comes to technology is to pursue relentlessly what they think is right and its approach to its communications programme is no different. The virtues of the brand that form the basis of the brand communications approach are engineering, openness, freedom in mindset, purposeful innovation, multiculturalism, vibrancy, being inviting and inclusiveness.[87] In South Africa, their television advertisements won the number one spot in Kantar Milward Brown's Best Liked Ads list for two years in a row (2016 and 2017). In 2016, their 'Sister' ad (which can be viewed at http://www.bizcommunity.com/Article/196/12/163021.html) used storytelling to engage and connect on an emotional level with viewers to showcase the phone innovations without getting involved in technical jargon. Samsung did it again in 2017 with their Knox-Seagull advertisement. They used 100% real footage for the ad to demonstrate the things people do with their work phones (ad can be viewed at http://www.bizcommunity.com/Article/196/12/175019. html). They chose another bird for the illustration of their Galaxy S8 phone. The entire clip is built around the ostrich's immersive Gear VR experience. When the ostrich finally starts to fly, the message becomes clear that 'we make what can't be made, so you can do what can't be done' (watch the ad at https://www.youtube.com/watch?v=H7ezU9MzaUE).

Samsung also used Twitter to create a fun, locally themed campaign for their Galaxy S7 and S8 phones. It used the hashtag #TheNextGalaxy to unlock daily cash prizes via tweets. They partnered with local radio stations @947 and @KFM to maximise exposure and increase immediacy. The campaign to discover 'what's in the box' successfully engaged the audience because as the value of the prizes in the box increased, so the number of retweets needed to unlock the prize also rose.[88]

Samsung also sponsored SA's Got Talent for its 8th season on e.tv. The programme showcases new and innovative talent each year and Samsung, that prides itself on being innovative and unlocking potential, was the perfect partner. The prize was the biggest in the show's history and Samsung made sure that the millions of viewers across Mzansi got the message that Samsung is enthusiastic about supporting dreams and South African talent. Marlon Davids, MD of e.tv, said the following: 'we are thrilled to have signed this exciting sponsorship deal between the country's biggest talent search and one of the world's biggest electronic brands'.[89]

Discussion questions

1. Samsung uses various elements in the promotion mix to build the brand image. Identify the elements mentioned in the case study and discuss how they help to communicate the virtues of the brand.
2. Access the links for the three advertisements mentioned, watch the ads and compare them on the effectiveness of conveying the message. Also choose your favourite one and support your choice with arguments from the theory discussed in the chapter.
3. In your opinion, which one of the elements mentioned in the case study is more effective in engaging consumers and building relationships? Motivate your answer.

ADDITIONAL RESOURCES

Visit the following websites for more information on some of the concepts and topics discussed in the chapter:

- http://www.bizcommunity.com/
- http://www.millwardbrown.com/
- https://www.facebook.com/
- https://twitter.com/
- http://mrfsa.org.za/
- https://www.adweek.com/
- http://themediaonline.co.za/
- https://www.iab.com/

REFERENCES

1 Adapted from Fortune.com 2017. Dove removes 'racist' ad that seemed to suggest black women were dirty. Available at: http://fortune.com/2017/10/09/racist-dove-facebook-ad-taken-down (accessed on 28 August 2018); Sepheka, T. 2017. The power of consumer insights (combined with woke strategy and creative). Available at: http://www.bizcommunity.com/Article/196/12/169057.html (accessedon 28 August 2018).
2 Solis, B. 2017. @BrianSolis. Available at: http://www.briansolis.com/ (accessed on 28 August 2018).
3 Li, C. & Bernhoff, J. 2008. *Groundswell: Winning in a world transformed by social technologies*. Boston, Massachusetts: Harvard Business Press.
4 Connected Consumer Research. 2017. Google reveals findings of the 2017 Connected Consumer Study. Available at: http://www.bizcommunity.com/Article/196/16/170329.html (accessed on 21 September 2018).

5   Kotler, P., Kartajaya, H. & Sertiawan, I. 2017. *Marketing 4.0: Moving from traditional to digital*. Hoboken, NJ: John Wiley & Sons.

6   Jackson, G. & Ahuja V. 2016. Dawn of the digital age and the evolution of the marketing mix. *Journal of Direct, Data and Digital Marketing practice*, 17(3): 170–186.

7   Lamb, C.W., Hair, J.F., McDaniel, C., Boshoff, C., Terblanche, N.S. & Elliot, R. 2015. *Marketing*, 5th ed. Cape Town: Oxford University Press, 270.

8   Kennedy, E. & Guzmán, F. 2015. Co-creation of brand identities: Consumer and industry influence and motivations. *Journal of Consumer Marketing*, 33(5): 313.

9   Bartl, M. 2013. Getting close to the consumer: How Nivea co-creates new product. Available at: http://www.michaelbartl.com/article/getting-closer-to-the-consumer-how-nivea-co-creates-new-products/ (accessed on 28 August 2018).

10 Koekemoer, L. 2011. *Introduction to integrated marketing communications*. Cape Town: Juta, 2.

11 Penstone, K. 2017. Inside Yuppiechef's omnichannel retail strategy. Available at: http://www.marklives.com/2017/11/inside-yuppiechef-omnichannel-retail-strategy/ (accessed on 28 August 2018).

12 O'Guinn, T.C., Allen, C.T. & Semenik, R.J. 2011. *Promo*, instructor ed. Mason, Ohio: South-Western Cengage Learning, 6.

13 Batra, R. & Keller, K.L. 2016. Integrating marketing communications: New findings, new lessons, new ideas. *Journal of Marketing*, 80(Special Issue): 122–145.

14 Clow, K.E. & Baack, D. 2010. *Integrated advertising, promotion, and marketing communications*, 4th ed. Upper Saddle River, NJ: Pearson Education, 33; Koekemoer, op. cit., 11; Ouwersloot, H. & Duncan, T. 2008. *Integrated marketing communications*, European ed. London: McGraw-Hill, 12.

15 Penstone, op. cit.

16 KFC – Add Hope. Available at: https://kfc.co.za/addhope (accessed on 21 September 2018).

17 De Statler, E. 2017. PoPI act could kill more than just spam. Available at: http://www.Bizcommunity.com/Article /196/459/173893.html (accessed on 28 August 2018).

18 Wings for Life. Available at: https://www.wingsforlifeworldrun.com (accessed on 21 September 2018).

19 Red Bull Media House. Available at: http://www.redbullmediahouse.com (accessed on 21 September 2018).

20 Koekemoer, op. cit., 25.

21 Adapted from Schiffman, LG. & Wisenblit, J.L. 2015. *Consumer behaviour*, 11th ed. Upper Saddle River, NJ: Pearson Prentice Hall, 200; Peter, J.P. & Olson, J.C. 2008. *Consumer behavior and marketing strategy*, 8th ed. New York: McGraw-Hill, 420; Babin, B.J. & Harris, E.G. 2012. *Consumer behaviour*, student ed. Mason, OH: South-Western Cengage Learning, 141.

22 Batra & Keller, op. cit.

23 Arens, W.L., Weigold, M.F. & Arens, C. 2011. *Contemporary advertising and integrated marketing communications*, 13th ed. New York, NY: McGraw-Hill, 11.

24 http:www//bmwblog.com/

25 Wu, P.C.S. & Wang, Y. 2011. The influences of electronic word-of-mouth message appeal and message source credibility on brand attitude. *Asia Pacific Journal of Marketing and Logistics*, 23(4): 452.

26 Dahiya, R. & Gayatri. 2017. A research paper on digital marketing communication and consumer buying decision process: An empirical study in the Indian passenger car market. *Journal of Global Marketing*, 31(2): 73–95.

27 Huete Alcocer, N. 2017. A literature review of word of mouth and electronic word of mouth: Implications for consumer behaviour. *Frontiers in Psychology*, 8: 1256.

28 Schiffman & Wisenblit, op. cit., 204.

29 Content Marketing Institute. 2017. Available at: http://contentmarketinginstitute.com/ (accessed on 30 August 2018).

30 Stokes, R. 2013. *eMarketing: The essential guide to marketing in a digital world*, 5th ed. South Africa: Quirk Education, 71.

31 Koekemoer, op. cit., 38.

32 Schiffman & Wisenblit, op. cit., 223.

33 Semenik, R.J., Allen, C.T., O'Guinn, T.C. & Kaufmann, H.R. 2012. *Advertising and promotions: An integrated brand approach*, international ed. Mason, OH: South-Western Cengage Learning, 19.

34 Schiffman & Wisenblit, op. cit., 200–203.

35 Geldenhuys, N. 2017. Top South African social media campaigns to learn from in 2017. Available at: https://www.mediaupdate.co.za/social/125551/top-south-african-social-media-campaigns-to-learn-from-in-2017 (accessed on 30 August 2018).

36 Tiger Brands. 2018. About Doom. Available at: http://www.tigerbrands.com/home-care/#Doom (accessed on 3 October 2018).

37 Tiger Brands. 2018. Doom insecticide. Available at: https://www.adforum.com/agency/6654372/creative-work/34554306/browser-history/doom-insecticide (accessed on 3 October 2018). TBWA\Hunt\Lascaris Johannesburg.

38 Wu & Wang, op. cit., 448.

39 Dahiya & Gayatri, op. cit.

40 Bruhn, M., Schoenmuller, V. & Schäfer, D.B. 2012. Are social media replacing traditional media in terms of brand equity creation? *Management Research Review*, 35(9): 770.

41 http://www.mediaupdate.co.za

42 Mulhern, F. 2009. Integrated marketing communications: From media channels to digital connectivity. *Journal of Marketing Communications*, 15 (2-3): 85–101.

43 Semenik et al., op. cit., 483.

44 South African Advertising Research Foundation. 2012. Average issue readership of newspapers and magazines. Available at: http://saarf.co.za/amps/readership.asp (accessed on 30 August 2018).

45 http://www.BRCSA.org.za

46 MCleod, D. 2018. Finally, digital TV era arrives in SA. TechCentral. Available at: https//techcentral.co.za/finally-digital-tv-era-arrives-in-sa/62948/ (accessed on 30 August 2018).

47 Information based on themediaonline's publication of a 'snapshot of the last AMPS results ever'. Available at: http://themediaonline.co.za/2016/04/snapshot-of-the-last-amps-results-ever/ (accessed on 30 August 2018).

48 Schiffman & Wisenblit, op. cit., 201–202.

49 Koenderman, T. 2013. *The future of media. Blueprint 2013.* OMD: Sandowne, 10.

50 Ryan, D. & Jones, C. 2009. *Understanding digital marketing: Marketing strategies for engaging the digital generation.* London: Kogan Page, 6.

51 Shelly, G.B. & Frydenberg, M. 2011. *Web 2.0. concepts and applications.* Boston, Massachusetts: Course Technology, Cengage Learning, 1.

52 Brijball, S., Parumasur, S. & Roberts-Lombard, M. 2012. *Consumer behaviour*, 2nd ed. Claremont: Juta, 369.

53 Penstone, K. 2017. Inside Yuppiechef's omnichannel retail strategy. Available at: http://www.marklives.com/2017/11/inside-yuppiechef-omnichannel-retail-strategy/ (accessed on 1 October 2018).

54 Stokes, op. cit., 149.

55 Ibid., 230.

56 Ibid., 294.

57 Harzenberg, L. 2018. Pricecheck Tech and E-commerce Awards 2018 winners revealed. Available at: http://www.bizcommunity.com/Article/196/394/181339.html (accessed on 1 October 2018).

58 Ryan & Jones, op. cit., 152.

59 https://www.facebook.com/pg/BMW/community/?ref=page_internal

60 Boeriu, H. 2017. BMW is the most successful Instagram channel among automotive brands worldwide. Available at: https://www.bmwblog.com/2017/02/09/bmw-successful-instagram-channel-among-automotive-brands-worldwide (accessed on 1 October 2018).

61 Arica, A. 2017. BMW test drives Snapchat's AR lenses in their 3D car ad. Available at: https://digitalagencynetwork.com/bmw-test-drives-snapchats-ar-lenses-in-their-3d-car-ad/ (accessed on 1 October 2018).

62 Adapted from Powell, G.R., Groves, S.W. & Dimos, J. 2011. *ROI of social media: How to improve the return on your social marketing investment.* Singapore: John Wiley & Sons, 16–20; Ryan & Jones, ibid., 169.

63 Babin & Harris, op cit., 204.

64 http://www.urbandictionary.com

65 Abraham, A. 2016. SA showed second highest growth in mobile video globally. Available at: http://themediaonline.co.za/2016/07/sa-showed-second-highest-growth-in-video-globally (accessed 3 October 2018).

66 Kalman, D.M. 2009. Brand communities, marketing and media. Terrella Media Inc. Available at: http://www.terella.com (accessed 20 September 2018).

67 http://www.linkhumans.com/Nandos

68 Shapsak, T. 2017. South Africa Has 21 Million Internet Users, Mostly On Mobile. Forbes.com. Available at: https://www.forbes.com/sites/tobyshapshak/2017/07/19/south-africa-has-21m-internet-users-mostly-on-mobile/#7d7fc8981b2d (accessed 3 October 2018).

69 Stokes, op. cit., 462.

70 Ibid., 478.

71 Adapted from Ornico. 2018. Inside the SA Social Media Landscape Report. Available at: http://website.ornico.co.za/2017/09/sa-social-media-2018 (accessed on 20 September 2018).

72 Batra, R. & Keller, K. 2016. Integrating marketing communications: New findings, new lessons and new ideas. *Journal of Marketing*, 80(6).

73 O'Guinn et al., op. cit., 311.

74 Arens et al., op. cit., 243.

75 O'Guinn et al., op. cit., 315.

76 IAB South Africa. Available at: https://www.iabsa.net/about-us/ (accessed on 20 September 2018).

77 Dicey, L. 2017. Siemens transforms brand identity in SA. *Financial Mail.* 12 September 2017. Available at: https://www.businesslive.co.za/redzone/news-insights/2017-09-12-siemens-transforms-brand-identity-in-sa (accessed on 3 October 2018).

78 Ryan & Jones, op. cit., 163.

79 Moloko, N. 2018. Consumer trends 2018. Available at: https://www.bluevinegroup.co.za/consumer-trends-2018/ (accessed on 20 September 2018).

80 Hartzenberg, L. 2017. Empowered customer experiences lie in multi-focused design. Available at: http://www.bizcommunity.com/Article/196/458/166335.html (accessed on 20 September 2018).

81 Penstone, op. cit.

82 Adapted from Tsele, L. Why the influencer marketing trend is catching on in SA and the names you should get to know. Available at: https://www.smesouthafrica.co.za/influencer-marketing-trend-catching-sa-names-get-know (accessed on 20 September 2018).

83 Viljoen, K.L., Dube, L. & Murisi, T. 2016. Facebook versus Twitter: Which one is more credible in a South African context? *South African Journal of Information Management*, 18:1–7.

84 Van Wyk, A. 2018. Why Facebook data scandal should scare you and what to do about it. Available at: https://www.enca.com/opinion/why-facebook-s-data-scandal-should-scare-you-and-what-to-do-about-it (accessed on 20 February 2018).

85 Verma. A. 2018. WhatsApp Co-founder Tells Everyone To Delete Facebook: "It Is Time". Fossbytes.com. Available at: https://fossbytes.com/whatsapp-cofounder-delete-facebook-time (accessed on 3 October 2018).

86 Kantar TNS. 2016. The 18th annual Sunday Times Top Brands Awards. Available at http://www.bizcommunity.com/Article/196/82/149985.html (accessed on 3 October 2018).

87 O'Leary, N. 2016. How Samsung embraced innovation to become a global master of brand marketing. Available at: http://www.adweek.com/contributor/Noreen-O-Leary (accessed on 15 March 2018).

88 https://marketing.twitter.com/emea/en_gb/success-stories/samsung-mobile-south-africa-generates-buzz-for-its-galaxy-s7.html (accessed on 3 October 2018).

89 eTV. 2017. Samsung joins SA's Got Talent as headline sponsor. Available at http://www.etv.co.za/news/2017/05/11/samsung-joins-sas-got-talent-headline-sponsor (accessed on 3 October 2018).

CHAPTER 13

CONSUMER DECISION MODELS

Alet Erasmus

LEARNING OBJECTIVES

After reading this chapter, you should be able to:

- discuss the value of a consumer decision model
- provide a brief overview of the origin of some of the earlier consumer decision models
- select a consumer decision model that would be appropriate to explain a specific decision process
- identify and discuss the different stages of an extensive consumer decision-making process and incorporate relevant terminology for every stage
- explain how the various stages of the consumer decision-making process differ for consumer decisions that vary in complexity.

Key terms

black box	Howard-Sheth model	post-purchase evaluation
cognitive dissonance	information processing	problem recognition
confirmation of expectations	information search	psychoanalytic motivations
consumer decision model	informed purchase decision	purchase decision
Engel-Kollat-Blackwell model	inputs	rational perspective
evaluation and selection of	Marshallian model	responsible purchase decision
alternatives	negative disconfirmation	Schiffman and Kanuk
evoked set	Nicosia's dyadic model of	consumer decision model
Freudian model	consumer behaviour	socio-psychological factors
Hawkins, Best and Coney	outputs	stimulus ambiguity
decision model	Pavlovian model	transformation phase
Hobbesian organisational	perceptual bias	Veblenian model
factors model	positive disconfirmation	

OPENING CASE STUDY

James and Andrew are both starting their first jobs after completing their studies. They are moving into apartments closer to where they work. James will be living on his own in a bachelor unit, while Andrew will be sharing a two-bedroomed flat with another young colleague. Both have to contribute certain items to furnish their new homes, including a refrigerator, kettle, crockery and bedding. James decides that his purchases need to be useful for an extended period of time as an investment towards his future home. He therefore decides to do some research with regard to which brands will offer the best in terms of quality and durability, also considering aesthetic properties such as stye and colour. Andrew, however, regards the purchases as merely functional and temporary, and therefore decides that he will purchase the cheapest options available. Although both of these young men are confronted with the same task, their decision processes differ considerably. Why is this so?

13.1 INTRODUCTION

Consumer decisions are seldom made without prior deliberation. Mostly, consumers think about a purchase for some time beforehand in order to identify possible alternatives. They may browse through magazines and brochures, surf the internet or look at window displays before making a purchase.

Any consumer decision involves a number of decision stages. Few consumers are aware of their progression through these stages (problem recognition, information search, evaluation of alternatives and product choice), which were discussed in Chapter 1. Relatively complicated consumer decisions such as purchasing an outfit for a special occasion or buying a new computer are usually fairly time consuming and even stressful because the consumer goes through all of the stages of the decision process.

A differentiation of the different stages of consumer decision making is useful for the following reasons:

* It gives marketers a better understanding of the intricacy of certain consumer decisions, that is, more complex versus less complex decisions.
* It helps explain why some consumer decisions are more involved than others.
* It allows us to see why some consumer decisions demand more attention and time.
* It encourages an understanding of why some consumer decisions impose more risk.
* It clarifies why some consumer decisions require a more extensive information search.

Over time, experts who have been particularly interested in consumer decision making have examined the associated literature in order to identify relevant concepts for every stage of the consumer decision process as well as to indicate the association among different stages and concepts in various decision processes. They have constructed models to present consumer decisions visually in order to aid our understanding of what happens during every stage and from one stage to the next for particular contexts.

A **consumer decision model** is therefore a structural representation of consumer decisions and contains all the concepts that are relevant during every stage. Some of these models may seem fairly intricate at first, but in essence they aim to do the following:[1]

- Visually represent the different stages of consumer decision making
- Specify relevant concepts for every stage of a consumer decision (the more concepts that are contained to explain activities that occur during every stage, the more intricate the model may seem for those who have not yet mastered the theory)
- Indicate how the concepts are integrated, which is useful in understanding the decision-making process

A consumer decision model integrates various factors that influence consumers' behaviour when buying products and services. For example, it could consider socio-cultural aspects (such as family ties, social class, and cultural and religious affiliations) and marketing aspects (such as price, product, place, promotion and sales personnel), both of which represent external influences to a consumer decision. These are then visually represented to show the relationship between them.

All of the renowned consumer decision models started out as flow charts, and then underwent rigorous testing to validate them. Much research was done to ensure that the relationships actually existed and the models could be trusted as truthful and reliable representations. Consumer decision models are therefore specific and cannot be used randomly, interchangeably or because one seems easier to interpret than another, although they may share certain concepts with the same meaning.

There are various reasons for the existence of different models, such as the following:

- Human behaviour is difficult to understand.
- Consumers tend to behave differently in different contexts.
- Experts have tried to make sense of consumer decisions from different viewpoints.

Intricate models are not necessarily more complex; they are mostly just conceptualised in more detail, which facilitates discussion and interpretation.

13.2 ADVANTAGES OF CONSUMER DECISION MODELS

Consumer decision models have the following important advantages in terms of understanding consumers' decision-making behaviour:[2]

- A consumer decision model provides a frame of reference for researchers as well as a schematic framework that clearly defines relevant concepts and their relationships within specific theoretical perspectives.
- Even if a researcher only investigates a specific aspect or part of the consumer decision-making process, such as the evaluation process, a consumer decision model makes it possible to integrate findings in terms of the entire decision process. Similarly, information from various literature sources and disciplines can be integrated in a logical way to produce more comprehensive discussions.

- Models are useful to construct theory because they provide a basis for the formulation of hypotheses that could be used to expand knowledge about selected phenomena, such as product evaluation or the information search.
- Even if specific components of a model are investigated (for example, which factors influence a specific consumer decision), the findings can be related to the entire model and thus elevate the discussion in terms of existing knowledge.

13.3 CAUTION ABOUT THE USE OF CONSUMER DECISION MODELS

A researcher first has to select an appropriate consumer decision model that follows the underlying theoretical approach of the research to ensure that the concepts and interactions are relevant. It is therefore useful to have some background about the model that will be used. Many of the models are simplified, which means that concepts are specified and linked, but not extensively delineated in terms of underlying concepts. This may create the impression that a consumer decision process is simple and straightforward. On the other hand, some of the concepts that are depicted in a model are difficult to distinguish, for example attitude and personality or needs and motives. A researcher therefore has to acquaint him- or herself with supporting theory and has to understand every concept that is depicted in a model to understand fully how the different sections of the model are aligned and influence one another.

13.4 THE EVOLUTION OF CONSUMER DECISION MODELS

Various consumer decision models exist.[3] Their application differs considerably, and critique expressed over time confirms scholars' interest in existing models and enthusiasm to expand the literature in this regard. It makes sense to understand the origin of consumer decision models and the rigour that is associated with model building because this will contribute to an improved comprehension of consumer or buyer models in general as well as the relevance of concepts when dealing with specific models.

13.4.1 Original models that attempted to describe a consumer's psyche

As discussed in Chapter 1, the most basic conception of the buying process is that it is a system of inputs (buying influences, for example pressure exerted by peers, limitation of personal finances and access to retailers) that are transformed in a buyer's mind in terms of a purchasing response (output, thus the final purchase decison). The individual is therefore viewed as an information processor where stimuli from the environment (for example, price and brand) are interpreted cognitively in memory, which instigates a particular response, for example to purchase or not to purchase.

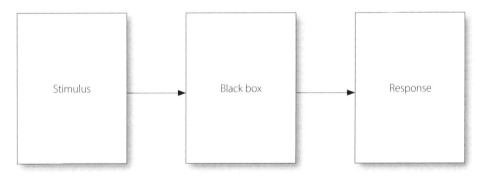

Figure 13.1 A simple presentation of how a consumer decision is made

Owing to the mysterious transformation of information in a buyer's psyche, facilitated by factors such as his or her ability to interpret information and differences in experience as well as the extreme difficulty to predict how a consumer will respond to external influences, a buyer's psyche is referred to as the '**black box**'.[4] The cognitive view of consumer decision making is illustrated simplistically in Figure 13.1.

Figure 13.1 indicates that a consumer's decision is influenced by stimuli, although no effort is made to indicate the type of stimuli and what they do. Other models that are discussed later in this chapter provide more detail. The purpose of this figure is merely to indicate that a consumer is exposed to and attends to stimuli from the environment, which are interpreted in memory (the black box), which results in some response, for example to buy or not to buy. More complex cognitive models that were designed later specify multiple influencing variables and allow researchers to conceptualise influences more explicitly.[5]

Over the years, various researchers have tried to explain consumer decisions within specific theoretical frameworks, for example **rational decision making** (or rational choice theory/ RCT), which is based on economic motivations.[6] In essence, RCT assumes that consumers/humans are rational beings who make informed decisions that they have carefully deliberated and that they understand their decisions and what they entail.[7] Firstly, a consumer methodically gathers and assimilates all information, including existing knowledge in memory based on prior experiences, of a product or service and the potential outcomes. The consumer then considers all the possible outcomes to identify pros and cons.[8] According to RCT, a rational person will choose the outcome that will potentially lead to the greatest reward[9] and discard those that may imply negative outcomes.[10]

The RCT as defined above[11] assumes the following:
- A consumer consciously tries to come to a decision.
- A consumer has all the information ('perfect market information') that is necessary to make a rational choice.[12]
- The possible outcomes can be ranked, thus no course of action is equal to another.

- The assumption of transitivity assumes that the individual has different preferences for the possible outcomes due to the rewards or punishments they entail. These preferences do not change should another relevant alternative be introduced.
- There are no institutional or psychological restrictions on the decision-making process.[13]

The RCT can be applied in terms of an understanding of the self-confidence of consumers who regularly purchase wine: self-confident consumers are clear about what they want and have enough personal knowledge and experience not to doubt the decision process. RCT assumes that humans are rational beings that make rational decisions. Thus, the decisions, albeit rational or emotional, of wine consumers when faced with the multiplicity of wine options available will depend on their level of consumer self-confidence (CSC). It is assumed that wine consumers with high CSC will make rational decisions. Conversely, wine consumers with low CSC will resort to heuristic approaches to decide on the most suitable wine. The researcher aims to investigate the relationship between RCT and wine consumers' CSC when selecting wine.

The existence of the various consumer decision models described below has been fundamental in terms of the theory that we use today.

The Marshallian model
The **Marshallian model** was developed by an English economist and one of the founders of economics, Alfred Marshall (1842–1924), and was based on economic motivations.[14] This particular model addressed consumer decisions from a **rational perspective**, more specifically a person's urge to maximise its utility/worth (usefulness), which presumes that a buyer would act in his or her own best interest.

This model was severely criticised for disregarding fundamental issues such as consumers' brand and product preferences during the decision-making process. It was also criticised for being too rigid and overly explicit, for example assuming that a drop in price would result in increased sales. Josiah Wedgewood (1730–1795), the famous English potter, demonstrated that the opposite of this assumption can also be true.[15] He intentionally increased the prices of his products when entering the luxury market and subsequently increased his market share because people then perceived his products to be superior and special.

Consumers therefore do not necessarily buy more if prices are cut. Discrepancies of this kind encouraged theorists to give further attention to the model-building process.

The Pavlovian model
The **Pavlovian model** originated from learning theory, and resulted from the work of Ivan Pavlov (1849–1936), the Russian psychologist and Nobel prize winner.[16] Pavlov's extensive experimental work evolved around phenomena such as learning, forgetting and a person's ability to discriminate stimuli (refer to chapters 3 and 4).

The results of these experiments, which were done on animals, culminated in the development of a stimulus–response model of human behaviour, which assumed that recognition of a stimulus would instigate specific behaviour. After several refinements of the theory, four central constructs were identified for this model:

- Drives (needs or motives), which may be primary, physiological or learnt
- Cues or stimuli in the environment, which activate specific behavioural responses
- A response, which depends on the anticipated award
- Reinforcement, which follows after a rewarding experience and which may result in repeat behaviour.

This model, which is applied extensively in advertising, specifies that learning facilitates behaviour and learning responses are generalised. Lack of reinforcement owing to non-use, for example if a consumer no longer sees a brand name because it is no longer advertised, may cause forgetting. Consumers must therefore be reminded about products continually, even if the retailer assumes that consumers are familiar with them.

The marketing application of this model assumes that consumers not only need to be exposed to stimuli (for example, through visual stimuli that are provided through advertisements), but they also have to try (test) products in order to have a rewarding experience. Free samples of products are often handed out so that consumers can experience products first hand. Similarly, prospective car buyers are encouraged to test drive new cars so that they can base their purchase decision on personal experience. Reinforcement through effective cues might then result in repeat purchases, for example if a consumer's eventual experience with the product echoes the product claims in the advertisement. That might result in repeat purchases and even in store or brand loyalty.

The Freudian model

The **Freudian model** was developed by Austrian-born Sigmund Freud (1856–1939).[17] Freud was a neurologist, physiologist and psychologist who became known as the founding father of psychoanalysis. His focus on consumer decisions reflects on consumers' **psychoanalytic motivations**.

The most significant contribution of the Freudian model is that it acknowledges the influence of symbolic as well as economic-functional concerns (for example, a consumer's concern during buying decisions that the money spent on an item will be worthwhile), while also admitting that consumer decisions are not necessarily logical or rational in nature. In terms of a practical example, the 'no name' generic or store brands (groceries) were originally designed to provide products of reasonable quality to consumers at affordable prices, especially aiming to cater for lower-income groups with the assumption that people in these groups could greatly benefit from it. However, empirical evidence shows that cheaper products are not necessarily appreciated (not even by lower-income groups) because such products are perceived to be of a lower quality and lower in status than more expensive brands.

Motivational research is generally complicated and time consuming, and usually involves qualitative techniques that use alternative methods that do not include structured questionnaires. For example, in-depth interviews and focus-group discussions (during which participants are given the opportunity to explain spontaneously in their own words why they behave in a particular manner) are used to allow a deeper understanding of consumers' thought processes.

The Veblenian model

The **Veblenian model** was designed by Thorstein Veblen (1857–1929), an American economist and social theorist.[18] His model of consumer decision making involves **socio-psychological factors** as a result of his particular interest in social anthropology. He postulated that man (a buyer) would, as part of a particular culture (for example, the African culture), conform to the norms of the group and the standards of sub-cultures that he associated with (for example, student groups on campus).

This approach concedes that a person's behaviour is shaped by the group with which he or she interacts or to which he or she aspires to belong, which explains the involvement of concepts such as prestige seeking and conspicuous consumption (where consumers consume products with the intention that they should be visible to others, for example shoes as opposed to sleepwear). Veblen's propositions drew the interest of prominent researchers such as Karl Marx (1818–1883), the German philosopher, economist and sociologist who is probably best remembered for being a revolutionary communist.

The Veblenian model admits the powerful influence of a group or groups on individuals' attitudes. It is hence relevant in sociology, cultural anthropology and social psychology in terms of an investigation of the influence of different cultures, sub-cultures, reference groups (for example, the leaders that people look up to) and membership groups (for example, social class or political group) on the buyer- and decision-making behaviour of individuals. However, it is important to allow for changes in attitudes over time and dominant attitudes at a specific point in time (for example, acknowledging that a consumer's attitude towards a product or service at a specific point in time is the result of previous encounters with that product or service).

The Hobbesian organisational factors model

The **Hobbesian organisational factors model** was compiled in 1651 by English philosopher Thomas Hobbes (1588–1679) to depict the behaviour of organisational buyers, who are appointed to buy merchandise on behalf of, and for, corporate companies (as opposed to the foregoing models, which focused on individual or family decisions).[19]

The Hobbesian model acknowledges the conflict experienced by organisational buyers. On the one hand, an individual's interest may be on a personal level, that is, the individual makes a decision that suits the company, but also secures the highest commission for him- or herself. Alternatively, the individual's interest could be primarily on an organisational level that is dominated by rational motives, which requires that he or she maximise quality at the best price for the company irrespective of the commission earned.

13.4.2 Systematic diagrammatic models of the post-1960 era

A growing interest in consumer behaviour research after World War II encouraged researchers to devote extensive efforts to compiling systematic diagrammatic consumer decision models that could be used to structure thought about consumer decision making in order to direct discussions for future research. A major influence was the formation of the Association for Consumer Research in 1969. This organisation has made a significant contribution towards consumer research in the world.

The following five systematic diagrammatic consumer decision models are discussed below:
* The Howard-Sheth model
* The Engel-Kollat-Blackwell model
* Nicosia's dyadic model of consumer behaviour
* The Schiffman and Kanuk model of consumer behaviour
* The Hawkins, Best and Coney decision model

13.4.2.1 The Howard-Sheth model

The first buying-decision model of Howard (1963) was based on learning theories. It was then revised and published in 1969 as the Howard-Sheth model of buying behaviour[20] to provide a comprehensive model that contained more variables and that indicated the interrelationship of variables more specifically than previous models. This model is suited to the investigation or discussion of consumers' evaluation of products.

The **Howard-Sheth model** is based on the assumptions that buying is a rational problem-solving exercise and that buyer behaviour can be explained as a systematic flow of activities. This model is theoretically based on the stimulus–response theory (see Figure 13.1), which postulates that decision making is prompted by stimuli (for example, a product advertisement on a billboard) and that repeated participation in consumer decisions increases an individual's knowledge and experience, which explains the model's association with theory related to learning. In essence, the model assumes that buying behaviour is mostly repetitive and that a consumer tends to simplify a task by storing relevant information. Decisions that are made frequently, for example purchasing fuel for your car, may thus become routine decisions.

The Howard-Sheth buying model distinguishes between extended, limited and routine buying behaviour, and is presented in terms of four distinct phases:
* Inputs
* Perceptual phase

- Learning phase
- Outputs

The unique value of this model is that it emphasises the influencing variables (input phase) and illustrates the way in which these influences are ordered during the decision-making process. The Howard-Sheth model distinguishes three types of stimuli:

- Marketing-related stimuli, such as quality, price, distinctiveness, service and availability
- Symbolic stimuli, such as elaborate packaging or specific brand names (which are also provided by the marketing environment, but which acknowledge differences in verbal communication and the value of images or symbols to convey messages)
- Social stimuli, which include the influences of the family, reference groups and social class

The Howard-Sheth model consists of two parts, namely perceptual and learning. The perceptual part (encompassing overt search; dealing with stimula ambiguity; attention and perceptual bias) specifically indicates how a consumer receives and processes information that is attained as inputs or that comes from the learning part of the model (which includes attitudes, motives and confidence that are inevitably based on prior experience). By including concepts such as '**stimulus ambiguity**' (vagueness) and '**perceptual bias**' (prejudice/confusion), this model acknowledges the following:

- The uncertainty that occurs during consumer decision making
- The non-significance of information to which a consumer does not pay attention
- The confusion created by information or stimuli that are contradictory or that do not support what a consumer already knows

The model does not account for the influence of external factors over which the individual has little control, for example the importance of the purchase, and time pressure.

The Engel-Kollat-Blackwell model

The initial **Engel-Kollat-Blackwell model**[22] of consumer decision making that was designed in 1968 was also subjected to thorough scrutiny over time to improve its descriptive ability. Revised editions were published in 1973 and 1978. This model is also based on learning theory and emphasises the first part of a product purchasing process, where information is acquired (information search process). It consists of four components:

- Central control unit
- Information processing
- Decision process
- Environmental influences

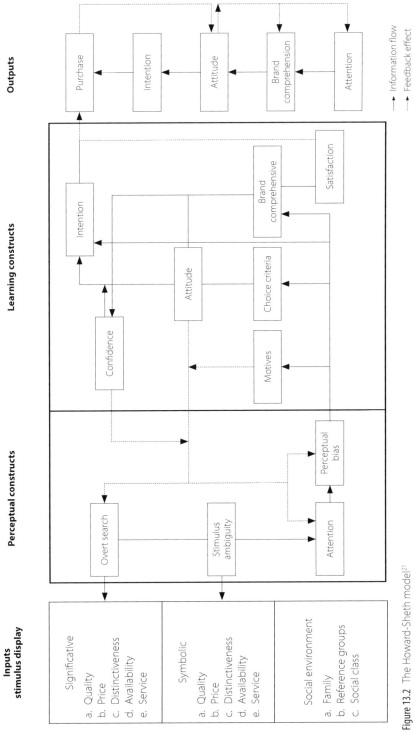

Figure 13.2 The Howard-Sheth model[21]

The central control unit is the core of the model. It defines four psychological characteristics that serve as filters for incoming stimuli and that determine how the consumer decision will proceed. The psychological characteristics are:

- stored information and previous experience, which provide a frame of reference when evaluating brands and products
- evaluation criteria, which represent a consumer's preferences during the evaluation process
- attitudes, which may influence the buying decision
- personality traits (for example, being a dogmatic consumer or an innovator), which may influence a consumer's responses to product alternatives.

Information processing refers to a consumer's attention, comprehension and retention of selected stimuli (that is, all product or brand information obtained from various sources). A precondition that is incorporated in this model is that a consumer must firstly be exposed to a product or brand, must attend to it, must comprehend it and must retain related information before a brand or product message can be filtered to the central unit. This model is therefore extremely useful in establishing what a consumer's information processing entails.

The decision component of the model defines five stages:

- Problem or need recognition
- An internal information search and evaluation (which refers to previous experience stored in memory)
- An external information search and evaluation (which may involve consultation of multiple information sources, for example published information and store visits)
- The purchase process
- Decision outcomes, which are realised as satisfaction or dissatisfaction

When using this model, marketers need to attend to the stages that are relevant to the specific consumer decision. For example, if a consumer is experienced and informed about a product, the external information search will be limited or absent. With extensive buying decisions or when a consumer is inexperienced, the individual may, however, go through all of the stages.

The fourth stage of the Engel-Kollat-Blackwell model involves an exclusive approach compared to other consumer decision models. It proposes that environmental influences, distinguished as income, culture, family, social class and physical influences (for example, whether a consumer is physically able to manoeuvre easily in the marketplace or the age of the individual) may affect a buying decision during various stages and may even block the process or interfere in the decision process. A very young consumer, for example, may not have access to all of the information sources or may not have the ability to interpret them.

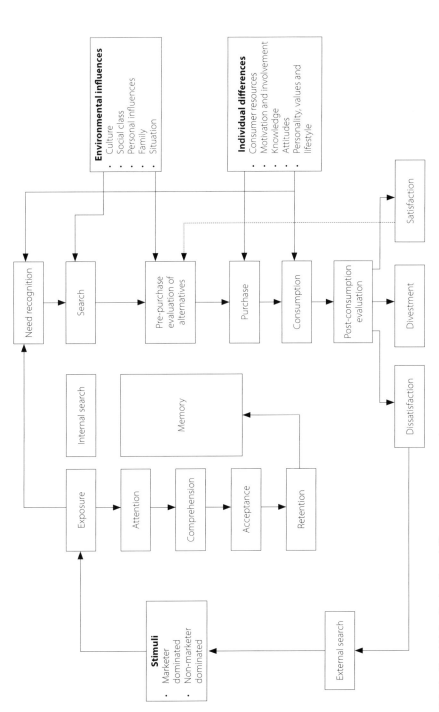

Figure 13.3 The Engel-Kollat-Blackwell model[23]

Nicosia's dyadic model of consumer behaviour

Contrary to most other consumer decision models, which reflect individuals' decision behaviour, the model that was developed by Francesco Nicosia is acknowledged as the first comprehensive model of buyer behaviour.[24] This model depicts interpersonal interaction, for example the consumer–retailer interaction or the salesperson–customer interaction. **Nicosia's dyadic model of consumer behaviour** distinguishes four fields[25]:

- *Field 1:* Depicts all the processes that convey messages from a company to a retailer, which includes advertisements and correspondence (to regular customers)
- *Field 2:* Represents a consumer's response to the message, which involves attitude formation, further investigations through consultation of different sources and the evaluation of alternatives
- *Field 3:* Represents a consumer's motivation to purchase (which can be either strong or weak)
- *Field 4:* Represents post-purchase feedback, which may include feedback to the company (positive or negative) as well as internal feedback (to memory, which would be influential in terms of future decision making). Subsequent decision-making experiences therefore change a consumer on a personal level, specifically that consumer's knowledge about a specific product or service, and subsequently also the consumer's self-concept. A decision that resulted in a favourable outcome or a memorable experience increases a consumer's self-confidence, which also enhances his or her self-concept. Positive post-purchase experiences may, for example, convert a 'consumer' who has had a positive purchase encounter into a 'customer'.

The Nicosia model suggests a cognitive problem-solving approach to consumer decision making and is useful because it shows that many steps are involved between attitude formation and the actual buying behaviour (action). The model also confirms an increase in consumers' personal attributes (for example, knowledge, attitudes, self-concept and motivation) as a result of product- or process-related experience, which acknowledges theory related to consumer socialisation. The model furthermore signifies intra-person feedback, that is, activity in consumers' thought processes that precedes decisions and/or actions.

The Schiffman and Kanuk model of consumer behaviour

The Schiffman and Kanuk consumer decision model[27] is presented as a system that involves the three phases that are typical of a system's theory approach:

- *Inputs:* This model proposes that a consumer is exposed to external influences or inputs. Two input categories are distinguished:
  - Marketing-related factors, which involve all the elements of an extended marketing mix (for example, product, price, place and promotions)
  - Socio-cultural factors (for example, family, social group and cultural group)
- *Transformation phase:* During this stage, all of the influences that may be relevant during a consumer's decision making are transformed internally

Figure 13.4 Positive disconformation exceeds expectation

with the aid of information that was stored in the form of cognitive frameworks in a consumer's memory during previous purchase experiences. Established cognitive frameworks in memory, also known as schemata, aid the consumer in recognising and interpreting stimuli, and subsequently influence new buying experiences. This means that a prior purchase experience facilitates similar purchase experiences in the future. Conversely, lack of experience complicates the purchase experience because a consumer has nothing in memory to support the process. While some decision models specify the internal influences (for example, attitude, motives and personality) as an input, the Schiffman and Kanuk model proposes that internal factors are fundamental as a mediating tool during the interpretation of external stimuli. The model also indicates that prior experiences expand memory. This model therefore acknowledges the influences of consumer socialisation (that is, the incurring process during which a consumer acquires the knowledge and skills that are required to function in the marketplace). The transformation phase incorporates concepts that are prominent in most other decision models.

- *Outputs:* A consumer's post-purchase evaluation is depicted as the output in the model. This involves the consumer's comparison of a product, brand or store's actual performance to what was expected. Expectations may be based on previous experience, marketing communication, salespeople's recommendations or the recommendations of friends. This comparison is not necessarily a conscious process, but during use of a product or a service (for example, when dining in a restaurant), a consumer inevitably deduces that he or she might purchase the same product or dine at the same restaurant again owing to a confirmation of his or her expectations (because **the product performed as expected**). There may even be **positive disconfirmation**, with the performance of the product or the service exceeding a consumer's expectations (for example, the food and the service in the restaurant were much better than expected). However, the consumer may also decide not to repeat the experience in the future because the product did not perform as expected. **Negative disconfirmation** is thus when a product or a service fails expectations and is disappointing. Confirmation or disconfirmation of expectations ultimately culminates as satisfaction or dissatisfaction (an emotion), which expands existing knowledge frameworks in memory and will influence future choice behaviour. The systems theory perspective refers to this experience 'storage' as feedback. The output of buying decisions will, however, also feed into a so-called control mechanism, which means that any consumer experience influences the way in which inputs are used in future consumer decisions. An experienced consumer would reconsider the use of certain information sources and/or consult alternative sources in an attempt to improve the outcome of subsequent consumer decisions.[28]

The Hawkins, Best and Coney decision model

Hawkins, Best and Coney[29] propose that consumers' lifestyles determine their behaviour in the marketplace. The **Hawkins, Best and Coney model** therefore considers the lifestyle and self-concept determinants that drive consumers' needs and desires and influence their buying decisions. Subsequent steps in this model coincide with the five prominent stages that appear in most of the other decision models and that were discussed in more detail in Chapter 1 (problem or need recognition, information search, evaluation of alternatives, choice and post-purchase evaluation).[30]

This model is ideal when status consumption and social aspects of consumption are investigated, therefore when studying consumers' consumption of goods to enhance or support their image in society. For example, it is appropriate for a discussion of the influence of consumers' buying practices on household debt.

13.5 UNDERSTANDING CONSUMER DECISION MODELS

The previous section provided background about the origin and content of some of the most prominent and established consumer decision models. The section that follows provides guidelines on interpreting them.

13.5.1 Identification of the important stages in a consumer decision process[31]

Despite apparent differences between consumer decision models (as explained in the previous section), certain stages of the consumer decision process are common to many of the so-called grand models, which were designed to reflect the consumer decision-making process from different perspectives and which are still acknowledged today as the start of the model-building process. Mostly, five prominent stages of consumer decision making can be distinguished.

These stages are discussed in more detail below.

Problem recognition

Problem recognition refers to a consumer realising the need for a particular product or service and the extent to which the need may be problematic.[32] For example, when a person's refrigerator breaks down in the middle of summer, he or she has to solve the problem quickly. The product in itself, however, requires some deliberation because it is expensive, involves complex technology and has to last for a considerable number of years. Alternatively, a consumer may need to replace a hairbrush, which is not nearly as involved a decision. The extent or significance of the problem determines the rest of the consumer decision process, that is, whether the process will be extensive, involving all the stages previously mentioned, or whether the process will be completed almost without conscious deliberation. This explains why discussions about consumer decision making are mostly product related and context related, and why the findings of one research endeavour are not necessarily applicable to every other consumer decision.

APPLICATION

Hint for researchers

Always specify the problem clearly and describe it in detail so that relevant supporting theory (for example, risk perception and consumer socialisation, which indicates a consumer's capability or demographics such as logistical problems) can be used to explain your discussion of the findings later on.

The information search

The information search deals with a consumer's quest for information to 'solve' the product need.[33] Inevitably, the consumer firstly reverts to memory to recall prior product or purchase experiences. This particular activity is dealt with extensively in models that are designed in terms of cognitive frameworks. For example, the Howard-Sheth model identifies perceptual and learning parts, and accommodates concepts such as stimulus ambiguity and perceptual bias to acknowledge the uncertainty or confusion that a consumer may experience. It also refers to the concept of non-significance of information (for example, when a restaurant is advertised as halaal and a consumer is not religious). Any discussion of a consumer's information search would necessarily have to refer to a consumer's expectations of the product and/or service because that would, for example, give clarity about the choice criteria used, the consumer's brand comprehension and subsequent affordability issues.

An information search process can involve personal sources of information such as friends, family members whose opinions are generally trusted or sales personnel, who are supposed to provide expert advice, but who are not necessarily trusted because consumers often think that their advice is motivated by sales incentives. A major advantage of personal information sources is that the consumer is able to ask for information selectively and to discuss it within his or her own frame of reference. Non-personal information sources include printed media (for example, advertisements, brochures, newspaper articles and technical reports), which can contain fairly detailed information such as product specifications. A major advantage of non-personal information sources is that consumers can refer to them multiple times and complicated information can be explained in some detail. This is not as viable in a personal conversation (for example, a discussion with a salesperson) because too much information may cause an information overload and confusion.

The Howard-Sheth model[34] and the Engel-Kollat-Blackwell model devote much attention to conceptualising the information search during consumer decision making.

RESEARCH BOX 14.1

Keep in mind that any discussion of an information search should acknowledge the characteristics of the sample (the consumers that are involved), such as:

- their cognitive abilities (for example, it would not make sense to expand your literature review in terms of various forms of written information if the research project involves consumers with a low level of literacy)
- their personality (for example, some consumers may prefer non-personal information sources because these sources do not involve personal contact and are therefore less threatening)
- the context (for example, do consumers potentially have access to all of the sources mentioned?)

The evaluation and selection of alternatives

The **evaluation and selection of alternatives** refers to the stage when a consumer identifies the products, services or brands that most closely incorporate the characteristics that are preferred or considered important.[35] The evaluation criteria that are used to identify suitable product alternatives may involve concrete product features such as size, capacity, colour and price, which may result in a rational prioritisation of products in accordance with features that are considered most important and even non-negotiable. For example, the product must not be more expensive than R1 000 because that is the maximum that can be afforded or the shoes must be black to match other outfits in the individual's wardrobe. Preferred product characteristics may, however, also involve emotional factors, for example:

- preferring a specific brand that is admired by friends
- preferring a specific brand because it reflects status
- choosing a brand that is familiar because it epitomises reliability within the frame of reference
- insisting on products that are environmentally friendly because of concern about the future of the planet.

Whatever the case, a consumer generally considers no more than seven product features and mostly limits the number of products that are scrutinised before a final decision is made to between three and seven products. This is referred to as a consumer's consideration set or an **evoked set** of products. Practically, this implies that a consumer should never be offered too many options from which to choose because that may be overwhelming and confusing. An over-enthusiastic estate agent who takes potential buyers to view too many properties for sale actually creates confusion. He or she should rather target an evoked set of three to seven homes that possess most of the required characteristics.

When selecting products, a consumer categorises the products firstly on a basic level, which groups together products that have a lot in common (for example, choosing desktop computers or laptop computers). On a subordinate level, all of the computers are then distinguished in terms of specific characteristics (for example, acceptable brands or all brands that are affordable). On a superordinate level, a consumer may distinguish brands in terms of characteristics that are more emotional in nature, such as computers with particular functional attributes (for example, a large hard drive). A consumer may, however, have a prototype in mind,[36] for example a mini-notebook.

A consumer could apply different strategies (or decision rules) to select the most suitable or appropriate product from the evoked set of products. Theoretical application of the different decision rules is explained in Chapter 1. The decision rule that is applied is not typical of a consumer or of a product. A decision rule is applied in context, that is, the same consumer might apply different consumer decision rules in different contexts.

The Engel-Kollat-Blackwell model[37] devotes much attention to the evaluation process.

APPLICATION

Application of decision rules

Any investigation that aims to identify the most popular product, feature or brand should take into consideration that different decision rules could be applied to make a final product decision. It is therefore important to formulate a question that will produce the type of answer that is required. For example, when product characteristics have to be ranked in order of priority and if 'brand name' was listed as the most important, it does not necessarily mean that a consumer will insist on the brand name that he or she had in mind unless the consumer was asked to indicate whether the characteristic was negotiable (in other words, whether a compensatory or a non-compensatory rule applied). Ranking will therefore merely give an indication of what consumers regard as highly important (or not), unless a laddering technique is used or the question is formulated differently. Here are some examples:

- When choosing a restaurant for a special function with your friends, which one of the following factors do you consider non-negotiable, irrespective of how favourable the other characteristics may be?
- When choosing a restaurant for a special function with your friends, which one of the following factors is highly preferable, although you might be willing to compromise if the other characteristics are acceptable?
- When choosing a restaurant for a special function with your friends, how important are the following attributes in terms of your final decision?

The purchase decision

The purchase decision refers to a consumer's final choice of product or service. Ultimately, a consumer's information search should result in the ability to make an informed, responsible purchase decision. 'Informed' refers to having all the information that would enable a consumer to feel in control of the evaluation process, that is, the ability to recognise product characteristics that are relevant and to comprehend the information. 'Responsible' refers to the fact that a consumer should take responsibility for that specific decision, that is, accept the consequences for the purchase decision (for example, preferring the cheaper product, despite the limited guarantee).

Purchase decisions that involve risk or uncertainty of some kind may create tension or anxiety immediately after the purchase is concluded.[38] For example:
* Will the product last that long? (performance risk)
* Will the holiday destination be safe to go to? (safety risk)
* Will my friends on social media approve of the purchase that I have just shared with them? (social risk)
* How might I feel if I purchase a brand that is less popular than others on the market? (psychological risk)
* Can I really afford this car? (financial risk)
* Will my personal detail be shared with other people (security risk)

Anxiety experienced immediately after a purchase is referred to as cognitive dissonance,[39] which is defined as a state of tension that is generated owing to a psychological inconsistency between a person's beliefs (about the product selected) and his or her behaviour (product decision) at a point (after purchase) when the transaction is irreversible. Several actions could be taken to reduce cognitive dissonance, for example:
* obtaining additional information from sales personnel or brochures to support the product choice
* obtaining additional information from friends or product specifications that confirm that the other available products would not have been appropriate in the situation
* gaining the approval or admiration of significant others by inviting them to look at the product and to make comments.

Post-purchase evaluation

Post-purchase evaluation is part of the purchase decision process. During this stage, a consumer starts using the product and gets the opportunity to compare the performance of the product to his or her expectations.[40] It is important to note that this comparison does not always occur consciously. A product that performs as expected confirms the consumer's expectations. Positive disconfirmation occurs when the product exceeds the consumer's expectations, which would result in consumer satisfaction, possible repeat purchases in the future and probably also in positive recommendations to acquaintances.[41] Negative disconfirmation occurs when a product does not meet a consumer's expectations. This usually causes dissatisfaction, which is a negative emotion that can be dealt with in several ways, for example private action (that is, disregarding the product in the future) or public action (that is, negative word-of-mouth communication, complaints or seeking redress). Whatever the outcome, every purchase experience becomes part of the consumer's experience framework in memory, which aids future purchase decisions. Extensive experience with a specific type of purchase (for example, being a frequent flyer on South African Airways) would therefore make purchase decisions easier to deal with in the future. This is referred to as product-related consumer socialisation. An experienced consumer is therefore not necessarily experienced in all product categories.

It is crucial to understand the five stages of the consumer decision-making process in terms of what every stage entails and to be aware that the various stages may differ in the following respects:

- Products and services vary in complexity and importance. For example, purchasing a new computer requires more intensive deliberation and progression through all of the stages than buying a pair of socks, which might require a limited information search or no information search at all.
- Consumers have different levels of experience. For example, the decision process of an experienced mountain biker who has been involved in the sport for several years will be different from that of a novice who now needs to buy a suitable bicycle to do mountain biking for the first time. If two couples need to select a new television for their homes, the decision may be easier for the couple who have been married for years and have bought televisions before, since they will have ample product-related experience that could help them throughout the decision process, whereas the newlyweds will probably have to search for a great deal of information and scrutinise several sizes and brands.
- Consumers have different levels of personal involvement in the product. For example, the decision process of an organisational buyer purchasing décor objects for the corporate office will be different from that of a person purchasing such items for his or her own home.
- Contexts differ. For example, the decision process will be more challenging when a product decision has to be made fast and under pressure (for example, when a refrigerator breaks down during a hot summer holiday) compared to the same task where there is no time pressure (for example, needing a refrigerator for a new home that will only be ready for occupation next month).

SUMMARY

Any consumer decision involves a number of decision stages, although consumers are not necessarily consciously aware that the decision is advancing through the stages of problem recognition, information search and evaluation of alternatives before an actual product choice is made. Differentiating between the stages of consumer decision making is useful in terms of our understanding of consumer decisions. The stages of the consumer decision-making process demonstrate how an individual proceeds through an intricate, high-risk decision that mostly requires more extensive personal involvement, more attention and a more extensive information search, which is time consuming. When relatively easy purchase decisions are made, certain stages of the decision process may be brief or even skipped, for example purchasing milk.

Over time, various consumer decision models have been constructed in order to present consumer decisions more visually. These models are structural representations of consumer decisions and contain all of the concepts that are relevant during every stage of the consumer decision to aid a better understanding of what happens during every stage and from one stage to the next for particular contexts. Every model aims to represent the different stages of consumer decision making for a specific context visually and to specify relevant concepts for every stage, as well as indicating how the concepts are integrated, which is extremely useful in understanding the decision-making process. Consumer decision models have important advantages in terms of an understanding of consumers' decision-making behaviour. They provide a frame of reference that clearly defines relevant concepts and their relationships within specific theoretical perspectives, making it possible to discuss decision making in terms of the entire decision process and to organise literature, which often only covers part of a decision process, in a logical way. It is important to have some background about a model before using it because models cannot be used interchangeably.

Many of the models are simplified, which means that concepts are specified and linked, but not extensively delineated in terms of underlying concepts. This may create the impression that a consumer decision process is simple and straightforward. Various consumer decision models exist and their application in an understanding of consumer decision making and marketing differs considerably. This chapter provides an overview of some of the original models and explains the underlying motivation for each model. Thereafter, some of the most renowned consumer decision models are presented to explain similarities and differences among various models, and how they can be used in discussions of consumer decision making.

SELF-ASSESSMENT QUESTIONS

1. How can a consumer decision model aid a researcher's discussion of a consumer decision-making process for a complex, high-risk decision?
2. How can a consumer decision model aid a marketer's understanding of the complexity of a consumer decision and subsequently the stages during which guidance would be useful?
3. Why did scholars refer to the cognitive process that occurs during consumer decision-making as the 'black box'?
4. Provide a practical example to explain why the Marshallian consumer decision model could not provide the ultimate explanation of consumer decision making.
5. Explain the value of the Pavlovian model in terms of efforts to communicate new information to consumers and to teach alternative behaviours, for example in advertising.
6. Which dimension did the Freudian model add to existing economic-rational approaches to consumer decision making? Explain.
7. Why is the Veblenian model particularly relevant in sociology, cultural anthropology and social psychology?
8. Why is it inappropriate to use a consumer decision model without understanding the fundamentals of its origin?
9. The Schiffman and Kanuk model is ideal for any discussion about the influence of previous experience in terms of a consumer decision. Explain.
10. What unique approach does the Hawkins, Best and Coney model add to discussions about consumer decision making?
11. Provide an example of a discussion where the four stages of Nicosia's interaction model would be useful to direct the narrative.
12. Identify and discuss each of the five prominent stages that are distinguished in any consumer decision model and explain how the various stages would differ for consumer decisions that vary in complexity.
13. What is meant by the output of a consumer decision?
14. How would the product evaluation stage be dealt with when a non-compensatory rule is applied?
15. How could cognitive dissonance that is experienced after a high-risk purchase be reduced by each of the following parties:
    - The salesperson?
    - The retailer?
    - The consumer?
16. Why does consumer satisfaction not necessarily imply that a product or a service is superior or excellent?

EXPERIENTIAL EXERCISE

You have been considering purchasing a new cellular phone because the functionality of your existing model is completely outdated.

1. Explain the product characteristics you would consider in coming to a final product replacement decision.
2. Do you think that familiarity with the Schiffman and Kanuk consumer decision model would help you in coming to a better decision? Explain why or why not.

CASE STUDY 1

The importance of a consumer decision context

Three potential customers enter a retail outlet that specialises in office furniture. The purpose of their respective store visits is as follows:

* Customer 1 represents the organisational buyer of a major corporate company. He needs to select suitable office furniture and lighting for a new open-plan office. His budget acknowledges the importance of the image of the company and the clients.
* Customer 2 wishes to purchase office furniture and lighting as part of the renovation of an existing study, but the new acquisitions have to match the built-in wall units.
* Customer 3 wishes to furbish a newly built home office for her retired husband who, as a professional, will still be consulting at home.

The product characteristics that the three consumers may consider in terms of their final product decisions are (in alphabetical order):

* aesthetics (materials and finishes)
* after-sales service
* environmental friendliness
* exterior design features (aesthetics)
* functionalitiy/suitability
* guarantee
* installation
* interior design features (practicality)
* price
* product performance characteristics (comfort, design)
* size (dimensions)

Discussion questions

1. Explain why the inputs phase of the Howard-Sheth model would be particularly appropriate to use in a discussion of the decision process of customer 1.
2. Explain why the transformation phase of the Schiffman and Kanuk model would be particularly appropriate to use in a discussion of the decision process of customer 2.
3. Explain why Hawkins, Best and Coney's lifestyle approach would suitably direct a discussion of the needs of customer 3.
4. Why would the transformation of the inputs (influencing factors) for customer 1 be less emotional and involving than for customer 2 and customer 3?
5. The outcome of a consumer decision depends on what the consumer wants to achieve (output), which is not necessarily consumer satisfaction. Choose at least one of the following constructs that would best describe the outcome of each of the three consumer decisions described (in other words, does customer 1 anticipate a suitable product, an impressive product, a status product or an affordable product and so on?):
   - Suitable product
   - Impressive product
   - Status product
   - Affordable product

- Exclusive product
- Reliable product

6. Using the outcome selected in question 5 for every consumer decision, briefly explain the five stages of the consumer decision process for each customer in order to demonstrate differences in the extensiveness of their decisions as well as their personal involvement in the decisions.

CASE STUDY 2

Interpersonal communication

Insurance company A recently launched a promotion to encourage households to switch their car insurance to its company. It offered financial incentives for consumers who contacted them during a predetermined period and who subsequently made the switch within one month. Consumers' text messages were responded to with a text message from the company, which included a reference number, after which a salesperson contacted interested consumers to acquire the relevant details with the hope of clinching a deal. Telephone calls to consumers were made without prior warning during office hours. Many consumers were working and therefore these calls did not always take place at a convenient time. The telephonic interviews took as long fifteen minutes to conclude and interviewers asked many questions that were not relevant to car insurance (as suggested in the advertisements). In some instances, calls had to be continued at a later stage because they took longer than expected, and when the salesperson made the second call, he or she had to repeat several personal enquiries to confirm the details of the prospective client. At long last, a quotation was provided, which meant a saving of R80 per month for the customer, provided that he or she switched to company A within one month. Some clients realised that the switch would mean the loss of their no-claim bonus, which was due some months later from their existing insurance company.

Discussion questions

1. Distinguish the four stages (fields) of interpersonal discussion according to Nicosia's model in the narrative.
2. Discuss field 2 in terms of how the process may have influenced the consumers' attitude formation.
3. Discuss field 3 in terms of the evidence from the narrative.
4. Discuss field 4 in terms of a consumer's interaction with friends about the experience.

Additional resources

For more information on the concepts discussed in this chapter, visit the following web sites:

- https://www.managementstudyguide.com/consumer-decision-making-process.htm (the consumer decision process explained)
- https://www.youtube.com/watch?v=kWHhA-1YjCw (consumer deicion models)
- http://www.managementstudyguide.com/consumer-decision-making-process.htm (stages in the consumer decision-making process)

- https://www.youtube.com/watch?v=fQaY3-SLBYI (Nicosia model)
- https://www.youtube.com/watch?v=zXooX8rsHXQ&t=21s (Howard Sheth model)
- http://www.amsreview.org/articles/giese01-2000.pdf (defining consumer satisfaction)
- http://cmsoforum.mckinsey.com/article/winning-the-consumer-decision-journey (winning the consumer decision journey)

Youtube videos:

- Consumer Decision Making Model - Realtime Explanation: https://www.youtube.com/watch?v=zbcvZi6aofg
- Consumer Decision Making Models: https://www.youtube.com/watch?v=KkXwwhfEaul
- Howard Sheth Model of Consumer Behaviour: https://www.youtube.com/watch?v=zXooX8rsHXQ
- Nicosia Model of Consumer Behaviour: https://youtu.be/q08faAdkKB4
- The Rational Decision Making Model: https://www.youtube.com/watch?v=dJARNLbe9NA
- Understanding consumer decision making process: https://youtu.be/cKGmETvpKEo

REFERENCES

1   Erasmus, A.C., Boshoff, E. & Rousseau, G. 2001. Consumer decision models within the discipline of consumer science: A critical approach. *Journal of Family Ecology and Consumer Sciences*, 29: 83–90.

2   Bray, J.P. 2008. Consumer behaviour theory: Approaches and models. Available at: http://eprints.bournemouth.ac.uk/10107/1/Consumer_Behaviour_Theory_-_Approaches_%26_Models.pdf (accessed on 14 June 2018); Lehmann, D.R., Farley, J.U. & Howard, J.A. 1971. Testing of buyer behavior models. Proceedings of the Second Annual Conference of the Association for Consumer Research. Available at: http://www.acrwebsite.org/volumes/display.asp?id=11962 (accessed on 14 June 2018).

3   Bray, ibid.; Erasmus et al., op. cit.; Kotler, P. 1965. Behavioral models for analyzing buyers. *Journal of Marketing*, 29(4): 37–45.

4   Duff, V. 2017 What is the importance of the black box model and its marketing implications? Available at: https://bizfluent.com/info-12157349-importance-black-box-model-its-marketing-implications.html (accessed on 14 June 2018); Hirschman, E.C. 1985. Cognitive processes in experimental consumer behavior. *Research on Consumer Behavior*, 1: 67–102.

5   Hirschman, E.C. 1985. Cognitive processes in experimental consumer behavior. *Research on Consumer Behavior*, 1: 67.

6   Erasmus et al., op. cit., 82.

7   Babin, B. & Harris, E. 2013. *CB5*. Mason, OH: South-Western Cengage Learning, 250; Solomon, M.R. 2018. *Consumer behavior: Buying, having, being*, 12th ed. Essex, England: Pearson Education, 339.

8   Solomon, ibid.; Van Hamersveld, M. & De Bont, C.J.P.M. 2007. *Market research handbook*. Chichester: John Wiley and Sons, 25; Jackson, T. 2005. Motivating sustainable consumption: A review of evidence on consumer behaviour and behavioural change. Guildford: University of Surrey.

9   Solomon, ibid.; Scott, J. in Browning, G, Halcli, A & Webster, F. 2000. *Understanding contemporary society*. Thousand Oaks, CA: SAGE, 128.

10 Jackson, op. cit.

11 Hoque, Z. 2006. *Methodological issues in accounting research: Theories, methods and issues.* London: Spiramus, 8.

12 Ibid.; Jackson, op. cit.

13 Hoque, ibid., 8, 9.

14 Asamoah, E.S. & Chovancová, M. 2011. An overview of the theory of microeconomics (consumer behaviour and market structures) in fast food marketing. Available at: Ekonomika a management, 2011 - vse.cz (accessed on 15 June 2018).

15 Trigg, A.B. 2001. Veblen, Bourdieau and conspicuous consumption. *Journal of Economic Issues*, 35(1): 99–114.

16 Jacoby, J. 2002. Stimulus–organism–response reconsidered: An evolutionary step in modelling consumer behaviour. *Journal of Consumer Psychology*, 12(1): 51–57.

17 Mittal, B. & Sheth, J.N. 2004. *Customer behavior: A managerial perspective*, 2nd ed. Ohio: Thompson, South-Western, 123.

18 Kastanakis, M. & Balabanis, G. 2012. Bandwagon, snob and Veblen effects in luxury consumption. *Advances in Consumer Research*, 38: 609.

19 Bunce, R.E.R. 2009. *Major conservative and libertarian thinkers – Thomas Hobbes*. London: Continuum International.

20 Howard, J.A. & Sheth, J.N. 1969. *The theory of buyer behavior*. New York: John Wiley, 32.

21 Ibid.

22 Engel, J.F., Blackwell, R.D. & Kollat, D.T. 1995. *Consumer behaviour*, 8th ed. Hinsdale: Dryden Press, 5.

23 Ibid.

24 For example, see Jones, D.G. B., Shaw, E. H. & McClean, P. A. 2011. The modern schools of marketing thought. In Maclaran, P., Saren, M., Stern, B. & Tadajewski, M. (Ed.), *The SAGE handbook of marketing theory*. London: SAGE.

25 Adapted from Nicosia, F.M. 1966. *Consumer decision processes*. Engelwood Cliffs, NJ: Prentice Hall, 156.

26 Nicosia, op. cit., 195.

27 Schiffman, L.G. & Wisenblit, J.L. 2015. *Consumer behaviour*, 11th ed. Malaysia: Pearson Education, 368.

28 Schiffman, L.G. & Kanuk, L.L. 2010. *Consumer Behavior*, 10th ed. New Jersey: Prentice Hall, 18.

29 Hawkins, I., Best, R.J. & Coney, K.A. 1989. *Consumer behavior: Building marketing strategy*, 4th ed. New York: Irwin/McGraw Hill, 2. Reprinted by permission of McGraw Hill Education.

30 Hawkins, I., Best, R.J. & Coney, K.A. 2001. *Consumer behavior: Building marketing strategy*, 8th ed. New York: Irwin/McGraw Hill. Reprinted by permission of McGraw Hill Education.

31 Cant, M.C., Brink, A. & Brijball, S. 2006. *Consumer behaviour*. Cape Town: Juta, 195.

32 Solomon, op. cit., 339.

33 Ibid.; Sonnenberg, N.C., Erasmus, A.C. & Donoghue, S. 2011. Significance of environmental sustainability issues in consumers' choice of major household appliances in South Africa. *International Journal of Consumer Studies*, 35(2): 153–163.

34 Howard & Sheth, op. cit., 32.

35 Solomon, op. cit., 339; Erasmus et al., op. cit., 648–658.

36 Solomon, ibid., 157, 356.

37 Engel et al., op. cit., 95.

38 Solomon, op. cit., 189, 358; Thakur, R. & Srivastava, M. 2015. A study on the impact of consumer risk perception and innovativeness on online shopping in India. *International Journal of Retail and Distribution Management*, 43(2):148–166; Dai, B., Forsythe, S. & Kwon, W.S. 2013. The impact of online shopping experience on risk perceptions and online purchase intentions: does product category matter? *Journal of Electronic Commerce Research*, 15(1): 13–24.

39 Solomon, op. cit., 176; Yeung, R.M.W. & Morris, J. 2006. An empirical study of the impact of consumer perceived risk on a purchase likelihood. *International Journal of Consumer Studies*, 30(3): 294–305.

40 Solomon, op. cit., 343; Peter, P.J., Olson, J.C. & Grunert, K.G. 2008. *Consumer behaviour and marketing strategy*. Singapore: McGraw Hill, 32.

41 Solomon, ibid., 397; De Los Reyes, A., Aldao, A. & Kundey, S.M. 2010. Compromised decision making and the effects of manipulating physical states on human judgments. *Journal of Clinical Psychology*, Jan., 1: 1–7.

CHAPTER 14

CONSUMERISM AND CONSUMERS AS CITIZENS

Alet Erasmus

LEARNING OBJECTIVES

After reading this chapter, you should be able to:

- describe the diverse meanings of consumerism
- describe the social movement that emerged in the US in 1962, and explain how it relates to the consumerism movement in South Africa and across the world today
- discuss consumerism in terms of its approach in less developed countries (LDC) versus more developed countries (MDC)
- list the eight internationally accepted consumer rights that direct the operations of consumer organisations in South Africa, then provide practical examples to demonstrate an understanding of how each mission statement protects consumers
- discuss consumers' responsibilities in the marketplace in terms of informed, responsible purchase decisions and the use of products and services
- explain consumers' social responsibility in terms of the consequences of product consumption and the environment in the long term
- explain the appropriate procedure on how consumers should act to address their complaints or concerns about products or services
- explain how consumers' involvement in consumer matters could enhance service delivery in the marketplace
- select appropriate channels through which consumers could be assisted to resolve problems that may be encountered in the marketplace.

Key terms

boycott group	consumerism life cycle	informed consumer decision
citizen self	pattern	making
complementary	consumer rights that are	materialism
technology	internationally endorsed	Nader network
Consumer Bill of Rights	consumers' responsibilities	perspective consciousness
consumerism	consumer self	responsible consumer decision
consumerism in a third-	Diderot effect	making
world context	global perspective	voluntary simplicity

Jane and Mary have moved into new apartments after completion of their college studies. Jane is renting an apartment that she saw advertised in a newspaper, while Mary was referred to a landlord by a friend. Jane had to sign a one-year contract that clearly stipulated the conditions of payment and the responsibilities of both parties (herself and the owner of the apartment). The contract indicated that the monthly rental fee could only be increased once a year, when the contract was due for renewal. Mary entered into a verbal agreement that only indicated the monthly rental and assurance that she could stay in the apartment for a year. This verbal agreement did not include a discussion regarding the possibility of an increase in the monthly rental fee.

After six months, both Jane and Mary were informed about an increase in the monthly rental. When complaining, the landlord told Mary that she could evacuate the flat if she was unhappy. Explain how both ladies should address the predicament that they are in, also referring to evidence that they can use to support their respective cases. Why will it be easier for Jane than for Mary to resolve the matter?

14.1 INTRODUCTION

Changes in the marketing orientation and subsequent changes in retailers' and industries' attention to the needs of consumers were discussed in Chapter 1. The consumer orientation highlighted the emergence of various organisations and strategies to protect and inform consumers, with the aim of encouraging **responsible consumer decision making** and to prevent exploitation in the marketplace. This chapter concludes this discussion with an elaboration of measures taken worldwide to protect, educate and inform consumers. Throughout this discussion, the emphasis is placed on the South African context.

14.2 THE CONCEPT OF CONSUMERISM

Consumers have been and always will be at the core of any marketing concept. Their buying power and loyalty are vital in order for businesses to survive. Consumers' influence in the marketplace was, however, elevated beyond their monetary influence when President J.F. Kennedy chose to promote **consumerism** as the primary drive of his presidential campaign in the US during the 1960s. When he was elected in 1962, his proclaimed **Consumer Bill of Rights**[1] became the centre of discussion in the marketplace. The enumerated consumer rights incorporated four basic rights:
- The right to choose
- The right to be informed
- The right to be heard
- The right to safety

Retail and industry had no option other than to reassess their modus operandi to acknowledge and accommodate the newly acclaimed status of 'the consumer as king'. Per definition, consumerism is a social movement that concerns itself with widening the range of activities of government, business and independent organisations that aim to protect individuals (consumers) from practices (of both business and government) that may infringe upon their rights as consumers. Also, consumerism is described as a social movement (a movement by people for people), seeking to extend the rights and powers of buyers (consumers) in relation to sellers;[2] or as a 'citizens' movement aimed at making broad-reaching social, ecological and political demands on companies (retailers) and manufacturers that supply goods and services.[3] Some definitions of consumerism also refer to the opportunity for consumers to raise (voice) their discontent after a negative product experience, the improvement of corrective actions[4] as well as 'efforts by the consumer himself, government or independent organisations to protect the consumer from unscrupulous practices of businesses in their quest for profit'.[5]

The phenomenon of consumerism literally took the world by storm and although it was formally launched in the US, the underlying principles were adopted and were even expanded on by organisations across the world soon after. The relevance of consumer organisations and related consumer rights are constantly scrutinised and updated to keep up with changes in the market place. For example, in March 2017, the World Consumer Rights Day 2017 celebration in South Africa involved the swearing in of ten new consumer affairs court officials to support 'consumer rights in the digital age'. This includes consumers' rights with regard to digital products and protection of data shared online.

14.2.1 The dual meaning of consumerism
In addition to the definitions mentioned above, consumerism may also refer to an excessive consumption of consumer goods that is associated with **materialism**, which refers to a consumer's obsession with accumulating goods and possessions.[6] This is similar to other '-isms', including alcoholism, pessimism and patriotism, which suggest excessive behaviour of some kind. Although the dual definitions of consumerism are vastly different at face value, the rest of the chapter will explain that these concepts are actually inseparable.

14.2.2 Progress of the consumer movement
Changes in marketing orientation (see Chapter 1) owing to a continual review of the role of the consumer in the marketplace over the years confirm the dynamic nature of the retail environment in which consumers operate. Simultaneously, consumer organisations (formal structures that are aimed at attending to consumer related issues – see section 14.3 for examples) have become an integral part of the shopping arena, joining forces with individuals and groups to solve matters that consumers find difficult to resolve on their own. The post-1960s era introduced several interpretations of the new consumerism movement, expanding to include social issues as well,[7] particularly people-oriented and highly specialised movements that focused on issues such as civil rights, labour practice and institutional reform.

Consumerism in developing countries
In a cross-national comparison of consumer attitudes toward consumerism in four developing countries, scholars[8] concluded that consumer protection in

more developed countries (MDC) such as the US and the UK has become quite advanced, while the same could unfortunately not be said for less developed countries (LDC) such as African countries. Many consumers in LDC are easily exploited owing to a lack of protection or because they are not aware of their consumer rights. Lower education levels inevitably limit the decision-making and negotiation skills of vulnerable consumers in these countries. Consumers with a low level of literacy are, for example, not able to read or comprehend complex product information, which is typical of product instructions that accompany new products, product label information and purchase contracts. Generally, these consumers are unable to interpret the written information and are even unable to do simple mathematical calculations to compare prices of products that differ in size, to select the best value for money alternatives.

Differences in the needs of consumers in LDC and MDC

As a result of differences in the profile of consumers in LDC and MDC, according to Darley and Johnson[9] it makes sense that consumer-related issues should be dealt with differently in different parts of the world, even if the same consumer rights are imposed. Owing to South Africa's consumer profile, with a majority of consumers still vulnerable and not necessarily able to fend for themselves in a competitive marketplace, the following priorities (which take into consideration the level of sophistication of consumers in different contexts) apply:

- To protect consumers because vulnerable consumers do not necessarily have the means, knowledge or resources to act on their own behalf
- To educate consumers so that they are empowered to become more vigilant
- To supply information to encourage responsible buying decisions (to consumers who are educated), and to remind them continually of their **responsibilities** and obligations in terms of their buying and consumption practices

The reverse order is proposed[10] for implementation in more developed countries (MDC) such as the US, namely to:

- firstly, provide consumer information to update consumers on new developments and to refresh their knowledge
- secondly, attend to consumer education when new issues arise, for example issues pertaining to the digital world
- finally, secure consumer protection in diverse forms such as consumer watch organisations and legal requirements.

Consumers from all walks of life need protection, although not necessarily to the same degree. Information that is provided in the marketplace may be overwhelming, confusing and even worthless if consumers are overloaded with information that they are not equipped to interpret and apply. Many of the measures established in South Africa in recent years, such as the National Credit Act 35 of 2005[11] that aims to protect consumers in the credit market so that credit and banking services are more accessible and less threatening, as well as the Consumer Protection Act 68 of 2008, confirm the need for the South African government to protect its citizens as a primary priority.

The consumerism life cycle pattern

Some researchers[12] argue that the progress of consumerism in a country follows a typical life cycle. It is further proposed that countries can be typified according to their consumer information and protection legislation as well as governments' involvement and support of these endeavours and consumer protection. Every country's situation can be distinguished in terms of progress along four distinct phases:

* **Crusading phase**, during which consumers are mostly left at their own mercy without any avenues for redress and with limited protection against exploitation, and subsequently start voicing their problems
* **Population movement**, which is common in developing countries, during which groups of consumers who share certain interests start voicing their concerns
* **Organisational or managerial phase**, where organisations are formed to act on behalf of consumer groups who share similar frustrations
* **Bureaucratic phase**, which is mostly characterised by consumers' arrogance, excessive and often unrealistic demands, and which may cause considerable tension between consumers and industry (a typical situation in highly developed countries such as the US

It is further argued that consumers in more advanced economies (for example, the US), where consumers have attained higher education levels, also have higher consumer expectations and are more inclined to express their dissatisfaction with products and services. This is typical of a bureaucratic society, while the contrary is true for developing countries, where consumers often do not have the knowledge or the confidence to act upon their frustrations because they are not aware of their consumer rights and do not know that legitimate problems, which they are not responsible for, can be addressed and resolved. It is therefore not surprising that researchers have come to the unfortunate conclusion that a negative relationship exists between consumer dissatisfaction and the level of education of consumers (thus that lower educated consumers are less inclined to express dissatisfaction, which may indicate that they are more satisfied), and that a strong positive correlation exists between consumer aspiration levels and degrees of economic development in a country (thus that consumers in more developed countries have higher aspiration levels).

DISCUSSION

Consumers' satisfaction with products and services does not necessarily mean that the products and services are of a good quality, and that retailers and industry can simply continue with 'business as usual'.

Discussion questions
* Why does consumer satisfaction not necessarily indicate that a product is of good quality?
* Considering the stages of the consumer life cycle, which stage has South Africa progressed to? Why do you think so?
* Why is it more difficult to please higher-educated consumers?

14.2.3 Organisations of the consumer movement

Several types of organisation with distinct characteristics that reflect their explicit area of interest are associated with the consumer movement.[13] This diversity has enabled consumers from different walks of life to become involved in some way with the common goal of attending to consumers' needs.

Local and state organisations

Irrespective of the country, local and state organisations differ in militancy while dealing with legislature, communicating consumer information and negotiating on behalf of individuals or society about consumers' complaints as well as price-, quality- and service-related issues. Personnel of these organisations are usually trained to operate as mediators to solve problems and to do investigations about issues of concern, for example reasons for price increases. Examples of such organisations in South Africa are Provincial Consumer Affairs Offices in the nine provinces (as discussed in section 14.3.1), include the following:

- National Consumer Commission (http://www.thencc.gov.za/)
- SA National Consumers Union (http://www.sancu.co.za/)
- Department of Trade and Industry (http://www.dti.gov.za/)
- Credit Ombudsman (http://www.osti.co.za/)
- Council for Medical Schemes (http://www.medicalschemes.com/)
- Consumer Goods and Services Ombud (http://www.cgso.org.za)

All of these organisations oversee specific interests of consumers and industries such as retailers. For more information, consult the following web sites: https://www.obssa.co.za/contact-us/ as well as http://www.cgso.org.za/

Boycott groups

Boycott groups are not unique to South Africa.[14] They have been instrumental in protests across the world, especially in the US, since the 1960s. The highly successful *Azikwelwa* (which means 'We will not ride') bus boycott was performed in 1957 in Alexandra in Johannesburg and Pretoria. As many as 70 000 township residents refused to use local buses for six months as a result of tariff increases.

Boycotts are generally organised to protest about issues of immediate concern such as price hikes, rather than long-term grievances. Specific boycott groups are therefore mostly short lived. Boycott groups may use several tactics to express their dismay, for example strikes, blockades, letter writing, media conferences and meetings. Complainants usually try to obtain as much media coverage as possible. Boycotts are usually performed during critical times to cause as much disruption as possible and to draw as much attention as possible. Participation in boycotts may be for personal gain (for example, not wanting to pay higher tariffs) or to help others (for example, to protest against farm murders).

Nader network

Ralph Nader[15] was a leader in the field of consumer advocacy in the US. He is still actively involved in the political arena, unafraid to voice his concerns about consumers and environmental issues, among others. His contribution towards the social consumer movement was evident through his persistent efforts to encourage the American public to support his pleas for the reform of product safety standards and government-driven regulatory processes. He used the settlement money from his successful lawsuit against General Motors in the 1960s[16] to finance his activities. His efforts focused on regulatory failures, product safety and environmental dangers, and he aimed at promoting 'business with a conscience' as well as instigating social and economic change. Nader was nicknamed the 'Lone Ranger of the consumer movement' because he operated independently of consumer organisations, although he enjoyed the support of the Consumer Union.

The success of Nader and his followers was ascribed to thorough research about pertinent issues and well-timed release of findings to the press. Today, product safety and safety standards in general in the US are amongst the most stringent in world.

Consumers Union and related organisations

The Consumers Union is a specific consumer organisation that was founded in the US in 1936. This organisation's primary interest is in consumer research. The union, which is an independent, non-profit testing and information organisation, refrains from policy prescription. It primarily provides information, education and product advice to consumers. In the US, it encourages technically based product testing and the findings are published in the Consumer Reports. The Consumer Union's sizeable budget allows it to provide financial assistance to several new consumer groups and publications, and it also helped to create Consumers International in 1974.

The first consumer movement in South Africa was founded in the 1950s by Mrs Dorothy van der Westhuizen, who became known as the 'grandmother of consumerism' in this country, although the movement as it is known today gained momentum under the leadership of Mrs Margaret Lessing, a strongly motivated public speaker who encouraged leading women's organisations to join in the movement's endeavours.[17]

The South African National Consumer Union[18] was established in 1961 as a voluntary autonomous body that acts with authority on behalf of South African consumers from all walks of life. Its members include, among others, leading women's organisations such as Women's Agricultural Unions, the National Council of Women of South Africa, the Association of Retired Persons and Pensioners, etc. The opinion of the South African Consumer Union is respected by manufacturers, retailers, the agricultural sector, the SA Bureau of Standards and government. The union's motto is: 'Consultation before confrontation'.

14.2.4   A conceptualisation of consumers' rights

Over the years, organisations have taken the liberty of expanding the four basic consumer rights that were proposed by the initial Consumer Bill of Rights in the US[19] in mission statements of their own. The section that follows discusses the expanded list of eight **consumer rights** with all of their associated implications (in other words, how consumers can benefit from each right) as **internationally endorsed**. Consumer organisations in South Africa may honour all of these rights or focus on selected rights, depending on their interests. For example, the Business Practices Committee advises the Minister of Trade and Industry regarding business conduct that may be harmful to consumers. Provincial Departments of Consumer Affairs in the country's nine provinces are responsible for implementing and monitoring Acts such as the Consumer Credit Act. The South African Bureau of Standards (SABS) is primarily concerned with promoting quality and the standardisation of products in the country.

The right to the satisfaction of basic needs

It is proposed that every consumer should have access to certain basic goods and services to secure **consumer well-being**. These include adequate food, clothing, housing, health care, education, clean water and sanitation. Government is therefore obliged to promote fair, reasonable and sustainable economic and social development in the country, and to prioritise areas that are vital to consumers' health, for example food, water and the supply of safe pharmaceuticals. Government therefore takes health-related issues very seriously. For example, it has measures in place to have food service systems inspected whenever there is any doubt about the safety and handling of food in restaurants, hostels, butcheries or wherever food is produced and prepared to be sold. The media frequently reports on such complaints and measures that are used to resolve pressing issues such as water quality and water supply, for example recent reports in 2017 on drought stricken areas in the Western Cape. *The Newspaper*, a free monthly printed publication in the Western Cape, recently reported on the low water levels in Cape Town. Attempts by the authorities to assist consumers to limit their water use and to penalise those who continued to waste water were accentuated.[20]

DISCUSSION

Consumers from all walks of life in South Africa are protected by various bills, acts, regulations and initiatives. For example, at an extremely basic level, products that are sold by retailers have to adhere to certain minimum safety standards.

Discussion questions
1. Discuss the implications if the water supply to your home was turned off for two weeks.
2. Discuss the implications of a long-term power failure compared to a long-term failure of the water supply to your home.
3. How do you see your own role in the preservation of water in your home in your specific geographic area?

The right to safety

The main concern in this instance is to ensure that consumers are appropriately informed about the potential dangers that may be associated with certain products. Manufacturers therefore have to take precautionary measures by introducing safety features into their products to prevent accidents such as electrical shocks, allergic reactions or poisoning. The underlying idea[21] is that consumers are entitled to purchase products without worrying that they may be hazardous or poisonous, or that a product may inflict any kind of bodily harm.

Government, business and civil society should thus ensure the safety and quality standards for goods that are sold and services that are rendered. In addition, they should encourage the development of facilities where essential consumer goods and services can be tested and certified in terms of:
- safety
- quality
- minimum performance standards.

For example, the South African Food Safety Initiative (FSI) of the Consumer Goods Council of South Africa (CGCSA) collaborates with stakeholders (in other words, industry and agriculture) to ensure that all the food that is produced and eventually sold in South Africa through official retail channels meets the highest standards of food safety and nutrition, and complies with legal requirements in our country. Recommendations and specifications are based on sound scientific evidence. Another example is South Africa's new food labelling regulations, which became law in 2010. The Department of Health thereby enforces stringent food labelling and safety requirements to ensure that the food that is sold in retail is safe for human consumption. If the safety of food is doubted for any reason whatsoever, it has to be withdrawn from sale. For example, with the recent listeriosis outbreak in South Africa in 2018, certain meat products were immediately withdrawn from retailers' shelves and consumers who had bought them already were encouraged to return these products for a refund.[22]

This kind of protection is not limited to food-related products. Policies require that manufacturers recall, replace, modify, substitute or compensate consumers for any hazardous or faulty products that may cause harm to or may threaten human life, such as faulty electrical appliances. Food labels are useful to identify batches or consignments of food that pose concerns. With the listeriosis incident, certain brand names were identified and clearly communicated in media to enable consumers to identify potentially harmful products.

A number of high-profile product safety events and product recalls in recent times have elevated public attention to, as well as interest in, the safety of the products that people consume, especially regarding the global supply chain and how that could cause or intensify safety risks scholars.[23] Fresh insights and new solutions to address these problems, such as updated regulations and standards, product life cycle management, traceability and recall management, as well as supplier relationships, are therefore inevitable.[24]

APPLICATION

Application of product safety regulations

In South Africa, product safety is regulated through specific minimum safety standards to which industry has to adhere.[25] When the cause of the listeriosis outbreak in 2018 was positively traced back to specific food products and brands, the problem was immediately brought to the attention of the public through communication in different types of media to ensure that consumers of all walks of life could be alerted. Consumers were instructed to return all products to the store for a refund – even products that were partly used – and to clean out their refrigerators with soapy water to prevent contamination.

Discussion questions

1. Why was the 'best before' date on food packaging irrelevant with regard to preserved meat products that were identified as unfit for consumption during the listeriosis outbreak?
2. Why would a retailer be unwilling to refund a consumer for preserved meat products other than those identified by the authorities during the listerioris outbreak?
3. Explain why consumers need not be hesitant to buy preserved meat products other than those identified by authorities during the Listeriosis outbreak.

The right to be informed

Ideally, consumers should not be exposed to incorrect, dishonest or misleading advertising and labelling. The Advertising Standards Authority of South Africa (also known as the ASA) is an independent body that is financed by the marketing communication industry. It has formulated a code of conduct for the local advertising industry that mostly relies on self-regulation (companies have to check their own operations carefully), although consumers may complain if any advertisements are found to be offensive. The ASA has a web site with clear links where complaints can be lodged (see the list of extra resources at the end of the chapter for the address of the web site). The body's code of conduct states that advertisements may not contain anything that does any of the following:

- Encourages or approves cruelty towards animals
- May cause harm (mentally, morally, physically or emotionally) to children or exploit them in any way
- Uses fear tactics without justifiable reason

In addition, it states that advertisements should be truthful and should not abuse consumers' trust or lack of knowledge. It is ultimately envisaged that consumers become empowered with factual information that enables them to make **informed consumer decisions**.[26] This inevitably depends on consumers' capability and willingness to search for relevant information as well as their insight in a specific product context so that they can raise their concerns if necessary.

DISCUSSION

Implications for the manufacturing and retail industry

The manufacturing and retail industry have to provide access to truthful product information, for example through proper labelling, brochures and by means of web sites. Regulations stipulate the type, format and content of the information that needs to be provided on the labels of various products. Of equal importance is the precondition that such information may not be misleading. Manufacturers may not, for example, claim that a product will contribute certain outcomes, such as hair growth, if this is not the case.

Any risks that may be associated with a product or its content should be stipulated, for example the presence of allergens in foods. The provision of correct and relevant information also applies to other product and consumption contexts, for example in terms of advertising and in contractual agreements, where confusing statements and false claims are not allowed.

Discussion questions

1. Look at the labels of three food products, for example a canned food, a frozen food and a dry food product such as sugar.
   - Compare the type of information on the different products and their labels.
   - Discuss the meaning and importance of the information on the various labels.
   - Discuss the usefulness of the product information for consumers with a relatively low level of education.
   - Discuss the implications when food carries no label at all.
2. Repeat the process for another product category such as clothing or household cleaning products.

The right to choose

Although a consumer's right to choose is supposed to be to an individual's advantage, it poses pertinent challenges and may be used as an excuse after irresponsible choice behaviour. For example, consumers can freely choose between imported and locally manufactured products, but may get annoyed when it takes longer to get parts to fix an imported product or when the spare parts are more expensive.

A major advantage is that consumers have the opportunity to choose from an array of products at competitive prices in the marketplace. The availability of products is not restricted without good reason and retailers stock local as well as imported goods and brands. Consumers are at liberty to purchase whichever product they prefer, but should take into consideration the consequences of their purchases and realise that imported goods have pertinent disadvantages, like those mentioned above.

Occasionally, goods are restricted by legislation, for example if it is evident that cheap child labour was used in the production process of certain textile products.

A challenge that is associated with freedom of choice is that a consumer needs to accept responsibility for the consequences of a purchase or product decision. For example, although various credit facilities are available for consumers who do not have the cash to secure an urgent transaction, a consumer should avoid more expensive credit options such as those provided by microlenders that charge excessive interest rates, even if the facilities are easy to access.[27] Consumers may enter into expensive credit agreements simply because they are enticed by the immediate pleasure that ownership of a desirable product offers (for example, owning a new smart phone) and do not take into account the stressful long-term implications (for example, coping with the increased financial demand of multiple monthly instalments that the new cell phone contract implies). Product choices may be restricted indirectly, for example when a consumer has a strong sense of social responsibility. A consumer may, for example, be committed to set personal, short-term preferences aside for the sake of others (for example, to support local businesses even if an imported alternative is more attractive), the environment (for example, choosing a product that consumes less electrical energy even if it is more expensive) or for long-term peace of mind (for example, saving up cash to purchase a cell phone later on to avoid using credit).

The Usury Act in South Africa allows microlending to the maximum of R10 000 per transaction, with a 36-month payback period, provided that loans are not settled using other forms of credit. The amount of interest required by the microlender is, however, not regulated, neither is it necessary for the lender to disclose all the additional charges. This is an example where consumers have the freedom to choose, but where they should be very cautious so as not to be trapped by high interest rates.[28]

DISCUSSION

In 2007, a restriction was imposed on the importation of textile products by South African retailers from Eastern countries in order to protect the South African textile industry, which was suffering owing to an increase of cheap imports from countries such as China.[29] For this restriction to succeed and to prevent a consumer uproar, measures had to be taken by local industry to ensure that their products were fit for their purpose, and that they met reasonable demands for durability, utility and reliability. In terms of imported goods, the consumer market needs the assurance that reliable after-sales service and spare parts are readily available for a considerable period of time (for example, spare parts for electrical appliances that may last up to 20 years).

Discussion questions
1. Are you aware of the country of origin of the clothing that you purchased most recently? Should this matter to you? Explain why.
2. Imagine your reaction if your local supermarket decided to offer only one brand and one size of each product on its shelves. Refer to chapters 4 to 6, which deal with individual and personal influences on consumer decision making and explain your feelings in terms of your personality, preferences, perceptions, attitude and product knowledge (previous experience).
3. Brands are not necessarily manufactured in the country of origin. For example, Pringle of Scotland (clothing) may be manufactured in South Africa and Swaziland, while Bernina of Switzerland (trains) may be manufactured in Japan. Why is this so?

The right to recourse and address
Ultimately, consumers should have the opportunity to voice concerns about products and services that do not perform adequately. Consumers' problems deserve sympathetic attention in the marketplace as well as at government level.[30] Government, business and civil society thus need to set up fair, inexpensive and accessible avenues for redress, and disputes should be resolved in a fair, efficient and informal manner.

Several avenues can be pursued by South Africans who wish to complain about poor service or product failure.[31] Some of the prominent organisations that can be contacted to lodge a formal complaint are listed and discussed in section 14.3.

DISCUSSION

Negative post-purchase product evaluations
When products (or services) do not perform adequately, consumers should receive compensation or a fair settlement of reasonable claims. Retailers therefore allow consumers to return faulty merchandise and/or to exchange and/or to repair it, provided there is proof of purchase. However, if consumers are unable to voice their concerns (for example, as a result of low literacy levels), assistance should be provided to resolve matters.

Discussion question
1. How can someone who purchases a new cell phone ensure that they get maximum benefit from the product guarantee and the service provider's after-sales service?
2. Share ideas about practical ways in which invoices could be filed for future use.
3. Share your experiences where the loss of an invoice has had dire consequences for you or your family.

14.2.4.6 The right to consumer education

Ideally, consumers should acquire structural (theoretical) and functional (how to) knowledge that empowers them to make informed, responsible decisions about goods and services. At the same time, they should be aware of their rights and responsibilities, and how to act on them. Inevitably some would need assistance to put a complaint in writing. Consumer education in schools (for example, in school subjects such as life orientation and consumer studies) and informative messages in the media (for example, in popular radio programmes, on news broadcasts and even on television programmes such as Carte Blanche) where issues are raised regularly, are very important to increase our awareness and knowledge about issues of everyday life that may be relevant to our consumer well-being. Such information can assist vulnerable consumer groups such as the young, inexperienced or those with lower education levels, provided they have access to the media.

DISCUSSION

The importance of consumer learning and experience

Consumer socialisation and product-related consumer socialisation occur over time as a result of exposure to and experience in the marketplace (in other words, informal learning). Formal learning (for example, notices in the media and educational television programmes that cover issues such as changes in interest rates and credit regulations) is necessary to expand consumers' knowledge frameworks in a dynamic marketplace where first-hand experience is not always possible.

Discussion questions

1. Discuss the effect of differences in product-related experience (specifically relating to electricity consumption) of two newlywed couples who are setting up their homes knowing that they will have to save on their electricity bills in order to make ends meet. One couple comes from an average-income household in an urban area, while the other couple comes from lower-income households which did not have electricity.
2. How does the product information provided to you by a friend, differ from the written information that can be acquired from a brochure?

The right to a healthy environment

Concern about the condition of the environment and how it may affect or threaten the health and well-being of consumers and future generations is acknowledged as a basic right. This pertains to the use of products.[32] It may, however, also be true for other situations, such as the short- and long-term implications of the production and storage of chemicals and potentially dangerous substances.[33] When new technologies are introduced (such as nano technology and radiation), they have to undergo rigorous testing to verify their safety for human consumption or use and to ensure that they will not cause problems such as cancer after long-term use. Even after thorough testing, concerned individuals or organisations may still voice their concerns about new products. This often leads to further investigation.

DISCUSSION

Diverse measures to encourage a healthy environment
Proper labelling and notices are required to warn consumers about potentially harmful situations or substances. South Africa, for example, requires clear notices of caution and safety precautions on products, in shopping malls and even on elevators. South Africa has also banned smoking – even vaping and E-cigarettes - in public areas through an Act that was passed in 1996, which restricts smoking in workplaces, restaurants and shopping malls, and which also prevents the advertising of tobacco products. The Act also stipulates penalties, which were implemented in 2001. The minimum legal age for purchasing tobacco products in South Africa, is 18 years. Further measures to curb smoking, include restrictions of smoking in the presence of children in enclosed spaces, including in private motor cars (https://www.iol.co.za/news/south-africa/western-cape/new-sa-smoking-laws-in-two-weeks-13640266).

Discussion question
1. Discuss the difference in the contributions of food legislation and anti-smoking legislation in terms of a consumer's health.
2. Discuss the apparent conflict between one's freedom to choose and restrictions against smoking in public places.

The right to representation

Not everybody possesses the skills or knowledge to negotiate or fend for themselves when problems arise, for example knowing how to address the problem when a newly purchased cell phone does not function as was explained by the service provider, or when the CD player of a newly purchased home theatre system stops working after a few months. Often, a consumer does not know how or where to seek assistance, and is not aware that they will be refunded if they raise the problem appropriately, at the service provider, with proof of payment.

Because it is impossible for consumers in general to be acquainted with all the legal aspects that are associated with product sales, consumers' interests are represented by means of government policy and through consumer groups or organisations (see section 14.3) that are able to act on consumers' behalf. The outcomes of long legislatory processes are then captured by legislation to which consumers have access, for example on web sites, and retailers and service providers have to honour these laws. Legislation is continually updated and revised if necessary.

14.3 SOUTH AFRICAN CONSUMER ORGANISATIONS

The most prominent consumer organisations that operate on different levels in South Africa are discussed below. Relevant consumer organisations can be identified through the following useful links: http://www.saconsumercomplaints.co.za/contact/ as well as https://www.icasa.org.za/pages/consumer-complaints-procedure

14.3.1 Provincial Consumer Affairs Offices

Provincial Consumer Affairs Offices operate countrywide.[34] Their role is to:

* investigate and resolve consumer complaints of alleged unfair business practices
* create awareness of consumer rights and responsibilities
* educate consumers on how they should proclaim their rights and protect their interests when buying products and services
* refer unresolved matters to the Consumer Affairs Court for adjudication.

Very importantly, they can disclose whether a specific company or contractor that a consumer intends doing business with (for example, a swimming pool contractor) has a previous history of complaints against it. They can be contacted to intervene in disputes over contracts and the quality of products or services.

The correct procedure to follow when a problem occurs is to approach the branch manager or customer care office of the organisation first. If the situation is not resolved, the nearest provincial consumer affairs office can be contacted. Trained staff can provide advice on consumer rights and intervene on behalf of consumers if necessary.

14.3.2 The Department of Trade and Industry

The Bill of Rights, which acknowledges the eight internationally recognised consumer rights (as listed previously) and which aims to protect the rights of every South African citizen, is a cornerstone of the Constitution of South Africa Act 108 of 1996. The Department of Trade and Industry (DTI) is involved in the implementation and protection of consumers' rights in South Africa, including legislative issues.[35] The DTI customer contact centre[36] handles consumers' enquiries. Consumers are also protected by legislation in the areas of industry regulation, consumer credit and product standards, as follows:

* The Competition Act 89 of 1998,[37] which was updated in 2016, promotes and upholds competition to ensure that consumers are offered ample product choices and competitive prices. It aims to provide all South Africans equal opportunity to participate fairly in the national economy and to achieve a more effective and efficient economy in South Africa. For example, the Competition Board would never allow any of the well-known supermarket groups or any of the prominent banks to take over one of their competitors, even if all parties agreed and they could afford to do so, because this would create a conglomerate that could manipulate prices to the detriment of consumers.
* The Consumer Protection Act 68 of 2008[38] promotes a fair, accessible and sustainable marketplace for consumer products and services, encourages responsible consumer behaviour and provides a reliable framework for consumer transactions and agreements. This act specifically forbids certain unfair marketing and business practices, and provides for advanced standards of consumer information as well as the co-ordination of laws that pertain to consumer transactions and agreements. It was enforced by the establishment of the National Consumer Commission.
* The Counterfeit Goods Act 37 of 1997[39] prevents trade in counterfeit goods to protect owners of trade marks, copyright and so on under the

Merchandise Marks Act 17 of 1941 and so safeguard intellectual property rights, for example counterfeit CDs and DVDs (also referred to as pirate copies) and knock-offs of sportswear, watches, handbags and perfumes that are all clever imitations of popular brands. Cases where counterfeit goods are seized upon arrival in harbours or where they are sold on the street and at flea markets are frequently brought to the public's attention. Consumers who willingly purchase these fake goods are, in fact, encouraging these illegal activities. In November 2017, a pirate copy of the book *The president's keepers* by Jaques Pauw was distributed to curious readers online and thousands of readers got access to it without paying for it. A summary of the act can be accessed at: https://ossafrica.com/esst/index. php?title=Summary_of_the_Counterfeit_Goods_Act%2C_no._37_of_1997

- The Estate Agency Affairs Act 112 of 1976[40] protects consumers who buy or sell property through estate agents from exploitation, misconduct and undue pressure to enter into contractual agreements. Estate agents have to abide by certain rules to prevent undue pressure, exploitation and confusion during their interaction with potential home buyers.
- The National Consumer Credit Protection Act 134 of 2009[41] that was signed in April 2009 has changed the way in which credit is obtained and issued in South Africa. It is intended to limit credit consumption, to curb credit abuse and to prevent consumer exploitation. The act aims to disallow reckless credit granting and to enable debt restructure for consumers who have become over-indebted; to regulate credit information; to establish registration of a credit bureau, credit providers and debt counselling services; to create national norms and standards relating to consumer credit; to promote a consistent enforcement framework for consumer credit; to establish the National Credit Regulator (NCR) and the National Consumer Tribunal;[42] to repeal the Usury Act 73 of 1968 and the Credit Agreements Act 75 of 1980; and to provide for related incidental matters.
- The National Gambling Act 7 of 2004[43] defines gambling to distinguish it clearly from electronic and board games and exerts pertinent limitations on gambling, for example the minimum age of gamblers, aiming to curb excessive gambling. The Gambling Act 33 of 1996[44] protects consumers against too much exposure to gambling. It restricts advertising of gambling in South Africa (similar to the restriction of the advertising of tobacco products).
- The Housing Development Schemes for Retired Persons Act 65 of 1988 guards the interests of retired people who have invested in housing development schemes to prevent the exploitation of this vulnerable market segment, who have limited opportunity to recover financially if a deal goes wrong. Information is available at: https://www.thedti.gov.za/business_regulation/acts/housing_act.pdf.
- The Liquor Act 59 of 2003 that came into being in 2004[45] and the Liquor Act 27 of 1989 ascribes where (for example, the type of store, restaurant or public facility), when (trading hours) and to whom (age limitation) liquor may be sold. The act emphasises social responsibility and aims to combat alcohol abuse.
- The Merchandise Marks Act 17 of 1941[46] was last amended in 2002 and aims to protect consumers against misleading packaging and labelling.

- The Property Time Sharing Control Act 75 of 1983[47] was introduced when time-sharing schemes became popular in the 1980s.
- The Sale and Service Matters Amendment Act 80 of 1995[48] updates the 1964 act to regulate lay-by agreements and controls the sale, display and marking of goods.

Several other important acts exist, indicating that South African consumers are well protected, although this does not negate consumers' responsibility to take ownership of their decisions prior, during and post their purchase of products and services.

14.3.3   The National Consumer Commission

The National Consumer Commission (NCC)[49] was established in terms of Section 85 of the Consumer Protection Act 68 of 2008. It operates as a state organisation within the public administration of South Africa, but also operates outside the public service with jurisdiction throughout the Republic of South Africa.

The NCC aims to promote a fair, accessible and sustainable marketplace for consumer products and services, and therefore establishes national norms and standards relating to consumer protection; attends to improved standards of consumer information; forbids certain unfair marketing and business practices; promotes responsible consumer behaviour; and provides a consistent legislation and enforcement framework relating to consumer transactions.

14.3.4   The National Consumer Forum

The National Consumer Forum (NCF)[50] investigates complaints on behalf of consumers. It is a non-profit and independent organisation that is devoted to the protection and promotion of consumer rights and interests in South Africa.

14.3.5   The South African National Consumer Union

In 1985, the South African National Consumer Union (SANCU) (also discussed in section 14.2.3) endorsed and adopted the eight basic consumer rights that are internationally recognised as the United Nations Guidelines for Consumer Protection. They propose certain requirements in terms of locally produced goods and services as well as imports, including physical safety; promotion and protection of consumers' economic interests; standards for the safety and quality of consumer goods and services; distribution facilities for essential consumer goods and services; measures enabling consumers to obtain redress; education and information programmes; and control measures relating to specific areas, for example food, water, pharmaceuticals, pesticides, chemicals and environmental information.

14.3.6   The National Consumer Tribunal

This independent body strives to attain fairness and justice for everyone in the consumer and credit market. It concerns itself with all credit-related issues in terms of the National Credit Act 34 of 2005, for example credit applications, applications for credit relief and complaints. A decision made by the National

Consumer Tribunal has the same status as one made by the High Court of South Africa. Anyone who disobeys an order of the tribunal can be fined or put in prison for up to ten years.

14.3.7   The National Credit Regulator

The introduction of the National Credit Regulator (NCR) (discussed in section 14.3.2) has changed the face of credit in South Africa since its introduction through the National Credit Act 34 of 2005. The NCR is responsible for the registration and regulation of credit providers, credit bureaus and debt counsellors. Before 2005, consumers were not really restricted in terms of the credit transactions that they were willing to adopt and no official credit record existed to monitor consumers' creditworthiness (for example, whether they honoured monthly instalments). Retailers therefore willingly offered credit to people irrespective of their financial circumstances.[51] Only when consumers were 'blacklisted' at credit bureaus because they fell into arrears did retailers refuse credit. When credit rates soared at the turn of the century, many households were in desperate financial circumstances, and some even lost their cars and homes as a result of excessive credit that they could not afford.

The Office of the Credit Ombud[52] attends to consumers' and businesses' complaints related to inaccurate or incomplete credit bureau information, or when a consumer has a disagreement with a credit provider. The Credit Ombud expects consumers to try to resolve their complaint with service provider or credit bureau first. When they are still unhappy or do not get satisfactory response within 20 working days, the Credit Ombud can be contacted by submitting the complaint and related evidence to them in writing.

14.3.8   Popular complaint sites

Several popular, easily accessible web sites exist where consumers are able to voice concerns, complaints and issues relatively painlessly, for example:
- Hello Peter (http://www.hellopeter.com; admin@hellopeter.com)
- GetClosure (http://www.getclosure.co.za)

Most newspapers have consumer columns and many also deal with consumer complaints, and their web sites may provide more details about their involvement, for example:
- the *Beeld* newspaper (e-mail complaints to totudiens@beeld.com)
- *Rapport* newspaper (e-mail complaints to http://www.ecommerceawards)
- the *Sowetan* newspaper (http://www.callupcontact.com/b/business/Sowetan/154634)

14.4 THE RESPONSIBILITIES OF CONSUMERS

The multiple measures that have been put in place over the years to protect the interests of South African consumers do not imply that consumers can refrain from accepting personal responsibility, commitment and involvement for their buying and consumption decisions.

14.4.1 Personal responsibilities

Consumerism is not meant to encourage the idea that retailers and industry are the only role-players who have an obligation to behave responsibly. Optimal performance in the marketplace also requires consumers to accept personal responsibility[53] for their buying and consumption behaviour.

Promoting a 'no excuse' culture

The underlying principles of consumerism reduce the risk that consumers may encounter in the marketplace and lessen anxiety because consumers are protected by systems that are meant to prevent disaster.[54] It remains important to ascertain that:

- consumers are well informed about products and services that they wish to purchase before entering into any purchase agreement or transaction
- consumers become more vigilant and co-operative to strengthen the voice of consumers in the marketplace, that is, socially driven activity that suggests participation in community-based organisations
- consumers need to become critically aware of consumer-related issues so that they become discerning shoppers who compare the quality of products, query prices and acquaint themselves with the terms and conditions of sales agreements and contracts
- consumers take action in the correct ways when problems arise so that matters can be resolved to prevent the reoccurrence of similar problems in the future and to prevent exploitation
- consumers behave in a socially responsible way[55] and understand the implications of their buying and consumption behaviour in terms of others and the environment.

Proper complaint procedures

Although consumers are encouraged to voice concerns and complaints when products or services are inferior or do not perform optimally, proper complaint procedures need to be followed[56] to ensure the expected outcome of the action.

A complainant is firstly required to try to solve the problem by bringing it to the attention of a responsible official or manager at the relevant organisation (for example, the store where the product was purchased). It might require a written report of the complaint that:

- indicates the nature of the complaint
- provides the background of the transaction and user experience
- specifies steps that were taken to prevent the problem or to solve it
- mentions the names of the personnel involved in the purchase transaction and previous attempts to raise the complaint (if possible)
- provides the date of the purchase or transaction
- includes reference to invoices and correspondence (if relevant) as well as personal contact details.

Facts should be presented in a logical order and should be relevant. Consumers are advised to allow approximately 30 working days (six weeks) to resolve a complaint that cannot be rectified immediately. If a consumer purchases an electric kettle and finds that it leaks, it may be returned to the store in its original packaging, with proof of purchase, within one week. It will most likely be replaced immediately. If, however, the kettle starts leaking after a few months while still under guarantee, the faulty kettle needs to be returned to the store with proof of purchase, after which it will be sent to the manufacturer to be checked and repaired or replaced. This will be done free of charge provided the kettle was used according to instructions and was not tampered with. The conditions of purchase of every product should be read carefully to ensure that a consumer abides with them and the instructions for use, otherwise the retailer and the manufacturer will show little empathy when problems occur.

The following tips and advice are provided by the Fair Trade Commission:[57]

- Shop around before purchasing. Businesses will not refund if a consumer finds a product cheaper elsewhere afterwards. They will only give redress under certain conditions, for example if a product is faulty or unfit for its intended purpose.
- 'No exchange, no refund' notices are illegal in any form – even for items that are on sale.
- Never sign a contract before reading its entire content and never trust a salesperson or representative to complete a blank form on your behalf after signing it.
- Always file receipts, cancelled cheques, instruction booklets and contracts that could be useful in problem solving.
- Customers have certain rights of redress, for example to have a faulty product repaired, replaced or to get a refund. It is not compulsory to accept a credit note.
- Customers deal with the seller of a product or service, never with the manufacturer. For example, if one experiences damage after a pest controller has sprayed your lawn, it is not your responsibility to argue with the manufacturer of the chemicals that are blamed for the disaster.
- Even when buying second-hand goods, potential problems have to be disclosed at the point of sale.

DISCUSSION

1. Give an example of a situation where a consumer will not be able to return a product to a retailer for a refund.
2. Give an example of products where the consumer would need professional assistance to install the product before use.
3. Give an example of 'proper maintenance of products'.
4. Share your thoughts on how consumers could logically file 'proof of purchase' of products for future use.
5. Share your thoughts about an incident where you (or a member of your family) neglected to read the preconditions of a purchase carefully OR when you benefitted from a store's return and exchange policy.

14.4.2   Social responsibilities

The emergence of consumerism has created a so-called 'blameless consumer',[58] where the idea is created that a consumer may never be found guilty despite having made many mistakes. For example, a consumer selects a cheaper radio in the retail store because it is a display model that could save him some money, and then later demands the same guarantee as is provided by the manufacturer for sealed units, even though the different purchase conditions were clearly explained beforehand. Such unfair claims create unnecessary problems for the retailer.

In recent years, much attention has been focused on the conflict between our **consumer selves** and our **citizen selves**, which is best explained in terms of concerns over environmental issues. Consumers, based on their citizen selves, generally agree that pollution should be controlled, and that damage to our rivers and natural habitat should be prevented.[59] However, despite the apparent awareness of South African consumers of the causes of environmental deterioration,[60] they struggle to accept the measures that are required to address these problems (due to their consumer selves), for example not wanting to pay higher prices for fuel substitutes that are environmentally friendly[61] or to buy fresh food products that are less than perfect as a result of alternative farming methods. In business markets, consumers contribute to global warming directly and indirectly. For example, they demand goods and services that put strain on our natural resources, and waste precious resources such as electricity and water. Many consumers also generate unnecessary waste by not participating in recycling because it takes effort.[62] Responsible consumption requires individuals to change from their 'consumer selves' into 'citizen selves',[63] which demands a new way of thinking and a willingness to adapt their lifestyles and cultivate behaviour patterns that support and enhance the necessary changes.[64]

To be socially responsible, consumers need to adopt a **global perspective** in terms of their buying and consumption behaviour. Consumers will have to become less materialistic and refrain from purchasing goods simply because they can afford to or want to, or because they enjoy accumulating things. Consumers will have to start behaving as citizens of the planet. Instead of focusing only on their own needs, they will have to learn to care about the consequences that their buying, consumption and disposal behaviour has for other individuals, other communities and their country as well as for the future and future generations. This process requires a mind shift and a life-long commitment to adapting their lifestyles. It may be trying in the beginning, but the outcomes promise to be extremely rewarding.[65] Here are some suggestions in this regard:

- Consumers should make a long-term commitment to reconsider their buying patterns and how they dispose of goods that have become redundant because they are broken, outmoded or no longer needed in order to reduce waste and pollution.
- Consumers should make objective, concrete product evaluation criteria (for example, price and brand) secondary to the implied advantages of a product for others and the environment, for example by considering a more expensive product because it might promote job creation in a poverty-stricken community.

- Consumers should question the merit of a purchase in terms of its origin and competitors in the market, for example country of origin or type of manufacturer, understanding that cheaper imported products may put local producers out of business, which will result in job losses. In the South African context, Afrocentricity refers to a value orientation where groups of people support each other and in so doing, form an inclusive group to reflect a unique collective African will. This is contrary to a Eurocentric approach, which in essence is associated with individualism and materialism. In an African context, the unique concept of *ubuntu* ('a person can only be a person through other people') illustrates the 'domino effect' of consumers' behavioural patterns (people are so supportive of each other that they are willing to stand and fall together).
- Ethical and moral concerns related to a purchase decision should take precedence over other concerns, that is human, social and environmental considerations should become more important than time and money, even if consumers can afford to pay more. For example, consumers must become willing to pay a reasonable price for a handcrafted product from an entrepreneur, rather than bargaining for the lowest price possible because they know that the crafters are desperate to sell their products.
- Consumers should guard against excessive and compulsive spending. They should prioritise saving and investing rather than borrowing.

In order to succeed in protecting our environment for future generations, the following assumptions of a global perspective[66] should guide consumers' everyday consumption choices:
- *Perspective consciousness:* People do not share the same sentiments and the same view of the world. A global perspective can therefore not be forced onto people whose own money is involved and who may have to make sacrifices to support the cause of saving the environment (for example, feeling obliged to purchase locally produced goods when they actually prefer the imported goods). Reluctant consumers will have to be convinced by the example of consumers who are in favour of a global perspective.
- *State-of-the-planet awareness:* Consumers should become mindful of current and emerging world conditions, for example understanding that certain packaging materials can harm the environment and that excessive electricity consumption increases pollution and depletes our resources. Consumers should thus be more willing to make sacrifices in using environmentally friendly alternatives such as energy-saving globes, although they prefer the brightness of the light produced by the other globes.
- *Cross-cultural awareness and diversity:* Lifestyles that seem socially desirable because they are promoted as such in the media should be avoided. Emerging consumers in developing communities are generally eager to adopt Westernised lifestyles to signify their status and progress. This has, however, resulted in major changes in the eating patterns of many cultural groups, for example the Chinese, and black population groups in South Africa, who have switched from traditional diets (which are low in fat and sugar, and high

in fibre) to Westernised diets (which include more refined and processed foods). As a result, problems such as tooth decay, obesity, hypertension, diabetes and cancer are now plentiful in communities that have not experienced such problems in the past.

- *Knowledge of global dynamics:* When consumers insist on imported brands (for example, clothing) for their so-called status value, money flows out of the country instead of supporting local structures.
- *Awareness of changing choices to reduce risks:* Technology has brought significant changes to agriculture and food production in recent years and has introduced revolutionary processes to improve food quality and to enhance crops. This has unfortunately also increased concerns about potential dangers associated with these processes (for example, irradiation of foods and genetic modification of crops), which have not necessarily been investigated completely. In order to make informed choices in terms of the consequences of such practices and the risks that might be involved, consumers have to insist on having access to the relevant information.
- *A balance between demand and supply:* At present, fresh produce is imported at ridiculous costs to meet consumer demands because consumers expect stores to have fruit and vegetables such as avocados available whether they are in season locally or not. The financial implication of these imports is higher prices, while they are also detrimental to our environment in terms of the carbon and methane gases produced during transportation and refrigeration (storage). Ideally, consumers should optimise the use of products that are locally produced and that are in season rather than demanding products that have to be sourced from other countries. This would also support the local economy.
- *Voluntary simplicity and more modest lifestyles:* This would make it much easier to promote socially responsible consumption behaviour, in other words, to motivate people to become more conscious about environmental issues. Often, money spent on cell phones and sophisticated technology purchased to impress others could have been used more appropriately for the household education and food budget.[67] The **Diderot effect** in the clothing industry refers to consumers' continuous replacement of clothing items to keep up with fashion trends. Consumers have to understand the implications of their choices and actions in terms of the global future and refrain from participating in a 'throw away' and 'replace' mentality. Buying second-hand items is something that is simply not done in higher socio-economic groups, while many useful items are simply discarded and wasted.
- *Complementary technology:* Support of local, indigenous technology should be encouraged in all our purchase decisions. However, globalisation fans consumers' desire to update products in their homes, for example to acquire the latest technology (such as a more sophisticated microwave oven) and to purchase well-known brands (which may be imported and are not necessarily better in terms of performance and style). Many consumers'

home situations do not necessarily merit the use of extravagant products. For example, a consumer may purchase a sophisticated washing machine, but only use the basic washing cycle. Money spent on extravagant features or products is therefore often wasted.

* *International reciprocity:* This means supporting the upliftment of poorer communities by paying reasonable prices for their produce and respecting their dignity rather than celebrating so-called bargains.

14.5 RESEARCH METHODS USED IN INVESTIGATING CONSUMERISM

The COPING scale[68] was developed to investigate the extent to which a consumer would cope with stress after a difficult encounter with a service provider. Information of this kind is extremely useful when a store is trying to improve its service and the support that it offers consumers. For example, this scale can be used to determine whether a specific sample (for example, consumers with a relatively low level of education versus more educated consumers) is able to cope with a specific situation, for example transportation to the Gautrain stations. Consumers' coping in general is determined by calculating the mean score (average) across the entire scale (including all of the items). Consumers' ability to cope with specific dimensions of the problem can be determined by calculating the mean score for each factor.

The original scale consists of three primary factors with sub-categories, which were identified through a specific statistical procedure called factor analysis and rigorously tested to ensure internal consistency. In the example below, only one of the three factors (*active coping*, which contains 16 items) is shown. This construct is further distinguished in terms of three sub-divisions: *actions taken* (7 items), *rational thinking* (5 items) and *emotions involved* (4 items). When used in research, the items are usually scrambled, so that the respondent (the person completing the questionnaire) cannot easily relate one statement to the next and is therefore not influenced by a previous statement. During analysis, the items that actually belong together as one dimension of the scale (for example, action) are then regrouped statistically for the purpose of calculations and interpretations. For example, calculating a mean score for Action by means of the average score across the 7 items for the sample, and this mean would range between 1 and 7 due to the 7 increments on the scale.

One hence has to calculate a mean for each of these dimensions individually (*action, rational thinking* etc.) to conclude, for example, that the overall mean of 4.6 suggests that a consumer's coping skills are slightly above average, but when looking at the individual dimensions, namely *action* (M = 5.0), *rational thinking* (M = 5.6) and *positive thinking* (M = 3.2), it is clear that a consumer's active coping is jeopardised by his or her lack of *positive thinking*. It is then easier to attend to the underlying shortcoming as one then knows what to attend to.

RESEARCH BOX 14.1

Read the scenario below, then complete the section of the scale that follows. For the purpose of this exercise, the items have not been scrambled. Once you have done that, calculate the mean (average) per sub-category. For example, for actions taken, calculate the total across the seven items and divide by seven. However, this merely indicates your own coping ability in that sub-category. When this scale is completed by a group of consumers, the means are calculated across the whole sample, for example all the students in the class (which would give you an idea of whether your ability to cope differs from that of the rest of the class) or for a much larger population (for example, all students on campus or all students in South Africa).

Scenario: Imagine that you recently purchased a new smart phone despite your tight budget. After two weeks, the phone started malfunctioning. When you took it back to the service provider, the salesperson indicated that your phone had been exposed to excessive moisture, which is not covered by the guarantee, and so the phone would not be replaced.

Higher-order factor 1: Active coping						
Action	Strongly disagree	Disagree	Unlikely	Uncertain	Probably	Agree	Strongly agree
1. Concentrate on ways the problem could be solved	1	2	3	4	5	6	7
2. Try to make a plan of action	1	2	3	4	5	6	7
3. Generate potential solutions	1	2	3	4	5	6	7
4. Think about the best way to handle things	1	2	3	4	5	6	7
5. Concentrate my efforts on doing something about it	1	2	3	4	5	6	7
6. Do what has to be done	1	2	3	4	5	6	7
7. Follow a plan to make things better	1	2	3	4	5	6	7
Rational thinking							
1. Analyse the problem before reacting	1	2	3	4	5	6	7
2. Try to step back from the problem and be objective	1	2	3	4	5	6	7
3. Try to control my emotions	1	2	3	4	5	6	7
4. Try to keep my feelings from controlling my actions	1	2	3	4	5	6	7
5. Would use restraint to avoid acting harshly	1	2	3	4	5	6	7
Positive thinking							
1. Try to look at the bright side of things	1	2	3	4	5	6	7
2. Focus on the positive aspects of the problem	1	2	3	4	5	6	7
3. Look for the good in what has happened	1	2	3	4	5	6	7
4. Try to make the best of the situation	1	2	3	4	5	6	7

SUMMARY

This chapter explained the different meanings of the term 'consumerism'. It considered consumerism as a social movement, and addressed concerns about the well-being of consumers and their ability to cope in a highly sophisticated global marketplace.

The original basic rights of consumers that were introduced in the US as part of J.F. Kennedy's presidential campaign (namely that consumers have the right to choose, to be informed and to be heard as well as to be safe) were discussed. Since then, attention has been focused on consumers' needs, vulnerabilities and responsibilities in countries across the world, including South Africa. This chapter presented information about consumer organisations and interest groups that are operational on various levels to oversee issues such as legislation, regulations and consumer complaints in our country.

The eight internationally accepted consumer rights that direct the operations of consumer organisations across the world were discussed in terms of practical examples in a South African context to explain the implications for consumers as well as manufacturers and retailers. Appropriate channels (names of organisations and the addresses of their web sites) through which consumers could be assisted in resolving problems experienced in the marketplace were discussed.

SELF-ASSESSMENT QUESTIONS

1. Why are the two definitions for 'consumerism' not entirely unrelated?
2. Briefly explain the expanded list of consumers' rights that has been adopted internationally and that also applies in South Africa.
3. Which of the approaches of consumer organisations that are explained by the authors Darley and Johnson in section 4.2.2.2 are particularly relevant to South Africa? Why?
4. Four phases of the consumer movement are distinguished. Based on evidence of established consumer organisations in South Africa, which phase has South Africa progressed to? Explain your view.
5. Describe a primary characteristic of a typical boycott group and provide an example.
6. How does a 'consumer's right to safety' apply to the marketing and sales of the following product categories: food products in supermarkets, food served in restaurants, electrical appliances, toys and pesticides?
7. Discuss the task of the National Credit Regulator and explain how that task impacts on South African consumers' use of credit.
8. Briefly explain what is meant by a 'no-excuse' consumer culture?
9. Explain the difference between a 'consumer self' and a 'citizen self'.

EXPERIENTIAL EXERCISE

1. You have seen that a small general dealer in your suburb sells cigarettes to children in their school uniforms. How would you appeal against this practice and where would you lodge your complaint other than to talk to the dealer, who refuses to take you seriously?
2. Having done some holiday work at a prominent clothing retailer, you have gained considerable experience in the customer care division where you have witnessed consumers' agony when they became over indebted and struggled to pay their monthly instalments. You are now concerned about your friends in class who have decided to enter into revolving credit accounts at this retailer to take advantage of the opportunity to pay for their purchases over an extended period of six months, interest free. How would you alert them about the danger associated with this type of credit? How relevant is the National Credit Regulator in terms of these types of credit?

CASE STUDY 1

Poor customer service

Ann purchased processed meats from her local supermarket for the month and stored them in the freezer as she normally does. When she became aware of the listeriosis outbreak, she took the products to the same retailer as she was advised to do. However, the retailer demanded proof of purchase and was not willing to refund packets of which the seals were broken. When she spoke to her friend Lisa later on, Lisa said that another salesperson at the same store attended to her product return very efficiently, without demanding proof of payment or any other demands as far as the products were concerned, as long as they were part of a selected list of brands.

Discussion questions

1. Which of Ann's consumer rights were violated? Explain.
2. What should Ann do to resolve the problem?
3. Ann's disappointment was directed at the store, but who was actually at fault?

CASE STUDY 2

Misleading advertising

A prominent hypermarket advertised 'specials' in the local community newspaper during the first week of September 2017, including a deal on two brands of wine. When arriving at the store on the first day that these wines were supposed to be available, a customer found that neither of them were on the shelves. A shop assistant explained to him that one wine was out of stock and that the store had never stocked the other wine. The customer was furious because he had driven quite a distance to purchase a box of each of the wine brands that he had selected. The store manager wanted to give him two bottles of wine to calm him down, but he refused.

Discussion questions

1. What did the store do wrong?
2. What actions could be taken by the customer to address this type of misconduct?
3. The customer rejected the two bottles of free wine. Was he being unreasonable? Explain.

EXPLANATORY VIDEOS

Find more information about legislation and organisations that are meant to protect and assist consumers by visiting the following web sites:

- SA CPA consumer intro: https://youtu.be/JKKbynfy2pA?list=PLKaKA_r2vI-CJPeOmWN5XJLnGE8AeBNHx
- Definitions you need to know: https://youtu.be/NxBl2OFQl2I?list=PLKaKA_r2vI-CJPeOmWN5XJLnGE8AeBNHx
- The 8 basic consumer rights: https://youtu.be/4YbPgCdiDNg?list=PLKaKA_r2vI-CJPeOmWN5XJLnGE8AeBNHx
- 8 basic consumer rights (Econ 20.1): https://youtu.be/e_X6ue0qoLU

INFORMATIVE WEB SITES

- Consumer Protection Act 68 of 2008: http://www.iol.co.za/news/south-africa/how-the-new-consumer-law-protects-you-1.1020996?pageNumber=1
- National Consumer Credit Protection Act 134 of 2009: http://www.comlaw.gov.au/Details/C2009A00134
- http://www.thedti.gov.za/ (activities of the Department of Trade and Industry relating to the following: Competition Act 89 of 1998, Consumer Protection Act 68 of 2008, Counterfeit Goods Act 37 of 1997, Estate Agency Affairs Act 112 of 1976, National Consumer Credit Protection Act 134 of 2009, Gambling Act 33 of 1996, Housing Development Schemes for Retired Persons Act 65 of 1988, Liquor Act 59 of 2003, Liquor Act 27 of 1989, Merchandise Marks Act 17 of 1941, Property Time Sharing Control Act 75 of 1983, Sale and Service Matters Act 25 of 1964, Trade Metrology Act 77 of 1973, Trade Practices Act 76 of 1976)
- National Consumer Commission: http://www.thencc.gov.za/
- Consumer Fair group, which involves two groups of companies: National Consumer Fair Consulting Enterprises and National Consumer Fair Financial Services: http://www.ncf.org.za/
- South African National Consumer Union: http://www.sancu.co.za/
- National Consumer Tribunal: http://www.thenct.org.za/
- National Credit Regulator: http://www.ncr.org.za

- The Credit Ombud: http://www.creditombud.org.za
- Popular consumers complaint sites such as Hello Peter (http://www.hellopeter.com) and the consumer columns of major newspapers, for example, *Beeld* (http://www.beeld.com/Suid-Afrika/Nuus/Die-klagtes-20091015)
- Advertising Association of South Africa: http://www.asasa.org.za
- The Restaurant Association of South Africa and the Consumer Protection Act: https://www.foodandhospitalityafrica.co.za/partners.php as well as https://www.yambu.co.za/ombudsman/

REFERENCES

1 Ede, F.O. & Calcich, S.E. African-American consumerism. Proceedings of the 2000 Academy of Marketing Science (AMS) Annual Conference, 113–122. Available at: https://books.google.co.za/books?isbn=3319118854 (accessed on 1 August 2018).

2 Armstrong, G., Kotler, P., Harker, M. & Brennan, R. 2009. *Marketing: An introduction.* Harlow, Essex: Pearson, 127.

3 McIlhenny, J.H. 1990. The new consumerism: How will business respond? *At Home with Consumers*, 11(5): 9–10.

4 Scott Maynes, E. 1972. Consumerism: Origin and research implications. Available at: http://www.econ.umn.edu/library/mnpapers/1972-17.pdf (accessed on 5 July 2018).

5 Onah in Kaynak, E. 1985. Some thoughts on consumerism in developed and less developed countries. *International Marketing Review*, 2(2): 15–30.

6 Jones, P., Hillier, D., Comfort, D. & Eastwood, I. 2005. Sustainable retailing and tourism. *Management Research News*, 28(1): 34–44.

7 Darley, W.K. & Johnson, D.M. 1993. Cross-national comparison of consumer attitudes toward consumerism in four developing countries. *Journal of Consumer Affairs*, 27: 37–54. doi:10.1111/j.1745-6606.1993.tb00736.x.

8 Ibid.

9 Darley & Johnson, op. cit.

10 Ibid.

11 https://www.legalrights.co.za/wp.../NATIONAL-CREDIT-ACT-NO.-34-OF-2005.pdf

12 Ibid.

13 Herrmann, R.O., Walsh, E.J. & Warland, R.H. 1985. The organisations of the consumer movement: A comparative perspective. In Maynes, S.E. *The frontier of research in the consumer interest.* Columbia: American Council on Consumer Interests, 469– 494.

14 Murtagh, C. & Lukehart, C. 2011. Co-op America's boycott organizer's guide. Available at: http://www.amerikaos.com/boycottguide.html (accessed 5 July 2018).

15 https://nader.org/

16 http://www.history.com/this-day-in-history/unsafe-at-any-speed-hits-bookstores

17 http://home.mweb.co.za/sa/sancu/more.html

18 http://www.sancu.co.za/

19 Ede & Calcich, op. cit.

20 https://www.thenewspaper.co.za/tag/western-cape-water-supply-system/

21 Purnhagen, K.P. 2013. Beyond threats to health: May consumers' interests in safety trump fundamental freedoms in information on foodstuffs? Reflections on *Karl Berger v Freistaat Bayern. European Law Review*, October. Available at: https://ssrn.com/abstract=2276899 (accessed on 5 July 2018); Kar H.L., Wuyang, H., Leigh, J. & Goddard, M.E. 2012. US consumers' preference and willingness to pay for country of origin labeled beef steak and food safety enhancements. *Canadian Journal of Agricultural Economics*, 61(1): 93–118; Polinsky, A.M. & Shavell, S. 2009. The uneasy case for product liability. Available at: http://www.law.harvard.edu/programs/olin_center/papers/647_Shavell.php (accessed on 5 July 2018).

22 http://www.who.int/csr/don/28-march-2018-listeriosis-south-africa/en/

23 Marucheck, A., Greis, N., Mena, C. & Cai, L. 2011. Product safety and security in the global supply chain: Issues, challenges and research opportunities. *Journal of Operations Management*, 29(7–8): 707–720.

24 Ibid.

25 https://foodfacts.org.za/regulation-food-safety-quality/

26 Clemonsa, E.K. & Gaob, G. 2008. Consumer informedness and diverse consumer purchasing behaviors: Traditional mass-market, trading down, and trading out into the long tail. *Electronic Commerce Research and Applications*, 7(1): 3; Skerlos, S.J. & Michalek, J.J. 2005. A step toward building a sustainable economy by informing consumer purchasing decisions at the point of sale. Available at: http://www.cmu.edu/me/ddl/AWARE/AWARE-EPA-P3-Final-Phase1-Report.pdf (accessed on 6 July 2018).

27 Vethecan, M. 2014.The problems (and promise) of microfinance. Available at: economicstudents.com/2014/04/the-problems-and-promise-of-microfinance/ (accessed on 6 July 2018); Mashigo, P. 2006. The debt spiral in the poor households in South Africa. *International Indigenous Journal of Entrepreneurship, Advancement, Strategy and Education*, 2(1): 59–79; Lin, Q.C. & Lee, J. 2004. Consumer information search when making investment decisions. *Financial Services Review*, 13: 319–332.

28 Debtcom. 2015. The rules of microlending. Available at: http://www.debtcom.co.za/the-rules-of-microlending-19032015/ (accessed on 6 July 2018).

29 Van Eeden, J. 2009. South African quotas on Chinese clothing and textiles economic evidence. *Econex. Trade Competition and Applied Economics*. Research note 9.

30 McKaiser, E. 2016. Money matters: Do South African consumers complain enough about prices? Available at: http://www.702.co.za/articles/193078/money-matters-do-south-african-consumers-complain-enough-about-prices (accessed on 6 July 2018); Panda, S. 2014. Post purchase consumer complaint behavior: A review of literature. *Business Management Dynamics*, 4(5): 1–7; Imai, M. 1985. Why consumer education in Japan? In Maynes, S.E., *The frontier of research in the consumer interest*. Columbia: American Council on Consumer Interests, 470– 495.

31 Donoghue, S. & De Klerk, H.M. 2009. The right to be heard and to be understood: A conceptual framework for consumer protection in emerging economies. *International Journal of Consumer Studies*, 33(4): 456–467.

32 Sonnenberg, N.C., Erasmus, A.C. & Donoghue, S. 2011. Significance of environmental sustainability issues in consumers' choice of major household appliances in South Africa. *International Journal of Consumer Studies*, 35(2): 153–163.

33 Follows, S.B. & Jobber, D. 2000. Environmentally responsible purchase behaviour: A test of a consumer model. *European Journal of Marketing*, 34(5/6): 723–746.

34 http://www.southafrica.info/services/consumer

35 Vuk'uzenzele. 2011. Know your consumer rights. Available at: http://www.info.gov.za/vukuzenzele/2011/number34/articles_1103_consumerrights.htm (accessed on 6 July 2018).

36 http://www.dti.gov.za/

37 http://www.wylie.co.za/wp-content/uploads/COMPETITION-ACT-NO.-89-OF-1998.pdf

38 https://www.acts.co.za/consumer-protection-act-2008/index.html

39 http://www.polity.org.za/article/counterfeit-goods-act-no-37-of-1997-1997-01-01

40 https://www.acts.co.za/estate-agency-affairs-act-1976/index.html

41 https://www.acts.co.za/consumer-protection-act-2008/index.html

42 https://www.thedti.gov.za/agencies/nct.jsp

43 https://www.thedti.gov.za/business_regulation/acts/National_Gambling.pdf

44 http://www.saflii.org/za/legis/num_act/nga1996156/

45 https://www.thedti.gov.za/business_regulation/nla_act.jsp

46 https://www.gov.za/documents/merchandise-marks-act-17-apr-1941-0000

47 https://www.acts.co.za/property-time-sharing-control-act-1983/index.html

48 http://www.saflii.org/za/legis/num_act/sasmaa1995313/

49 http://www.thencc.gov.za/

50 http://www.thencc.gov.za/

51 Erasmus, A.C. & Mathunjwa, G.C. 2010. Idiosyncratic use of credit facilities by consumers in an emerging economy. *International Journal of Consumer Studies*, 35(3): 359–371.
52 http://www.creditombud.org.za/
53 Henry, P.C. 2010. How mainstream consumers think about consumer rights and responsibilities. *Journal of Consumer Research*, 37(4): 670. Available at: https://doi.org/10.1086/653657 (accessed on 7 July 2018); Olson, L.O. & Wiley, P. 2006. Benefits, consumerism and an 'ownership society'. *Benefits Quarterly*, 22(2): 7–14.
54 Strong, C. 1996. Features contributing to the growth of ethical consumerism – a preliminary investigation. *Marketing Intelligence and Planning*, 14(5): 5–13.
55 Littrell, M.A. & Dickson, M.A. 1999. Social Responsibility in the global market: fair trade of cultural products. Thousand Oaks, CA: Sage,.
56 Kolkailah, S.K., Aish, E.A. & El-Bassiouny, N. 2012. The impact of corporate social responsibility initiatives on consumers' behavioural intentions in the Egyptian market. *International Journal of Consumer Studies*, 36(4): 369–384; Erasmus, A.C., Kok, M. & Retief, A. 2001. Adopting a global perspective in consumer science. *Journal for Family Ecology and Consumer Sciences*, 29: 116–122; McGregor, S.L.T. 1998. Towards adopting a global perspective in the field of consumer studies. *Journal of Consumer Studies and Home Economics*, 22(2): 111–119.
57 http://www.ftc.gov.bb/index.php?option=com_content&task=view&id=49&Itemid=66
58 Morgan, F.W. 1989. The evolution of punitive damages in product liability for unprincipled marketing behavior. *Journal of Public Policy and Marketing*, 8(1): 279–293.
59 Ibid.
60 Dos Santos, M.A. 2012. Investigating consumer knowledge of global warming based on Rogers' knowledge stage of the innovation decision process. *International Journal of Consumer Studies*, 36(4): 385–393.
61 Morgan, op. cit.
62 Dos Santos, op. cit.
63 Morgan, op. cit.
64 Shiva, V. 2008. *Soil not oil: Climate change, peak oil and food insecurity*. London: Zed, 6, 43.
65 Kolkailah et al., op. cit.; Erasmus et al., op. cit.
66 Erasmus et al., ibid.
67 McGregor, op. cit.
68 Duhachek, A. 2005. Coping: A multidimensional, hierarchical framework of responses to stressful consumption episodes. *Journal of Consumer Research*, 23(June): 41–53.

CHAPTER 15

CHANGES IN RETAILING

Alet Erasmus

LEARNING OBJECTIVES

After reading this chapter, you should be able to:

- discuss changes to the retail scene in South Africa since 2000 in terms of the emergence of alternative shopping modes/channels
- describe the advantages associated with online shopping
- explain why online shopping is not necessarily an attractive shopping channel for all consumers
- discuss the various forms of risk that are associated with online shopping and how this could be reduced to enhance consumers' peace of mind
- explain the advantages of brick-and-mortar shopping that are difficult to replicate with online shopping
- explain the concept 'experiential retailing' in terms of how it addresses consumers' needs
- name and describe at least one experiential retail format that is operational in South Africa and explain why it is experiential in nature.

Key terms

brick-and-mortar retailing	online shopping platforms
controllable elements in store design	partly experiential retailers
escapism	retail/shopping modes/channels
experiential retail	risk perception
fully experiential retailers	retail channels
functional product needs	subjective experiences
hedonistic experiences	uncontrollable elements in store design
online shopping	

Two friends, Sipho and Eric, joined a new outdoor adventure club when they enrolled at their college. They now wish to purchase the right equipment and protective clothing to go mountain climbing with the group during the summer holidays. Both are inexperienced in this activity and need to purchase everything they need from scratch. Sipho uses the internet to gain as much information as possible and decides to order everything he needs online as the merchandise will then be delivered to him free of charge. Eric, on the other hand, uses Uber to visit an experiential retailer that specialises in outdoor and sports equipment. How will the information gathered by the two students differ? Explain the difference in time and effort made to secure the purchases, and how their eventual purchases might differ in terms of suitability.

15.1 INTRODUCTION

The retail environment has changed considerably since the turn of the century. On the one hand, it has had to cope with economic pressure and the influx of popular global brands into the South African retail scene, something which has seriously impacted even established retailers. Furthermore, traditional brick-and-mortar (B&M) retailers have had to cope with the introduction and growing popularity of alternative **shopping channels/modes** such as online shopping that have emerged as a consequence of persistent technological progress.[1]

Due to a wider choice, consumers have become more discerning – specifically with regard to B&M retail stores. Undoubtedly it can be more convenient to shop online, from the comfort of your own home, with multiple **shopping platforms** available 24 hours a day, seven days a week, all year round. In order to attract consumers and to retain customers, B&M retailers have had to adapt to meet discerning consumers' elevated expectations. Empirical evidence shows that contemporary consumers nowadays expect B&M stores to offer a 'total shopping experience' that integrates non-negotiable fundamental practical/utilitarian value (the vital, hands-on characteristics expected when in a store, such as changerooms to try on clothing or demo models of TVs to inspect) as well as hedonic value (emotional value such as pleasure and enjoyment).[2]

The changing face of retail has created exciting new opportunities for consumers in terms of *where* to shop. For example, one can shop at more traditional B&M stores, driving around to compare the various options, or online, accessing multiple platforms that even include international suppliers. One can also choose *how* to pay for goods, for example cash, credit card, lay-by, revolving credit or electronic fund transfer (EFT).[3] From B&M retailers' point of view, these changes have introduced major challenges in terms of how to retain customers and how to attract the attention of consumers amidst fierce competition in the marketplace.

This chapter devotes attention to the pros and cons of online versus B&M shopping, and indicates how the retail environment has had to adapt to survive, specifically through the introduction of experiential retail.

Figure 15.1 Shopping can now be done without personal interaction.

15.2 BRICK-AND-MORTAR SHOPPING CHALLENGED

Brick and mortar (B&M) retailing refers to physical retail stores that can either be stand-alone stores or incorporated in shopping malls. Location is a crucial element of the retail strategies of traditional B&M stores, due to the importance of being accessible and within close proximity of their target markets.[4]

15.2.1 Advantages of B&M retail stores

Certain characteristics of B&M stores are highly appreciated in terms of customer experiences, for example:

* Products are tangibly arranged in organised displays for consumers to see, touch, try on (such as clothing) and test (such as cosmetics) before purchasing.[5] Sometimes products are even skilfully arranged or grouped for consumers to make decisions easily, for example displaying garments with suitable accessories in one aisle in the store.
* The presence of in-store displays, graphics and demonstrations is not only attractive, but also useful when purchasing complex products such as electronics.[6]
* Face-to-face interaction with sales personnel is a major advantage, particularly when guidance is needed during the product search and evaluation process. When problems arise, the merchandise can be returned to the store where the consumer can personally express his or her dismay and solve the problem on the spot.[7] In ideal circumstances, with well-trained and supportive personnel, interaction between consumers and employees enhances the level of trust in a retailer which is conducive for store loyalty and consumer satisfaction.[8] Employee training is extremely important to improve customer–employee interaction because this allows the opportunity for products to be demonstrated before the purchase is made.[9]
* Consumers experience instant delight, because they immediately take ownership of a product after purchase without having to await delivery.[10]

* A physical store can usually accept a wider range of payment options and more monetary instruments, including lay-by options, compared to online stores.[11]

15.2.2   Growth or demise of traditional B&M retailing?

Evidence of multiple new shopping mall developments and the upgrading and expansion of existing shopping malls is somewhat confusing, considering recent evidence of the growth of online shopping. Presently, South Africa has more than thirty shopping malls per million people, which is the highest in the world.[12]

The difference, however, is that, over time, the face of retail has had to change to accommodate consumers' needs. The importance of comfort in B&M stores in terms of consumer spending is increasingly acknowledged through the clever design of particular elements of retail stores and shopping malls to encourage customers' prolonged stay in the store and as well as their future return. Comfortable in-store temperature, good lighting, parking facilities and short queues are some of the ways that are used to make customers' shopping experiences more pleasant and to encourage them to browse, stay longer and hopefully spend more.[13]

Research indicates a positive relationship between consumers' experience of comfort in a store and **hedonic value** (enjoyment and pleasure) that are derived from a shopping experience.[14] Retailers and marketers have thus come to admit that shopping is a multisensory experience, not simply the purchasing of goods (focusing on the utilitarian benefits). Therefore modern B&M stores are much more accommodating in terms of amenities such as comfortable restrooms than what they used to be.[15] B&M retail stores now have to make considerable effort to convince consumers to come to their stores rather than to opt for convenient online shopping.[16] The hedonic value achieved from physically going to a retail store to do shopping cannot be replicated online. The creative visual merchandising, window displays, music and lighting collectively evoke emotions within consumers, resulting in a sense of pleasure and enjoyment. Retailers are becoming increasingly aware of consumers' demand for entertainment in addition to the usual functional benefits of shopping and this has brought about a novel approach to B&M shopping.

Another possible solution for existing B&M retailers is to have an online presence as well. Many retailers offer multi-channel options for shopping, for example Woolworths, Truworths and Builders Warehouse customers/account holders can easily order products online rather than to go to a physical B&M store. This works especially well if consumers are already familiar with the products and know exactly what they want.

With the onslaught of alternative shopping modes, of which the increased popularity of online shopping is undeniable, the ability of B&M retailers to secure memorable experiences by means of pleasant store environments and the opportunity for interaction has emerged as a pertinent concern,[17] indicating that retail as we have traditionally known it is no longer viable.

The following represents a summary of an article that was recently published by BusinessTech regarding the future of online shopping in South Africa.[18]

The Mastercard South African SpendingPulse report that was released worldwide on a wide range of consumer financial transactions, including those by cash, electronic transfer and credit card, revealed insightful results. Apparently, over 80 billion transactions are processed in 210 countries every year, which provides a good idea of consumers' spending habits. It became evident that one of the biggest changes in shopping trends occurred after the 2008 recession, when it no longer became acceptable for consumers to flaunt their wealth by making impressive purchases. Rather, consumers opted for an appearance that suggests being wealthy. This coincides with the increase of millennials' (consumers who were born more or less after 1980) purchasing power, and their inclination to buy experiences, and to 'buy time' rather than to spend their money on products. Eating out and travelling have, for example, become more popular among young adults.

With respect to online shopping, South Africans are primarily purchasing commodity goods such as electronics online, because these products have specific specifications that they can evaluate beforehand. This is contrary to clothing items, where the size and colour or style might cause some doubt before placing an order, or food, where quality is of concern. This issue is universal and online retailers around the world are struggling to create an ideal platform with manageable logistics. For online retailers, it is costly to deal with deliveries and returns as well as to offer the same level of service to everyone. Ultimately, the more successful online retailers are those that are product specific or that sell niche products, provided they have a reputation of excellent service.

In terms of retail in general, marketing specialists concur that it is nowadays important for retailers to design and construct experiences carefully so that they will capture consumers' attention and create positive impressions.

Discussion questions

1. Explain why B&M retailers are still popular despite the convenience of online shopping.
2. Explain how retailers could enhance the atmosphere/ambience in their B&M stores to increase the pleasantness of shopping.
3. Discuss the importance of sales personnel in B&M stores.

15.3 ONLINE SHOPPING AS AN ALTERNATIVE

Technology has been instrumental in increasing consumer convenience and value across the multiple retail modes/ channels that are available today.[19] It is nowadays much easier and more convenient for consumers and retailers to connect online, even across national borders. Consumers can browse across multiple web sites in the comfort of their own homes any time of day, any day of the week or year.[20]

Online shopping (e-commerce), whereby goods or services are purchased through the internet,[21] has become a global phenomenon since around 2000.[22] Developing countries like South Africa have, however, been slower to adopt this way of shopping for several reasons (see section 15.3.2). For instance, in certain geographic areas, the internet connection is problematic and consumers do not necessarily have data to access web sites. Lack of experience with using the internet and distrust of delivery services may cause hesitance to do online shopping. Some of these problems are more characteristic of developing countries such as South Africa where the infrastructure that is needed to do trouble-free online shopping is not as advanced yet as in developed countries. Nevertheless, online shopping is expected to grow notably in South Africa in the near future,[23] based on evidence of a consistent annual growth of 20% in South Africa since 2000, and double between 2016 and 2020.[24]

15.3.1 Benefits of online shopping

Probably the most important advantage of online shopping is convenience. In the convenience of one's home, a consumer is able to do price comparisons, find special offers and read product reviews. Online shopping is not restricted by trading hours, holidays or geographic location. It is even possible to order products and highly sought-after brands from elsewhere in the world.[25] When shopping online, one does not have to queue and products are delivered, mostly without additional costs. Often, online retailers' prices are lower than B&M retailers, who have to cover other unavoidable overhead expenses such as rent, electricity and salaries of trained store personnel.

15.3.2 Factors that may influence consumers' adoption of online shopping

Several factors may influence consumers' willingness and capability to adopt online shopping as indicated in the following section. When more than one of these deterrents is present, it further complicates the decision to shop online:

* *The product category:* Complex purchase decisions are better dealt with in B&M stores, where consumers can physically see, touch, inspect and evaluate products such as furniture, major household appliances, musical instruments and formal clothing. Tangibility of products also determines the preferred retail format: it is non-threatening to purchase items such as movie tickets, airline tickets and books online, while a consumer might be more hesitant to purchase less standard products such as clothing that has to fit well.[26] Online shopping lacks opportunity to touch information, which makes online purchases intangible and more complex.[27] Sensory evaluation is vital in product categories such as apparel, shoes and interior décor.[28] Research suggests that as consumers gain experience with online purchases, the likelihood of making more complex purchases increases.[29]
* *Consumer demographics:* Millennials, thus adults who were born after 1980, have grown up in an era of technology and with it being an important part of school curricula. This group is therefore more likely to shop online than older consumers.[30] In South Africa, millennials have the highest

literacy levels compared to previous generational cohorts due to changes in the socio-political climate in the country, and due to the competence required to shop online, more highly educated consumers will be better equipped to adopt internet usage and online shopping.[31] However, notwithstanding a consumer's age and level of education, in South Africa, one has to be fluent in English to shop confidently online because that is the most-used medium of communication. Online shopping can be more complicated if one is not familiar with the terminology used or the instructions.[32] This explains the slower adoption of online shopping in South Africa, seeing as there is still a large number of citizens who are not fluent in English, compared to other countries and societies to date. It might therefore be worthwhile to browse a few retailers' web sites first to familiarise yourself with the steps of an online shopping process. Even when you have registered as a shopper, a transaction is only concluded after you have provided and confirmed payment details and therefore a mock transaction will do no harm.

- *Payment options:* A consumer mostly has to have some form of bank card or electronic transfer ability to shop online, a facility that consumers in lower socio-economic groups may not necessarily have.[33] Alternative payment options are possible, for example PayPal, where a consumer can link PayPal to an existing bank account. The money is then transferred securely through your bank with an online transaction, not requiring ownership of a credit card. Other payment options include Bitcoin, while some companies, such as TakeAlot, offer cash-on-delivery transactions, but this is the exception.

- *Internet connection and electronic devices such as a computer or smartphone:* Inevitably, a consumer has to have access to the relevant technology to purchase online, which is difficult to acquire for lower socio-economic groups. Not only is internet connectivity often unstable in certain geographic areas in the country, but one also has to have data, and this may be expensive and even unaffordable for some consumers.[34] Internet cafes, where customers can browse the internet at a fixed cost for a particular time, may be a solution. Alternatively, some companies and retailers offer free Wi-Fi, provided one buys a cup of coffee or shops in the store.

- **Risk perception**: This encompasses the degree of uncertainty that consumers experience, including concern about possible negative outcomes of the purchase decision.[35] Different types of risk are distinguished in literature. The types of risk that are specifically associated with online shopping are as follows:

  - *Financial risk* refers to the likelihood of financial loss due to a purchase. With online purchases, one has to provide sensitive financial information and this could cause concern[36] about, for example, falling prey to credit card fraud. Third party online payment systems, such as PayPal, can reduce financial risk perception.[37] Worry about additional delivery and return costs also contributes, which is seldom relevant to B&M shopping.

Financial risk perception is higher when consumers' disposable income is lower.[38]

- *Functional and performance risk* refers to the possibility that a product will not perform as expected and is even more problematic when consumers do not have the opportunity to examine products physically beforehand.[39] Lower-educated consumers tend to experience online purchases as more complex due to difficulty in evaluating intangible product attributes and gathering relevant product information.[40] Good return policies can negate this concern.

- *Psychological risk* is relevant when consumers are concerned that they might not cope doing the online transaction or that the purchase will be inferior, thus tarnishing their self-image, for example purchasing an unfamiliar brand of which the characteristics are uncertain.

- *Social risk* is defined as the possibility that one's peers or social group will not approve the purchase and will regard it as inferior.[41] Purchases are generally discussed in social circles and on social media, thus exposing a consumer to negative social judgement.[42] Social risk perception is related to age: younger consumers' social risk perception, for example millennials, is generally more pertinent.[43]

- *Time or effort risk* refers to anxiety about the possibility of wasted time.[44] While online shopping saves time in terms of commuting to B&M stores and queueing at pay points, browsing on web sites may also be time consuming, especially for inexperienced consumers and with poor internet connectivity.[45] Inexperienced and lower-educated consumers may also experience difficulty to use the technology and to navigate online platforms.[46] Because online shopping is a remote transaction, the time delay until product delivery also increases time risk.[47]

- *Privacy risk* relates to potential misuse of consumers' personal information by online retailers,[48] such as tracking of online shopping habits. When purchasing clothing, consumers generally have to share extensive personal information to ensure that the correct products are delivered at the correct location, while the same is not required at B&M retailers.

- *Security risk* refers to doubt about the way in which a consumer's personal and financial information may be shared with other companies, and stored.[49] Many online consumers experience extreme security concerns when entering bankcard information.[50] Fear of the illegal capture of financial details by unauthorised parties is also a reality.

- *Health risk* relates to concern about one's physical safety as well as health concerns that may be relevant during the production and delivery of online products, for example concern about the way in which products were packaged and treated for delivery, and transported.[51] For example, when ordering food and groceries online, one may be concerned about the temperature at which food was kept while being transported to various customers.

The following statistics emerged from the 2017 E-commerce industry report.[52] The survey, involving 8751 respondents, revealed that 80% of online shoppers had either maintained or increased their online shopping habit during the past year, while 46% of offline shoppers intended to make an online purchase within the coming year.

More specific results for online shopping:
As many as 46% of respondents had shopped online (25% were older than 60 years; 63% were younger than 40 years). Online shoppers were mostly well-educated (more than 65% possessed education beyond matriculation), high-income earners with full-time jobs (more than 35% earned above R30 000 monthly). The most popular online purchases were items such as travel tickets, books, shows/sporting event tickets and hotel reservations that didn't require delivery time. Respondents indicated that convenience and price were the primary benefits of online shopping. However, major barriers and causes of unease were distrust in the payment method, lack of a pleasant shopping experience, complexity of certain web sites, and lack of product information. Delivery was apparently not a matter of concern for online shoppers, and almost 90% were fairly or very satisfied with the speed of delivery. Interestingly, approximately 30% of online shoppers browsed in-store before concluding a purchase online. Importantly, 43% indicated that they would feel more comfortable shopping online if they could pay with cash.

In terms of offline (B&M) shoppers:
The majority (60%) earned less than R20 000 monthly; 44% stated matriculation as their highest level of education; 12% had completed a university degree, and 60% were younger than 35 years. Compared to online shoppers, fewer off-line shoppers worked full time. Just like online shoppers, they indicated that a trusted payment method would encourage them to shop online. Concerns about online shopping included the following: 43% preferred to transact with cash; 13% felt that some sites might not be trustworthy; 32% were concerned about returns and return guarantees.

Discussion questions
1.   Explain the 'time convenience' associated with online shopping.
2.   Explain why younger consumers might be more enthusiastic to try online shopping.
3.   Discuss the possibility that online shopping might lead to overspending.
4.   Explain why it is easier to purchase certain product categories such as books and perfume online, compared to product categories such as jewellery and furniture.

Bearing in mind the 2017 E-commerce industry report summarised above:
1.   Make a summary of the students in your class, expressed in terms of male and female, of:
     * those who have shopped online before
     * the type of products that they have purchased

- problems that they may have encountered with online shopping
- the payment methods used when purchasing online.

2. Make a summary of students in your class who have purchased online before, and who would do so again in the future

3. Make a summary of students who prefer to shop offline (in physical stores), indicating:
   - reasons why they prefer to purchase offline
   - payment methods used when purchasing offline
   - factors that might persuade them to purchase online.

4. Make a summary of students who browse in physical stores before purchasing online.

5. Discussion topic in general: how would you feel if physical stores no longer existed?

15.4 THE INTRODUCTION OF EXPERIENTIAL SHOPPING

Undoubtedly, online shopping has multiple advantages for those who have mastered the technology (see section 15.3.1), but modern consumers, who are often over-exposed to and consumed by technology for the better part of their daily lives in their work environments, long for more. Research indicates that consumers have of late developed a need for **hedonistic (pleasure seeking) experiences** that allow them the opportunity to escape from every day responsibilities (at least for a while) and to have fun.[53] Indications are that, potentially, B&M retail environments can provide this solution, although in a self-serving way.

Although experiential consumption has not received much attention in scholarly textbooks to date, its relevance in terms of our understanding of consumer behaviour was already noted in 1982, by researchers who acknowledged consumers' need for fantasy, expression of their feelings, and fun when shopping.[54] Soon after, other scholars also expressed concern about retail environments, specifically B&M retailers that no longer met consumers' needs and demands in terms of shopping experiences.[55] The mutual conclusion was that it was imperative for retailers who wished to secure long-term relationships with their customers to pay more attention to store atmosphere[56] and consumers' in-store shopping experiences.[57]

Experiential retail as a phenomenon has attracted the attention of several researchers in recent years as it addresses consumers' need for distraction while also providing opportunity for B&M stores to distinguish and augment their service offerings on a level that alternative shopping modes such as online platforms would find difficult to replicate. A fundamental assumption is that the context in which interaction takes place, thus the in-store environment, influences consumers' thoughts and feelings,[58] and subsequently alters their shopping experience.[59] Today's retailers and manufacturers therefore have no choice other than to generate value-added retail experiences in addition to adding value to merchandise features.[60]

Figure 15.2 A typical Build-a-Bear workshop

15.4.1   Characteristics of experiential retail

Initial attempts to introduce entertainment to the shopping experience have
included the incorporation of social spaces in shopping malls with tables and
chairs, plants and play areas for kids, often also with artwork, live music, food
stalls and restaurants around, where people can meet and relax in a comfortable environment.[61] The idea with experiential retail, however, is to transform the
entire shopping environment, including the product and service offerings, into a
total consumption experience that has the potential to satisfy consumers' emotional and expressive desires over and above their rational or functional needs.[62]
Generally, a B&M retailer's in-store environment is transformed in some way to
create excitement, surprise and enjoyment by introducing unique products or
service components, and activities that are complementary to the destination.[63]
For example, in Magnum stores, consumers get the opportunity to create their
own ice creams, and in an outdoor shop, consumers get the opportunity to try
out different guns in an indoor shooting range. Mostly, experiential retailers sell
limited edition products or memorabilia that provide some exclusivity so that
visitors can purchase something as a reminder of the pleasant experience.

Experiential retailing aims to capture consumers' attention by means of
carefully selected stimuli that will influence a consumer's senses.[64] Atmospheric
stimuli/ambient cues, such as lighting, appropriate background music, a comfortable in-store temperature and a pleasant scent, are used to create retail
environments that will attract consumers and engage them in pleasant ways.[65]
Retailers can therefore create aesthetically sensitive and emotionally pleasing
environments by manipulating ambient cues to enhance consumers' value perceptions positively.[66] The event is not supposed to stagnate, so the environment
is adapted frequently to retain some level of surprise and excitement, even for

those who return to the venue soon after. Eventually, the image of the store and consumers' perception of it distinguishes it from other stores.[67] Some experiential retailers are only temporary, in the form of **pop-up stores**, for example a Christmas decoration store that is erected in the hallway of a shopping mall for a restricted period of time, where customers can decorate their own parcels using available stock and examples as inspiration.

Joshi and Kulkarni[68] suggest that a pleasant store atmosphere is not created by a single factor, for example attractive store displays. When in the store, consumers evaluate the entire situation, which subsequently influences their cognitive, affective, emotional, social as well as physical responses to the controllable as well as uncontrollable elements in the retail environment. **Controllable elements** include atmospheric cues such as smell, music/noise and merchandise cues, for example product range and price. **Uncontrollable elements** that retailers literally have to manage as they arise are, for example, electricity failure, the influence of other customers in the store, crowding in certain areas and noise created by children in the store.[69]

Retailers can be **partly experiential,** that is when sections of a store are converted to be experiential, or they can be **fully experiential**. Examples of fully experiential retailers in South Africa, are the following:[70]

- Hard Rock Café,[71] where regular performances are held by rock bands while visitors enjoy their drinks and signature hamburgers
- Pestaurant[72] (Gauteng; Western Cape), a restaurant that was introduced by Rentokil to educate people about the health benefits of an insect-rich diet. Entomophagy (eating of insects) is a protein rich diet that is enjoyed by millions across the globe, promoting the idea that edible insects are much more environmentally friendly because they require less food and water and have a lower carbon footprint than traditional forms of protein
- Die Blou Hond[73] (Gauteng), a theatre come restaurant where the audience bark when applauding to support the theme of the venue
- Build-a-Bear,[74] a toy store where each child/visitor makes their own stuffed animal friend and where guests can 'pawsonalis' their new furry friends with a range of outfits and accessories
- Cape Union Mart Adventure Centre (KZN, Western Cape),[75] where visitors can experience the outdoors indoors through exposure to a rain as well as a cold weather chamber where the temperature goes down to −19°C, can try wall and rock climbing under supervision, and get advice about appropriate clothing. Cape Union Mart is a leading South African retailer in outdoor equipment.

In order to be successful, experiential retailers need to attend to the store atmosphere and all the elements that collectively contribute to the consumers' experience. They therefore have to ensure that the interaction between customers and sales personnel (service interface) is appropriate for the occasion and also have to ascertain that the product assortment and merchandising appeal to consumers' senses, feelings, intellect, curiosity and self-image so that the visit, and consumers' efforts to get to the venue, is worthwhile.[76]

15.4.2 Consumers' behaviour in experiential retail environments

Although every experiential retail venue offers an exclusive experience, the overall aim is to stimulate consumers' inherent desires for excitement, surprise and uniqueness. However, consumers' reactions to the same stimuli will differ, depending on their state of mind upon arrival (a good mood or not) and the reason why they have entered the store. An experiential venue can be visited for personal pleasure, joining as a member of a group for a social occasion, or to purchase a unique gift, knowing that the experience will probably not be repeated.[77] It is difficult to plan or predict one's behaviour in an experiential retail environment because one never knows what to expect.

The introduction of fun, interactive activities and captivating displays is purposively and skilfully done to stimulate consumers' senses and to encourage some form of participation that could take the form of product tastings; spontaneous participation in live activities, such as singing or dancing; or mere spectatorship. In essence, a visit to an experiential destination should be so engaging and pleasurable that consumers/patrons pay attention and are even willing to pay an entry fee because they do not want to miss out.[78] When visiting an experiential retailer, consumers derive hedonic value from the shopping experience in the form of enjoyment, even though they might not necessarily purchase anything.[79]

Hedonic value is therefore derived from the uniqueness, symbolic association, or the emotional arousal and imagery that culminate from the retailer, the merchandise and/or the service.[80] Visual appeal and entertainment are non-negotiable in securing a pleasant shopping experience and to encourage positive response behaviours. Intrinsic enjoyment is, for example, derived from adventure, socialisation and additional value-bearing activities such as bargain hunting for discounted items or wine tasting.[81] **Escapism**, which is another outcome of experiential shopping, refers to activities that consumers can freely engage in and that allow them to 'escape' momentarily from their daily duties where they can pretend without feeling guilty.[82] Cognitive pleasure may result when consumers imagine product use scenarios (for example, when visiting the Cape Union Mart Adventure Centre as described in 15.4.1) or where they envision the customisation of merchandise (for example, when visiting Build-a-Bear, as described in 15.4.1). Merchandise in a store or an experience in a retail outlet may evoke fond memories and nostalgic thoughts.[83]

Ultimately, consumers' subjective (personal) experiences of the retail environment are the consequence of their reaction to a combination of stimuli that are presented in the form of tangible as well as intangible elements of the retail environment.[84] These stimuli are meant to induce positive emotions,[85] such as delight, interest and enthusiasm,[86] that will encourage consumers' purchase behaviour (impulse purchases), consumer satisfaction as well as the time and amount of money spent in the store.[87] Social cues in a retail environment that might influence consumers' value perceptions include the presence of other people in the store[88] as well as other social variables such as the number of store employees and their physical appearance.

Shopping experiences are highly influential in terms of consumer decision making, for example consumers' purchase and return intentions as well as their satisfaction and mood.[89] Positive experiences translate as so-called 'approach behaviour', which reflects eagerness to remain in the store and to further explore the store environment.[90]

Unequivocally, consumers' retailer preferences, in other words whether they purchase online or in B&M stores, and patronage intentions are determined by their value perceptions.[91] High levels of perceived value are associated with positive behavioural intentions, that is the likelihood that a person will purchase something or spend more time in the store, or participate in activities. The contrary is true when perceived value is low, in which case a consumer will avoid the store or refrain from purchasing.[92] In the same vein, consumers might rush to get an anticipated negative experience over and done with to escape the anxiety that is associated with it.[93] Research indicates that consumers who are in a negative mood are more inclined to make impulsive purchases once they are in the store to lift their mood, while consumers who are in a good mood might not need a new purchase to feel better and thus only browse around as a form of relaxation.[94] Ultimately, pleasant in-store shopping experiences are essential for B&M retailers to beat competition from other retail formats as well as other B&M retailers in the marketplace.

DISCUSSION

In experiential retail environments, certain key factors are taken into consideration during the design to drive sales, to cultivate a brand relationship and to secure long lasting customer loyalty:

- The creation of a multi-sensory experience that is impossible to achieve through any online platform, for example pleasant aromas, impressive lighting design and tactile elements that allow customers to interact with products and services such as a cooking lesson; the incorporation of scents that can be linked to memory and recalled to ensure lasting memories.
- Value-added retail experiences where customers can partake in certain activities, for example an in-store repair service or training experience such as rock climbing
- Human touch points to encourage interpersonal interaction, for example a seated consultation area, a demonstration space, sampling table, demonstrations to encourage personal connection with a brand

Discussion questions

1. Explain ways in which experiential retailing can be introduced partially in a large supermarket.
2. Discuss reasons for the success of experiential retailing.
3. Identify experiential retailers in your area/city/province.

SUMMARY

This chapter highlighted the dilemma of traditional B&M retailers in terms of the competitive advantage that online shopping has in terms of its convenience. Consumers' risk perception with regard to online shopping is explained to gain an understanding of their loyalty to B&M shopping, which is more prevalent in certain product categories. Consumers' needs with regard to B&M shopping are explained in the context of changes in modern consumers' exposure, increased education levels and time scarcity due to long working hours. Subsequently, the reaction of B&M retailers to counteract the onslaught of online shopping is discussed, namely increased attention to store atmosphere through attention to sensory stimuli.

The attraction of experiential retail is explained and discussed in terms of ways in which consumers can be lured back to B&M shopping.

SELF-ASSESSMENT QUESTIONS

1. Explain the specific advantages of B&M stores for less experienced consumers.
2. How have B&M retailers adapted to keep consumers' attention?
3. Explain why urban consumers would find it easier to shop online.
4. Explain the security risk that is associated with online shopping and indicate how this risk can be reduced.
5. Explain the attraction of experiential retail in modern times.
6. Use the example of the Build-a-Bear company to make suggestions on how an established sports retailer could revamp its stores to become fully experiential.
7. Provide examples of how modern shopping malls have adapted to meet consumers' need for pleasurable shopping experiences.
8. Why is social risk perception prevalent when doing online shopping?

EXPERIENTIAL EXERCISE

You are appointed as a visual merchandiser of a toy store in a shopping mall in July, which is six months before Christmas. As a new initiative, you wish to erect a temporary pop-up store in a small vacant space around the corner from the main store, applying the basic principles of a fully experiential retailer. Explain how you would achieve this.

CASE STUDY 1

Buying nursing textbooks

Lindiwe will be returning to college for her fourth academic year to complete her qualification in nursing. She has received notification of the textbooks that will be required for the next academic year and also has to do some preparation in advance, using these books. Lindiwe lives in a small village in Mpumalanga and will not be able to visit an academic B&M bookstore and therefore appreciates that she will be able to order the books online. She can do so either from the academic division of TakeAlot (https://www.takealot.com/books/academic) or from Pimp My Book, which offers second-hand books (www.pimpmybook.co.za/).

Discussion questions

1. Explain the steps that Lindiwe needs to follow when she wishes to inquire about the books' prices on both websites.
2. Lindiwe has no credit card facility. Explain the alternative payment options that she can use if she wishes to order her books from TakeAlot, and also explain the delivery options provided by both companies.
3. One of the text books are available through both companies, the second-hand book being significantly cheaper than the new book. Explain the types of risk that may have convinced Lindiwe to rather buy all three books from TakeAlot.

CASE STUDY 2

Kilimanjaro expedition

Peter's friend Tony will be visiting him in Johannesburg before they leave on a Kilimanjaro mountain climbing expedition. Both still need some essential clothing items and equipment before they go, and Peter decides to take advantage of the new experiential concept store of Cape Union Mart (http://www.climbing.co.za/2009/12/cape-union-mart-brings-outdoors-indoors-with-experiential-concept-store/) rather than to purchase what they need from a traditional Cape Union Mart store in the nearest shopping mall. Tony has never done this extreme type of mountain climbing before.

Discussion questions

1. Explain the advantages of visiting the experiential concept store, rather than going to a similar retailer in the closest shopping mall.
2. Apart from advice about the most appropriate clothing items and equipment, what would they have learnt after an encounter at the experiential store that they might not have known beforehand?

EXTRA RESOURCES

- A travel to experience the Store of the Future in Chicago: an immersive retail experience that combines the sensory benefits of B&M with the high-tech features of online shopping
  The Store of the Future: https://youtu.be/IKouQFI1aM4
- Retail innovation demonstrated through the transformation journey of Telstra's flagship store in George Street, Sydney Innovation to improve in-store experience [Telstra Case Study]: https://youtu.be/yXfqDBe9kyU
  For more information, download: telstra.com/innovateretail
- A look at the in-store moment and how to convert it to be more experiential, using a shopper five-senses model
  Experiential Retail: The need for positive disruption: https://youtu.be/6Qo945hCHt8
- Images of the shopping experience: digitising in-store browsing and selection, creating a fast checkout experience

- • Experiential retail redefined: the consumer of tomorrow, so what are the retail spaces of tomorrow: https://youtu.be/Gboh4pARFiw
- • Rachel Shechtman – Reinventing Retail: Experience-Driven Commerce: https://youtu.be/M_ ZSg07_FBY
- • Immersive Retail Experiences: https://youtu.be/P77zQJO6Rpg
- • Emerson and global retail market experts Euromonitor provide new research-based insights on the grocery, convenience, foodservice and mixed retail markets. Five trends are highlighted.
- • Experience-Shopping Trends Still Driving Retail: https://youtu.be/SK-qzJeGXBc (published on 31 January 2017)
- • Experiential Retail – 2017: https://youtu.be/rUDa2X6TeXU
- • Proposing what a bricks and mortar store of the future may look like to satisfy Millennials' needs. Inside The Retail Store Of The Future At Millennial 20/20: https://youtu.be/3f_tOORo9w4

REFERENCES

1 Davis, L. & Hodges, N. 2012. Consumer shopping value: An investigation of shopping trip value, in-store shopping value and retail format. *Journal of Retailing and Consumer Services*, 19: 229; Garvin, A.N. 2009. *Experiential retailing: Extraordinary store environments and purchase behaviour.* Master's thesis. Eastern Michigan University. Ypsilanti, Michigan; Janse Van Noordwyk, H. 2008. *The development of a scale for the measurement of the perceived importance of the dimensions of apparel store image.* PhD Dissertation. University of Stellenbosch. Stellenbosch.

2 Kim, J., Fiore, A.M. & Lee, H.H. 2007 Influences of online store perception, shopping enjoyment, and shopping involvement on consumer patronage behavior towards an online retailer. *Journal of Retailing and Consumer Services*, 27.

3 Otto, J.R. & Chung, Q. 2000. A framework for cyber-enhanced retailing: Integrating e-commerce retailing with brick-and-mortar retailing. *Electronic Markets*, 1–7.

4 Barkworth, H. 2014. Six trends that will shape consumer behaviour this year. Forbes. Available at: http://www.forbes.com/sites/onmarketing/2014/02/04/six-trends-that-will-shape-consumer-behavior-this-year/Build-a-bear (accessed on 1 August 2018); http://www.buildabear.co.za/ (accessed on 1 August 2018).

5 Holmqvist, J. & Lunardo, R. 2015. The impact of an exciting store environment on consumer pleasure and shopping intentions. *International Journal of Research in Marketing*, 32: 117; Riteshkumar, D., Singh, R.H. & Atul, P. 2010. Key retail store attributes determining consumers' perceptions: An empirical study of consumers of retail stores located in Ahmedabad (Gujarat). *SIES Journal of Management*, 7(1): 20–34; Gaur, X. 2009. Consumer comfort and its role in relationship marketing outcomes: an empirical investigation. *Advances in Consumer Research*, 8: 296.

6 Holmqvist & Lunardo, ibid., 119; Walsh, G., Shiu, E., Hassan, L.M., Michaelidou, N. & Beatty, S. E. 2011. Emotions, store-environmental cues, store-choice criteria, and marketing outcomes. *Journal of Business Research*, 64: 737–744; Seock, Y. 2009. Influence of retail store environmental cues on consumer patronage behavior across different retail store formats: An empirical analysis of US Hispanic consumers. *Journal of Retailing and Consumer Services*, 16: 329; Laroche, M., Yang, Z., McDougall, G. & Bergeron, J. 2004. Internet versus bricks-and-mortar retailers: an investigation into intangibility and its consequences. *Journal of Retailing*, 81(4): 256.

7 Vieira, V.A. 2012. An evaluation of the need for touch scale and its relationship with need for cognition, need for input, and consumer response. *Journal of International Consumer Marketing*, 24(1-2): 57–78.

8 Donoghue, S. & De Klerk, H.M. 2009. The right to be heard and to be understood: A conceptual framework for consumer protection in emerging economies. *International Journal of Consumer Studies*, 33: 456; Yoon, S. 2002. The antecedents and consequences of trust in online-purchase decisions. *Journal of Interactive Marketing*, 16(2): 47; Chen, Q., Griffith, D.A. & Wan, F. 2004. The behavioural implications of consumer trust across brick-and-mortar and online retail channels. *Journal of Marketing Channels*, 11(4): 61.

9   Seock, op. cit., 331; Mathwick, C., Malhotra, N. & Rigdon, E. 2001. Experiential value: Conceptualization, measurement and application in the catalogue and internet shopping environment. *Journal of Retailing*, 77: 52; Chen et al., ibid.; Erasmus, A.C. & Gothan, A.J. 2004. The complex role of a salesperson in an appliance sales context. *Journal for Family Ecology and Consumer Sciences*, 32: 100–102.

10 Walsh et al., op. cit.; Seock, ibid., 334.

11 Walsh et al., ibid.; Otto & Chung, op. cit., 3.

12 Moneyweb. 2015. SA's brick & mortar retailers safe, for now. Available at: https://www.moneyweb.co.za/investing/property/sas-brick-mortar-retailers-safe-for-now/ (accessed on 15 July 2018).

13 Ainsworth, J. & Foster, J. 2017. Comfort in brick and mortar shopping experiences: Examining antecedents and consequences of comfortable retail experiences. *Journal of Retailing and Consumer Services*, 35: 27; El-Adly, M.I. 2007. Shopping malls attractiveness: A segmentation approach. *International Journal of Retail Distribution Management*, 35(11): 936.

14 Arnold, M.J. & Reynolds, K.E. 2003. Hedonic shopping motivations. *Journal of Retailing*, 79: 77; Rintamäki, T., Kanto, A., Kuusela, H. & Spence, M.T. 2006. Decomposing the value of department store shopping into utilitarian, hedonic and social dimensions: Evidence from Finland. *International Journal of Retail & Distribution Management*, 34(1): 8.

15 Foster, J. & McLelland, M. 2015. Retail atmospherics: The impact of a brand dictated theme. *Journal of Retailing and Consumer Services*, 22: 196.

16 Ibid.

17 Barkworth, op. cit.

18 BusinessTech. 2017. The future of online shopping in South Africa is not quite what you think. Available at: https://businesstech.co.za/news/technology/199898/the-future-of-online-shopping-in-south-africa-is-not-quite-what-you-think/ (accessed on 17 July 2017).

19 Grewal, D., Roggeveen, A., Compeau, L. & Levy, M. 2012. Retail value-based pricing strategies: New times, new technologies, new consumers. *Journal of Retailing*, 88: 1–6.

20 Gaur, op. cit., 297; Chiu, H.-C., Hsieh, Y.-C. & Kuo, Y.-C. 2012. How to align your brand stories with your products. *Journal of Retailing*, 88(2): 262–275; Grewal, D., Roggeveen, A., Puccinelli, N.A. & Spence, C. 2014. Retail atmospherics and in-store nonverbal cues: An introduction. *Journal of Psychology and Marketing*, 31(7): 469.

21 Business Dictionary. 2017. Online shopping. Available at: http://www.businessdictionary.com/definition/online-shopping.html (accessed on 17 July 2018).

22 Mahlaka, R. 2016. Online shopping: Shifting purchasing realms. Available at: https://www.moneyweb.co.za/in-depth/ecommerce/online-shopping-shifting-purchasing-realms/ (accessed on 17 July 2018).

23 Ibid.; WorldWideWorx. 2016. Online retail in South Africa 2016: Executive summary. Available at: http://www.worldwideworx.com/retail2016/ (accessed on 17 July 2018).

24 WorldWideWorx, ibid.

25 Chiu et al., op. cit.; Soopramanien, D.G.R. & Robertson, A. 2007. Adoption and usage of online shopping: An empirical analysis of the characteristics of 'buyers', 'browsers' and 'non-internet shoppers'. *Journal of Retailing and Consumer Services*, 14(1): 73–82.

26 Erasmus, A.C., Donoghue, S. & Dobbelstein, T. 2014. Consumers' perception of the complexity of selected household purchase decisions. *Journal of Retailing and Consumer Services*, 21(3): 293.

27 Vieira, op. cit., 57.

28 Wankhade, L. & Dabade, B. 2010. Quality uncertainty due to information asymmetry. In *Quality Uncertainty and Perception*. Heildelberg: Physica-Verlag, 20.

29 Spake, D.F., Beatty, S.E., Brockman, B.K. & Crutchfield, T.N. 2003. Consumer comfort in service relationships: Measurement and importance. *Journal of Service Research*, 5(4): 316; Kim, Y. & Krishnan, R. 2015. On product-level uncertainty and online purchase behavior: An empirical analysis. *Management Science*, 61(10): 2449.

30 Parment, A. 2013. Generation Y vs. Baby Boomers: Shopping behavior, buyer involvement and implications for retailing. *Journal of Retailing and Consumer Services*, 20(2): 189, 199.

31 Effective Measure. 2016. South Africa e-commerce industry report – June 2016. Available at: http://hello.effectivemeasure.com/thank-you-sa-ecommerce-2016?submissionGuid=59ebf686-a0b0-4a47-83c9-b7ccf5e731d7 (accessed on 17 July 2018); PWC. 2012. South African retail and consumer products outlook 2012–2016. Available at: https://www.pwc.co.za/en/publications/retail-and-consumer-outlook.html (accessed on 17 July 2018).

32 Naseri, M. & Elliot, G. 2011. Role of demographics, social connectedness and prior internet experience in adoption of online shopping: Applications for direct marketing. Available at: http://link.springer.com/article/10.1057/jt.2011.9 (accessed on 17 July 2018).

33 Otto & Chung, op. cit., 1–7.

34 Turtle, B. 2014. 8 amazing things people said when online shopping was born 20 years ago. Available at: http://time.com/money/3108995/online-shopping-history-anniversary/ (accessed on 17 July 2018).

35 Featherman, M.S. & Pavlou, P.A. 2003. Predicting e-services adoption: A perceived risk facets perspective. *International Journal of Human–Computer Studies*, 59(4): 451.

36 Vos, A., Eberhagen, N., Giannakopoulos, G., Skourlas, C., Marinagi, C. & Trivellas, P. 2014. Electronic service quality in online shopping and risk reduction strategies. *Journal of Systems and Information Technology*, 16(3): 170.

37 PWC, op. cit.

38 Erasmus et al., 2014, op. cit., 300.

39 Dimoka, A., Hong, Y. & Pavlou, P.A. 2012. On product uncertainty in online markets: Theory and evidence. *MIS Quarterly: Management Information Systems*, 36(2): 395.

40 Erasmus et al., 2014, op. cit., 293.

41 Zhao, A.L., Hanmer-Lloyd, S., Ward, P. & Goode, M.M.H. 2008. Perceived risk and Chinese consumers' internet banking services adoption. *International Journal of Bank Marketing*, 26(7): 505.

42 Vos et al., op. cit., 170.

43 Parment, op. cit., 189.

44 McGuire, K.A., Kimes, S.E., Lynn, M., Pullman, M.E. & Lloyd, R.C. 2010. A framework for evaluating the customer wait experience. *Journal of Service Management*, 21(3): 269.

45 Luo, L. & Sun, J. 2016. New product design under channel acceptance: Brick-and-mortar, online-exclusive, or brick-and-click. *Production and Operations Management*, 2014; Kakava, N.Z. & Erasmus, A.C. 2012. Waiting as a determinant of store image and customer satisfaction: A literature review. *Journal of Family Ecology and Consumer Sciences*, 40(1): 99; Janakiraman, N., Meyer, R.J. & Hoch, S.J. 2011. The psychology of decisions to abandon waits for service. *Journal of Marketing Research*, 48(6): 970.

46 Thakur, R. & Srivastava, M. 2015. A study on the impact of consumer risk perception and innovativeness on online shopping in India. *International Journal of Retail and Distribution Management*, 43(2): 148.

47 Kunze, O. & Mai, L.W. 2007. Consumer adoption of online music services: The influence of perceived risks and risk-relief strategies. *International Journal of Retail & Distribution Management*, 35(11): 862.

48 Kesh, S., Ramanujan, S. & Nerur, S. 2002. A framework for analyzing e-commerce security. *Information Management and Computer Security*, 10(4): 149.

49 Kolsaker, A. & Payne, C. 2002. Engendering trust in e-commerce: A study of gender-based concerns. *Marketing Intelligence & Planning*, 20(4): 206.

50 Horrigan, J.A. 2008. Online shopping. *Pew Internet & American Life Project Report*, 36: 1–24. Available at: http://pewresearch.org/pubs/733/online-shopping (accessed on 17 July 2018).

51 Chen, S.J. et al. 2010. Brominated flame retardants in house dust from e-waste recycling in China. *Environmental International*, 36(6): 535–541.

52 effectivemeasure. n.d. e-Commerce industry report 2017. Available at: https://cdn2.hubspot.net/hubfs/2622125/2017%20South%20Africa%20E-Commerce%20Industry%20Report.pdf (accessed on 1 August 2018).

53 Barkworth, op. cit.

54 Holbrook, M.B. & Hirschman, E.C. 1982. The experiential aspects of consumption: Consumer fantasies, feelings and fun. *Journal of Consumer Research*, 9, 132–140.

55 Singh, R. 2006. *An empirical investigation into the effects of shopping motivation on store environment– value relationship*. PhD dissertation. Florida State University. Florida. Available at: http://diginole.lib.fsu.edu/islandora/object/fsu:176203/datastream/PDF/view (accessed on 1 August 2018); Fiore, A.M. & Kim, J. 2007. An integrative framework capturing experiential and utilitarian shopping experience. *International Journal of Retail and Distribution Management*, 35(6):421.

56 Schmitt, B. 2010. Experience marketing: Concepts, frameworks and consumer insights. *Foundations and Trends® in Marketing*, 5(2): 55. Available at: http://dx.doi.org/10.1561/1700000027 (accessed on 1 August 2018).

57 Grewal et al., 2014, op. cit., 469.

58 Kumar, A. & Kim, Y.-K. 2014. The store-as-a-brand strategy: The effect of store environment on customer responses. *Journal of Retailing and Consumer Services*, 21: 685.

59 Same, S & Larimo, J. 2012. *Marketing theory: Experience marketing and experiential marketing*, 7th International Scientific Conference 'Business and Management 2012' May 10-11, 2012, Vilnius, Lithuania: 480-487. ISSN 2029-4441 print / ISSN 2029-929X online ISBN 978-609-457-116-9 CD doi:10.3846/bm.2012.063 http://www.bm.vgtu.lt © Vilnius Gediminas Technical University, 480.

60 Grewal et al., 2014, op. cit., 469.

61 Evans, M. 1999. Let us entertain you. *Journal of Property Management*, Mar/Apr: 54.

62 Arnold, M.J. & Reynolds, K.E. 2003. Hedonic shopping motivations. *Journal of Retailing*, 79: 77; Kim, H. & Kim, Y. 2007. Shopping enjoyment and store shopping modes: The moderating influence of chronic time pressure. *Journal of Retailing and Consumer Services*, 15(2008): 410.

63 Oh, H., Fiore, A.M. & Jeoung, M. 2007. In measuring experience economy concepts: Tourism application. *Journal of Travel Research*, 46: 119.

64 Grewal et al, 2014, op. cit., 469

65 Verhoef, P.C., Lemon, K.N., Parasuraman, A., Roggeveen, A., Tsiros, M. & Schlesinger, L.A. 2009. Customer experience creation: Determinants, dynamics and management strategies. *Journal of retailing*, 85(1): 31; Rahimi, F., Nadaf, M. & Cheaghi, M. 2014. The relationship between the internal environment stimulus of the store and customers' behavioural intention. *International Journal of Modern Management & Foresight*, 1(2): 88.

66 Kumar, A. 2010. *The effect of store environment on consumer evaluations and behaviour toward single-brand apparel retailers*. PhD dissertation. University of Tennessee, Knoxville, 685.

67 Joshi, J.V. & Kulkarni, V.R. 2012. A factorial study of impact of store atmospherics in organized retail chain stores on customers shopping experience. *Journal of Management Insight*, 8(2): 89.

68 Joshi & Kulkarni, ibid.

69 Joshi & Kulkarni, ibid.; Verhoef et al., op. cit.

70 Retief, M. 2018. *Experiential retailing*. PhD thesis. University of Pretoria.

71 http://www.hardrock.com/cafes/pretoria/

72 https://www.rentokil.com/pestaurant/

73 https://blouhond.co.za/

74 http://www.buildabear.co.za/

75 Lawson, J. 2009. Cape Union Mart brings outdoors indoors with experiential concept store. Climb ZA. Available at: http://www.climbing.co.za/2009/12/cape-union-mart-brings-outdoors-indoors-with-experiential-concept-store/ (accessed on 1 August 2018).

76 Schmitt, op. cit., 55.

77 Pine, B.J. & Gilmore, J.H. 1998. Welcome to the experience economy. *Harvard Business Review*, July/ August: 96; Same & Larimo, op. cit., 480; Bagdare, S. & Jain, R. 2013. Measuring customer experience. *International Journal of Retail and Distribution Management*, 41(10): 790–804; Srivastava, M. & Kaul, K. 2014. Social interaction, convenience and customer satisfaction: The mediating effect of customer experience. *Journal of Retailing and Consumer Services*, 21: 1028–1037.

78 Pine, B.J. & Gilmore, J.H, 2002. Differentiating hospitality operations via experiences: Why selling services is not enough. *The Cornell Hotel and Restaurant Administration Quarterly*, 43(3): 87; Pegg, S. & Patterson, I. 2010. Rethinking music festivals as a staged event: Gaining insights from understanding visitor motivations and the experiences they seek. *Journal of Convention & Event Tourism*, 11(2): 85.

79 Sullivan, P., Kang, J. & Heitmeyer, J. 2012. Fashion involvement and experiential value: Gen Y retail apparel patronage. *The International Review of Retail, Distribution and Consumer Research*, 22(5):459–483.

80 Ha, J. & Jang, S. 2010. Perceived values, satisfaction, and behavioural intentions: The role of familiarity in Korean restaurants. *International Journal of Hospitality Management*, 29: 2.

81 Arnold, M.J. & Reynolds, K.E. 2003. Hedonic shopping motivations. *Journal of Retailing*, 79: 77.

82 Mathwick et al., op. cit., 39.

83 Fiore, A.M. & Jeoung, M. 2007. Measuring experience economy concepts: Tourism applications. *Journal of Travel Research*, 46: 95.

84 De Farias, S.A., Aguiari, E.C. & Melo, F.V.S. 2014. Store atmospherics and experiential marketing: A conceptual framework and research propositions for an extraordinary customer experience. *International Business Research*, 7(2): 87.

85 Harris, L.C. & Ezeh, C. 2008. Servicescape and loyalty intentions: An empirical investigation. *European Journal of Marketing*, 42 (3/4): 390.

86 Henning-Thurau, T., Groth, M., Paul, M. & Gremler, D.D. 2006. Are all smiles created equal? How emotional contagion and emotional labour affect service relationships. *Journal of Marketing*, 70(3): 58.

87 Morrisson, M., Gan, S., Dubelaar, C. & Oppewal, H. 2011. In-store music and aroma influences on shopper behaviour and satisfaction. *Journal of Business Research*, 64: 558.

88 Baker, J., Parasuraman, A., Grewal, D. & Voss, G.B. 2002. The influence of multiple store environment cues on perceived merchandise value and patronage intentions. *Journal of Marketing*, 66 (2): 120.

89 Puccinelli, N.M., Goodstein, R.C., Grewal, D., Price, R., Raghubir, P. & Stewat, D. 2009. Customer experience management in retailing: Understanding the buying process. *Journal of Retailing*, (85): 15.

90 Kawaf, F & Tagg, S. 2012. Online shopping environments in fashion shopping: An S-O-R based review. *Marketing Review*, 12(2): 161.

91 Hassan, Y., Muhammad, N.M.N. & Bakar, H.A. 2010. Influence of shopping orientation and store image on patronage of furniture stores. *International Journal of Marketing Studies*, 2(1): 175.

92 Hanzaee, K.H. & Rezaeyeh, S.P. 2013. Investigation of the effects of hedonic value and utilitarian value on customer satisfaction and behavioural intentions. *African Journal of Business Management*, 7(11): 818.

93 Shah, A.K. & Alter, A.L. 2014. Consuming experiential categories. *Journal of Consumer Research*, 41(12): 965.

94 Retief, op. cit.

INDEX

Please note: Page numbers in *italics* refer to images, tables and figures.